# Company Law For Accountants

# Company Law For Accountants

**C D Thomas** LLB, Dip Ed
Barrister, Senior Lecturer in Law at Liverpool Polytechnic

London
Butterworths
1985

| England | Butterworth & Co (Publishers) Ltd, 88 Kingsway, LONDON WC2B 6AB |
|---|---|
| Australia | Butterworths Pty Ltd, SYDNEY, MELBOURNE, BRISBANE, ADELAIDE, PERTH, CANBERRA and HOBART |
| Canada | Butterworth & Co (Canada) Ltd, TORONTO and VANCOUVER |
| New Zealand | Butterworths of New Zealand Ltd, WELLINGTON and AUCKLAND |
| Singapore | Butterworth & Co (Asia) Pte Ltd, SINGAPORE |
| South Africa | Butterworth Publishers (Pty) Ltd, DURBAN and PRETORIA |
| USA | Butterworth Legal Publishers, ST PAUL, Minnesota, SEATTLE, Washington, BOSTON, Massachusetts, AUSTIN, Texas and D & S Publishers, CLEARWATER, Florida |

**British Library Cataloguing in Publication Data**

Thomas, Colin
   Company law for accountants.
   1. Corporation law——Great Britain
   I. Title
   344.106'66     KD2079
   ISBN Softcover 0–406–00960–0

Typeset by Phoenix Photosetting, Chatham
Printed by Biddles Ltd, Guildford, Surrey.

To Rita

# Preface

This book is designed for students studying the company law syllabuses of the various accountancy bodies. I also hope that other students will find the text of value.

Company law resembles a vast jigsaw with one piece examined at a time. At the end of the day one hopes that a complete picture will emerge.

I would like to thank the members of the staff at Butterworths for their assistance with the preparation of this book.

C D Thomas

# Acknowledgments

Grateful acknowledgment is made to the following for permission to reproduce material in the Appendices:

Marks and Spencer plc for permission to reproduce their Memorandum of Association in Appendix B and their Accounts in Appendix E.

Grieveson Grant, 59 Gresham Street, London for permission to reproduce their list of shareholders' concessions in Appendix C.

The Association of Certified Accountants; The Institute of Chartered Accountants in England and Wales; The Institute of Chartered Secretaries and Administrators; and The Institute of Cost and Management Accountants for permission to reproduce examination questions in Appendix C.

# Contents

# Table of The Companies Acts 1985

# List of Statutes

# Table of Cases

# Chapter 1

# The incorporation of a company

A company is a corporation and as such has an existence, rights and duties distinct from those who are from time to time its members. A corporation may be formed in one of three ways:–

(a) by the grant of a Royal Charter,
(b) by incorporation by special Act of Parliament,
(c) by registration under the Companies Acts. This is the normal method of incorporating a commercial company i e a 'company limited by shares under the Companies Acts'. It is also used by non-commercial concerns who wish to avail themselves of a corporate status.

These three types of corporations are classified as corporations aggregate as they have more than one member. This chapter deals with companies registered under the Companies Acts.

Corporations (a) and (b) are dealt with in chapter 2.

## PROCEDURE FOR REGISTRATION

The procedure for the registration of a company under the Companies Acts is relatively simple. The promoters or their advisers draw up the company's constitutional documents – namely the memorandum of association and the articles of association (if articles are to be submitted). These and other documents are submitted to the Registrar of Companies who will register the documents on payment of certain fees and stamp duties.

A company whose registered office is in England or Wales submits the documents and fees to the Registrar of Companies for England at Cardiff, while a company whose registered office is in

Scotland submits the fees and documents to the Registrar of Companies for Scotland at Edinburgh.

The following documents must be submitted to the Registrar.

1. A memorandum of association.
2. The articles of association. (If no articles are delivered the articles contained in Table A will apply to the company).
3. A certified English translation where the memorandum states that the company's registered office is to be situated in Wales and the memorandum and articles are in Welsh.
4. A statement of directors and secretaries which must be signed by or on behalf of the subscribers to the memorandum. It must contain a consent signed by each of the persons named in it as a director, as secretary or as one of joint secretaries to act in the relevant capacity. A notice of the address of the company's registered office must also be included in the statement.
5. A statement of nominal capital (Form PUC 1), unless the company is formed without a share capital.
6. A statutory declaration in the prescribed form by a solicitor engaged in the company's formation, or by a person named as a director or secretary of the company in the statement of first directors and secretary, that the requirements of ss 117 and 118 have been complied with. The Registrar may accept such a declaration as sufficient evidence of compliance.

The Registrar is under a duty to examine the documents to ensure that the statutory requirements have been complied with. He must ensure that:–

(a) The memorandum is signed by at least two persons.
(b) The articles (if submitted) are signed by the signatories to the memorandum. No objection can be raised to the fact that the signatories are nominees of one person or that the signatories are foreign nationals who are resident abroad, or to the fact that one of the signatories is a minor.
(c) The proposed company is formed for a lawful purpose.
(d) The memorandum and articles are in the form required by the Act.
(e) The proposed name of the company is not prohibited.

## THE CERTIFICATE OF INCORPORATION

The Registrar will issue a certificate of incorporation on being satisfied that:

(a) the documents are in order.
(b) the appropriate fees have been paid.
(c) stamp duty has been paid.

He must also publish a notice in the London Gazette that a certificate of incorporation has been issued.

The certificate is in the following form:

(i) *Private company*

I hereby certify that ............... Limited is this day incorporated under the Companies Act 1985 and that the Company is Limited.
Given under my hand at Cardiff this ............... day of
...............

(ii) *Public company (entitled to do business)*

I hereby certify that ............... public limited company having complied with the conditions of s 117 of the Companies Act 1985, is entitled to do business.
Given under my hand at Cardiff this ............... day of
...............

The issue of a certificate of incorporation is conclusive evidence that:

(a) The requirements of the Companies Act in respect of registration have been complied with.
(b) The company is authorised to be registered and is duly registered.
(c) The company is a public company if the certificate contains a statement to that effect.

From the date of incorporation the company becomes a body corporate which is known by the name contained in the memorandum of association. It is capable of exercising all the functions of an incorporated body from the day of incorporation.

**Jubilee Cotton Mills Ltd v Lewis** (1924)

A company's memorandum and articles were accepted by the Registrar on the 6 January 1920 and the certificate of incorporation was dated on that day.

The certificate was not signed by the Registrar until 8 January, 1920. The company allotted shares on the 6 January. It was held that the allotment was valid as a company is deemed to be incorporated from the first moment of the day of the date on its certificate of incorporation.

If a company has obtained registration and it is subsequently discovered that some objects of the company are illegal, the issue of the certificate prevents any doubts being raised as to the legal personality of the company. It does not however validate an illegal object. The certificate 'prevents anyone alleging that the company does not exist' – per Lord Dunedin in *Bowman v Secular Society Ltd* (1917).

The Registrar will refuse to register a company if he is of the opinion that the company's objects are illegal.

### R v Registrar of Joint Stock Companies (1931)

The Registrar refused to register a company whose objects were to sell Irish Hospital sweepstake tickets in the United Kingdom. This was authorised in the Irish Free State but was illegal as a lottery in the United Kingdom.

An appeal may be made from the Registrar's decision to the Queen's Bench Divisional Court by way of an order of mandamus ie ordering him to register the company.

## COMMENCEMENT OF BUSINESS

A private company may commence business and exercise its borrowing powers from the date of its incorporation.

A company registered as a public company 'on its original incorporation' may not do business or exercise any borrowing powers unless the Registrar issues the company with a s 117 certificate. The Registrar must be satisfied that the nominal values of the company's allotted share capital is not less than the authorised minimum, currently £50,000. If the Registrar does not do so the company must re-register as a private company.

A statutory declaration must be delivered to the Registrar and signed by a director or secretary of the company. It must state that:

(a) The nominal value of the company's allotted share capital is not less than the authorised minimum.

(b) The amount paid up, at the time of the application, on the allotted share capital of the company.

(c) The amount or estimated amount of the preliminary expenses of the company and the persons by whom any of these expenses have been paid or are payable.

(d) Any amount or benefit paid or given or intended to be paid or given to any promoter of the company, and the consideration for the payment or benefit.

A share allotted in pursuance of an employees' share scheme may be taken into account in determining the nominal value of the company's allotted share capital if it is paid up at least as to one quarter of the nominal value of the share and the whole of any premium on the share.

A s 117 certificate is conclusive evidence that the company is entitled to do business and exercise any borrowing powers. If a company enters into a business transaction or exercises its borrowing powers without such a certificate both the company and any officer of the company in default is guilty of an offence, but the transaction is nevertheless valid. Should the company fail to meet its obligations under such a transaction within 21 days of being asked to do so by the other party, the directors of the company are jointly and severally (collectively and individually) liable to indemnify the other party to the transaction in respect of any loss or damage suffered by him due to the company's failure to comply with those obligations (s 117).

The Secretary of State may present a petition to wind up a public company which has not been issued with a certificate if more than a year has elapsed since its registration as a public company.

## THE CHARACTERISTICS OF A COMPANY

### 1. SEPARATE LEGAL ENTITY

On the issue of its certificate of incorporation a company becomes a body corporate i e it is a legal person separate and distinct from its members. This was authoritatively established by the House of Lords in 1897 in the case of *Salamon v Salamon & Co Ltd* (1897).

### Salomon v Salomon & Co Ltd (1897)

Salomon, a wholesale boot manufacturer, formed a limited company to acquire his business. The company paid £39,000 to Salomon for his business. He received 20,000 shares, £9,000 in cash and debentures for £10,000. His wife and five children received one share each. The company later encountered financial problems and a liquidator was appointed. It had assets of £6,000 and owed £7,800 to trade creditors as well as the £10,000 owed to Salomon under the debenture. The trade creditors claimed to have priority over the payment of the assets on the grounds that the company was a one man company and a sham.

It was held that the company was a body corporate distinct from its members. The debentures were valid and Salomon was entitled to the remaining assets in part payment of the debentures.

## Lee v Lee's Air Farming Ltd (1960)

Lee formed a private company to carry on a crop spraying business. He held 2,999 of the company's 3,000 shares, was the company's governing director and was also employed as the company's chief pilot. He was killed while piloting the company's aircraft. His widow claimed compensation for his death under the New Zealand Workers' Compensation Act 1922 which required an employer to pay compensation on the death of a worker. It was held that Lee was an employee of the company, and that a person may perform a dual function both as a director and employee of the same company.

## Multinational Gas & Petrochemical Co v Multinational Gas & Petrochemical Services Ltd (1983)

Three oil companies, incorporated in the United States, France and Japan, formed the plaintiff company as a joint venture for dealings in petroleum and gas products. The plaintiff company was incorporated in Liberia and the defendant company was incorporated in England to act as an agent and adviser to the plaintiff company. Both companies were wound up. The liquidator of the plaintiff company sought to claim against the oil companies for breaches of the duty of care which they owed the plaintiff as persons exercising the powers of management and direction in connection with the plaintiff company's decisions. It was held that the plaintiff was in law a different legal person from the subscribing oil company's shareholders and was not their agent.

A company's property therefore belongs to the company and no individual member has any insurable interest in the property.

## Macaura v Northern Assurance Co Ltd (1925)

Macaura, who owned a timber estate, formed a company and sold the timber to the company. The shareholders consisted of Macaura and various nominees. He later effected an insurance policy on the timber in his own name, and not in the company's name or as an agent for the company. The timber was later destroyed by fire. It was held that Macaura could not claim as he could not have an insurable interest in the company's assets, since the company was a separate legal entity.

## 2. LIMITED LIABILITY

As a company is a separate person it is liable, without limit, for its debts. The majority of companies are formed on the basis of limited liability (either by shares or guarantee) and the shareholders of such companies are not required to contribute in a winding up, more than the amount outstanding on their shares (if any) or the amount of their guarantee. A member of an unlimited company is a guarantor of the company's debts and obligations in a winding up, without any restriction on the amount.

### 3. PERPETUAL SUCCESSION

A company has perpetual succession in that its existence is independent of its members. A change in the membership of a company as a result of a transfer of ownership or death of a member is not a change in the company itself. The company's existence will not be affected should the membership fall below the statutory minimum of two. (In such a situation an application will be made to the court to convene a meeting of the company).

### 4. PROPERTY

A company's property is clearly distinguished from that of its members. A member has no proprietary right to a company's property but merely to his shares. A change in membership with the consequent transfer in shares does not affect a company's property. A claim by a company's creditor lies against the property of the company, not against its members.

A company has the same capacity to hold land as a natural person as long as this is not inconsistent with its objects.

It may take action in the courts to enforce its legal rights and it may be sued for breach of its legal duties i e it may sue and be sued.

### 5. CONTRACT

A company has the same freedom as a natural person to enter into contracts as long as it is acting 'intra vires' (i e within its powers) as laid down by its memorandum.

### 6. TORT

A company may, as a plaintiff, sue for all torts (civil wrongs) committed against it. Companies frequently take action against third parties who infringe companies rights.

A company has the capacity to commit a tort. It is therefore liable for the tortious acts of its employees as long as the employee is engaged, within the scope and course of his employment, in an intra vires activity.

### Limpus v London General Omnibus Co (1862)

A company was held liable for the actions of its employees who had engaged in a race with other horse drawn buses and had caused injury to certain passengers when the buses overturned.

If an employee engages in an ultra vires activity without express authority, the company will not be liable for his actions.

If an employee engages in an ultra vires activity with the company's authority, the courts have held that the ultra vires doctrine does not apply and the company is liable for the employee's acts.

### 7. CRIMINAL LIABILITY

A company is treated as having a mind capable of committing a criminal offence i e it has 'mens rea'. As the company is an abstract personality the mental state of its agents in senior managerial positions is synonymous with that of the company. A senior employee may therefore be regarded as possessing 'the directing mind and will of the company'.

### Tesco Supermarkets Ltd v Nattrass (1971)

A shop manager contravened the Trade Descriptions Act (1968) by charging a customer more for an article than the price specified in the special offer poster. The company was prosecuted but was found not guilty of an offence under the Act as the manager was not a senior official of the company and was one of the hands of the company and not part of its brain.

The mental state of the company's controllers will not be attributed to the company in certain cases e g where the controllers conspire to act in breach of various provisions laid down by statute to protect companies.

Both the company and its officers are liable for criminal offences occasioned by the acts or defaults of the company's officers.

There are certain crimes which a company is regarded as incapable of committing e g bigamy, perjury and offences for which the only punishment is imprisonment.

### 8. BORROWING

A company is able to grant an effective form of security in the form of a floating charge in order to raise money for its activities ie a lender may obtain an effective security on a company's present and future undertakings and assets.


9. CONSTITUTION

A company must have a written constitution in the form of its memorandum and articles of association.


10. MANAGEMENT

The management of a company lies in the hands of its directors. A member has no right to be appointed as a director although he has the power to appoint a director (and may appoint himself).

A member has no right to make contracts on the company's behalf as its agent, although if a director he may enter into such contracts if power has been delegated to him by the company.


11. TRANSFERABLE SHARES

A member's share constitutes an item of property which is freely transferable, subject to any restrictions imposed by the company's articles.


12. MEMBERSHIP OF OTHER BUSINESS ORGANISATIONS

A company may be a member, director, secretary or manager of another company and may also be a partner in a partnership. It may not be an auditor of another company.


## THE VEIL OF INCORPORATION

Generally the courts have considered themselves bound by the concept of a company as a separate legal personality distinct from its members ie a veil is drawn between a company and its members.

There are however certain circumstances when the courts have disregarded this concept and lifted the veil of incorporation. These have related mainly to questions involving the actual control of a company or a group of companies. No consistent principle has been followed but the courts have intervened where there is a flagrant disregard for justice, to prevent fraud and to protect the Revenue. The effect of the intervention has been to enforce company legislation and the prevention of fraud or other evasion of legal obligations.

The following are examples of situations where the veil has been lifted:

(a) If a company carries on business without having at least two members and does so for more than 6 months the remaining member is jointly and severally liable with the company for the company's debts for the whole or any part of the period it carries on business after these six months, if at that time:
   (i) he is a member of the company; and
   (ii) knows that it is carrying on business with only one member (s 24).
(b) If in the course of winding up it appears that the company's business has been carried on with intent to defraud creditors or for any fraudulent purpose the courts may declare that any persons (e g the directors) who were knowingly parties to that fraud shall be personally responsible (without limitation of liability) for the company's debts or other liabilities (s 630).
(c) The courts will not allow s 428 (compulsory purchase of minority's shares) to be abused and will prohibit the formation of a new company by members holding nine-tenths of the shares in an existing company if the new company is formed solely to expropriate the shares of the minority shareholders (*Re Bugle Press* (1961) (see p 384)).
(d) Where a private company is founded on a personal relationship between its members the court may order its winding up under the just and equitable rule (s 517(g)) if the relationship has soured, or there is a breakdown in mutual confidence between the parties, or one party has acted inequitably. As many small companies are in fact quasi-partnerships, the court will have regard to the actual substance and reality of the association rather than to its particular form (*Re Yenidje Tobacco Co* (1916); *Ebrahimi v Westbourne Galleries* (1973)).
(e) To determine whether the relationship of holding company and subsidiary exists. This is important for the following reasons:
   (i) The general rule is that a holding company must produce group accounts in which the profits or losses, assets and liabilities of subsidiary companies are 'consolidated' i e treated as if they belonged to a single undertaking (the holding company) (s 229).

(ii) As a general rule a subsidiary company may not hold shares in its holding company.

(iii) An inspector appointed by the Department of Trade to investigate a company's affairs under ss 431 or 432 may, if he thinks necessary, also investigate any other company which is or has at any relevant time been the company's subsidiary or holding company (or a subsidiary of its holding company or a holding company of its subsidiary).

(iv) Where a subsidiary is considered to be acting as the agent for its holding company.

### Smith, Stone and Knight Ltd v Birmingham Corporation (1939)

The business premises of a company were compulsorily acquired by a local authority. Although the company carried on the business at those premises, its parent company controlled its activities and kept its books and accounts. It was held nevertheless that the parent company was the real occupier of the premises and was entitled to claim compensation for removal and disturbance as a result of the compulsory purchase order.

(v) Where the holding company and subsidiary company (or companies) are involved in carrying on a single business to the extent that they are regarded as an economic entity.

### DHN Food Distributors Ltd v Tower Hamlets Borough Council (1976)

A company carried on business in premises owned by its subsidiary, a holding company which did not engage in any commercial activity. Both companies had the same directors. The premises were purchased compulsorily by the local authority under the Land Compensation Act 1961, which requires compensation to be made for the value of land and disturbance to a business. The local authority paid compensation to the subsidiary company for the land but refused to compensate for disturbance as the subsidiary did not occupy the land. It refused to compensate the holding company on the grounds that the company had no interest in the land, but was at best a licensee of its subsidiary. It was held that compensation for disturbance should be paid as the holding company and its subsidiary were an economic entity ie the ownership of the premises and the business activities were under the control of a single group.

(f) In the law relating to trading with the enemy. The test of control is adopted to determine whether a company is an alien enemy.

Under the Trading with the Enemy Act 1939 a company is to be regarded as an enemy company if it is enemy controlled, incorporated by an enemy state or if it carries on business in enemy territory.

### Daimler Co Ltd v Continental Tyre and Rubber Co Ltd (1916)

All the members of a tyre company, incorporated in England were, with one minor exception, German nationals. It was held that as the persons in control of the company were enemy aliens, the company could not take action in the English courts (1915) to enforce the payment of a debt.

(g) Where an officer of a company signs on its behalf a bill of exchange, promissory note endorsement, cheque or order for money or goods in which the company's name is not mentioned, he is personally liable in respect of those transactions for the amount thereof, unless it is paid by the company (s 349).

(h) In the law of merger control. The Fair Trading Act 1973, provides that a merger situation arises when two or more enterprises, of which at least one was carried on in the United Kingdom, cease to be direct enterprises. This occurs if they are brought under common ownership or common control; or if one of them ceases to be carried on at all as a result of an arrangement or transaction entered into to prevent competition between the enterprises.

Article 86 of the EEC treaty may be used in certain circumstances to control mergers. It prohibits any abuse by an undertaking of its dominant position within the common market or in any substantial part of it in so far as it may affect trade between member states. Secondary legislation has also decreed that a holding company and its subsidiary should be regarded as an economic unit.

(j) Where a company is formed for a fraudulent purpose.

### Re FG Films Ltd (1953)

A company was incorporated in England with a capital of £100 in £1 shares. Ninety shares were held by the president of a United States film company while the remainder were held by a British director. The company contended that it was the maker of a film which should be registered as a British film. The court held that the company was the nominee of the United States film company which had provided the capital for making the film. The company had been formed for the sole purpose of enabling the film to qualify as a British film which could be registered under the Cinematograph Films Act 1938.

### Gilford Motor Co Ltd v Horne (1933)

Horne, the managing director of the plaintiff company convenanted that he would not solicit the company's customers when he left their employment. On termination of his employment he formed a company with his wife and an employee to carry on a competing business and this company solicited the customers of the Gilford Motor Co. The plaintiff company was granted an injunction against Horne and the company which he had formed as a cloak for his activities.

### Jones v Lipman (1962)

A man who had entered into a contract to sell his house sought to avoid his obligations by conveying the property to a company of which he was the controlling shareholder. It was held that a decree of specific performance would be granted to compel him to fulfill his contractual obligations as the company was both a 'device and sham'.

(k) In revenue matters a company's residence is one of the main factors in determining a company's liability for corporation tax. The location of a company's central management and control determines its residence.

### Unit Construction Co Ltd v Bullock (1960)

A United Kingdom company had three Kenyan subsidiaries which were incorporated in Kenya. The subsidiaries were in theory separate from the parent company and had independent boards of directors. The parent company in fact controlled their activities although it had no constitutional authority to do so. It was held that for tax purposes, the subsidiaries were resident in the United Kingdom where their central management and control was located.

## LIMITED COMPANIES AND PARTNERSHIPS

The owners of a company may elect to trade as a partnership or form a company. In many cases the choice is determined by an individual's tax liability.

The inclusion of the word 'company' in a company's name is not essential. Its use in a name does not necessarily signify that such an association is a company, as many partnerships include the word in their names.

The advantages and characteristics of both forms of business associations may be illustrated by a comparison of the two.

1. A company is an artificial legal person with perpetual succession. A partnership is not a separate entity, but represents the sum of its members.

2. A company is created by registration under the Companies Acts. Various documents must be delivered to that Registrar and stamp duty and registration fees are payable.
   A partnership may exist without any form of written agreement. Although most partnership agreements are in writing, or in the form of a deed the existence of a partnership may be implied from the conduct of the parties.

3. Shares in a company are freely transferable unless the articles provide otherwise.
   A partner may not transfer his share in a partnership without the consent of the other partners. He may assign his share but the assignee does not become a partner and is only entitled to the assigning partner's share of the profits.

4. A company may issue shares of different classes with different rights.
   In the absence of an agreement to the contrary all the partners have equal rights in the firm's affairs and share equally in the capital and profits of the firm. They must also contribute equally towards the firm's losses.

5. The management of a company is in the hands of the company's directors. The members are not the company's agents and may not enter into contracts on the company's behalf.
   A general partner has the right to participate in the management of the partnership and may bind the partnership by his actions.
   A member of a company may enter into a contract with a company but a partner may not contract with the partnership.

6. The liability of a member of a company may be limited either by shares or by guarantee.
   A general partner is however liable, without limit, for the debts of the partnership.

7. A company's property is vested in the company itself while the partnership property belongs to the partners.
   A change in the partnership is a change of ownership of the partnership property.

8. A limited company is subject to rules relating to the raising and maintenance of its share capital which may only be increased or reduced by following the procedures laid down in the Companies Act.

The amount of the capital in a partnership may be altered, at will, by the partners.

9. The scope of a company's powers are determined by its objects clause, the Companies Act and the law in general.
The doctrine of ultra vires does not apply to a partnership which may engage in any lawful activity, decided upon by the partners.

10. The death or bankruptcy of a member of a company does not affect the company ie a company has perpetual succession.
The death or bankruptcy of a partner automatically dissolves the partnership (unless there is an agreement to the contrary).

11. The winding up of an insolvent company does not bankrupt the company's members. The bankruptcy of a partnership means the bankruptcy of every partner (with the exception of a limited partner under the Limited Partnership Act 1907).

12. A company may not be wound up except with the consent of the majority of members. A partnership may be dissolved by a general partner at anytime on giving due notice (unless the partnership was entered into for a fixed time).

13. A company must have a minimum of two members, but there is no upper limit.
A partnership may not consist of more than twenty partners, with the exception of certain groups of professional partnerships e g solicitors, accountants, stock brokers, surveyors, patent agents, consulting engineers, auctioneers, estate agents.

14. A company's accounts (with the exception of unlimited and small companies) are open to public inspection.
Partnership accounts are never subject to public scrutiny.

15. A company is subject to regulation and supervision by the Registrar of Companies, the courts and the Department of Trade and Industry. Documents have to be submitted to the Companies Registry.
There is no supervision of a similar nature of the activities of a partnership.

16. A company has greater facility for borrowing than a partnership e g it may borrow on debentures and may create a floating charge over its assets as security for a loan e g stock, book debts.
A partnership may not borrow on debentures or create a floating charge over its assets.

## COMMUNITY LAW AND COMPANY LAW

As a result of entry into the European Communities, the United

Kingdom has become subject to the provisions of community law. This consists of original and amending treaties and secondary legislation.

Secondary legislation consists of regulations, directives, decisions and other measures adopted by the various institutions of the Community. As a general rule regulations are binding on member states 'without further enactment' while directives, although binding in principle, require legislation by the member states to bring them into operation.

In keeping with the concept of a common market the Council of Ministers of the European Economic Community have approved various measures designed to harmonize company law throughout the European Community.

Various directives have been approved and other draft directives are under consideration.

The first directive deals with the disclosure of information and the validity of obligations entered into by a company. This was implemented by the European Communities Act 1972, which modified the ultra vires doctrine, regulated pre-incorporation contracts and also provided for the disclosure of certain information and documents.

The second directive deals with company formation and the maintenance, increase and reduction of capital. This directive was implemented by the Companies Act 1980.

The third directive deals with the co-ordination of provisions regulating internal mergers of companies within a member state. This includes take-overs, mergers by the formation of a new company and the take-over of a company by another company which is its sole shareholder. It does not extend to United Kingdom take-over procedure, although there is a proposed directive on take-over bids. The third directive is due to be implemented by member states before 1 January 1986.

The fourth directive deals with the contents of the annual accounts and the disclosure of financial information. This directive was implemented by the Companies Act 1981.

The fifth draft directive deals with the organisation and structure of public limited companies. It requires employee participation in public limited companies which are not co-operatives and which alone or with subsidiaries employ 1,000 or more workers. It provides for the division of boards into two tier or single tier boards containing a majority of non-executive directors. The directive also deals with directors' duties and their enforcement, the functions and liability of auditors and the conduct and power of general meetings.

The draft Vredeling directive contains procedures for the supply of information to, and consultation with, employees of large companies.

The sixth directive dealing with the merger and demerger of companies is due to be implemented by member states before 1 January 1986.

The seventh directive on consolidated accounts is due to be implemented by member states before 1 January 1986.

The draft eighth directive deals with the qualifications of auditors. Its objective is to enable auditors to audit the accounts of companies of member states other than the state in which they are qualified to act.

There are three directives on Stock Exchange matters dealing with:

the requirements for admission of securities to listing,
the contents of documents containing listing particulars,
the information to be supplied by listed companies.

These were due to be implemented in 1983.

A draft directive on prospectuses may be revived in the near future.

A draft Regulation on European Co-operation Grouping proposes the establishment of a corporate entity for joint ventures between companies and firms in different member states. As the regulation will be made under Article 23 of the Treaty of Rome it will bind the United Kingdom, as a member state, without the need for implementing legislation.

There is also a long standing draft Regulation for the creation of a European company, which would be governed by the provisions of a European company statute and have the status of a national company in every member state. It would be formed by two or more national companies already operating in different countries, amalgamating, or forming a holding company or a joint subsidiary. The company would be registered in the European Commercial Register kept at the European Court in Luxembourg. Its share capital would be expressed in European Units of Account (EUA). The management of such a company would be exercised by a management board, whose activities would be subject to general supervision by a supervisory board. The supervisory board would consist of one-third shareholder representatives, one-third employee representatives and the remaining one-third representation would be co-opted by the shareholders and employee representatives.

Chapter 2

# The classification of companies

Various types of companies have evolved over the past century to meet the needs of businessmen, promoters and investors. Although the Act provides for three basic types of companies (namely companies limited by shares, companies limited by guarantee and unlimited companies) and two forms of companies (public and private companies) it also recognises other types of companies.

## CHARTERED COMPANIES

Chartered companies are formed by the grant of a charter by the Crown under its special statutory powers or its prerogative powers. Charters are used to incorporate learned societies, professional bodies, universities and colleges.

In the past the Crown granted royal charters to trading companies (eg the Russia Company in 1555; the East India Company in 1600; the Hudson Bay Company in 1670) and to banks (eg The Bank of England in 1694) and insurance companies (eg The London Assurance in 1720).

There are however certain commercial organisations which operate under charters and seven such companies are listed in the Stock Exchange Year Book. Certain sections of the Companies Act apply to such companies which are carrying on business for gain.

A chartered company has similar powers to an individual to enter into contracts and deal with property. These powers cannot be modified or restricted by the charter ie the ultra vires doctrine does not apply to chartered companies. The Crown may however annul the charter if the limits of the charter are disregarded by the company.

Members of a chartered company created by the Royal prerogative are not liable for the company's debts. If a company is granted a charter under the provisions of the Chartered Companies Act 1837, the charter usually provides that a member is liable to a specified extent in respect of his shares for the company's debts.

## STATUTORY COMPANIES

Statutory companies are incorporated by special Act of Parliament. Such companies may be incorporated by a private (or local) Act or by a (special) public Act.

The formation of a company by private Act of Parliament was frequently used in the past by canal, railway, water, gas, electricity and harbour undertakings. These companies were usually granted compulsory powers to purchase land and commit what would otherwise be a nuisance. They were also granted a monopoly in a specific area.

As the provisions of these private Acts were found to be similar, several public statutes were passed containing general regulations applicable to these companies. The regulations were then incorporated by reference to the Act creating the company, e g The Companies Clauses Consolidation Act 1845 defines the liability of shareholders, regulates borrowing powers, and the company's constitution. The Land Clauses Consolidation Act 1845 deals with the compulsory purchase of land, conveyance of land and the payment of purchase money.

The powers of a statutory company are limited by the private Act under which it is incorporated. If a statutory company acts outside those powers it ceases to act as a legal person and the acts are null and void. A member's liability is limited to the extent that his shares are not paid up. He is liable to contribute to the extent of the amount unpaid on his shares if the company is unable to pay its debts.

A public or special Act is used to create a public corporation. These corporations are formed to own and manage the various nationalised industries and new industries promoted by the state e g The Atomic Energy Authority, the National Coal Board, The British Gas Corporation, the Central Electricity Generating Board, the Post Office, the British Transport Commission.

The characteristics of these bodies was outlined by Denning LJ in *Tamlin v Hannaford* (1950). He described the British Transport Commission as

'. . . a statutory corporation of a kind comparatively new to English law. It has many of the qualities which belong to corporations of other kinds to which we have been accustomed. It has, for instance, defined powers which it cannot exceed; and it is directed by a group of men whose duty it is to see that those powers are properly used. It may own property, carry on business, borrow and lend money, just as any other corporation may do, so long as it keeps within the bounds which Parliament has set. But the significant difference in this corporation is that there are no shareholders to subscribe the capital or to have any voice in its affairs. The money which the corporation needs is not raised by the issue of shares but by borrowing and its borrowing is not secured by debentures, but is guaranteed by the Treasury. If it cannot repay, the loss falls on the Consolidated Fund of the United Kingdom; that is to say, on the taxpayer. There are no shareholders to elect the directors or fix their remuneration. There are no profits to be made or distributed. The duty of the corporation is to make revenue and expenditure balance one another, taking, of course, one year with another, but not to make profits. If it should make losses and be unable to pay its debts, its property is liable to execution, but it is not liable to be wound up at the suit of any creditor. The taxpayer would, no doubt, be expected to come to its rescue before the creditors stepped in. Indeed, the taxpayer is the universal guarantor of the corporation.'

## UNLIMITED COMPANIES

An unlimited company is defined as 'a Company not having any limit on the liability of its members' (s 1). The name of the company will not contain the word 'limited' and the memorandum will not contain a limitation of liability clause.

It is the only permitted form of company for certain types of business organisations e g the Stock of Exchange will not allow a company to become a member unless the company's members are personally liable for its debts. Certain exemptions granted to unlimited companies are attractive to companies that do not wish to publish their accounts.

As the members of an unlimited company are liable without limit for the company's debts, such companies are comparatively rare. However, an unlimited company possesses two major advantages over other forms of companies:

(i) it is not required to file its accounts, directors and auditors reports with the Registrar;
(ii) it may purchase its own shares.

These two advantages are now of minor importance. Since 1981 all companies may purchase their own shares (if so authorised by their articles) and a small company is no longer required to file its profit and loss account or directors' report.

The exemption from filing its accounts does not apply if the company has, during its accounting reference period, been to its knowledge:

(i) a subsidiary of a limited company; or
(ii) jointly controlled by two or more limited companies; or
(iii) the holding company of a limited company; or
(iv) carrying on business as the promoter of a trading stamp scheme (s 241).

A members liability will only arise if the company is wound up and is unable to meet its debts. The members will be liable to contribute to the company's debts and the costs of winding up without limitation of their liability. It is however possible for the members to restrict or avoid liability by the device of a company issuing a policy or another contract whereby the liability of individual members on the policy or contract is restricted, or the company funds are solely liable in respect of the policy or contract.

An unlimited company is a private company and may be formed with or without share capital. The memorandum and articles have to be in the form set out in Table E or as near to as circumstances admit.

An unlimited company is not governed by the rules relating to the maintenance of capital as are other types of companies (s 135). It may therefore reduce its capital and return capital to its members without the approval of the court.

An unlimited company may re-register as a private limited company if the following steps are taken:

(i) A special resolution is passed. It must state whether the company is to be limited by shares or by guarantee. If the company is to be limited by shares it must state what the share capital is to be. It must also provide for the necessary alterations and additions to the memorandum and articles.
(ii) An application is submitted to the Registrar, (in the prescribed form) signed by a director or secretary of the company accompanied by printed copies of the memorandum and articles as altered. The Registrar then issues a certificate of incorporation. The status of the company is then changed and the additions and alterations to the memorandum and articles then take effect.

An unlimited company may not re-register as a public company. If a company wishes to effect this conversion it must do so in two stages. It must first re-register as a private limited company with a share capital and then re-register as a public company. Both stages may be achieved in one process.

A private limited company may re-register as an unlimited company. It must submit an application in the prescribed form, signed by a director or secretary of the company, to the Registrar. The application must provide for the necessary alterations and additions to the memorandum and articles. The application must be accompanied by the following documents:

(i) the prescribed form of assent to the company being registered as unlimited subscribed by or on behalf of all the members of the company.

(ii) a statutory declaration by the directors that the subscribers constitute the whole membership and if any member has not subscribed the form himself that the directors have taken all reasonable steps to satisfy themselves that each person who subscribed it on behalf of a member was lawfully empowered to do so.

(iii) a printed copy of the memorandum and articles (if registered) incorporating the alterations set out in the application.

The Registrar will then issue a certificate of incorporation which alters the status of the company from limited to unlimited, and the alterations to the memorandum and articles then take effect.

## COMPANIES LIMITED BY GUARANTEE

A company limited by guarantee has 'the liability of its members limited by the memorandum to such amount as the members may . . . undertake to contribute to the assets of the company in the event of its being wound up (section 1.') The members liability to contribute only arises if the company is wound up.

The memorandum must also contain a clause stating the extent of the members guarantee. For example,

> 'Every member of the company undertakes to contribute to the assets of the company in the event of its being wound up while he is a member, or within one year afterwards, for payment of the debts and liabilities of the company, contracted before he ceases to be a member, and the costs, charges and expenses of winding up the same and for the adjustment of the rights of the contributories amongst themselves, such amount as may be required, not exceeding £20.'

The amount of the guarantee specified in the memorandum may not be increased or reduced. It cannot be changed by the company while the company is a going concern.

A member's liability under the guarantee for the debts and liabilities of the company and the cost of winding up only arises after the commencement of winding up. A past member may be liable if he ceased to be a member within a year of the commencement of winding up, but only for debts and liabilities contracted by the company before he ceased to be a member.

The company's articles must state the number of members with which the company proposes to be registered. Any increase beyond the registered number must be notified to the Registrar within 15 days.

A guarantee company formed before 1981 could be either a private or a public company and could be formed with or without a share capital. A guarantee company having a share capital was able to re-register as a public company if it satisfied the requirements relating to public companies.

Since 1980 no company may be formed, or become, a company limited by guarantee with a share capital.

The majority of guarantee companies are formed by professional associations, trade associations clubs and societies who wish to obtain the benefits of incorporation without incurring personal liability. The vast majority will be exempt from using the word 'limited' as part of the company's name (s 30(2)).

A guarantee company must register articles of association with the memorandum (s 7). If it does not have a share capital its memorandum and articles must correspond with the form set out in Table C. If it has a share capital its memorandum and articles must correspond with Table D.

A guarantee company is similar to a share company in that the liability of its members is limited. It differs in that a member of a share company may be required at any time during the company's existence to pay any amounts outstanding on his share, while a member of a guarantee company's liability under the guarantee only arises after the commencement of winding up and even then only subject to certain conditions. Members of a guarantee company with a share capital have a dual liability – to pay for their shares and to honour their guarantee in the event of the company being wound up.

A guarantee company with a share capital must submit an annual return as required by the Act. A guarantee company without a share capital submits a modified annual return.

The provisions of the Act apply to guarantee companies, unless specifically excluded by the Act.

## COMPANIES LIMITED BY SHARES

A company limited by shares is defined by s 1(2) as 'a company having the liability of its members limited by the memorandum to the amount, if any, unpaid on the shares respectively held by them'. The capital clause of the memorandum of such a company provides that the share capital is divided into shares of a fixed amount. This amount determines the memorandum liability of the shareholder. A holder of a fully paid share therefore incurs no further liability. Should the company be wound up, he will not be liable to contribute to the payment of its debts.

## PUBLIC AND PRIVATE COMPANIES

A public company is a limited company with a share capital, whose memorandum states that it is a public company which has either been registered or re-registered as a public company. This includes companies limited by shares and companies limited by guarantee having a share capital.

A private company is any company that is not a public company.

A company must satisfy the following requirements before it can register as a public company.

1. It must state in its memorandum that it is a public company. A clause to that effect must be inserted in its memorandum.
2. Its name must end with the words 'public limited company' or the permitted abbreviations, ie plc, ccc (Welsh abbreviation).
3. Its memorandum must be in the form set out in Schedule 1 of the Act.
4. It must have a minimum authorised share capital of £50,000.

### RE-REGISTRATION OF A PRIVATE COMPANY AS A PUBLIC COMPANY

A private company may re-register as a public company if it complies with s 43.

1. The company must pass a special resolution at a general meeting that it should be re-registered.
   The special resolution must:
   (a) alter the memorandum to the form of memorandum of a public company ie change of name, statement that it is a

public company. Its memorandum must be in the form specified by the Secretary of State or as near to that form as circumstances admit.

(b) make such alterations in the company's articles as are required in the circumstances.

2. An application in the prescribed form, and signed by a director or secretary of the company is delivered to the Registrar accompanied by the following documents.

(a) a printed copy of the memorandum and articles as altered in pursuance of the resolution;

(b) a copy of a written statement by the auditors of the company that in their opinion the balance sheet (prepared not more than 7 months before the application) shows that at the balance sheet date the amount of the company's net assets was not less than the aggregate of its called-up share capital and undistributable reserves;

(c) a copy of the relevant balance sheet, together with a copy of an unqualified report by the company's auditors in relation to that balance sheet;

(d) a copy of any report relating to the valuation of a non-cash asset accepted between the date of the balance sheet and the special resolution, in payment or part payment for any of the company's shares.

(e) a statutory declaration by a director or secretary of the company:
 (i) that certain conditions relating to the valuation of non cash assets and nominal capital have been complied with and
 (ii) that, between the balance sheet date and the application of the company for re-registration, there has been no change in the financial position of the company that has resulted in the amount of the company's net assets becoming less than the aggregate of its called-up share capital and undistributable reserves.

The statutory declaration must state that:

(i) the special resolution has been passed.
(ii) a valuation (if required) has been properly carried out.
(iii) the nominal value of the company's allotted share capital is not less than the authorised minimum £50,000).
(iv) every allotted share is paid up to the extent of at least one quarter of its nominal value plus the whole of any premium on it.

(v) where any shares have been allotted as fully or partly paid up on the basis of an undertaking for work or services, the undertaking must have been performed or otherwise discharged.

(vi) where shares have been allotted as fully or partly paid on the basis of an undertaking to transfer a non-cash asset to the company, the undertaking must have been performed or otherwise discharged or there is a contract which provides for the transfer within five years (ss 44, 45).

If the Registrar is satisfied that the application and other documents are in order he will issue the company with a certificate of incorporation stating that the company is a public company. The issue of a certificate of incorporation is conclusive evidence that the requirements for re-registration have been complied with and that the company is a public company (s 47).

RE-REGISTRATION OF A PUBLIC COMPANY AS A PRIVATE COMPANY

A public company may re-register as a private company. To do so it must:

(a) Pass a special resolution that it should be re-registered.

(b) Deliver an application in the prescribed form to the Registrar, together with a printed copy of the memorandum and articles of the company as altered by the resolution. The application must be signed by a director or secretary of the company (s 53).

If the Registrar is satisfied that the application and other documents are in order he will issue the company with a certificate of incorporation appropriate to a company that is not a public company. The issue of a certificate of incorporation is conclusive evidence that the requirements for re-registration have been complied with and that the company is a private company (s 55).

Minority shareholders who are opposed to the re-registration of a public company may apply to the court to cancel the resolution within 28 days of it being passed.

Application may be made by:

(i) shareholders holding 5 per cent of the issued share capital or any class of capital.

(ii) not less than five per cent of the company's members of a company is not limited by shares

(iii) not less than 50 of the company's members.

An application may not be made by any member who has consented to or voted in favour of the resolution.

The court may confirm the resolution, or cancel the resolution or confirm the resolution subject to such terms and conditions as it thinks fit. It may also provide for the purchase by the company of any shares of members and for the consequent reduction of capital and alteration of the memorandum and articles.

A company may not re-register until 28 days have elapsed from the passing of the resolution, to allow a minority the right to object.

The company must give immediate notice to the Registrar if an application is made opposing the re-registration of the company. When the court order is made the company must within 15 days deliver an office copy of the order to the Registrar (s 54).

COMPARISON OF PUBLIC AND PRIVATE COMPANIES

1. (a) A public company must have an allotted share capital of at least £50,000.
   (b) A private company is not required to have a minimum capital.
2. (a) A public company must not enter into a business transaction or exercise its borrowing powers until it has been granted a section 117 certificate by the Registrar.
   (b) A private company may commence business and borrow on receipt of its certificate of incorporation.
3. (a) A public company may raise capital by offering its shares or debentures to the public.
   (b) A private company is not permitted to do so.
4. (a) A public company must have a minimum of two directors (unless registered before 1 November 1929).
   (b) A private company requires only one director.
5. (a) A director of a public company must retire on reaching the age of 70 (unless otherwise resolved).
   (b) This rule does not apply to a director of a private company, unless the company is a subsidiary of a public company.
6. (a) Directors of public companies other than the first directors must be voted into office individually at a general meeting.
   (b) Two or more directors of a private company may be voted into office by a single resolution.
7. (a) A public company must publish its accounts in full.
   (b) A private company (if it satisfies the small or medium company definition) may have partial exemption from publishing its full accounts.

8. (a) A public company must convene an extraordinary general meeting if its net assets fall to half its called up share capital.
   (b) A private company is not subject to this rule.
9. (a) A member of a public company may appoint more than one proxy to represent his interests. A proxy may vote but, unless the articles provide otherwise, may not address the meeting.
   (b) A member of a private company may only appoint one proxy, but the proxy may vote and address the meeting.
10. (a) A public company may not make an allotment of shares unless at least one-quarter of the nominal value and the whole of any premium has been paid.
   (b) A private company is not subject to these provisions.
11. (a) A public company must provide for unrealised capital losses before making a distribution.
   (b) A private company is not required to make such a provision.
12. (a) A public company may not give financial assistance to enable a person to purchase the company's shares.
   (b) A private company may provide such financial assistance.
13. (a) Shares may not be allotted by a public company in consideration for services, or for an undertaking to be performed more than five years after allotment.
   (b) A private company is not subject to a restriction on the consideration for the purchase of its shares.
14. (a) The secretary of a public company must have the requisite knowledge, experience and possess an appropriate professional qualification.
   (b) The company secretary of a private company is not required to be qualified.

## OVERSEA COMPANIES

An oversea company is a company incorporated outside Great Britain which has established a place of business within Great Britain (s 691). For the purpose of this section Great Britain is defined as England, Wales and Scotland, but not the Channel Islands or the Isle of Man. An oversea company incorporated in the Channel Islands or the Isle of Man is known as an island company.

A company establishes a place of business if it has a share-transfer or registration office in Great Britain, but not if it merely acts through agents resident in Great Britain.

An oversea company must, within one month of establishing a place of business within Great Britain, file with the Registrar:

  (i) A certified copy of its charter or memorandum and articles;
 (ii) A list of directors and secretary;
(iii) The name and address of at least one person resident in Great Britain authorised to accept service of process on behalf of the company.

Any alteration of the above particulars must be notified to the Registrar.

Every oversea company must prepare a balance sheet and profit and loss account in respect of each accounting reference period. If the company is a holding company it must also prepare group accounts in such form as if it had been incorporated in Great Britain. Copies of these documents must be delivered to the Registrar. A certified English translation must be annexed to any document that is not written in English. These provisions do not apply if the form of the company is such that it would be regarded as an unlimited company if it had been incorporated in Great Britain.

Every oversea company must state the country in which it is incorporated in every prospectus inviting subscriptions for shares or debentures in Great Britain. The content and format of such a prospectus is very similar to a prospectus issued by a company registered in England (s 693).

It must also conspicuously exhibit in every place where it carries on business in Great Britain the name of the company, the country in which it is incorporated and (if applicable) that it is a limited company. This information must also appear in all the company's bill-heads, letters, notices and other official publications.

An oversea company must also register all charges created on property in England.

Any process or notice will be effectively served if addressed to the person whose name and address has been delivered to the Registrar as authorised to accept service of process on the company's behalf, and left at or sent by post to that address (s 695).

## HOLDING AND SUBSIDIARY COMPANIES

It is often necessary to determine whether a company is a subsidiary of another. Section 736 lays down three situations where a company is deemed to be a subsidiary.

 (i) if another company (H) is a member of it (S) and controls the composition of its (S) board of directors; or

(ii) if another company (H) holds more than half in nominal value of its (S) equity share capital; or

(iii) if (S) it is a subsidiary of any company (A) which is in turn a subsidiary of another company (H).

(i) The other company (H) must be a member of the company (S) i e it must be the registered holder of at least one share. It must control the composition of the company's (S) board of directors. Section 736 provides that the test of control is that the other company (H) can without the consent or concurrence of another person appoint or remove all or a majority of the directors. In particular the necessary control exists if:

(a) a person cannot be appointed to the board (of S) unless the other company (H) exercises a power in his favour;

(b) a person's appointment as a director (of S) follows automatically from his appointment as director of the other company (H);

(c) the directorship is held by the other company (H) or a subsidiary of it.

(ii) Equity share capital is defined as a company's issued share capital having an unrestricted right to participate in the distribution of a dividend and/or a return of capital. It includes a company's ordinary share capital as well as any participating preference shares (i e preference shares having an unrestricted right to participate in a distribution) issued by a company.

(iii) Any shares held, or powers exercisable by a company are disregarded for the purpose of establishing the relationship of holding company and subsidiary

e g where a company acts as a nominee for another party

where a company holds shares as a trustee.

where a company holds debentures of another company and is given certain powers (e g to appoint directors) under the terms of the debentures.

## SMALL AND MEDIUM-SIZED COMPANIES

A company may be classified for accounting purposes as a small or medium-sized company (s 248).

A company qualifies as a small or medium-sized company if it satisfies, for the financial year in question and the preceding year, two of the following conditions:

FOR A SMALL COMPANY

(i) Its turnover (or annual equivalent) must not exceed £1,400,000.
(ii) Its balance sheet total must not exceed £700,000;
(iii) The average number of employees, in a financial year, does not exceed 50.


FOR A MEDIUM-SIZED COMPANY

(i) Its turnover (or annual equivalent) must not exceed £5,750,000.
(ii) Its balance sheet total must not exceed £2,800,000;
(iii) The average number of employees, in a financial year, does not exceed 250.

A company cannot qualify as a small or medium-sized company if it is a public company or an insurance, banking or shipping company or a member of a group which contains such a company.

The directors of small and medium sized companies may deliver modified and less detailed versions of their company's accounts to the Registrar, which must be accompanied by an audit report which states that in the auditors opinion the requirements for exemption are satisfied.

A small company may group together some of the items which are required to be shown separately on the standard balance sheet and is not required to file a profit account or the directors' report. A medium-sized company is permitted to file a modified profit and loss account which does not disclose turnover and group accounts.

The full accounts of both classes of companies must be laid before their shareholders at the general meeting.

Any company which qualified as a small or medium-sized company will not lose its status if it is unable to fulfil the criteria for one year. If it loses its status it will take two years of satisfying the criteria to re-establish it as a small or medium-sized company, as the case may be.

Group accounts may also be prepared in a modified form if the holding company and its subsidiaries together fulfil the small or medium-sized company criteria.

Companies which do not qualify as small or medium-sized companies, public companies, and insurance, banking and shipping companies must prepare their accounts fully in accordance with the Act.

# Chapter 3

# The memorandum of association

The memorandum of association contains a company's constitution and lists the minimum requirements for its incorporation and continued existence. It not only determines a company's name, domicile, liability of its members and the amount of its share capital, but also the objects which it may pursue either expressly or impliedly. All other activities undertaken by a company are ultra vires and consequently void.

While the memorandum governs the company's external activities the articles of association contain the rules and regulations which relate to the company's internal management.

The memorandum is the dominant document. Section 1 of the Companies Act provides that any two or more persons may form an incorporated company by subscribing their names to a memorandum of association and otherwise complying with the requirements of the Companies Act in respect of registration.

The memorandum has priority over the articles and in the case of conflict between the provisions of the articles and the contents of the memorandum, the memorandum will prevail.

## THE MEMORANDUM MUST CONTAIN THE FOLLOWING CLAUSES:

1. *The name of the company*: The name of a private company which is limited by shares or guarantee must end with the word 'limited', and that of a public company with the words 'public limited company'. The Welsh equivalent of these words may be used and certain abbreviations are permitted.
2. Whether the company's *registered office* is to be situated in England and Wales, Wales or Scotland.
3. The *objects* of the company.

4. That the *liability* of its members is limited if the company is limited by shares or by guarantee.
5. That each member, of a *company limited by guarantee*, undertakes to contribute to the company's assets in the event of its being wound up while he is a member (or within one year after he ceases to be a member) such amount as may be required, but not exceeding a specified amount.
6. If the company is a *limited company* having *share capital*, it must state the amount of share capital with which it proposes to be registered and the division of that capital into shares of a fixed amount.
7. The memorandum must be signed by at least two persons ie the subscribers to the memorandum, in the presence of at least one witness who must attest the signature. Each subscriber must take at least one share and must write opposite to his name the number of shares he takes.

A company having its registered office in Wales may have its memorandum and articles in Welsh but these documents must be accompanied by a certified translation into English. It may use the words 'cyfyngedig' for limited and 'cwmni cyfyngedig cyhoeddus' for public limited company.

Certain abbreviations are permitted – Ltd, plc, cyf, and CCC.

TABLE F: MEMORANDUM OF ASSOCIATION (PUBLIC COMPANY LIMITED BY SHARES)

1. The company's name is 'Western Electronics Public Limited Company'.

2. The company is to be a public company.

3. The company's registered office is to be situated in England and Wales.

4. The company's objects are the manufacture and development of such descriptions of electronic equipment, instruments and appliances as the company may from time to time determine, and the doing of all such other things as are incidental or conducive to the attainment of that object.

5. The liability of the members is limited.

6. The company's share capital is £5,000,000 divided into 5,000,000 shares of £1 each.

We, the subscribers to this memorandum of association, wish to be formed into a company pursuant to this memorandum; and we agree to take the number of shares shown opposite our respective names.

| Names and Addresses of Subscribers | Number of shares taken by each Subscriber |
|---|---|
| 1. James White, 12 Broadmead, Birmingham. | 1 |
| 2. Patrick Smith, 145A Huntley House, London Wall, London EC2. | 1 |
| Total shares taken | 2 |

Dated 19

Witness to the above signatures,
Anne Brown, 13 Hute Street, London WC2.

TABLE B: MEMORANDUM OF ASSOCIATION (PRIVATE COMPANY LIMITED BY SHARES)

1. The company's name is 'The South Wales Motor Transport Company cyfyngedig'.

2. The company's registered office is to be situated in Wales.

3. The company's objects are the carriage of passengers and goods in motor vehicles between such places as the company may from time to time determine and the doing of all such other things as are incidental or conducive to the attainment of that object.

4. The liability of the members is limited.

5. The company's share capital is £50,000 divided into 50,000 shares of £1 each.

We, the subscribers to this memorandum of association, wish to be formed into a company pursuant to this memorandum; and we agree to take the number of shares shown opposite our respective names.

| Names and Addresses of Subscribers | Number of shares taken by each Subscriber |
|---|---|
| 1. Thomas Jones, 138 Mountfield Street, Tredegar. | 1 |

2. Mary Evans, 19 Merthyr Road,                     1
   Aberystwyth.

                        Total shares taken          2

Dated              19

Witness to the above signatures,
Anne Brown, "Woodlands", Fieldside Road, Bryn Mawr.


TABLE C: MEMORANDUM OF ASSOCIATION (COMPANY LIMITED BY
GUARANTEE NOT HAVING A SHARE CAPITAL)

1. The company's name is 'The Dundee School Association
Limited'.

2. The company's registered office is to be situated in Scotland.

3. The company's objects are the carrying on of a school for boys
and girls in Dundee and the doing of all such other things as are
incidental or conducive to the attainment of that object.

4. The liability of the members is limited.

5. Every member of the company undertakes to contribute such
amount as may be required (not exceeding £100) to the company's
assets if it should be wound up while he is a member or within one
year after he ceases to be a member, for payment of the company's
debts and liabilities contracted before he ceases to be a member,
and of the costs, charges and expenses of winding up, and for the
adjustment of the rights of the contributories among themselves.

We, the subscribers to this memorandum of association, wish to be
formed into a company pursuant to this memorandum.

Names and Addresses of Subscribers.

1. Kenneth Brodie, 14 Bute Street, Dundee.

2. Ian Davis, 2 Burns Avenue, Dundee.

Dated              19

Witness to the above signatures,

Anne Brown, 149 Princes Street, Edinburgh.

TABLE D: MEMORANDUM OF ASSOCIATION (PUBLIC COMPANY LIMITED BY GUARANTEE HAVING A SHARE CAPITAL)

1. The company's name is 'Gwestai Glyndwr, cwmni cyfyngedig cyhoeddus'.

2. The company is to be a public company.

3. The company's registered office is to be situated in Wales.

4. The company's objects are facilitating travelling in Wales by providing hotels and conveyances by sea and by land for the accommodation of travellers and the doing of all such other things as are incidental or conducive to the attainment of those objects.

5. The liability of the members is limited.

6. Every member of the company undertakes to contribute such amount as may be required (not exceeding £100) to the company's assets if it should be wound up while he is a member or within one year after he ceases to be a member, for payment of the company's debts and liabilities contracted before he ceases to be a member, and of the costs, charges and expenses of winding up, and for the adjustment of the rights of the contributories among themselves.

7. The company's share capital is £50,000 divided into 50,000 shares of £1 each.

We, the subscribers to this memorandum of association, wish to be formed into a company pursuant to this memorandum; and we agree to take the number of shares shown opposite our respective names.

| Names and Addresses of Subscribers | Number of shares taken by each Subscriber |
|---|---|
| 1. Thomas Jones, 138 Mountfield Street, Tredegar. | 1 |
| 2. Andrew Smith, 19 Merthyr Road, Aberystwyth. | 1 |
| Total shares taken | 2 |

Dated              19

Witness to the above signatures,
Anne Brown, "Woodlands", Fieldside Road, Bryn Mawr.

TABLE E: MEMORANDUM OF ASSOCIATION (AN UNLIMITED COMPANY HAVING A SHARE CAPITAL)

1. The company's name is 'The Woodford Engineering Company'.

2. The company's registered office is to be situated in England and Wales.

3. The company's objects are the working of certain patented inventions relating to the application of microchip technology to the improvement of food processing, and the doing of all such other things as are incidental or conductive to the attainment of that object.

We, the subscribers to this memorandum of association, wish to be formed into a company pursuant to this memorandum; and we agree to take the number of shares shown opposite our respective names.

| Names and Addresses of Subscribers | Number of shares taken by each Subscriber |
|---|---|
| 1. Brian Smith, 24 Nibley Road, Wotton-under-Edge, Gloucestershire. | 3 |
| 2. William Green, 278 High Street, Chipping Sodbury, Avon. | 5 |
| Total shares taken | 8 |

Dated          19

Witness to the above signatures,
Anne Brown, 108 Park Way, Bristol 8.


THE NAME CLAUSE

The promoters select the company's name. Various restrictions are imposed on their freedom of choice by statute, regulations and common law.

The Registrar may refuse to register a Company by a name:

(i) Which includes the words 'limited', 'unlimited', 'public limited company', their abbreviations or Welsh equivalents, other than at the end of the name;

(ii) which is the same as a name appearing on the index of company names kept by the Registrar;

(iii) the use of which by the company would in the opinion of the Secretary of State constitute a criminal offence;
(iv) which in the opinion of the Secretary of State is offensive (s 26(1).

THE INDEX OF NAMES

The Registrar keeps an index of the names of:

   (i) All companies registered under the Companies Act 1985 and under earlier Companies Acts.
       This also includes the names of the companies registered in Scotland and Northern Ireland.
  (ii) Oversea companies.
 (iii) Limited partnerships registered under the Limited Partnership Act 1907.
  (iv) Registered industrial provident societies, including those registered in Scotland and Northern Ireland.

CHANGE OF NAME

1. A company may change its name by special resolution. A copy of the resolution must then be sent to the Registrar within 15 days. As the change of name effectively alters the memorandum, a copy of the memorandum as altered must accompany the copy of the resolution (s 28(1)).
2. The Secretary of State may, within 12 months of a company's registration, direct a company to change its name if its name is the same as or, (in his opinion), too like a name appearing in the index, or is too like a name which should have appeared in the index at the time of registration (s 28(2)).
3. The Secretary of State may, within 5 years of registration, direct a company to change its name if it appears that the company has provided misleading information in order to be registered by a particular name, or has given undertakings or assurances that have not been fulfilled (s 28(3)).
4. The Department of Trade may direct a company to change its name if it is of the opinion that the name gives so misleading an indication of the nature of the company's activities as to be likely to cause harm to the public (s 32).

A direction must be complied with within 6 weeks or such longer period as the Department of Trade may allow. A company has a right to appeal to the court against the direction. An appeal must be lodged within 3 weeks of the date of the direction. The court may set aside the direction or confirm it.

On a change of name, the Registrar enters its new name on the register and issues a new certificate of incorporation.

A change of name does not affect any of the company's rights or obligations. Any legal proceedings by or against the company may be continued or commenced by its new name.

RESTRICTIONS ON THE USE OF CERTAIN WORDS

Certain statutes forbid the use of words in a company's name which imply an association or connection with charitable organisations e g The Chartered Associations (Protection of Names and Uniforms) Act 1926 forbids the use or imitation of the names of 'Boy Scouts', 'Girl Guides Association', the 'Order of St John of Jerusalem'.

'Red Cross' may not be used without the authority of the Army Council – Army Council (Geneva Convention) Act 1957.

Other words whose use is forbidden include: Building Society – unless registered as a Building Society (Building Societies Act 1962). Bank – unless recognised as such by the Bank of England (Banking) Act 1979.

A company may not be registered by a name which is likely to give the impression that it is connected in any way with the Government or with any local authority – except with the approval of the Secretary of State.

Approval is also required for the use of any words or expressions listed in the appropriate regulations i e The Company and Business Names Regulations 1981. These Regulations list some 79 words and expressions which range in alphabetical order from 'Abortion' to 'Windsor'. They can only be used with the approval of the Secretary of State, or the appropriate government department, or other body e g Assurer, English, Giro, Ireland, Patentee, Scottish, Trust, United Kingdom, Wales, (approval of the Secretary of State), Duke, Police, Royal, Windsor (approval of the Home Office) Dental, Dentistry (approval of the General Dental Council).

EXEMPTION FROM USING THE WORD 'LIMITED'

A company which is, or about to be, registered as a private company limited by *guarantee* will be exempt from using the word 'limited' in its name if its objects are 'the promotion of commerce, art, science, education, religion, charity or any profession and anything incidental or conducive to any of those objects' (s 30).

The memorandum or articles must:

(i) require its profits (if any) or other income to be applied in promoting its objects.
(ii) prohibit the payment of dividends to its members.
(iii) provide that if the company is wound-up its assets will be transferred to another body with similar objects or charitable objects.

A private company limited by *shares*, formed for charitable and social purposes, and licenced by the Department of Trade before 26 February 1982 continues to be granted exemption.

A statutory declaration made by a solicitor engaged in the company's formation, or by a director or secretary of an existing company that the company satisfies the exemption requirements is sufficient to obtain the exemption.

PUBLICATION AND DISPLAY OF NAME

Various Acts deal with the publication and display by a company of its registered name.

1. *Publication of name*
A company's name must appear legibly

(a) On the outside of every office or place in which it carries on business, in a conspicuous position.
(b) Engraved on its seal.
(c) In all its business letters, notices and official publications.
(d) In all bills of exchange, promissory notes endorsements, cheques and orders for money or goods signed on its behalf.
(e) In all its receipts and letters of credit (s 349, 350).

A company and its officers may be fined for not complying with these provisions.

In addition any officer or person acting on the company's behalf who signs or authorises the signature of any bill of exchange, promissory note, cheque or order for money or goods will incur personal liability if the company's name is incorrectly mentioned in the bill of exchange etc. This liability will only arise if the company is unable to pay.

**Atkin v Wardle and Others** (1889)

The South Shields Salt Water Baths Co Ltd was described in a bill of exchange as the Salt Water Baths Co Ltd. The directors were held personally liable on the bill for this misdescription.

**Barber & Nicholls v R & G Associates (London) Ltd** (1982)

A director who signed a cheque for the defendant company was held personally liable on the cheque as he had omitted (London) from the company's name.

### 2. *Company identification*
Section 349 provides that every company is to mention the following particulars in all its business letters and order forms:

(a) The place of registration and its registered number.
(b) The address of its registered office.
(c) An investment company must state that it is such a company.
(d) A limited company, which is exempt from the obligation to use the word 'limited' as part of its name, must state that it is a limited company.

### 3. *Business name*
A company carrying on business under a business name which does not consist of its registered name is subject to the Business Names Act 1985

(i) It may not use any of the words or phrases listed in the regulations made under the Business Names Act 1985 without the written consent of the Secretary of State.
(ii) It must state its registered name and address for the service of documents on all its business letters, written orders for goods or services, invoices, receipts and written demands for payment of debts.
It must also display its name and address, in a prominent position, in any business premises to which customers and suppliers have access, so that they may be easily read by those customers and suppliers.
(iii) It must supply its name and address to any person with whom anything is done or discussed in the way of business, if so requested by that person.

PASSING OFF

A party who considers that his rights have been infringed by the use of a name may bring an action at common law for passing off to restrain another party from using that name. It is a tort to sell an article or carry on a business under a name which misleads the public into believing that the article or business is that of another party. The injured party may seek an injunction to prevent further violation and either damages or an account for all the profits made as a result of the deception.

### Ewing v Buttercup Margarine Co Ltd (1917)

The proprietor of the Buttercup Dairy Co, a company retailing dairy products in Scotland and Northern England obtained an injunction preventing a newly formed company carrying on business under the name of the Buttercup Margarine Co Ltd. Although the new company was formed to manufacture and deal in margarine it was held that the names were so similar as to cause confusion.

### Exxon Corporation v Exxon Insurance Consultants Ltd (1981)

The Exxon Corporation obtained an injunction restraining the defendant company from using the word 'Exxon' as part of its name. The name had been coined by the Esso Petroleum Company who therefore had a prior and exclusive claim to its use.

Neither an individual nor a company may claim the exclusive use of a word which is in general usage, nor the use of a name which includes the personal name of an individual connected with a firm.

### Waring & Gillow Ltd v Gillow and Gillow Ltd (1916)

The plaintiffs, who were furniture and carpet retailers and auctioneers, sought an injunction to restrain the defendant company from carrying on the business of carpet auctioneers under the name of Gillow & Gillow Ltd. The action failed as the defendant had purchased the business from LC Gillow and was permitted to use his name so as to take advantage of the goodwill purchased.

## THE REGISTERED OFFICE CLAUSE

A company must at all times have a registered office to which all communications and notices may be addressed (s 287). The memorandum must state whether the registered office is to be situated in England, Wales or Scotland (s 2(b)). A company which states in its memorandum that its registered office is situated in England may, if its registered office is situated in Wales, by special resolution alter its memorandum to provide that the registered office is to be situated in Wales.

The address of the registered office must accompany the documents sent to the Registrar on the company's incorporation.

The situation of the registered office determines a company's nationality and domicile e g a company with a registered office in England has British nationality and an English domicile. It does not determine a company's residence for taxation purposes, as this can only be determined by establishing where a company's control and management lies.

All business letters and order forms of a company must state, in legible characters, the location of its registered office (s 351).

A document (including a writ, or notice) may be served on a company by leaving it at or sending it by post to its registered office (s 725).

A company may change its address within its domicile and must notify the Registrar of the change within 14 days. The Registrar must then publish, in the London Gazette, notice of the receipt by him of the change of address. Until the publication of this notice any document delivered to the company's previous address will be deemed to have been validly delivered, unless the person concerned was aware of the change (s 42).

REGISTERS

Certain registers and documents are kept at the company's registered office:

 (i) The register of members and, if the company has one, the index of members. If the register is made up at another office of the company, they may be kept at that office. If the register and index is made up by an agent, they may be kept at the agent's office (ss 352, 353).
 (ii) The register of directors and secretaries (s 288).
(iii) The register of directors interests in shares in, or debentures of, the company or associated companies together with the index of names in the register (if the company has an index). If the register of members is not kept at its registered office, this register may be kept where the register of members is kept (ss 324, 325, 327).
(iv) The register of substantial interests (5% of more) in shares carrying unrestricted voting rights and an index of names (if the company has an index). This must be kept at the same

place as the register of director's interests (ss 211, 213).

 (v) A copy of each director's service contract, and if the contract is not in writing a memorandum of its terms. These may be kept at the place where the register of members is kept, or at the company's principal place of business (s 318).

 (vi) The minute books of general meetings (s 383).

 (vii) The register of debenture holders (if a register is kept). If the register is made up at another office, it may be kept at that office. If the register is made up by an agent, it may be kept at the agent's office (s 190).

(viii) The company's register of charges affecting the property of the company (ss 407, 409).

 (ix) A copy of every instrument creating any change requiring registration under ss 396, 400, 406.

 (x) A declaration of solvency and auditors' report where a private company intends to purchase or redeem its shares out of capital (s 175).

 (xi) All these documents may be inspected without any charge by members during business hours.

Other persons have the right, usually on payment of a nominal fee (5p), to inspect all these documents apart from the minute book and the directors service contracts. There is also a right in most cases to be supplied with a copy of entries in documents on payment of a small fee (usually 10p per 100 words).

## THE OBJECTS CLAUSE

Every memorandum must contain an objects clause (s 2). This clause determines the capacity of the company to enter into contracts ie '. . . it must specify the objects . . . it must delimit and identify the objects in such plain and unambiguous manner as that the reader can identify the field of industry in which the corporate activities are to be confined', per Lord Wrenbury in *Cotman v Brougham* (1918).

The statement of the company's objects serves a dual purpose:

 (i) It protects the subscribers to the memorandum who are made aware of the purposes for which their money can be applied; and

 (ii) It protects persons dealing with the company who are thereby aware of the extent of the company's contractual powers.

Any transaction outside the limits of the objects clause is ultra vires (ie beyond the company's powers) and void.

### Ashbury Railway Carriage & Iron Co v Riche (1875)

The company was incorporated to carry on the business of 'mechanical engineers and general contractors'. The directors entered into a contract to purchase a concession to construct a railway in Belgium, and their decision was ratified by the shareholders in general meeting. It was held that the contract was not within the company's objects and was therefore void. Such a contract could not be ratified by the shareholders.

### Simmonds v Heffer (1983)

The main object of the League against Cruel Sports, a company limited by guarantee, was the prevention of cruelty to animals. The company donated £80,000 to the Labour Party which had pledged, in its manifesto, to ban hare coursing and deer and stag hunting if elected. £50,000 was given without any conditions being attached to the gift, while the remaining £30,000 was to be used for publicising the manifesto pledge on animal welfare. It was held that the gift of £50,000 was ultra vires while the remaining gift was intra vires.

The ultra vires rule also applies to statutory companies, but not to chartered companies. A member of a chartered company may apply for an injunction to restrain a company from exceeding its stated objects.

A company's objects must be distinguished from the powers which it can exercise in furtherance of these objects and which are incidental to those objects.

### Rolled Steel Products (Holdings) Ltd v British Steel Corpn (1982)

The plaintiff company (RSP) gave the British Steel Corporation (BSC) a guarantee for a debt owed by another company (S) and later issued a debenture secured by a floating charge in favour of BSC. In return RSP received a sum of money from BSC which enabled it to pay a debt owed to S, and this sum was paid to S. The objects clause of RSP provided that the company could:

'lend and advance money or give credit to such persons, firms or companies and on such terms as may seem expedient, and in particular to customers of and others having dealings with the company, and to give guarantees or become security for any such persons, firms or companies?

It was held that this clause was a power and not an object. Such a power had to be exercised for the company's benefit. As this was not the case the transaction was held to be ultra vires and void.

The objects of the Western Electronics plc (as set out in the specimen memorandum are 'the conveyance of passengers and goods in ships or boats between such places as the company may from time to time determine'. The objects clause concludes with a power to do 'all such things as are incidental to the attainment of the above object' – thus enabling the company to attain its objects. Some powers are expressly stated in the memorandum while certain powers are implied.

> 'Anything reasonably incidental to the attainment or pursuit of any of the express objects of the company will, unless expressly prohibited be within the implied powers of the company' per Buckley LJ in *Re Horsley & Weight Ltd*.

The Western Electronics plc would most certainly have the powers to:

Hire and dismiss employees
Borrow money
Purchase, lease or sell property
Aquire similar businesses
Bring and defend actions
Draw and accept bills of exchange
Pay pensions to its ex-employees
Buy and hire all manner of transport
Pay directors' remuneration
Acquire shares in another company.

The courts have always insisted that a power which is implied must be exercised for the benefit of the company.

### Parke v Daily News (1962)

The majority shareholders of a company which had been sold proposed to distribute the whole of the purchase price as ex gratia payments to its redundant employees. It was held that such payments were ultra vires as they were not for the benefit of the company.

(Section 719 now provides that a company has the power to make provision for the benefit of its employees and former employees on its transfer or winding up – even though such payments may not be in the company's best interests).

A company may carry on an additional business if that business is incidental to the company's main objects, and thereby benefits the company.

### Deuchar v The Gas Light & Coke Co (1925)

A company formed to extract gas from coal had the power to manufacture and supply gas, deal with and sell by-products, and convert the by-products into a marketable state. The plaintiff, a secretary of a company which supplied the defendant with caustic soda sought a declaration that the manufacture of caustic soda and chlorine by the defendant and the erection of a factory for that purpose was ultra vires the company. The company used the caustic soda to convert certain residuals of gas-making into chlorine, a by-product of caustic soda was converted into bleaching power. It was held that the manufacture of both products was fairly incidental to the company's powers.

An act which is expressed to be, and is capable of being an independent object of the company is intra vires the company.

### Re Horsley & Weight Ltd (1982)

A company's objects included a power to grant pensions to its present and past employees and to its directors. The company purchased a pension policy for a director and employee who was about to retire. After his retirement the company was wound up and the liquidator sought a declaration that the payment was ultra vires. It was held that the power to grant pensions was a substantive object of the company and was therefore valid.

A company may not convert a subordinate power into an independent object, as the power is dependent on the objects clause. Thus a power to borrow money cannot convert that power to an independent activity.

### Introductions Ltd v National Provincial Bank Ltd (1970)

A company was formed to provide accommodation and entertainment for overseas visitors. The objects clause empowered the company to borrow or raise money in such manner as it deemed fit and provided that each of the objects was an independent object. A bank lent money to the company to finance the company's sole activity, pig breeding, and took debentures as security for the loan. It was held that the loan was for an ultra vires activity, and the debentures were void.

It is usual for a company to insert express powers in its object clause to:

(a) make gifts;
(b) provide gratuities and pensions for employees and former employees;

(c) provide for employees and former employees on the cessation or transfer of a business;
(d) give guarantees in respect of the liabilities of 3rd parties.

The inclusion of such powers removes the need to rely on an implied power to make gifts and provide gratuities etc. The exercise of such a power must however be considered in relation to the company's activities.

It was held in *Re Lee Behrens & Co Ltd* (1932) that for a gift to be valid it must

(i) be reasonably incidental to carrying on the company's business;
(ii) be a bone fide transaction;
(iii) done for the benefit of and to promote the company's prosperity.

### Evans v Brunner, Mond & Co Ltd (1921)

A chemical manufacturing company made gifts to universities and other bodies engaged in scientific research. The objects clause included a power that the company could do 'all such business and things as may be incidental or conducive to the attainment of the above objects, or any of them'. It was held the gifts were conducive to the company's main objects as the company would benefit from scientific research and the increase in the number of scientists.

### Re Lee Behrens (1932)

A company's objects clause conferred a power to grant pensions to widows and other dependants of employees and former employees. Three years before the company was wound up the directors covenanted to pay a pension of £500 p.a. to the widow of a former managing director. It was held that the three conditions (set out above) had not been satisfied.

(See also *Re W & M Roith* (1967), p 205).

These 3 conditions have been questioned in later cases in so far as they apply to the interpretation of express powers.

In *Charterbridge Corporation v Lloyds Bank* (1970) Pennycuick J rejected (i), and it is thought that such a condition need not be fulfilled in the case of a gift made under an express power.

In *Re Horsley & Weight Ltd* (1982) Buckley LJ rejected (iii) and stated

'. . . if the memorandum of association expressly or by implication provides that an express object only extends to acts which benefit or promote the prosperity of the company, regard must be paid to that limitation; but where there is no such express or implied limitation, the question whether an act done within the terms of an express object of the company will benefit or promote the prosperity of the company, or of its business is, in my view, irrelevant'.

The payment of a gift may nevertheless be challenged as constituting an unlawful return of capital.

### Re Halt Garage Ltd (1964) Ltd (1982)

A husband and wife were the sole shareholders and directors of a company. The articles of the company provided that the directors were not entitled to remuneration unless it was voted by the general meeting. The liquidator claimed that payments made by way of directors' remuneration were gratuitous as the payments were made to the wife after she became ill and was no longer active in the business and the husband's drawings exceeded the market value of his services. It was held that the liquidator could recover part of the payments made to the wife as they amounted to a gratuitous distribution out of capital.

A power is given to directors to make political and charitable contributions which must be listed in the director's report (Sch 7).

INTERPRETATION OF THE OBJECT CLAUSE

The object clause of the majority of companies consists of some 20 to 30 paragraphs, containing objects and powers, often intermingled, which enable companies to engage in a variety of activities. The format and the contents of objects clauses are fairly standardised, and most companies adopt similar clauses. Under the original Companies Act 1862, the objects clause was unalterable and prior to the Companies Act 1948 a company had to seek the court's approval before it could alter its objects clause. A company would therefore include in its object clause the power to engage in all types of business and activities and the facility to enter into every kind of commercial transaction.

In the light of these developments the courts sought to restrict a wide and liberal interpretation of the objects clause.

### (a) *The main objects clause*

The ejusdem generis rule was applied to the construction of an objects clause ie where a memorandum contains a company's objects in a series of paragraphs, and the first paragraph or series of paragraphs appear to embody the company's main object, the other paragraphs are regarded as being limited by, and ancillary to this main object.

### (b) *Failure of the company's substratum*

If all the company's main objects have failed, the substratum of the company is said to have gone and the shareholders may petition for the company to be wound up under the just and equitable rule.

### Re German Date Coffee Co (1882)

A company was formed to manufacture coffee from dates, using a German patent. Other objects included the acquisition and use of any other invention for a similar purpose, and the import and export of all descriptions of produce for the purpose of food. The German patent was not granted but the company acquired a Swedish patent and successfully manufactured coffee in Hamburg. Two shareholders petitioned for the company to be wound up. It was held that the company's substratum had failed, as the company's main object was the manufacture of coffee using a German patent.

### Re Amalgamated Syndicate (1897)

A company was formed to erect stands, let seats and promote entertainments in connection with Queen Victoria's Diamond Jubilee (1897). It was also given powers in its memorandum to invest in other companies and proposed to carry on business under these powers. It was held that its substratum had failed as the main object had ceased at the end of the Diamond Jubilee.

Companies have sought to avoid the effect of these rules by inserting various paragraphs in their object clause.

(a)  A concluding paragraph stating that each sub-clause should be considered an independent main object, not limited or restricted by reference to any other paragraph or the company's name.

### Cotman v Brougham (1918)

A company formed to develop rubber estates abroad included in its object clause various sub-clauses, including the power to promote companies and deal in shares of other companies. The final clause of the objects clause provided that each of the thirty sub-clauses should be considered a separate and independent main object. The company underwrote shares in another company. It was held that the underwriting contract was valid as the transaction was authorised by the memorandum.

### Anglo-Overseas Agencies Ltd v Green (1961)

A company whose main object was to act as importers and exporters of goods, sought to acquire a valuable building lease under a sub-clause in the memorandum. This clause provided that the company was empowered to 'acquire any concessions, rights . . . and to turn to account, maintain and sell, dispose of and deal with the same'. The concluding paragraph of the object clause provided that the objects specified in any paragraph were not to be limited or restricted by reference to or inference from the terms of any other paragraph in the object clause. It was held that the proposed acquisition was valid as the concluding paragraph excluded the operation of the main objects rule.

### Re New Finance Mortgage Co Ltd (1975)

A company was empowered to act as financiers, capitalists, concessionaries, bankers, commercial agents, mortgage brokers, financial agents and advisers, exporters, importers of goods and merchandise of all kinds and merchants generally. The objects clause concluded with a statement that each subclause was to be read independently of the others. It was held that the words 'merchants generally' gave the company the authority to operate a chain of garages and the company was therefore liable to the Total Company for petrol supplied to its garages.

### Newstead v Frost (1980)

A television entertainer and performer in the United Kingdom decided to exploit his talents in the United States while retaining residence in the United Kingdom. He carried out his overseas activities as a partner in a partnership between himself and a company incorporated in the Bahamas. The objects of the company were 'to carry on Business as bankers, capitalists, financiers, concessionaries and merchants and to undertake and carry on and execute all kinds of financial trading or other operations . . .' It was held that the words 'all kinds of financial trading or other operations' were wide enough to empower the company to carry on the business of the partnership.

(b) A clause at the end of the memorandum giving a company the power 'to do such other things as are incidental or conducive to the attainment of the objects above specified'.

(c) A clause permitting a company to 'carry on any other trade or business which can in the opinion of the Board of Directors be advantageously carried on by the Company in connection with or as ancillary to any of the above business or the general business of the company'.

### Bell Houses Ltd v City Wall Properties Ltd (1966)

A company agreed, for a procuration fee, to introduce another company to a financier to enable that company to obtain a short term loan for property development. The court held that this subsidiary business of mortgage broking was valid. The test as to what the directors considered to be advantageous to the company was subjective and in the absence of bad faith or improper motive such an activity was intra vires.

SECTION 35

Section 35 implements the first Directive on Company Law which requires that 'acts done by organs of the company shall be binding upon it even if these acts are not within the objects of the company.'
   Section 35 provides:

'In favour of a person dealing with a company in good faith, any transaction decided on by the directors is deemed to be one which it is within the capacity of the company to enter into, and the power of the directors to bind the company is deemed to be free of any limitation under the memorandum or articles. A party to a transaction so decided on is not bound to enquire as to the capacity of the company to enter into it or as to any such limitation on the powers of the directors, and is presumed to have acted in good faith unless the contrary is proved'.

This section does not abolish the ultra vires doctrine – it modifies the doctrine in certain situations.
   A party who contracts with the company will be protected if the following conditions are satisfied:

(a) The person entering into the contract with the company must have acted in good faith. A party is presumed to have acted in good faith, unless the company is able to prove that he knew that the act was outside the company's objects or, he could not (in view of the circumstances) have been unaware that he was a party to an ultra vires transaction.
(b) It must be a transaction. It would appear that this section would not cover a situation where a company carries on an ultra vires course of business, and not a single transaction.
(c) The transaction must be decided on by the directors. The acts of a sole director come within the scope of s 35 as will the acts of a managing director where the board has properly delegated powers to him. It would appear that delegation to a sole effective director also comes within the scope of s 35. This view

was expressed in *International Sales and Agencies Ltd v Marcus* (1982).

## THE ULTRA VIRES DOCTRINE

Although the ultra vires doctrine has been modified by the European Communities Act and its effect modified by careful drafting of the objects clause there are nevertheless occasions when the doctrine is important.

(a) A person who enters into a contract with a company and who is aware of the ultra vires nature of the contract, may not enforce the contract. However, if he enters into a contract which could be within a company's objects clause (eg the sale of machinery) but the contract in question is, unknown to him, outside these objects it is nevertheless an intra vires contract. Such a contract will only be deemed to be ultra vires if the party in question knew that the goods supplied were being used for an ultra vires purpose. A contract is also valid if goods are supplied for an intra vires purpose, but are used by the company for an ultra vires purpose.

### Re David Payne & Co Ltd (1904)

A company was lent £6,000 and issued a debenture as security for the loan. The money was used by a director of the company to finance his own company. The company was later wound up and the liquidator claimed that the debenture was void as the money had been used for an ultra vires purpose. It was held that the debenture was valid, as the loan was within the company's powers, and the lender was under no obligation to enquire as to the use of the loan.

(b) Neither a company, its directors or members may enforce an ultra vires contract.
(c) A director may be liable to compensate a company for any loss incurred by the company if he parts with any money or property for an ultra vires purpose.
(d) A company, in general meeting, cannot ratify and make valid an ultra vires contract (*Ashbury Railway Carriage & Iron Co Ltd v Riche* (1875) (see p 45)).
(e) A member may apply to the court for an injunction to restrain a proposed act of the company on the grounds that it is ultra vires.

Although no action can be brought under an ultra vires contract there are certain *remedies* available to a third party who has entered into such a transaction with a company.

(a) Tracing. He may trace property if that property remains in the possession of the company.
He may also trace any money resulting from an ultra vires borrowing if that money has been paid into a fund or has been used to purchase a particular asset ie it can be identified. However, this remedy does not lie against a purchaser who has taken any asset bone fide for value, in good faith and without notice of any third party rights.

### Sinclair v Brougham (1914)

A building society developed a banking business which was not within its objects clause and therefore ultra vires. It borrowed large sums of money for this activity from its bank customers. When the company was put into liquidation it was held that although the bank customers could not sue to recover their money they were nevertheless able to trace their funds into the society's monies.

(b) If tracing is not possible, the other party is entitled in a liquidation to share in the distribution of any surplus assets after certain creditors have been paid and winding up costs have been met.

(c) Subrogation. If a company borrows money on an ultra vires contract and uses the money wholly or partly for the payment of intra vires debts the lender is entitled to rank as an unsecured creditor in respect of money used for the payment of these intra vires debts.

### Cunliffe, Brooks & Co v Blackburn Building Society (1884)

An agreement between a bank and a building society was deemed ultra vires. The money advanced by the bank was used to discharge intra vires debts of the building society. It was held that the ultra vires lender (the bank) was entitled to be subrogated to the position of intra vires creditors paid off with the money borrowed from the bank.

(d) A claim in quasi-contract. Mocatta J suggested in *Bell Houses Ltd v City Wall Properties Ltd* (1966) that an action for money had and received might well succeed in a situation where a company paid money to another party under an ultra vires contract and the other party relied on the ultra vires character of the contract to avoid his obligations under the contract.

(e) Enforce a guarantee or other security provided by the company or other interested party.

### Garrard v James (1925)

The plaintiff purchases 1,500 shares in a company to advance a scheme for the appointment of a relative as business-manager to the company. It was agreed that if the relative should leave the company's employment the company would re-purchase the shares and two of the company's directors entered into a guarantee for the re-purchase. The relative left the company and the company refused to re-purchase the shares. It was held that although the contract entered into by the company to re-purchase the shares was ultra vires and void, nevertheless the guarantee was enforceable.

#### ALTERATION OF THE OBJECTS CLAUSE

A company may alter its object clause by special resolution (s 4). A copy of the resolution must be submitted to the Registrar within 15 days (s 380). The Registrar must then publish a notice in the London Gazette acknowledging receipt of the copy. If there is no objection to the alteration the company must then deliver a copy of the memorandum as altered to the Registrar between 21 and 36 days after the passing of the resolution (a 21 day period is allowed for minority shareholders to object) (s 6).

A company is permitted to alter its objects clause:

(a) To enable it to carry on its business more economically or more efficiently. As there is no alteration to the company's business, the alteration must be as to the method of conducting that business.

### Re Consett Iron Co Ltd (1901)

A company altered its objects to enable it to acquire shares in companies carrying on a similar business to its own, to promote such companies and enter into partnership or profit sharing agreements with such companies. It was held that the alteration was valid.

(b) To attain its main purpose by new or improved means.
(c) To enlarge or change the local area of its operations.

### Re Egyptian Delta Land and Investment Co (1907)

A company, whose main object was to acquire land in Egypt was entitled to alter its memorandum to acquire land in the Sudan. The court directed the company to change its name to the Egyptian Delta and Sudan Land and Investment Co to reflect the change in its area of operation.

(d) To carry on some business which under existing circumstances may conveniently or advantageously be combined with the business of the company.

### Re Parent Tyre Co Ltd (1923)

A company was incorporated to manufacture tyres, vehicle parts and to invest in companies which manufactured these goods. A resolution was passed to enable the company to carry on business as bankers, financiers, underwriters and deal in real and personal estate. It was held that the alterations were valid, even though the new business bore no relation to the company's existing business. (The company had never manufactured tyres, and had always operated as a holding company).

(e) To restrict or abandon any of the objects specified in the memorandum.

### Re Hampstead Gardens Suburb Trust Ltd (1962)

A company's memorandum provided that any surplus in a winding up should pass to an institution having similar objects, or in default to any charity. The company altered its memorandum to provide that in a winding up its sole beneficiary should be the Hampstead Garden Suburb Community Trust Ltd, whose objects were charitable. It was held that the alteration should be cancelled as it did not fall within the scope of the section.

(f) To sell or dispose of the whole or any part of the undertaking of the company.

(g) To amalgamate with any other company or body of persons.

*Rights of dissenting shareholders*
Minority shareholders who did not vote for the alteration may petition the court, within 21 days, for relief. The dissentients must hold at least 15 per cent of the company's issued capital or 15 per cent of any class of share (where the company has more than one class of share).

Application may also be made by debenture holders holding 15 per cent of any debentures issued before December 1947.

The court may confirm the resolution in whole or in part (subject to any conditions it thinks fit) or it may cancel the alteration. It may also adjourn the proceedings to allow the majority the opportunity of purchasing the shares of the dissenting minority, or it may provide for the purchase by the company of the shares and for the consequent reduction of the company's capital.

If an application is made to the court to cancel the alteration the company must immediately notify the Registrar. A copy of the court order, either confirming or cancelling the alteration, must be delivered to the Registrar within 15 days of the order being made. If the court confirms the alteration the company must also file a copy of the memorandum as altered (s 6).

## LIMITED LIABILITY CLAUSE

The memorandum of a company limited by shares or guarantee merely states that the liability of the members is limited. A company which is exempt from using the word 'limited' as part of its name must nevertheless state, in its memorandum, that the liability of its members is limited.

The consequences of limited liability are as follows:

(i) A member of a company limited by shares cannot be called upon to contribute more than the nominal amount of his shares, or as much as remains unpaid on the shares. There is no liability if the shares are fully paid up.

(ii) A member of a company limited by guarantee, not having a share capital cannot be called upon to contribute a sum in excess of his guarantee.

(iii) A member of a company limited by guarantee, having a share capital cannot be called upon to contribute a sum in excess of his guarantee and the amount (if any) unpaid on his shares.

A typical guarantee clause is found in the specimen memorandum on page 35.

These provisions which limit a member's liability are of fundamental importance as this right cannot be abrogated by the company or by a majority of members. A member cannot be compelled, by altering the memorandum or the articles, to accept an increase in liability to contribute money or take up further shares. Such a purported alteration is null and void.

There are, however, certain circumstances where a member's liability may be increased:

(i) If he agrees, in writing, to take up more shares or increase his liability (s 16).

(ii) If a company carries on business without having at least two members and does so for more than 6 months, the surviving member who, for the whole or any part of the period it carries on business after these six months is aware of this fact is liable (jointly and severally with the company) for the payment of the company's debts during that period, or that part of it (s 24).

(iii) If every member agrees in writing to the re-registration of a private limited company as an unlimited company (s 49). (An unlimited company may by special resolution re-register as a limited company). A company may only make a change from limited to unlimited and vice versa on a single occasion.

(iv) A company may, if authorised by its articles, alter its memorandum by special resolution so as to make the liability of its directors, managers or managing directors unlimited (s 306).

## THE CAPITAL CLAUSE

The capital clause sets out the amount of nominal capital, the number of shares into which it is divided and the amount of each share, eg the share capital of a company is £200,000 divided into 200,000 shares of £1.

The promoters will determine the amount of capital required by a company. Private companies have been registered with a capital of less than £2, while the capital of many public companies is in excess of £10,000,000.

Various factors are taken into consideration in determining the capital required by a company, eg a company is formed to acquire an existing business for £120,000. The purchase price is to be paid in cash and in shares (£60,000 in paid up shares, £60,000 in cash). Shares to the value of £50,000 are kept in reserve to be issued as and when the company requires further capital. A further £30,000 is needed for working capital. The capital is therefore fixed at £200,000.

Although a company may issue shares of any value the most common value is a £1 share.

The capital may consist of different classes of share eg ordinary, preference, deferred shares. The rights attaching to the various classes are usually to be found in the articles or in the terms of issue of the shares.

The capital may be altered at a later date with the consequent alteration of the capital clause. An increase of capital requires an ordinary resolution (s 121) a reduction of capital requires a special resolution and confirmation by the court (s 135).

## THE ASSOCIATION CLAUSE

The memorandum of a company limited by shares concludes with a clause in which the subscribers declare that they desire to be formed into a company and agree to take shares.

The name, address and description of each subscriber and the number of shares subscribed for follows in tabular form.

The memorandum must be signed by each subscriber in the presence of at least one witness who must attest the signature. Each subscriber writes opposite to his name the number of shares he agrees to take, with a minimum subscription of one share.

The subscribers thus become the first members of the company. They also sign the articles and appoint the first directors and the company secretary.

### OTHER CLAUSES

Clauses are sometimes inserted in the memorandum which are usually found in a company's articles. Such clauses may provide for the rights of different classes of shareholders with regard to dividend, voting rights and participation in the company's assets on a winding up.

These clauses may be altered by special resolution, unless the memorandum prohibits the alteration, or provides for some other method of alteration or a condition in such a clause relates to the variation or abrogation of class rights.

The holders of 15 per cent of the issued capital of the company may object to the alteration. The procedure to be followed is similar to that laid down for the alteration of the objects clause in s 4 (s 17).

# Chapter 4

# The articles of association

A company's articles of association contain regulations for the internal management of the company's affairs. A company may submit articles to accompany the memorandum of association when it seeks registration. The articles are subsidiary to the memorandum. In the case of conflict the memorandum prevails. The articles are subject to the requirements of the Company's Act and must not contravene the common law.

The articles must –

(a) be printed,
(b) be divided into paragraphs numbered consecutively and,
(c) be signed by each subscriber to the memorandum in the presence of at least one witness who must attest the signature (s 7(3)).

The Act contains model sets of articles for various types of companies.

(i) Table A – companies limited by shares.
(ii) Table C – guarantee companies not having a share capital.
(iii) Table D – guarantee companies having a share capital.
(iv) Table E – unlimited companies having a share capital.

A company limited by shares need not submit articles, when applying for registration. In that case the articles contained in Table A will apply to the company. (The articles referred to in the text are the articles found in Table A.)

Most public companies will submit their own articles as the Stock Exchange requires that a listed company includes certain articles which are not found in Table A.

A company may set out its own articles and adopt part of Table A. This is the course which is often adopted by a private company to modify or exclude certain articles found in Table A and insert articles which are relevant to the company's specific needs.

A company may expressly exclude Table A. If Table A is not expressly excluded, it will apply to matters which are not dealt with in the company's articles.

Some modification of Table A is usually found to be necessary, as companies seek to exclude, amend or enlarge provisions relating to shares, voting at meetings, director's rights etc.

The major Companies' Acts since 1862 have included a set of model articles in the form of Table A. The particular Table A which applies to a company is the one in force at the time of the company's incorporation. The major Companies Acts were passsed in 1862, 1908, 1929, 1948, 1985, e g a company formed in 1926 is governed by Table A of the Companies Act 1908.

Guarantee companies and unlimited companies must always register articles, as both types of companies must state the number of members with which they propose to be registered. The articles of a guarantee company must correspond with Tables C or D and an unlimited company must correspond with Table E or as near thereto as circumstances admit.

A company's articles are subordinate to, and controlled by the memorandum as the memorandum contains the conditions upon which the company is granted incorporation. Any article that goes beyond the powers contained in the memorandum is inoperative and anything done under the authority of such an article is void and incapable of ratification.

### Guinness v Land Corporation of Ireland (1882)

A company's memorandum declared its objects to be the development of land in Ireland and activities incidental thereto. The company provided in its articles that part of its capital was to be invested in order to provide income to be used as a guarantee fund for the payment of dividend to preference shareholders. It was held that this provision was void as the memorandum stipulated that the whole of the capital should be used to further the company's objects.

A provision in an article may be used to clarify an ambiguity in the memorandum, but it may not be used to extend the company's objects.

### Rainford v James Keith and Blackman and Co (1905)

A memorandum of a trading company empowered the company to do all things incidental to the attainment of its objects. It was held that a provision in the articles which gave the company power to lend money entitled the company to lend money to its employees.

## THE CONTENTS OF THE ARTICLES

The articles usually include provisions dealing with the following:

Share capital and variation of rights
Lien and calls on shares
Transfer and transmission of shares
Forfeiture of shares
Conversion of shares into stock
Alteration of capital
General meetings
Notice of general meetings
Proceedings at general meetings
Votes of members
Borrowing powers
Appointment, power and duties of directors and managing director
Disqualification of directors
Proceedings of directors
Secretary
Dividends and reserves
Accounts and audit
Capitalisation of profits
Special provisions relating to winding up.

## ALTERATION OF THE ARTICLES

A company may alter its articles by passing a special resolution at a general meeting. It is also possible to alter a company's articles without a special resolution if the consent of all the members is obtained.

In *Cane v Jones* (1981) all the members agreed to change an article which gave the chairman a casting vote. They did not formally meet to sanction the change or sign a document to that effect. Nevertheless it was held that the article had been changed and the chairman no longer had a casting vote.

The alteration must not conflict with the Act or the company's memorandum e g by stipulating that an article may only be altered by a 90% majority, as the Act provides that any article may be altered by a three-quarters majority.

A company may not deprive itself of the power to alter its articles (s 9). It is not unlawful to provide in the articles that a specific article may only be changed with the consent of a named person. Such an article may be altered by passing a special resolution and the named person may not prevent this.

An alteration which requires a member to take or subscribe for more shares, and to increase his liability to contribute to the company's share capital, or otherwise pay money to the company is not binding unless he agrees to this in writing (s 16).

A company is entitled to alter its articles even though the minority shareholders consider their interests to be prejudiced by such an alteration. An alteration is valid if it is bone fide for the benefit of the company as a whole.

This test places a heavy burden on a minority shareholder who seeks to oppose an alteration. The Courts of Appeal in *Greenhalgh v Arderne Cinemas* (1951) took the view that:

(a) bone fide in the company's interests means that the majority are regarded as best qualified to determine what is in the company's interests, and
(b) the company as a whole means the general body of shareholders. An alteration would be set aside if it discriminated between majority and minority shareholders, so as to give the majority an advantage which was denied to the minority. Would the individual hypothetical member, in the opinion of the majority, benefit from such an alteration?

### Greenhalgh v Arderne Cinemas (1951)

The majority shareholders wished to sell their shares to an outsider. The articles provided that any shareholder who wished to sell his shares must first offer them to the other members of the company at a fair price before selling them to an outsider. The articles were altered to allow the sale of shares to an outsider if approved by an ordinary resolution of the company. The majority could therefore sell their shares to an outsider on passing an ordinary resolution, while the minority would have to sell their shares to the other members if the majority exercised their rights under the articles. It was nevertheless held that the alteration benefited the company as a whole as all the members would be able to sell their shares to an outsider.

### Sidebottom v Kershaw, Leese and Co (1920)

A private company's articles were altered so as to give the directors power to require any member who engaged in a business which competed with that of the company to transfer his shares at a fair value to nominees of the directors. Sidebottom, a shareholder, who was in competition with the company contended that the alteration was invalid. It was held that the alteration was valid and for the company's benefit as a company should not be obliged to have as members 'persons who are competing with them in business and who may get knowledge from their membership which would enable them to compete better' (per Lord Sterndale MR).

### Rights and Issues Investment Trust Ltd v Stylo Shoes Ltd (1965)

A company had a nominal capital of £2 million divided into 8 million 25p (5/-) shares. The issued capital consisted of 3.6 million 25p ordinary shares and 4 million 25p management shares carrying 8 votes each. The management shares represented 47 per cent of the company's total voting power. Resolutions were passed to create and issue 4.8 million shares to members of another company in a takeover and to double the voting rights of the management shareholders. Each management share would carry 16 votes and would represent 45 per cent of the company voting power. The management shareholders did not vote in respect of their shares or cast votes in respect of ordinary shares held by them. It was held there had been no discrimination against the minority, as the members had decided that it was for the company's benefit to preserve the existing balance of control.

The minority may seek to prove that the alteration was not made bona fide for the benefit of the company on the grounds that the actions of the majority:

(i)   are motivated by malice, or
(ii)  discriminate against the minority.

Malice is a desire to harm or injure a person by depriving him of his rights under the articles or excluding him from the company. It was held in *Sidebottom v Kershaw Leese & Co* (1927) that the alteration of the articles to provide a power of expulsion was not malicious. In *Shuttleworth v Cox Bros & Co* (1927) the articles were altered to permit a company to disqualify a director if requested to resign by the other directors. Shuttleworth, a director, was entitled to hold office for life unless disqualified on other specific grounds. It was held that the alteration which subsequently deprived Shuttleworth of his directorship was in the company's best interests as he had failed on 22 occasions in 12 months to account for money received on the company's behalf.

A discriminatory act is an act which benefits a section of the company, without necessarily benefiting the company as a whole. The majority are not entitled to 'sacrifice the interests of the minority without any reasonable prospect of advantage to the company as a whole' (per Eve J in *Sidebottom v Kershaw Leese & Co* (1927)).

### Brown v British Abrasive Wheel Co (1919)

A public company required further capital. The holders of 98 per cent of the company's share capital were willing to supply the additional capital if they could buy out the minority. The minority refused to sell and the company proposed to alter the articles to provide that a shareholder was bound to transfer his shares on the written request of the holders of 90 per cent of the issued capital. This clause could have been validly inserted in the original articles. It was held that the alteration was invalid as it was not for the benefit of the company as a whole, but for the benefit of the majority.

### Dafen Tinplate Co v Llanelly Steel Co (1920)

A company was controlled by directors who were appointed by a number of steel firms who were among its shareholders. The company sought to alter its articles to enable the shares of the existing shareholders to be bought out at a fair price, to be determined by the company's board. The proposed alteration was held to be invalid as it conferred an unrestricted power on the majority to expropriate the shares of the minority. It was far wider than necessary to protect the company's interests.

A company may undertake not to alter its articles or a specific article. Such an undertaking does not bind a company, and the courts will not grant an injunction restraining a company from effecting an alteration. If the alteration results in a breach of contract, the company may be liable in damages.

### Southern Foundries (1926) Ltd v Shirlaw (1940)

Shirlaw was appointed by contract in 1933 to be the company's managing director for ten years. The articles stipulated that the managing director (subject to his contract with the company) could be removed from office in the same manner as the other directors and that his appointment would automatically terminate if he ceased to be a director. As a result of a merger the articles were altered to give the company power to remove any director from office. Shirlaw was removed from office in 1937 and ceased to be managing director. It was held that the company could not be precluded from altering its articles, but it was liable for breach of its contract of service with Shirlaw.

If an alteration of the articles results in the re-structuring of the company it may nevertheless be regarded as valid, unless expressly forbidden by the memorandum.

### Andrews v Gas Meter Co (1897)

A company altered its articles in order to issue preference shares, and then issued preference shares. It was held that the alteration was effective as it had not been forbidden by the memorandum. It was immaterial that the preference shares had priority over the ordinary shares.

An alteration is valid even though its effect is retrospective.

### Allen v Gold Reefs of West Africa (1900)

A company had a lien on partly paid shares only. The articles of a company give a lien on all shares that were not fully paid up in respect of calls due to the company. A shareholder, the only holder of fully paid shares, died owing money to the company for calls due on other shares. The company altered its articles to delete the words 'not fully paid up' so as to give it a lien over the deceased shareholder's shares. It was held that such an alteration was valid.

The court has no jurisdiction to rectify a drafting error in the articles. The proper course is for a company to alter the articles by passing a special resolution. If a court alters a company's articles as the result of a petition brought by a minority shareholder under s 459), it cannot then be altered by the majority to nullify the court's alteration unless the leave of the court is first obtained.

## THE EFFECT OF THE MEMORANDUM AND THE ARTICLES

Section 14 provides that the memorandum and articles shall when registered bind the company and its members to the same extent as if they had been signed and sealed by each member and contained covenants on the part of each member to observe all the provisions of the memorandum and of the articles.

The memorandum and articles therefore have a contractual effect, between the company and each member and also between the members themselves.

The effect of the memorandum and articles may be considered under the following headings:

1) A contract between the company and the members.
2) A contract between the members and the company.
3) A contract between the members themselves.
4) In relation to the members in some other capacity.
5) The articles as evidence of a contract.
6) The articles do not bind the company to outsiders.

### (1) THE CONTRACT BETWEEN THE COMPANY AND ITS MEMBERS

Each member is therefore bound to the company by the provisions found in the articles. A shareholder is bound to pay the amounts outstanding on his shares when requested to do so by the company. A member of a guarantee company is bound to pay the amount of his guarantee if requested to do so, on the winding up of the company.

These are speciality debts, i e debts which may be recovered by the company within twelve years.

The provisions in the articles bind each member in his capacity as member, and not in any other capacity, e g as a director who is also a shareholder.

### Hickman v Kent or Romney Marsh Sheep-Breeders Association (1915)

A company's articles provided that any dispute between a member and the company should be submitted to arbitration. Hickman, a member, was in dispute with the company, which threatened to expel him. He then, in breach of the articles, brought an action in court to prevent his expulsion. It was held the action would be stayed as the articles constituted a contract between the company and the members in respect of their rights as members. The matter should therefore, be referred to arbitration.

### Beattie v Beattie Ltd (1938)

The articles of a private company provided that any dispute between the company and its members relating to any act or default of the directors should be submitted to arbitration. Proceedings were commenced by a company against its managing director for the recovery of money improperly paid to him. The managing director sought to have the action stayed and the matter submitted to arbitration. It was held that as the claim was against the individual in his capacity as a member (not as a director), he could not rely on the arbitration clause in the articles.

### (2) THE CONTRACT BETWEEN THE MEMBERS AND THE COMPANY

A company is bound to its members and must not deny him those rights accorded to the members in the articles and the memorandum.

### Oakbank Oil Co v Crum (1882)

A company declared a dividend in proportion to the amount paid up on its shares, i e a holder of a £1 share with only 5/- (25p) paid up was only entitled to a quarter of the declared dividend. It was held that the dividend must be 'apportioned and paid proportionately to the amounts paid upon the shares . . .' (Article 104).

## Wood v Odessa Waterworks Co (1889)

A company declared a dividend and proposed to pay it by issuing debentures to its shareholders in lieu of a cash payment. The company was prevented from doing so as the articles empowered the company to declare a dividend 'to be paid' to its shareholders, ie paid in cash.

## Pender v Lushington (1877)

A company's articles provided that a member was not entitled to cast more than one hundred votes, regardless of the number of shares held. Pender, a shareholder, transferred shares to nominees to circumvent this provision. The chairman refused to accept the votes cast by the nominees and a resolution proposed by Pender was declared lost. It was held that the company was contractually bound by the articles to recognise the votes of its members and the chairman's ruling was invalid.

### (3) THE CONTRACT BETWEEN THE MEMBERS THEMSELVES

The articles constitute an agreement between the members themselves. This agreement must normally be enforced through the company or through a liquidator representing the company.

In certain circumstances a provision in the articles or memorandum may be interpreted as a personal undertaking by a member and the other members may sue on this undertaking.

## Borland's Trustee v Steel Brothers and Co (1901)

The articles of a company provided that the shares of any member who was declared bankrupt should be sold to certain persons at a fair price, not exceeding par. On Borland's bankruptcy his trustee contended that he was not bound by the articles. It was held that the articles were a personal contract between Borland and the other members and his trustee must sell the shares in accordance with the articles.

## Rayfield v Hands (1960)

The articles of a private company required every director to be a shareholder and provided that if a member intended to transfer his shares he should inform the directors who will take the said shares equally between them at a fair value. The directors refused to purchase the plaintiff's shares. It was held that the articles bound the members and the member-directors in relation to their holdings of the company's shares.

### (4) RIGHTS GIVEN TO MEMBER IN OTHER CAPACITY

If a member is given rights in the articles, other than in his capacity as a member (e g as a director), he cannot sue on the articles, i e treat the articles as a contract by the company with him. He must make out a contract outside the articles.

### Eley v Positive Government Security Life Assurance Co (1876)

The company's articles were drafted by Eley and provided that he should be employed for life as a solicitor to the company and should only be removed for misconduct. He became a member of the company after its incorporation. The company ceased to employ him as its solicitor and he sued for breach of contract. It was held that he could not rely on the articles as it was a contract between the company and its members and he was not seeking to enforce any rights as a member.

### (5) THE ARTICLES AS EVIDENCE OF A CONTRACT

A provision in the articles may be referred to if it supplies the necessary terms to a contract entered into by a company.

### Re New British Iron Co ex parte Beckwith (1898)

The articles of a company provided that the directors should be paid fees of £1,000 per annum to be divided amongst themselves as they saw fit. The company was wound up and the directors claimed arrears of fees. It was held that although the articles did not constitute a contract, its terms could be implied into the contract between the directors and the company, and the directors were entitled to recover the arrears.

### (6) THE ARTICLES DO NOT BIND THE COMPANY TO OUTSIDERS

A company is not bound to outsiders by a provision in its articles.

### Re Rotherham Alum and Chemical Co (1883)

The articles of a company provided that all expenses incurred in the formation of the company should be paid by the company. A solicitor claimed a sum in respect of the expenses incurred in the formation of the company. It was held that an article giving a company authority to pay promotion expenses, was not a contract on which a promoter could sue the company for payment of these expenses.

# Chapter 5

# The promoter

A promoter has been defined, by Cockburn CJ in *Twycross v Grant* (1877), as

'one who undertakes to form a company with reference to a given project and to set it going and who takes the necessary steps to accomplish that purpose'.

Bowen LJ described the term promoter as

'a term not of law but of business, usefully summing up in a single word a number of business operations, familiar to the commercial world, by which a company is generally brought into existence'.

The Companies Act does not define the term 'promoter' and a person's role in relation to a company's formation must be examined to determine whether he is a promoter. The following have been held to be the acts of a promoter:

(i) taking procedural steps to form a company by giving instructions to draw up the memorandum and articles of association;
(ii) inviting other persons to become directors;
(iii) negotiating contracts for the purchase of property by the company;
(iv) issuing a prospectus;
(v) agreeing to place shares.

A person may become a promoter after the company's incorporation e g if he undertakes to raise capital for a newly formed company.

A person who merely acts in a professional capacity on behalf of a promoter e g a solicitor who draws up a memorandum of articles of association, an accountant or valuer who prepares a set of accounts or a valuation on behalf of a promoter will not be regarded as a promoter (s 67(3)). If, however, he puts his client in touch with a person who may be interested in taking shares in the newly formed company, he may then be regarded as a promoter.

## DUTIES OF A PROMOTER

A promoter is not an agent for a company as it does not exist until incorporation. He is not a trustee as he is not forbidden to profit from the promotion as long as he makes proper disclosure. Nevertheless his relationship to the company is of a similar nature to that of agency and trusteeship. He is regarded as being in a fiduciary relationship to the company and may not make a secret profit for himself or otherwise benefit at the company's expense.

A promoter who acquires property with the intention of forming a company to acquire and develop that property is entitled to retain any profit he makes on the resale of the property, as long as he discloses to the company on its formation that the vendor of the property and the promoter are one and the same person. Any profit made by a promoter after the company's incorporation or the benefit of any contract which he enters into during the time belong to the company.

A promoter must disclose any profit which he makes from promoting a company to either an independent board of directors or to the present and future shareholders.

Disclosure to an independent board of directors is rarely possible as the promoters are usually the company's first directors. Disclosure is usually made to the shareholders by means of a prospectus or in some other way so that 'the real truth is disclosed to those who are induced by the promoters to join the company' (Lindley MR in *Lagunas Nitrate Co v Lagunas Syndicate* (1899).

## REMEDIES AGAINST THE PROMOTER

If a promoter fails to make full disclosure of any profit or benefit obtained by him the following *remedies* are available to the company.

### (a) RESCISSION OF THE CONTRACT

The effect of this is to return the parties to their former position ie the property is returned to the promoter and the purchase price is returned to the company.

### Erlanger v New Sombrero Phosphate Co (1878)

Erlanger purchased for £55,000 the lease of an island in the West Indies reputed to contain large quantities of phosphate deposits. The lease was held in the name of a nominee. Erlanger then formed a company to purchase the lease for £110,000. The board of directors were nominees of Erlanger. The profit made by the promoters was not disclosed in the prospectus issued by the company. The original directors were removed from office and replaced by others who sued for rescission of the contract. It was held the contract should be rescinded as there had not been a disclosure to an independent board of directors or to the members.

Rescission is only possible if the parties can be restored to their former position. If a company has re-sold the property rescission is not possible. The right to rescind will be lost if it is not exercised within a reasonable time.

### (b) RECOVERY OF SECRET PROFIT

The company may compel the promoter to account for any secret profit made by him.

### Gluckstein v Barnes (1900)

A syndicate purchased property for £140,000 and then formed a company which purchased the property for £180,000. The members of the syndicate were the first directors of the company and disclosed the profit of £40,000 in a prospectus. The prospectus also mentioned that the promoters had 'intermediate transactions' but no further details were given. This was a reference to debentures which the syndicate had purchased from the previous company at a low price knowing that these would be repaid at par if the sale materialised. The syndicate made a profit of £20,000 on the debentures. It was held that there was no adequate disclosure of this profit and the promoters were bound to pay it to the company.

### (c) DAMAGES FOR BREACH OF FIDUCIARY DUTY

The company may sue the promoter for damages for breach of his fiduciary duty.

### Re Leeds and Hanley Theatres of Varieties Ltd (1902)

A company purchased two music halls for £24,000 intending to sell the properties to a new company when formed. In the meantime it conveyed the properties to a nominee. It then promoted this new company and instructed the nominee to sell the properties to this company for £75,000. A prospectus was issued which gave the nominee as the vendor of the property and did not disclose the interest of the first company. The board of directors of the second company was not an independent board. It was held that the prospectus should have disclosed the interest of the first company, and the promoters were liable in damages for the profit which they had made.

A promoter who makes a secret profit out of the company's promotion, apart from selling property to the company, must account for that profit to the company. He is however entitled to deduct from his profit any expenses properly incurred e g solicitors and accountants' fees, printing expenses.

Proceedings may be brought in a winding up against a promoter (amongst others) who has misapplied, or retained, or become liable or accountable for any money or property of the company or has been guilty of any misfeasance or breach of trust in relation to the company. He may be ordered to repay or compensate or make restitution to the company (s 631).

A promoter is liable to compensate a person who has suffered loss as a result of subscribing for shares on the basis of a prospectus containing an untrue statement (s 67).

## REMUNERATION OF PROMOTERS

A company does not have the legal capacity, prior to incorporation, to enter into a legally binding contract with a promoter to pay for promotion services or for any expenses incurred in the promotion.

The promoter should therefore enter into an express agreement with the company after its formation. The agreement must be under seal as the consideration given to the company will be past consideration i e the services have already been rendered.

A company's articles usually give authority to the directors to pay promotion expenses. This is not legally binding, but in practice the promoters are invariably re-imbursed as the promoters or their nominees are usually the company's first directors.

## PRE-INCORPORATION CONTRACTS

A company is often formed to acquire an existing business or property, to develop a patent, to work a mining concession or undertake a financial business.

The promoters of the company will need to enter into certain preliminary agreements e g a contract with the owner of the business or the vendor of the property to sell that business or property to the company. The company cannot make a binding contract until it has been incorporated.

In the majority of cases this problem will not arise as the promoters are the owners of the business or the vendors of the property. In other cases the promoter will seek to ensure that the company will, after incorporation, re-imburse him for any expenses incurred prior to incorporation.

A company is not bound by a contract made on its behalf prior to its incorporation. Although a company is entitled to ratify a contract (i e adopt an unauthorised contract made on its behalf as if there had been prior authorisation), ratification is only possible if the company was in existence at the time of making the contract. Therefore an agent who contracts on behalf of the company in respect of a pre-incorporation contract is treated as if he were contracting on his own behalf.

### Kelner v Baxter (1866)

Three individuals entered into a contract for the supply of wines and spirits to a hotel company which at that time had not been incorporated. The wines were subsequently delivered and consumed. It was held that the three individuals who contracted on the company's behalf were personally liable on the contract.

Section 36 provides that:–

'where a contract purports to be made by a company, or by a person as agent for a company, at a time when the company has not been formed, then subject to any agreement to the contrary the contract has effect as one entered into by the person purporting to act for the company or as agent for it, and he is personally liable on the contract accordingly.'

The agent is therefore personally liable on the contract. The basis of his liability is contractual in that 'he is personally liable on the contract'. It therefore follows that he will also be able to enforce the contract against the other party.

An agent will be able to exclude his personal liability on a pre-incorporation contract, but he must do so expressly and clearly. Merely signing a contract 'as agent' will not exclude liability as this is insufficient to infer 'an agreement to the contrary'.

### Phonogram Ltd v Lane (1982)

A contract was made by Lane with Phonogram Ltd 'for and on behalf of Fragile Management Ltd'. It was intended to form this company to manage a pop group, but it was never subsequently incorporated. It was held that Lane was personally liable for the £6,000 advanced in respect of Fragile Management Ltd, as s 36 is not confined to the situation where the company is already in the course of formation.

A company is not bound by a pre-incorporation contract.

### Re English and Colonial Produce Co Ltd (1906)

A solicitor drafted a company's memorandum and articles prior to its formation. After incorporation it refused to pay his charges for the work undertaken. It was held that although it had taken the benefit of the work it was not liable to pay the charges as the contract was made before the company was formed.

A company cannot enforce a pre-incorporation contract against the other party to the contract.

### Natal Land and Colonisation Co v Pauline Colliery & Development Syndicate Ltd (1904)

The agent for the Pauline Colliery Syndicate had, before the company's incorporation, entered into a contract with the Natal Land Co for an option to lease certain land. When the company was formed it sought to enforce the contract against the Natal Land Co. It was held that the contract was not enforceable.

A promoter may seek to avoid liability for pre-incorporation by taking one of the following steps:–

(a) Not entering into a contract until the company is incorporated.
(b) Making a contract with a trustee for the company before the company's incorporation. The company's memorandum will contain as one of the objects that it will adopt this preliminary agreement. The trustee will be personally liable on the contract until the company enters into a new agreement on the basis of the preliminary agreement. A trustee can however avoid liability by including a power of rescission in the contract.
(c) Entering into a contract with a third party and assigning the benefit of the contract to the company on its formation. The disadvantage of such an assignment is that the promoter remains liable for any undertaking given by him prior to the assignment. A promoter should therefore ensure that the

company enters into an identical contract with the third party, with the additional stipulation that the promoter's obligations should cease on the company entering into an identical contract.

(d) Taking an option on the property. The promoter will then assign the benefit of the option to the company or enforce the contract for the company's benefit. The promoter incurs no liability if the company does not wish to purchase the property or does not adopt the contract within the time specified in the option.

It is also possible to assert that a company has entered into a new contract if a company by its conduct treats itself as bound by a provisional agreement entered into on its behalf prior to its incorporation ie a novation. There must be evidence of a new contract.

### Re Northumberland Avenue Hotel Co (1886)

A promoter entered into a contract for the grant of a building lease, prior to the company's incorporation. After incorporation the company entered onto the land to commence building operations. It did not enter into a new contract as the company believed that the agreement was binding upon it. It was held that the contract could not be ratified as there was no evidence of the formation of a new contract.

Evidence of a new contract was found in:–

### Howard v Patent Ivory Manufacturing Co (1888)

The vendor of property agreed to sell the land to a company which was about to be formed. After the company had been incorporated the terms of the contract were modified and the vendor agreed to take part of the purchase price in debentures instead of in cash as previously agreed. It was held that the modification of the previous agreement was evidence of the formation of a new contract.

# Chapter 6

# Raising capital

There are various methods by which companies may raise capital. A private company is prohibited from offering its shares or debentures to the public, but a public company may do so by means of a prospectus. Stringent rules are laid down as to the contents of a prospectus, its publication and the liabilities which may be incurred by directors and others if the contents of such a prospectus are untrue.

## PRIVATE COMPANIES

A private limited company may not offer its shares or debentures to the public (s 81(a)). This restriction does not apply to a guarantee company which does not have a share capital ie it may offer its debentures to the public; or to an unlimited company which may offer its shares or debentures to the public. (A guarantee company with a share capital is a private limited company).

A private limited company is therefore restricted as to the ways in which it may raise its capital.

It may do so in one of the following ways:

1. A rights issue ie offering shares to its existing members in proportion to their current shareholding. The offer is made by means of a letter of rights, which must be non-renouncable ie a member is not allowed to renounce his rights to a person outside the company.
2. A private placing ie entering into contracts with various individuals for the allotment of shares.
3. Offering its shares or debentures, or inviting its shareholders, debenture holders, employees or certain members of their respective families to subscribe for shares or debentures. (This

includes a person's spouse, widow, widower or children).
4. Offering its shares or debentures for subscription under an employees' share scheme.

A company may allow its shareholders, debenture holders and employees to renounce their rights in favour of those relatives, listed above, and may allow a person entitled to hold shares under an employees' share scheme to renounce in favour of another person holding shares or debentures under that scheme.

## PUBLIC COMPANIES

A public company may raise capital in any of the following ways:–

1. *A direct offer to the public.* A company may invite the public to subscribe for its shares or debentures. Such an offer must be in the form of a prospectus and contain the information required by the 3rd Schedule to the Act.
   A direct offer is comparatively rare and is mainly confined to large issues of shares by public companies who are exempt from making a rights issue. Such an issue will normally be underwritten ie underwriters agree, for a commission, to take up any securities not taken up by the public.
2. *An offer for sale.* A company sells the issue to an issuing house which then offers the shares for resale to the public. There is deemed to be an offer for sale to the public if either:–
   (i) the offer is made within 6 months after the allotment or an agreement to allot; or
   (ii) at the date when the offer is made the company has not received the whole of the consideration due from the issuing house.
   An offer for sale of this kind is a prospectus for which the company and the issuing house are responsible. In addition to the particulars required to be disclosed in a prospectus such an offer for sale must also state:–
   (i) the net amount to be received by the company.
   (ii) the place and time at which the contract between the company and the issuing house may be inspected (s 58(4)).
3. *Rights issue.* A company may offer shares to its members in proportion to their current shareholding. A circular, known as a letter of rights, is sent to each member inviting him to subscribe for further shares. A form of acceptance or renunciation may be attached to the letter, or a company may anticipate acceptance

by sending a provisional letter of acceptance to each member. In the latter case a member may reject the offer and renounce his rights in favour of a third party.

4. *Placing.* An issuing house will undertake to place securities with certain clients e g institutional investors. If the placings are to a small, restricted number of select investors a prospectus will not be required. If the shares are offered to a wider clientele by means of a circular letter or some other general communication a prospectus will be required.

5. *Offer by tender.* Investors are invited to bid for the shares, subject to a certain minimum price. The shares will then be allotted to the highest bidder. The aim of this procedure is to benefit the company and not a stag (a certain type of speculator) when an issue is oversubscribed.


## PROSPECTUS

A prospectus is defined as 'any prospectus, notice, circular, advertisement or other invitation offering to the public for subscription or purchase any shares or debentures of a company' (s 744).

(i) A prospectus is not an offer but an invitation to treat and may take various forms e g a newspaper advertisement, a circular. An individual who applies for shares in a company makes an offer to the company which the company is free to accept or reject. The application form usually includes the following clause 'I agree to accept such shares and any smaller number that may be alloted to me.' If this clause is not inserted and the company signifies its acceptance of an offer by the allotment of a smaller number of shares than that originally applied for, an applicant would be entitled to reject the shares, i e as the company is making a counter offer.

(ii) 'Public' includes any section of the public, whether selected as members or debenture holders of the company or as clients of the person issuing the prospectus or in any other manner.

### Re South of England Natural Gas Co (1911)

A promoter of a gas company distributed a circular to 3,000 shareholders in other gas companies in which he was interested. The circular was headed 'for private circulation only' and offered shares for subscription. It was held that the circular was a prospectus which offered shares to the public.

(iii)  An offer is not to be regarded as having been made to the public if it is not calculated to result directly or indirectly in shares or debentures becoming available for subscription or purchase by persons other than those receiving the offer, or otherwise as being a matter of domestic concern of the person making and receiving it (s 60).

**Nash and Lynde** (1929)

A director sent a document to a solicitor containing details of the issue of shares in a company. Although the document was marked 'strictly private and confidential' it stated that anyone who was interested should contact the director. The solicitor gave it to a client who handed the document to a relative. It was held that as the document had passed between parties who were known to each other there had been no publication. The document was not a prospectus as there had been no offer to the public.

An issue of shares is not made to the public if it is directed to specified persons and is not calculated to result in shares or debentures becoming available to other persons e g:–
where an issuing house places the whole or part of a new issue privately with a few institutional investors who have agreed to hold the securities as long term investments;
where a business is converted into a company and shares are issued by the vendor to a small circle of friends, relatives or select customers. In particular an offer of shares or debentures in a private company or an invitation to subscribe for shares is of domestic concern only if made to
(a)  an existing member of the company,
(b)  an existing employee of the company,
(c)  a member of the family of such a member or employee, or
(d)  an existing debenture holder (s 60).

(iv)  There must be an invitation to purchase the new company's unissued shares or to subscribe for shares i e taking or agreeing to take shares for cash.

**Governments Stock and Other Securities Investment Co Ltd v Christopher** (1956)

A shipping company offered to acquire all the shares in two other companies in exchange for its own shares. A circular was sent to the members of the two companies concerned accompanied by a form of acceptance and transfer. It was held that the circular was not a prospectus as it was not an offer to the public or an invitation to purchase or subscribe the shares.

(v) 'of a company'. A prospectus applies to offers made by a company and other parties e g a promoter, an issuing house, a broker, a holder of a company's shares.


## THE CONTENTS OF A PROSPECTUS

The general rule is that every prospectus issued by or on behalf of a company or promoter must state the matters specified in the Third Schedule and set out the reports contained in that Schedule; whether the prospectus is issued on the company's formation or subsequently (s 56(1)).

### DETAILS OF SHARES AND DEBENTURES

(a) The number of founders or management or deferred shares, if any, and the nature and extent of their interest in the company's property and profits. (This type of share is rarely created by companies. Such a share has a small nominal value in relation to the total capital of the company, but it may be entitled to a large proportion of the profits above a stated figure).

(b) If the company's capital is divided into different classes of share, the voting capital and dividend rights of each class of share.

(c) The amount payable on application and allotment on each share including the amount, if any, payable by way of a share premium. In the cases of a second or subsequent offer of shares, the amount offered for subscription on each previous allotment made within the two preceding years, the amount actually allotted and the amount paid on the shares allotted including the amount, if any, paid by way of premium.

(d) Particulars of any option to subscribe for shares or debentures, the period during which it is exercisable, the price to be paid, the consideration given for the option and the persons entitled to exercise the option.
(The option price is not necessarily the market price at the time of exercising the option. It can therefore represent a valuable right if the option price is below the market price and is given for an inadequate consideration.)

(e) The number and amount of any shares or debentures issued within the previous two years for a consideration other than cash and the nature of the consideration.
(Sections 102–116 of the Act ensure that such a consideration is adequate).

### THE COMPANY'S FINANCIAL HISTORY

(a) If a company has carried on business for less than three years, or if the business to be acquired has been carried on for less than three years, the length of time the company or business has been carried on.
(b) The company's auditors must submit a *report* with respect to:–
  (i) The company's profits and losses in the five financial years preceding the issue of the prospectus.
  (ii) The company's assets and liabilities at the date of the last accounts.
  (iii) The rates of dividend (if any) paid in respect of each class of share in the last five financial years.
  (iv) The company's subsidiaries (if any). It must deal either with the combined profits or losses of the subsidiaries, or with the profits and losses of each subsidiary separately in so far as these matters concern the members of the company. Alternatively the company's profits or losses may be dealt with in conjunction with the combined profits or losses of its subsidiaries. The report must either deal with the combined assets and liabilities of the subsidiaries or deal with the assets and liabilities of each subsidiary separately. It must also indicate the allowance to be made for persons other than the company's members.

### DETAILS OF ANY PROPERTY OR SHARES TO BE ACQUIRED

(a) Where the company proposes to use the whole or part of the proceeds of the issues for the purchase or acquisition of property, details must be given of:–
  (i) the names and addresses of the vendors;
(ii) the amount payable in cash, shares and debentures to the vendors;
(iii) particulars of any transaction relating to the property in the preceding two years in which any vendor, promoter, director or proposed director had any direct or indirect interest (apart

from contracts entered into in the ordinary course of business, or where the amount of the purchase money is not material).

A vendor is defined as a person who has entered into any contract, absolutely or conditionally for the sale or purchase, or for any option to purchase any property to be acquired by the company, where:–

(i) the purchase money is not fully paid at the date of issue of the prospectus;

(ii) the purchase money is to be paid wholly or partly out of the proceeds of the issue of shares or debentures offered by the prospectus;

(iii) the contract depends for its validity or fulfilment on the result of that issue.

(b) A *report* by named accountants as to the profits or losses and assets and liabilities, in respect of each of the five financial years preceding the issue of the prospectus, of any business to be purchased with the proceeds of the issue of the shares or debentures.

(c) A *report* by named accountants if the proceeds of an issue are to be applied in acquiring a controlling interest in the shares of another company. The profits and losses of that company in the five financial years preceding the issue of the prospectus must be disclosed, as well as its assets and liabilities at the last date at which its accounts were made up. The report must also contain information (including profits or loss, assets and liabilities) relating to any subsidiaries of that company.

THE COMPANY'S FINANCIAL REQUIREMENTS

(a) The minimum subscription ie the minimum amount which in the directors' opinion must be raised by the issue of those shares to provide for:

(i) the purchase price of any property purchased or to be purchased which is to be defrayed wholly or partly out of the proceeds of the issue;

(ii) any preliminary expenses payable by the company and any underwriting commission payable;

(iii) the repayment of any moneys borrowed for those purposes;

(iv) working capital.

(b) The time of the opening of the subscription lists. No allotment of shares may be made until the third day after the issue of the prospectus or until such later date as the prospectus may provide. This is to prevent 'stagging'.

DIRECTORS

(a) The names, descriptions and addresses of the directors or proposed directors. (This will reveal whether the directors are men of standing in the commercial world.)
(b) Details of the interest of every director in the promotion of the company or property to be acquired by the company, with a statement of all sums paid or agreed to be paid to induce a person to become a director, or to qualify as a director, or for services in connection with the promotion or formation of the company.
(c) The number of shares, if any, fixed by the articles as director's share qualification and any provision in the articles as to the directors remuneration. Companies occasionally provide that a person is not qualified to act as a director unless he holds a certain number of shares. This indicates the extent of a director's financial interest in the company.

PROMOTERS

Any amount or benefit paid or given within the two preceding years or intended to be paid or given to any promoter, and the consideration for such payment or benefit.

AUDITORS

The names and addresses of the company's auditors.

If the prospectus contains a statement purporting to be made by an expert, the prospectus may not be issued unless:

(a) the expert has given and has not, before delivery of a copy of the prospectus to the Registrar for registration, withdrawn his written consent to the inclusion of the statement; and
(b) the statement that he has given and not withdrawn that consent appears in the prospectus (s 61).

## ABRIDGED PROSPECTUS

A prospectus need not contain the matters set out in Part 1 of

Schedule 3 (the contents of a prospectus), or the reports required by the Schedule.

(a) the prospectus is issued to existing members or debenture holders (whether or not the applicant will or will not have the right to renounce in favour of other persons)
(b) the prospectus relates to shares or debentures which are or are to be in all respects uniform with shares or debentures previously issued and for the time being listed on a prescribed stock exchange (s 56(5)).

## PROSPECTUS NOT REQUIRED

An application for shares or debentures may be issued without a prospectus where:

(a) there is a bona fide invitation to a person to enter into an underwriting agreement with respect to the shares or debentures;
(b) the shares or debentures are not offered to the public;
(c) the shares or debentures are offered to existing members or debenture holders (whether or not the applicant will or will not have the right to renounce in favour of other persons);
(d) the issue relates to shares or debentures which are or are to be in all respects uniform with shares or debentures previously issued and for the time being listed on a prescribed stock exchange (s 56).

### REGISTRATION OF PROSPECTUS

No prospectus may be issued by or on behalf of a company, or in relation to an intended company unless on or before the date of its publication, a copy of the prospectus has been delivered to the Registrar for registration. It must:

(a) be signed by every person who is named in it as a director or proposed director of the company or by his agent authorised in writing
(b) have endorsed on or attached to it any consent to the issue required from any person as an expert (s 64).

When the prospectus is issued generally (ie to persons who are not existing members or debenture holders of the company) the copy of the prospectus delivered to the Registrar must also have endorsed on or attached to it a copy of any material contract (or a memorandum giving full particulars of it). If the persons making any report required by the prospectus, or have (without giving reasons) indicated in it any adjustments as respects profits, losses, assets or liability, the copy of the prospectus delivered to the Registrar must include a written statement signed by them setting out the adjustments and giving the reasons for them (s 64).

The prospectus must be dated and that date is taken as its date of publication, unless the contrary is proved (s 63).

## UNDERWRITING

It is usual for a company, when offering shares or debentures to the public, to enter into a contract with an issuing house, brokers, insurance company or bank to have the issue underwritten.

The promoters (on the formation of a company) or the directors of a company, (when an existing company is issuing new shares or debentures), will enter into an agreement, before the shares are offered to the public, that in the event of the public not taking up the whole of the issue of the number specified in the agreement, the underwriter will for an agreed commission, take an allotment of these shares or debentures as are not taken up by the public.

The terms of the agreement may be contained in a formal agreement, or set out in an underwriting letter.

As the underwriting agreement may be based on a draft prospectus it is usual to insert a clause to the effect that the underwriter will be bound by the terms of the agreement even if the draft prospectus is subsequently altered before its issue to the public.

Underwriting commission is calculated on the number of shares or debentures underwritten, and is payable whether the underwriter is subsequently called upon to take up the shares or debentures. An underwriter may enter into a 'firm' agreement i e he will take an allotment of shares regardless of whether the issue is over or under subscribed by the public.

Section 97 provides that a company may only pay commission if the following conditions are satisfied:

(i) Payment is authorised by the articles.
(ii) The commission does not exceed 10 per cent of the issue price of the shares or the amount or rate authorised by the articles, whichever is less.
(iii) The amount or rate agreed to be paid is disclosed in the prospectus (if shares are offered to the public) or in other cases

disclosed in a statement filed with the Registrar.
(iv) The number of shares which the underwriters have agreed to subscribe for absolutely (ie firm) is disclosed.

Section 363 and the Fifteenth schedule provided that 'the total amount of the sums (if any) paid by way of commission in respect of any shares or debentures' shall be stated in the annual return, while the Ninth, Schedule, para 3, provides that 'any expenses incurred in connection with any issue of share capital or debentures' shall be stated, unless written off.

Underwriters usually enter into sub-underwriting agreements with other persons to relieve them wholly or partly from liability. The commission paid by the underwriters to the sub-underwriters is known as an over-riding commission, and need not be disclosed in the prospectus.

## BROKERAGE

This is a sum paid to an issuing house or brokers in return for placing a company's shares or debentures. Brokerage does not involve the brokers in any risk, as they do not subscribe to the issue. The amount paid by way of brokerage must be reasonable, in the ordinary course of business (one-quarter per cent is regarded as reasonable), and must be disclosed in any prospectus within two years of any issue.

## LIABILITY FOR MISREPRESENTATION AND NON-DISCLOSURE IN A PROSPECTUS

Section 71 of the Companies Act provides that a statement in a prospectus is deemed to be untrue if it is misleading in the form and context in which it is included.

Various remedies are available at common law and at statute, under the provisions of the Companies Act, to a person who suffers damage as a result of incorrect information in a prospectus.

The two main remedies at common law are

(a) Rescission
(b) Damages.

### (a) RESCISSION

A person who is allotted shares (the allottee) may seek rescission of the contract i e a repudiation of the contract to take up shares, and the restoration of the parties to their former positions. The allottee is entitled to recover his subscription money (with interest at four per cent to the time of payment) and to have his name removed from the register of members.

In order to succeed in an action for rescission the allottee must prove that:–

(a) The prospectus contained a material false statement of fact.
(b) The statement induced him to subscribe for shares in the company.
(c) On discovering the misrepresentation he took immediate steps to set aside the contract.

### (a) *Material false statement of fact*

(i) The misrepresentation must be material i e likely to influence a reasonable man in deciding whether or not to apply for shares.

#### City of Edinburgh Brewery Co v Gibson's Trustee (1869)

A prospectus stated that 'a large number of gentlemen in the trade and others have become shareholders'. When the register was compiled it was found that only 10 or 12 of the 55 shareholders were connected with the trade. Nevertheless it was held that the misrepresentation was not sufficiently material to justify rescission of the contract.

The statement must be a statement of fact, not of opinion e g a statement that the company's profits are expected to be in excess of £2m in the current year would be a statement of opinion.

(ii) A statement of intention may be held to be a misrepresentation if it can be shown that the person making the statement did not intend to pursue that particular course of action.

#### Edgington v Fitzmaurice (1885)

The directors of a company stated that a loan would be used to improve the company's buildings and expand its business. Their intention was to use the money to pay off existing debts, as creditors were pressing for payment. It was held that there had been a misrepresentation.

'It is true that it is very difficult to prove what the state of a man's mind at a particular time is, but if it can be ascertained, it is as much a fact as anything else. A misrepresentation as to the state of a man's mind is, therefore, a mis-statement of fact'. (per Bowen LJ)

(iii) A statement of opinion may amount to a misrepresentation if it can be shown that there are no reasonable grounds for holding that opinion.

### Aaron's Reefs Ltd v Twiss (1896)

A prospectus stated that a mine to be acquired by a company 'had proved rich' when in fact the mine had been worked unsuccessfully by three previous companies. The reports quoted in the prospectus were three years old and the amount to be raised by the issue of shares after payment for the mine would not have provided sufficient capital to work the mine. It was held that the statement was a misrepresentation as the directors could not honestly have held that opinion.

(iv) A statement which is literally true may nevertheless be regarded as a false statement of fact if it is misleading in the context in which it is used.

### R v Kylsant (1932)

A prospectus issued by the Royal Mail Company stated that the company had paid dividends for the last seventeen years (from 1911–1927). This was literally true, but what was not stated in the prospectus was that the company had suffered trading losses from 1921–7 and was only able to declare a dividend by using accumulated profits and tax rebates. It was held that the prospectus was false in a material particular.

(v) Non disclosure of a material fact may amount to a misrepresentation if the nature of the omission makes that which is stated misleading.

### Coles v White City (Manchester) Greyhound Association Ltd (1928)

A prospectus described a piece of land as 'eminently suitable' for greyhound racing. The land was however subject to a planning resolution by a local authority which would have entitled the local authority to acquire the land and buildings without paying compensation unless prior consent had been given for the erection of any buildings. The local authority refused to consent to building a greyhound stadium. It was held that 'eminently suitable' was misleading in view of the omission of other relevant facts and the shareholders were entitled to rescission.

(vi) If a company adopts or relies on or authenticates the report of an expert, which is referred to in a prospectus, it will incur liability if the report proves to be false. A company that does not wish to issue shares on the basis of facts stated in a report must clearly and unequivocally disassociate itself from the contents of such a report.

### Re Pacaya Rubber Co (1914)

A prospectus issued by a company included a report by an expert on the number and condition of the rubber trees on an estate. The report was inaccurate. It was held that the company was liable for misrepresentation as the value of the rubber estate was based on this report and the company had not disclaimed responsibility for the accuracy of the report.

(b) *The statement was material*
That is it influenced the plaintiff in deciding to subscribe for shares.

### Smith v Chadwick (1884)

The plaintiff sought damages on the basis of a misrepresentation in a prospectus, which stated that a Mr J J Grieves MP was a director of a company, whereas he had withdrawn his consent the day before the issue of the prospectus. It was held that although the statement was untrue, it was not material, as the plaintiff had never heard of Mr Grieves.

A plaintiff is not obliged to make enquiries in respect of a prospectus and will not be debarred from obtaining a remedy by reason of a failure to make inquiries or inspect documents.

### Central Railway Company of Venezuela v Kisch (1867)

A prospectus of a railway company stated that the engineer's report, maps and plans could be inspected at the company's offices. If these documents had been inspected, the company's true position would have been revealed i e that it was undercapitalised. It was held that as the plaintiff had chosen to rely on the prospectus he was entitled to rescission of his contract to take shares in the company.

(c) *There is no delay in seeking rescission*
The right to rescind the contract will be lost if the plaintiff:–
(i) Delays in seeking rescission. A plaintiff must seek rescission within a reasonable time of discovering the misrepresentation.
In *Heymann v European Central Railway Co* (1868) a delay of three months after the discovery of the misrepresentation, was held to debar a plaintiff who sought rescission.
In *Re Scottish Petroleum Co* (1883) the plaintiff delayed for 15 days after being informed by the company of the falsity of

the prospectus. It was held that the plaintiff had forfeited his right of rescission by the delay.
(ii) Affirms the contract after discovering the false statement(s) in the prospectus e g:
by voting at a meeting of shareholders,
by receiving and retaining dividends,
by entering into a contract to sell part or all of his shareholding.
(iii) Commences an action for rescission after the commencement of a winding up. In this situation the rights of the creditors rank before those of the shareholders.

(d) *It is not possible to restore the parties to their previous positions.*

## Refusal of rescission

A court has the power to refuse rescission of a contract and declare it binding even though a party has entered into the contract as the result of an innocent misrepresentation and is therefore entitled to rescission. The court will therefore award damages in lieu of rescission.

A court may only exercise this power if it is of the opinion that it would be equitable to do so, having regard to the nature of the misrepresentation, the loss which would be incurred if the contract was upheld, and the loss which rescission would cause to the other party (Misrepresentation Act 1967, s 2(2)).

### DAMAGES FOR FRAUDULENT MISREPRESENTATION

An allottee who is induced by fraud to take shares may sue for the tort of deceit. He must establish that the prospectus contained a statement of fact which was false, or which the defendant did not honestly believe to be true, or was made recklessly or without care whether it was true or false. He must also prove that it was intended that he should act upon the statement, and that he did act upon it to his detriment ie he has suffered loss or damage. Fraud is extremely difficult to prove and for that reason few actions are brought under this heading.

A director will not incur liability or a false statement if he honestly believes in its truth, even though there are no reasonable grounds for his belief.

## Derry v Peek (1889)

A company was granted the right, by special Act of Parliament, to operate horse drawn trams and, on obtaining the consent of the Board of Trade, steam driven trains. A prospectus was issued which stated without qualification that the company had the right to use steam driven trams. The Board of Trade refused its consent and the company was wound up. A shareholder who had subscribed for shares on the basis of the prospectus sued the directors for fraud. It was held that the directors were not liable for fraud as they honestly believed that the statement as to the use of steam power was true.

### Akerhielm v De Mare (1959)

It was stated in a circular letter, which induced an individual to subscribe for shares in a company formed in Kenya, that 'about one-third of the capital had already been subscribed in Denmark'. This referred to shares allotted as fully paid for services rendered in connection with the company's formation. It was held that the statement was not fraudulent as the representer honestly believed the representation to be true in the sense in which he understood it.

As a general rule only the original allottee may bring an action for deceit i e the person to whom the prospectus was directed.

### Peek v Gurney (1873)

The plaintiff purchased shares from the original purchaser after reading the company's prospectus. It was held that as he was not the original purchaser, the prospectus was not addressed to him and he had no remedy against the company.

If a purchaser of shares proves that a false prospectus has been circulated with a view to inducing persons to purchase shares in the market, he may sue for damages for fraud, whether he originally subscribed for the shares or purchased them in the open market.

### Andrews v Mockford (1896)

A prospectus was issued for the Sutherland Reef Company, a non-existent gold mining company. It was later followed by a newspaper report of rich discovery by the company, which was also untrue. Andrews bought shares in the market in reliance on this information. In an action for damages it was held that he could rely on the misleading prospectus as part of the fraud.

THE FOLLOWING MAY BE SUED

### 1. *The Company*
A company is liable for the acts of its officers if they are aware of the false nature of a statement published in a prospectus or in an offer for sale after allotment for that purpose by the company.

An allottee must first rescind the contract before he can sue for damages for fraud. If he is unable to obtain rescission he cannot recover damages for fraud against the company.

An allottee who obtains rescission of the contract will find it unnecessary to claim damages for fraud, as on rescission he will be entitled to the return of his money with interest.

## 2. *The directors and other persons responsible for the issue of the prospectus (e g promoters, expert)*

An allottee may be able to bring an action against the directors and other responsible persons, even though he is unable to sue the company for fraud e g where he is unable to rescind the contract. If he is able to rescind, but unable to recover the money from the company due to its insolvency, he may nevertheless sue the directors and other responsible persons.

## 3. *An issuing house*

An issuing house, its directors or partners may incur liability if the prospectus is an offer for sale. The measure of damages is the difference between the price paid for the shares and their real value at the date of allotment.

## DAMAGES UNDER THE MISREPRESENTATION ACT 1967

An action for damages may be brought against a company for any loss suffered as a result of an innocent misrepresentation made by or on behalf of a company.

It is a defence to show that the company, or those acting on the company's behalf had reasonable grounds to believe, and did in fact believe up to the time of the allotment that the facts represented were true.

The basis of the claim and the possible defence to this action is very similar to that found in ss 67 and 68 of the Companies Act. However, an action under the Misrepresentation Act is confined to companies, while s 67 is confined to natural persons e g directors and experts.

The usual claim in respect of an innocent misrepresentation is for rescission of the contract. A court may however award damages in lieu of rescission (Misrepresentation Act 1967, s 2(2) ).

## DAMAGES FOR NEGLIGENCE

It may be possible to bring an action for damages caused by a negligent mis-statement as long as a duty of care is owed by the maker of the statement to its recipient.

### Hedley Byrne and Co v Heller and Partners Ltd (1964)

The House of Lords held that an action lies against a person who negligently makes a false statement in circumstances where as a reasonable man he should have foreseen that another party would rely on the statement to his detriment.

Few cases are likely to be contested under this heading as s 67 provides a satisfactory remedy in respect of a mis-statement in a prospectus.

An action for negligence may however provide a remedy where a document offering shares for cash is not a prospectus, or shares are offered for a consideration other than cash. In neither case will the sections of the Act relating to investor protection apply.

A duty of care is owed to a party where a representation concerns a business or professional transaction, where the nature of the transaction makes clear the importance of the inquiry and the answer to that inquiry.

### Dimond Manufacturing Co Ltd v Hamilton (1969)

A company's auditors were held liable to a purchaser of the company's shares as they had given a copy of the company's audited balance sheet to his agent for use in the negotiations. This amounted to an implied representation as to the correctness of the balance sheet, which was later found to be incorrect.

COMPENSATION UNDER THE COMPANIES ACT (S 67)

A director, a person who has authorised himself to be named as a director or future director, a promoter and every person who has authorised the issue of a prospectus is liable to compensate all persons who subscribe for any shares or debentures on the faith of a prospectus for loss or damage sustained by reason of any untrue statement contained in the prospectus.

An expert who has given his consent to a statement in a prospectus may be liable, if the statement is untrue, as a person who has authorised the prospectus. He is only liable in respect of the statement contained in the prospectus. 'Expert' includes an engineer, valuer, accountant and any other person whose profession gives authority to a statement made by him.

A statement is deemed to be untrue if it is misleading in the form and context in which it is included.

A plaintiff may find it easier to bring an action in respect of a mis-statement under this heading, rather than pursuing an alternative remedy. It may be brought where a mis-statement is made innocently or fraudulently, and the burden of proof is less stringent than that of fraud at common law.

The liability of a defendant is not strict and the following defences are available to a person (other than an expert) under this section:

(i) He had withdrawn his consent to become a director before the prospectus was issued and it was issued without his consent; or

(ii) It was issued without his knowledge or consent and on becoming aware of the issue, he gave reasonable public notice of this fact; or

(iii) After issue, but before allotment, and on becoming aware of the untrue statement he withdrew his consent and gave public notice of its withdrawal and the reason for it; or

(iv) He had reasonable grounds to believe and did up to the time of allotment believe the statement to be true; or

(v) The statement was fairly represented and made by an expert. He believed the expert competent and the expert had given his consent; or

(vi) It was a correct and fair representation of a statement made by an official, or a correct and fair copy of an extract from a public official document (s 68).

A director is liable for not disclosing a material contract, of whose existence he was aware. He cannot avoid liability by professing ignorance of the contents or materiality of the contract or by alleging that he left the matter to his legal advisers.

An expert who has given his consent to the inclusion of a statement which proves to be untrue may avoid liability if he proves that:–

(i) Having given his consent, he withdrew it in writing before delivery of a copy of the prospectus to the Registrar; or

(ii) After delivery of a copy of the prospectus for registration but before allotment, on becoming aware of the untrue statement, he withdrew his consent in writing and gave reasonable public notice of the withdrawal and the reasons for it; or

(iii) He was competent to make the statement and that he had reasonable grounds to believe, and up to the time believed the statement to be true.

DAMAGES FOR NON-COMPLIANCE WITH S 56

A prospectus must contain the matters and reports set out in the Third Schedule to the Act.

A subscriber may bring an action against a director or other person responsible for the prospectus if these requirements are not complied with, even if the ommission does not make a prospectus false or misleading.

A director or other person responsible for a prospectus may avoid liability if he can prove that:–

(i)   He did not know of the matter not disclosed; or
(ii)  Non-compliance arose from an honest mistake of fact on his part; or
(iii) Non-compliance was not material or was otherwise such as ought in the court's opinion reasonably to be excused (s 66).

A person acting in contravention of this section is liable to a fine.

CRIMINAL LIABILITY

Any person who authorises the issue of a prospectus which includes an untrue statement is guilty of an offence and is liable to imprisonment and/or a fine unless he can prove:–

(i)  that the statement was immaterial or
(ii) that he had reasonable ground to believe and did, up to the time of the issue of the prospectus, believe that the statement was true.

The Theft Act 1968 provides that if an officer of a company, with intent to deceive its members or creditors about its affairs, publishes or concurs in publishing a written statement or account which to his knowledge is or may be false or misleading in a material particular, he is liable on conviction on indictment to imprisonment for a term not exceeding seven years.

## PREVENTION OF FRAUD (INVESTMENTS) ACT (1958)

The prospectus provisions of the Companies Act apply primarily to the public issue of shares and debentures by a company. The Companies Act does not provide protection against:

(i) fraud in subsequent dealings of shares and debentures;
(ii) the private offer of sales and debentures in companies which have not filed a prospectus;
(iii) the purchase of shares and debentures for a consideration other than cash;
(iv) share hawking ie circulating letters or hawking application forms from door-to-door offering shares or units for sale.

The Prevention of Fraud (Investments) Act seeks to exercise a measure of control in these areas.

It provides that:–

1. Any person carrying on the business of dealing in securities or issuing circulars regarding securities is required to hold a licence issued by the Department of Trade (s 1).
   A licence is not required by the following:–
   (i) members of any recognised stock exchange.
   (ii) members of a recognised association of dealers in securities.
   (iii) the Bank of England, any statutory corporation or municipal corporation, industrial and provident society or building society.
   (iv) any person acting in the capacity of manager or trustee under an authorised unit trust scheme (s 16).
2. Any person making any statement, promise or forecast which he knows to be misleading, false or deceptive or dishonestly concealing material facts to induce, or attempt to induce another person to acquire, dispose of or underwrite securities is liable to a term of seven years imprisonment (s 13, as amended by the Banking Act 1979).
3. Any person (other than those listed in 1) who distributes, or has in his possession for the purpose of distribution circulars which to his knowledge invite persons to acquire, dispose of or underwrite securities is liable to a term of imprisonment or a fine or both.
   This prohibition does not apply to:–
   (a) a prospectus which complies with the requirements of s 56 and Sch 3 of the Companies Act.
   (b) any distribution of documents required, authorised by or under any other Act (s 14).

This section does not prohibit the distribution or possession of a circular by reason only that it contains information relating to securities made or given by or on behalf of:–

members of a recognised stock exchange;
the Bank of England;
exempted dealers;
a company to its members, employees, creditors or subsidiaries;
a building society;
a manager under an authorised unit trust scheme;
a trustee to beneficiaries under a trust;
or in a prospectus of securities sold by auction.

A circular may be in the form of a newspaper, journal, magazine or other periodical publication.

# Chapter 7

# The allotment of shares

## THE APPLICATION FOR SHARES

The general law of contract applies to contracts to take shares in a company. An offer is made by an applicant submitting an application form to the company, which the company is free to accept or reject. The company signifies its acceptance by sending a letter of allotment to the applicant.

In a rights issue (an issue of new shares in proportion to a member's existing holding) the letter of rights sent by the company to holders of existing shares is an offer which on acceptance by the shareholders, constitutes a binding contract. If the letter is an 'open offer' (an invitation to shareholders to apply for any number of new securities), it is an invitation to treat and the member's reply constitutes an offer which the company may accept or reject.

### Jackson v Turquand (1869)

A circular was distributed to the shareholders of the Leeds Banking Co. giving them an option to subscribe for additional shares on a one to five basis. The circular also invited them to apply for any remaining shares. Jackson applied for 29 shares on the basis of the option (he already held 145 shares) and a further 6 surplus shares. The company informed Jackson that he had been allotted a total of 35 shares, but he never replied to the company's letter. It was held that there was a binding contract in respect of the 29 shares, but not in respect of the 6.

### CONDITIONAL APPLICATIONS

An application may be made subject to:–
(a) *A condition precedent* ie a conditional application.
   An allotment made without regard to the condition may be

99

repudiated by the allottee i e there is no contract where there is a conditional application and an unconditional allotment.

### Shaw's Case (1876)

Shaw, who owned 20 shares in a company, applied for a further 30 shares to qualify as a director. At a general meeting the shares were alloted, he was appointed a director and paid a deposit on the shares. He was later informed that as the meeting was improperly constituted he had not been appointed as a director. It was held that Shaw was entitled to repudiate the additional shares as the allotment was conditional on his being appointed a director.

(b) *A condition subsequent* i e a collateral agreement.
   If an application is subject to a collateral agreement the applicant agrees to become a member, and has a right to enforce the collateral agreement against the company.

### Elkington's Case (1867)

E applied for shares in a company and paid £1.50 (30/-) per share on allotment. He refused to pay a further call on the grounds that the shares were taken on an understanding that until goods to the value of £3,000 had been taken and paid for by the company no further calls would be made. It was held that the agreement to purchase goods was a collateral agreement, and he must pay the call. His remedy lay in an action against the company for damages.


## THE NOTICE OF ALLOTMENT

The notice of allotment is generally sent by post, as an application in the usual form impliedly authorises acceptance by post. The general rule is that there is an acceptance on posting the letter of allotment, even though the letter may be delayed or even lost in the post.

### Household Fire Insurance Co v Grant (1879)

Grant applied for 100 £1 shares in a company and deposited £5, and agreed to pay the balance within 12 months of allotment. The company posted a letter of allotment which was not received by the defendant. It was held that the defendant was liable to pay the balance owing on the shares, as acceptance was complete when the letter of allotment was posted.

Recent dicta (*in Holwell Securities Ltd v Hughes* (1974)) suggests that an acceptance by post must normally be communicated to effect a binding contract. Only in exceptional cases, where the parties clearly intend, is posting sufficient to make the contract effective.

Communication of an allotment may be made in other ways e g by a letter demanding payment of an instalment on the shares (*Forget v Cement Products of Canada* (1916)).

An acceptance must be communicated within a reasonable time, otherwise the offer will lapse. Therefore an application to take shares lapses if an allotment is not made within a reasonable time.

### Ramsgate Victoria Hotel Co Ltd v Montefiore (1866)

M and another applied for 50 £20 shares in the plaintiff company in June 1864. No allotment of shares was made until November of that year. M refused to accept the shares or pay any calls. It was held that the offer had lapsed as the allotment was not made within a reasonable time.

An offer may be revoked (ie withdrawn) before communication of the acceptance. The revocation is not effective until it is brought to the company's notice e g a letter of revocation is of no effect unless it reaches the company before the letter of allotment is posted.

An application for shares made in pursuance of a prospectus issued generally (ie to persons other than existing shareholders and debentureholders) may not be revoked until the expiration of the third day after the opening of the subscription lists (s 82). This is to prevent 'stags' revoking their applications before allotment if it appears that the issue is not successful. The company has usually posted the letters of allotment before the expiration of this third day.

## POWER TO ALLOT SHARES

The directors of a company may only issue shares or grant the right to convert securities into shares if they are given express authority to do so in the articles or by a resolution passed in general meeting.

The authority must:

(a) be for a period of not more than 5 years from the date of the company's incorporation, or if given at a later date, 5 years from that date;
(b) state the maximum amount of shares that may be allotted.

These minimum requirements are set out in s 80 and a company may impose additional conditions or stipulations. Such an authority may be revoked, varied or renewed by ordinary resolution in general meeting.

These restrictions do not apply to:

(a) shares allotted under an employees' share scheme
(b) shares to be taken by subscribers to the memorandum.

When the authority expires it may be renewed for a further period not exceeding five years.

A copy of any resolution relating to such an authority must be filed at the Companies Registry within 15 days of it being passed (s 380). Notice of the resolution must also be published in the London Gazette.

An allotment made in contravention of s 80 is nevertheless valid, but any director who knowingly and wilfully contravenes or permits or authorises a contravention of the section is liable on conviction to a fine.

PRE-EMPTION RIGHTS

A company which proposes to make an allotment of ordinary 'equity' shares must first offer those shares to its existing ordinary shareholders in proportion to their existing shareholding (s 89). This provision seeks to ensure that the rights of a company's ordinary shareholders are not affected by a further issue of ordinary shares by a company.

The offer must be open for at least 21 days and must be notified to the members concerned in the same manner as notification of a general meeting of the company.

A private company may permanently exclude pre-emption rights by a provision to that effect in its memorandum or articles.

Any public or private company may exclude pre-emption rights from all its allotments if it has already granted the directors authority to issue shares under s 80. It may confer this power upon the directors by a provision to that effect in the articles or by a special resolution.

A company may exclude pre-emption rights from a particular allotment by passing a special resolution to that effect. The special resolution may not be proposed unless it is recommended by the directors and there has been circulated (with the notice of the meeting) a written statement by the directors setting out:

(a) their reasons for making the recommendation;
(b) the amount to be paid to the company in respect of the allotment;
(c) the directors' justification of that amount (s 95).

## CONSIDERATION FOR ALLOTMENT

1. Shares allotted by a company and any premiums payable on them may be paid up in money or money's worth (which includes goodwill and knowhow). This allows a company to make an allotment of bonus shares to its members, or to pay up, with available sums any amounts unpaid on any of its shares.
2. A public company may not accept, in payment of its shares or any premiums payable on them, an undertaking given by an allottee that he or another person should do work or perform services for the company or for any other person. (This prohibition does not apply to private companies). If such an undertaking is accepted as part payment by a public company, the allotment is not invalid. The company may enforce the undertaking, and any holder of shares is liable to pay the company an amount equal to the nominal value of the shares, together with any premium payable on them (s 99).
   Any subsequent holder of such shares will incur similar liability unless:
   (a) he is a purchaser for value who did not have actual notice of the contravention at the time when he purchased the shares; or
   (b) he derived his title to the shares (directly or indirectly) from a person who became a holder of the shares after the contravention and who was not subject to the statutory liability (s 112).
3. The subscribers to the memorandum of a public company must pay for their shares in cash (s 106).
4. A public company must not enter into an agreement with a subscriber to the memorandum to acquire from him a non cash asset, within the first two years of its existence, unless the consideration given by the company is at least equal in value to one tenth of the company's issued share capital at that time (s 104).
5. A public company must not make an allotment of shares unless at least ¼ of the nominal value and the whole of any premiums have been paid (s 101).

## ALLOTMENT OF SHARES BY PUBLIC COMPANIES – NON-CASH CONSIDERATION

Where a public company makes an allotment of shares for a non-cash consideration eg an undertaking to transfer property, the company must ensure that the undertaking is performed within five years of the date of the allotment (s 102).

Where a company allots shares in contravention of this rule the allottee is liable to pay the company a sum equal to the nominal value of the shares, the premium (if any) plus interest. If he fails to fulfil his undertaking within the five year period he becomes subject to similar liabilities unless:

he is a bone fide purchaser of the shares without knowledge of the contravention; or
derives his title from such a bone fide purchaser.

A public company may not make an allotment for a non-cash consideration unless it has received a report on the value of the consideration during the six months preceding the allotment.

The valuation and report must be made by an independent person who is qualified, at the time of making the report, to be appointed as the company's auditor (s 103).

The report must state:

(a) the nominal value of the shares to be wholly or partly paid for by the consideration,
(b) the amount of any premiums payable on those shares,
(c) a description of the consideration and the methods used to value it,
(d) the extent to which the nominal value of the shares and any premium are to be treated as paid up by the consideration and in cash.

A copy of the report must be sent to the proposed allottee of the shares and filed with the Registrar (ss 108, 109).

A public company may not, within 2 years of the issue of the certificate of incorporation, acquire assets from subscribers to the memorandum having an aggregate value of 10 per cent or more of the nominal value of the company's issued capital unless:

(a) the valuation rules in ss 108, 109 are complied with.
(b) the transaction is approved by an ordinary resolution.

A copy of the resolution must be filed within 15 days of its passing (s 111).

These rules do not apply to an allotment of shares to shareholders of another company in exchange for their shares on a takeover or merger with that other company ie the first company need not obtain a valuation of the shares of the second company.

## ALLOTMENT OF SHARES BY PRIVATE COMPANIES – NON-CASH CONSIDERATION

These provisions do not apply to private companies who may issue shares for a consideration other than cash e g transfer of property to the company, or rendering a service to the company.

There must be consideration for such an agreement. It must not be given for past services i e past consideration.

### Re Eddystone Marine Insurance (1893)

A company which proposed to convert into a public company allotted fully paid shares to the value of £6,000 to its directors and shareholders as payment for services rendered in the company's formation. No such services had been rendered. It was held that the allottees must pay for the shares as no consideration had been given. Had any services been rendered they would have been of no value, as the consideration would have been past.

The courts will not inquire into the adequacy of the consideration as long as the directors have acted honestly and reasonably in the valuation of assets.

### Re Wragg (1897)

W & M, the proprietors of a livery stable business sold the business for £46,300 to a newly incorporated company, Wragg Ltd, formed by themselves. £20,000 of the purchase price was paid in shares, the balance in cash and debentures. The company went into liquidation, the liquidator contended that the shares were not fully paid up as certain assets had been overvalued i e the horses and carriages which were valued at £27,000 were shown to be worth only £15,000 at the time of the sale. It was held that the courts would not examine the adequacy of the consideration as W & M had relied on an expert's valuation and he had valued the business at £46,300.

The courts will however inquire into an agreement if the contract is fraudulent, or if the consideration is illusory or inadequate.

### Hong Kong and China Gas Co Ltd v Glen (1914)

A company agreed to allot G 400 fully paid shares and one fifth of any future increase in the company's capital in return for a concession to supply gas to one of the cities in Hong Kong. It was held that the provision as to the future increase in capital was not binding on the company, as it had agreed to give an indefinite and unlimited value for the purchase of the concession i e the value of the concession bore no relation to the value of the shares.

When shares are issued for a non-cash consideration the company must deliver to the Registrar for registration the contract (*or* if it is not in writing particulars of the contract), within one month of the allotment. If the company defaults the allotment is nevertheless valid, but the officers of the company are liable to a fine and a further fine for each day the company is in default (s 88).

## ISSUE OF SHARES AT A DISCOUNT

A company must not issue shares at a discount (s 100), and any allottee must pay the full nominal value of the share, plus the interest on the discount.

### Ooregum Gold Mining Co of India Ltd v Roper (1892)

A company whose £1 ordinary shares stood at 12½p (2/6) in the market, proposed to issue £1 preference shares with 75p (15/-) credited as having been paid, leaving a liability of only 25p (5/-) per share. It was held that the issue was ultra vires and the original allottees were liable to pay the 75p unpaid on the shares when called upon to do so by the company.

Any subsequent holder of the shares may also be liable for the payment of the discount, unless he is a bone fide purchaser for value of the shares and does not have notice of the contravention or derives his title from such a person.

An attempt to issue shares at a discount by indirect means is also prohibited.

### Mosely v Koffyfontein Mines (1904)

A company proposed to issue £1 debentures at 80p (16/-). The holders of the debentures were to be given the right to exchange the debentures for fully paid shares at any time before the debentures were repaid. It was held that this would amount to an issue of shares at a discount as a shareholder would be able to exercise this right immediately and obtain a £1 share in exchange for a £1 debenture which had been purchased for 80p.

It is not an issue of shares at a discount to exchange a debenture for a fully paid up share whose nominal value is equal to the issue price of the debenture.

An exception is permitted by s 97 in that the allottees of shares may deduct or be paid underwriting commission for subscribing for shares.

The issue of debentures at a discount is not prohibited by the Act.

# ISSUE OF SHARES AT A PREMIUM

A company may issue shares at a premium ie it may require allottees to pay a price above the nominal value of the share. The difference between the issue price of such a share and its nominal value is called the share premium.

This is not a trading profit and s 130 provides that the premium must be transferred to a share premium account, and may only be used for certain purposes. The share premium is by its very nature capital and may only be reduced as if it were share capital. It may not be used for the payment of dividends.

A share premium may also arise if shares are issued for a non-cash consideration and the value of the consideration exceeds the nominal value of the shares. In these circumstances the value of the consideration must be transferred to a share premium account.

### Henry Head and Co Ltd v Ropner Holdings Ltd (1952)

RH Ltd was formed to acquire the issued share capital of two shipping companies. The authorised capital of RH Ltd was £1,799,606 which was equal to the aggregate capital of the two shipping companies. The amalgamation was effected by issuing one share of RH Ltd for each share of the two companies. The assets of two companies were valued at £6,826,112. It was held that the surplus of £5,066,506, could not be distributed as a dividend and must be transferred to the share premium account as this sum was the premium on the new shares.

The share premium account may be used for:

(i) paying up fully paid bonus shares to be issued by the company to its members (s 130).
(ii) writing off preliminary expenses, or the expenses of, or underwriting commission on, the issue of shares or debentures (s 130).
(iii) the provision of any premium payable on the redemption of any debentures (s 130).
(iv) paying off the premium on a redemption or purchase by a private company of its own shares (s 171).

Relief is granted from the provisions of s 130 in certain situations involving mergers and group reconstructions:

(i) Where an acquiring company obtains a 90 per cent equity holding in another company by way of share exchange, the premiums do not have to be credited to the share premium account (s 131).

(ii) Where a wholly owned subsidiary acquires shares in another subsidiary in return for an allotment of its shares to its holding company or to another wholly owned subsidiary, only the minimum premium value has to be transferred to the share premium account. The minimum premium value is the difference between the nominal value of the shares issued, and either the cost of the shares being transferred or the amount at which they stood in the company's records (whichever is the lower) (s 132).

## RESTRICTIONS ON ALLOTMENT BY PUBLIC COMPANIES

A public company issuing a prospectus is subject to certain statutory restrictions on the allotment of its shares.

1. Where a public company for the first time issues a prospectus it may not make an allotment of shares unless the minimum subscription has been taken up by the applicants and the application money has been received by the company (s 83) (The minimum subscription is the minimum amount which in the directors opinion is required by the company to pay for the purchase of property, preliminary expenses, repayment of loans and the provision of working capital).

    This only applies to a first invitation by a company, whether it occurs on the company's formation or at a later date. It does not apply to a second or subsequent invitation or to any invitation to subscribe for the company's debentures.

    Section 84 also provides that no allotment of the shares can be made unless:

    (a) the capital is subscribed in full; or
    (b) the prospectus states that the allotment can be made subject to any specified conditions.

    If the minimum subscription is not subscribed within 40 days of the issue of the prospectus, all money received must be repaid to the applicants within the following 8 days. If repayment is delayed beyond the 48th day, the directors are jointly and severally liable to repay the money with interest at 5 per cent per annum.

    A director may avoid liability if he can show that the delay was not due to any misconduct or negligence on his part (s 101).
2. A public company may not make an allotment of shares unless at

least one quarter of the nominal value of the shares and the whole of any premium due has been paid (s 101).
3. A public company may not make an allotment until the beginning of the third day after the issue of the prospectus, or until any later time stated in the prospectus (s 82).
4. If a prospectus states that an application has been made or will be made for permission to be listed on any Stock Exchange any allotment is *void*:
   (i) if permission has not been applied for before the third day after the issue of the prospectus; or
   (ii) if permission is refused before the end of three weeks or longer period (not exceeding six weeks) granted by the Stock Exchange from the date of the closing of the subscription lists (s 86).

The application money received by the company must be kept in a separate account. It does not form part of the general assets of the company and is not subject to a floating charge on the company's assets.

Where permission has not been applied for within the requisite time or has been refused, the application moneys must be returned forthwith to the applicants, and if not repaid within 8 days the directors are jointly and severally liable for the repayment with interest at 5 per cent per annum. A director may only avoid liability if he can prove that the default in repayment is not due to his misconduct.

IRREGULAR ALLOTMENTS

An allotment made in contravention of:

(1) Section 83 (ie before the minimum subscription has been subscribed, or after 40 days from the first issue of the prospectus) is *voidable* at the option of the allottee. If an allottee wishes to retain the shares, a company cannot insist on repaying the application moneys.

   An allottee who seeks to avoid the allotment must inform the company, within one month of his intention (s 85). His rights will not be affected, even though a company goes into liquidation during this period.

(2) Section 101 (ie as to one-quarter of its nominal value plus premium has not been paid) is valid. Each share allotted is treated as paid as if s 101 had been complied with and the

allottee and any subsequent holder is liable to pay this amount. (A bona fide purchaser without notice of the breach of his successor in title is not liable).

(3) Section 82 (ie an allotment made before the 3rd day) is valid, but the company and its officers in default are liable to a fine.

(4) Section 86 (ie failure to apply to The Stock Exchange for permission to deal, or a refusal of application) is void.

## RETURN AS TO ALLOTMENTS

When a company limited by shares or a company limited by guarantee and having a share capital makes an allotment of its shares, it must within one month deliver to the Registrar:

(a) A return of the allotments stating the number and nominal amount of the shares, the names and addresses of the allottees and the amount (if any) paid or due on each share whether on account of the nominal value of the shares.

(b) In the case of shares allotted otherwise than in cash
   (i) a contract constituting the title of the allottee to the allotment together with any contract for sale or for services or other consideration in respect of which that allotment was made, and
   (ii) a return stating the number and nominal amount of shares so allotted, the extent to which they are to be treated as paid up, and the consideration for the allotment (s 88).

# Chapter 8

# Share capital

The term 'capital' is used in various ways and has a variety of meanings.

1. Nominal or authorised capital ie the full nominal value of the shares which a company may issue under its memorandum of association.
2. Issued capital ie the nominal value of shares actually allotted by the company, in cash or for some other consideration, whether paid up or not.
3. Paid up capital ie the amount actually received in cash or other consideration by the company on the shares issued.
4. Uncalled capital ie the total amount remaining unpaid on the shares issued.
5. Subscribed capital ie the total number of shares taken up, or agreed to be taken up, whether paid up or not.
6. Reserve capital ie that part of the uncalled capital which may only be called up on winding up (s 120).
7. Equity share capital ie that part of the issued capital which gives an unrestricted right to participate in dividends and the distribution of capital. It normally consists of ordinary and deferred shares.
8. Circulating capital ie property acquired or produced by a company with a view to re-sale or sale at a profit.
9. Fixed capital ie property acquired by a company and intended for retention and employment with a view to profit.

The capital of a company may be divided into various classes of shares, or it may consist partly or wholly of stock. It is not necessary for the shares to be uniform or have equal rights. The memorandum and the articles may provide for the issue of different classes of shares with different attributes and different rights. Article 2 provides that 'without prejudice to any rights attached to any existing shares, any share may be issued with such rights or restrictions as the company may by ordinary resolution determine.'

If a company is not given the power either in the articles or in its memorandum to divide its shares into classes or subdivide its shares it may alter its articles to enable it to do so (*Andrews v Gas Meter Co* (1897)).

## TYPES OF SHARE CAPITAL

1. Ordinary shares.
2. Preference shares.
3. Deferred or founders' shares.
4. Redeemable shares.
5. Employers' shares

## ORDINARY SHARES

The holders of ordinary shares are entitled to the surplus profits after prior interests have been met eg the payment of a fixed dividend on preference shares.

The ordinary shareholders are also entitled to a fixed rate of dividend before any payment is made to the holders of deferred shares. They may also be entitled to a proportion of the company's profits after payment of a fixed percentage to the deferred shares, or share in any surplus profits with the deferred shareholders.

The ordinary shareholders are entitled in a winding up to the surplus profits assets remaining after the payment of the company's liabilities and the return of capital to all other classes of share, unless the company's preference shareholders are given the right to participate in the distribution of any surplus assets.

A company may issue non-voting ordinary shares, which form a separate class of shares.

## PREFERENCE SHARES

There is no precise legal definition of the term 'preference share'. The term is used generally to denote shares which confer certain preferential rights upon their holders. The principal rights are the right to a dividend at a fixed rate before the payment of a dividend to other classes of shareholders and the right to receive a proportionate part of the capital or to participate in the distribution of the company's assets.

1. The rights of the preference shares are usually set out in the articles, but may be found in the memorandum or the terms of issue of the shares. If the rights are clearly and fully set out, the relevant provisions must be examined in each case, to determine the rights of the preferential shareholders.
2. The right to receive a specified rate of dividend in priority to other shareholders, only exists if a dividend is declared by the company. It is not a right to compel a company to pay a dividend, but to preferential treatment if and when a distribution is made.
3. Unless otherwise stated a preferential dividend is deemed to be cumulative i e if dividends are not declared in any year because of insufficient profits, the arrears in respect of those shares are to be made good in subsequent years before any dividend is paid to any other class of shareholders.

   If the share is non-cumulative, this must be clearly stated, but it may be inferred in certain cases.

   In *Staples v Eastmam Photographic Materials Co* (1896) it was stated that the preference shares should be paid 'out of the profits of each year'. It was held that the shares were non-cumulative.
4. A company may also designate a fund out of which a preference dividend is payable.
5. Preference shares may be participating or non-participating i e participating in any surplus profits after payment of their fixed dividend. In *Re Isle of Thanet Electricity Supply Co* (1950) a Company's preference shareholders were given the right to participate further in the company's profits after a dividend of 6 per cent had been paid on the ordinary shares.

   Preference shares are presumed to be non-participating unless participating rights are given in the articles, memorandum or terms of issue.
6. The general rule in a winding up is that all shares rank 'pari passu' in respect of dividend and capital, and the rule is only displaced if the articles, memorandum or terms of issue state otherwise.

AREARS OF DIVIDEND

(i) There is no right to any arrears of dividend on a winding up unless: the dividends have been declared before the commencement of a winding up; or
(ii) the articles contain express provision to this effect, or on the

construction of the words the shares are preferential as to payment of dividend on a winding up.

### Re EW Savory Ltd (1951)

The articles of the company provided that: 'The preference shares . . . shall confer on the holders the right to a fixed cumulative preferential dividend at the rate of £6 per annum on the capital paid up thereon and shall rank both as regards dividend and capital in priority to all other shares, both present and future.' It was held that the priority as to capital referred to a winding up and the reference to a dividend must refer to arrears of dividend in a winding up (as the word would otherwise be unnecessary and superfluous).

RETURN OF CAPITAL

Preference shareholders are not entitled in a winding up to the repayment of capital in priority to the ordinary shareholders, unless there is a provision to this effect. If there is no provision the preference shares rank pari passu with the ordinary shares in the repayment of capital.

If the preference shares are granted priority as to return of capital, the preference shareholders are not, unless otherwise stated, entitled to participate with the ordinary shareholders in any surplus assets remaining after the repayment of capital to the ordinary shareholders.

It is for the preference shareholders who claim further rights to prove additional entitlement in respect of the shares.

### Re Isle of Thanet Electricity Supply Co (1950)

The preference shareholders were given priority over the ordinary shareholders in respect of a 6 per cent dividend, arrears of dividend, and the repayment of capital in a winding up. It was held these rights were exhaustive and they were not entitled to share in surplus assets on the winding up of the company.

## DEFERRED SHARES

These shares are sometimes called founders or management shares, and are rarely issued today. They were often issued to a promoter or a vender of a business, who demonstrated his confidence in the venture by taking shares as payment for the business, or for his services. Most deferred shares have been converted into ordinary shares.

The holders of deferred shares are not entitled to the payment of a dividend until a dividend at a specified rate has been paid to the ordinary shareholders.

A prospectus issued by a company must state the number of founders shares, their voting rights, their interest in the Company property and profits (Sch 3).

## REDEEMABLE SHARES

A company limited by shares, or a company limited by guarantee and having a share capital may issue shares which may be redeemed at the option of the company or the shareholder (s 159). Article 3 provides that 'shares may be issued which are to be redeemed or are to be liable to be redeemed at the option of the company or the holder on such terms and in such manner as may be provided by the articles'.

The following conditions must be satisfied:

(i) The company must be authorised to do so by its articles (s 159(1)).

(ii) The company must, at the time of the issue of the shares have other shares which are not redeemable (s 159(2)).

(iii) The shares may not be redeemed unless they are fully paid (s 159(3)).

(iv) The terms of redemption must provide for payment on redemption ie repayment may not be postponed beyond the date of redemption (s 159(3)).

(v) The shares may only be redeemed out of distributable profits or out of the proceeds of a fresh issue of shares made for the purpose of redemption (s 160(1)).

(vi) The premium payable on redemption must be paid out of distributable profits, unless the shares that are being redeemed were originally issued at a premium. In that case a proportion of any premiums payable on their redemption may be paid out of the proceeds of an issue of shares made for the purposes of redemption (s 160(2)).

(vii) If the shares are redeemed out of distributable profits, an amount equal to the nominal amount of the shares redeemed must be transferred to a capital redemption reserve (s 170(1)).

(viii) A company may issue shares up to the nominal amount of the redeemed shares, without being regarded as increasing its share capital, if it redeems its old shares within one month of the issue of its new shares.

(ix) A private company may redeem shares out of capital if authorised to do so by its articles (s 173).

(x) The redemption of shares does not amount to a reduction of the company's authorised share capital, as the redeemed shares remain part of the company's nominal capital and must be shown in the balance sheet.

If a company fails to redeem its shares, a shareholder has a right of action for breach of contract in respect of that failure. However, the company will not be liable in damages for this breach. Neither will the court grant an order of specific performance unless it can be shown that the company is able to meet the cost of redemption out of distributable profits.

If a company is wound up after the obligation to redeem shares has arisen the shares are to be treated as cancelled. The shareholder will be treated as deferred creditor in the winding up ie he will be paid after all the other creditors, but before the other shareholders (ss 159, 160, 171).

A company must give notice of the redemption of shares to the Registrar within one month (s 122).

## EMPLOYEES' SHARES

Many companies encourage their employees to have a direct interest in the company's affairs by becoming shareholders. Companies have devised schemes where part of the profits have been set aside to assist employees to purchase the company's shares.

An employees' share scheme is a scheme for encouraging or facilitating the holding of securities in a company by or for the benefit of:

(i) bona fide employees or former employees of the company or a related company.

(ii) the wives, husbands, widows, widowers, infant children of such employees or former employees.

A company usually appoints trustees to administer an employees' share scheme. The trustees purchase shares on the employee's behalf either on the Stock Exchange or by subscribing for new shares. The total value of the shares is related to the company's

profits and that cost is deducted from the company's profits or
distributable profits (if a public company).


## SHARE WARRANTS

A company limited by shares may, if the shares are fully paid up and
it is given authority by its articles, issue a share warrant stating that
the bearer is entitled to the shares specified therein (s 188).

On the issue of a share warrant the member's name is struck off
the register, and the following particulars entered in the register:

(i)   the fact that a warrant has been issued;
(ii)  a statement of the shares included in the warrant;
(iii) the date of issue of the warrant.

The bearer of the warrant is, subject to any provision in the
articles, entitled to have his name entered as a member in the
register of members on surrendering his warrant for cancellation (s
355).

The holder of a share warrant is a shareholder, but not a member,
unless the articles specify otherwise. The articles usually provide
that the holder of a warrant may not vote, requisition a meeting or
give notice of resolutions unless he deposits his share warrant with
the company before a general meeting. The share warrant is
returned to him at the conclusion of the meeting.


## VARIATION OF CLASS RIGHTS

A company may seek to amend or vary the rights attaching to one or
more of its classes of shares. These rights are usually concerned with
dividends, voting or the distribution of assets in a winding up of the
company.

The class rights are usually found in the company's articles, but
may also be found in the memorandum or the terms of issue of the
shares or occasionally in the terms of a special resolution (*Re Old
Silkstone Collieries Ltd* (1954)).

The following rules apply to the variation of class rights:

(1) A company may alter the rights of unissued shares by passing
    the appropriate resolution at a general meeting. The articles
    will specify the type of resolution required to sanction the
    alteration.

(2) If a company has only one class of shares, the rights attaching to those shares may be varied by special resolution if the rights are contained in the articles. If the rights are contained in the memorandum they may be altered, subject to the procedures laid down in section 17.

(3) If the class rights are set out in the articles, which provide for a variation procedure, that procedure must be followed. The articles generally provide that the rights attaching to any class may be varied with the written consent of the holders of three quarters of the issued shares of that class, or with the sanction of an extraordinary resolution passed at a separate general meeting of the holders.

Class rights created by the terms of issue of the shares or by a special resolution must be treated in the same manner as those defined in the articles (s 9).

### Re Old Silkstone Collieries Ltd (1954)

The assets of a nationalised colliery company were vested in the National Coal Board under the Coal Industry Nationalisation Act 1946. Various rights were reserved in favour of the preference shareholders by a resolution in general meetings on a redemption of the preference shares. The company later resolved to repay the preference shareholders without regard to those rights. It was held that the resolutions of the general meeting created special rights and these rights could only be varied by consent of a qualified majority of the preference shareholders.

(4) If a company has different classes of shares, the variation of class rights is subject to the provisions of s 125 which stipulates that:
  (a) where rights are attached to a class of shares other than in the memorandum, and the articles do not contain a provision as to the variation of those rights, they may be varied only if:
    (i) holders of three quarters in nominal value of the issued shares of that class consent in writing to the variation.
    (ii) an extraordinary resolution is passed at a separate meeting of the holders of that class sanctioning the variation.
  (b) where the rights are attached to a class of shares by the memorandum or otherwise and the variation of those rights is connected with the powers of the directors to allot shares; or with a reduction of capital those rights may only be varied as in 1(a).
  (c) where the rights are attached to a class of shares by the

memorandum or otherwise and the articles contain a provision for their variation, the class rights may only be varied in accordance with those provisions.

(d) where the rights are attached to a class of shares by the memorandum and the memorandum and articles do not contain provision for varying those rights, they may only be varied if all the members of the company agree to the variation.

(e) Consent to the variation of class rights may only be given at a class meeting which must comply with the Act as to notice and procedure. The quorum for such a meeting must be two persons holding or representing by proxy at least one third in nominal value of the shares of the class in question. Any holder of shares of the class in question, present in person or by proxy, may demand a poll.

(5) Any alteration to the procedure for variation of class rights is regarded as a variation of those rights and is subject to the rules previously listed.

(6) If there is no provision for variation, the consent of the court may be obtained to a scheme of arrangement under section 425, where a company enters into a binding compromise or arrangement with a class by members.

(7) The method by which class rights may be varied depends on the source of those rights.

(a) Where the class rights are contained in the articles, the rights may be varied by a special resolution (in accordance with section 9).

(b) Where the class rights are contained in the memorandum, the memorandum usually prescribes the appropriate resolution.

(c) Where the class rights are contained in the terms of issue of the shares, an ordinary resolution will be sufficient (unless otherwise stated).

A company need only follow the procedure for variation of these class rights if its proposals amount to a variation of class rights. In the following situations there is no such variation.

a. The issue of new shares or a new class of share ranking equally with the existing shares.

### White v Bristol Aeroplane Co Ltd (1953)

The company's issued capital consisted of 660,000 £1 preference shares and £3,300,000 ordinary stock. The articles provided that class rights could only be altered with the sanction of an extraordinary resolution passed at a separate meeting of members of that class. The company proposed to issue 600,000 £1 preference shares as bonus shares to the ordinary shareholders, ranking pari passu with the existing preference shares. It was held that although the issue of additional preference shares altered the value of the voting power of the existing preference shares it did not affect their rights. The company's proposals therefore did not require the approval of the existing preference shares.

b. The subdivision of shares of one class under a power in the articles, which has the effect of increasing the voting rights of those shares.

### Greenhalgh v Arderne Cinemas (1951)

The Company had two classes of ordinary shares of 10p (2/-) and 50p (10/-); each share carried one vote. The company passed a resolution to sub-divide the 50p shares into five 10p shares. It was held that there had been no variation of class rights, as each of the original 10p shares carried one vote, as before.

c. The cancellation of shares where those shares were entitled to priority in the repayment of capital in a winding up.

### Scottish Insurance Corporation v Wilsons & Clyde Coal Co (1949)

A company which was to go into voluntary liquidation, after the nationalisation of its assets, proposed to reduce its capital by the repayment in full of its 7 per cent preference stock. The articles provided that in a winding up the preference stockholders were entitled to the repayment of capital in priority to the ordinary shareholders. It was held that the repayment would be approved as the preference shareholders would not be entitled to share in the surplus assets on a winding up. They received the same amount as they would on the proposed liquidation.

### Re Saltdean Estate Co Ltd (1968)

A company which had two classes of shares, namely ordinary and preference shares, proposed to repay the preference shareholders and so eliminate that class of shares. The preference shares were entitled to priority as to return of capital on a winding up, but had no other rights over the ordinary shares. It was held that this was not a variation of class rights, as the company could pass a resolution to wind up at anytime. In the event the preference shareholders would only be entitled to a return of capital as in the company's proposals.

If class rights are varied under a procedure contained in the memorandum or articles of a company, whose share capital is divided into different classes of shares, the dissenting members of that class may apply to the court to have the variation cancelled.

(i) The dissenters must hold not less than 15 per cent of the issued shares of that class.
(ii) They must not have consented to or voted in favour of the resolution.
(iii) They must apply to the court within 21 days of consent being given or the resolution being passed.
(iv) The variation is of no effect unless and until it is confirmed by the court (s 127).

The court may either confirm or cancel the alteration. It will adopt the latter course if it is satisfied that the variation would unfairly prejudice the majority e g if the majority who vote in favour of the variation act on grounds of self interest, rather than considering the interests of the general body of members of the class.

**Re Holders Investment Trust** (1971)

A company proposed a reduction of capital by cancelling its 5 per cent cumulative redeemable preference shares and allotting an equivalent amount of unsecured loan stock to those preference shareholders. Trustees holding 90% of the preference shares voted in favour of the resolution at a class meeting as they also held 52% of the ordinary shares in the company. They had been advised that the trusts would benefit from the change. It was held that the resolution at the class meeting was invalid as the trustees had not been concerned with the interest of the preference shareholders as a class, and the issue of the loan stock had not been shown by the company to be fair and equitable.

The consent of the holders of a class is only required, and the right of the minority to object may only be exercised if a company's proposals constitute a variation of class rights.

The company must send a copy of the court order to the Registrar, within 15 days of the order being made (s 127).

## ALTERATION OF SHARE CAPITAL

A limited company may, if authorised by its articles, alter the conditions of its memorandum so as to:

  (i) Increase its share capital by creating new shares
 (ii) Consolidate and divide all or any of its share capital into shares of a larger denomination.
(iii) Convert all or any of its paid up shares into stock and re-convert that stock into paid up shares of any denomination.
 (iv) Subdivide its shares, or any of them, into shares of a smaller amount.
  (v) Cancel shares which at the date of the passing of the resolution have not been taken or agreed to be taken by any person and diminish the amount of its share capital by the amount of the share so cancelled.

This capital re-organisation may only be accomplished by passing the appropriate resolution in general meeting. Unless otherwise specified, an ordinary resolution is sufficient (s 121).

Notice must be given to the Registrar within one month, if a company

  (i) consolidates and divides its shares; or
 (ii) converts its shares into stock; or
(iii) reconverts stocks into shares; or
 (iv) subdivides its shares; or
  (v) redeems any redeemable shares;
 (vi) cancels any shares (other than in a reduction of capital) (s 122).

If the articles do not authorise the company to increase or alter its capital, it may alter its articles by special resolution to enable it to do so. The alteration of the articles and the capital may be effected by a single resolution.

Notice must be given to the Registrar of any increase of capital within 15 days of passing the resolution authorising the increase (s 123).


REDUCTION OF CAPITAL

A limited company may, by special resolution, reduce its share capital in any way provided that:

 (i) Authority is given by the articles.
(ii) The reduction is confirmed by the court (s 135). Three methods of reduction are specifically referred to in this section.
   (a) To extinguish or reduce liability on partly paid up shares e g if a company has £1 shares of which 75p has been paid up it may eliminate the outstanding liability of 25p on each

share, by reducing the share to 75p. Capital is not returned by the company.

(b) To cancel paid up capital which has been lost or which is not represented by available assets, e g a company has £1 fully paid shares, but its assets only represent a value of 50p per share. The company may seek to reduce the nominal value of its shares to 50p. It would then be able to make a distribution out of future profits without having to make good past losses.

(c) To pay off any paid up share capital which is in excess of the company's needs. This often occurs when a company sells part of its understanding, and intends to restrict its activities to the remaining part of its business.

A company may adopt other methods to effect a reduction of capital e g by issuing debenture stock to its shareholders (*Re Holders Investment Trust Ltd* (1971)); by cancelling all or part of its capital reserves.

## Carruth v Imperial Chemical Industries (1937)

A company's capital consisted of £1 ordinary shares and 50p deferred shares, both fully paid up. As the market value of the deferred shares stood at 25p, the company proposed to reduce the deferred shares to 25p per share fully paid and concert and consolidate every four deferred shares into one ordinary £1 share. The company's articles permitted a reduction of capital by specified ways or otherwise as may seem expedient. The reduction was upheld by the court as it effectively strengthened the company's financial structure and had been approved by the requisite majority of ordinary and separate shareholders at separate class meetings.

The articles usually provide the necessary authority for a reduction of capital. (A typical article granting authority is Article 34). If the authority is not contained in the articles they must be altered by special resolution. The special resolution giving the company the authority to effect a reduction must be passed before the special resolution reducing the capital can be passed.

A company must first pass a special resolution to reduce its share capital and then apply to the Court, by petition, for an order confirming the reduction.

REDUCTION WHICH DOES NOT INVOLVE CREDITORS

A reduction which does not involve creditors is of domestic concern only.

The only questions which concern the court are:
(i) Should permission for the reduction be refused out of regard to the interests of those members of the public who may be induced to take shares in the company?
(ii) Is the reduction fair and equitable as between different classes of shareholders?

An appropriate form of reduction where there is a loss of capital is an all round reduction i e the same percentage should be reduced or cancelled or paid off in respect of each share, whatever the class of the share.

(a) The courts have regarded an all round reduction as appropriate where there are several classes of shares.
(b) Where the preference shareholders have priority as to capital, the loss should be borne first by the ordinary shareholders.
(c) Where the preference shareholders have priority as to dividend, but not capital, the loss will be borne rateably by both ordinary and preference shareholders.
(d) Where capital is surplus to requirements the class of shares entitled to priority in a winding up will be paid first, even though, if participating as to dividend, this may deny them an opportunity to participate in a future dividend.

## Prudential Assurance Co Ltd v Chatterley-Whitfield Collieries Ltd (1949)

A coal company with an equal number of ordinary shares and preference shares had a surplus of capital as a result of nationalisation. The articles gave the preference shareholders priority as to repayment of capital in the event of a winding up, but no further right to participate in any surplus assets. A special resolution was passed for a reduction of capital by paying off the preference shares. It was held that the reduction was fair and equitable as the preference shareholders had no right to a continuance of their rate to a dividend, if the company decided that they should be paid off and had the means to do so. It was immaterial that as a result they would be unable to share in any excess assets in a winding up.

A debenture holder is not entitled to object if the reduction does not involve either the reduction of liability or the return of capital.

### REDUCTION INVOLVING CREDITORS

If a reduction involves a reduction of liability in respect of uncalled capital (as in (a)) or a return of capital (as in (c)) the court:
(i) must settle a list of creditors entitled to object with the nature and amount of their debts and claims.

(ii) may publish notices fixing a day or days on which creditors not entered on the list are entitled to be heard in respect of their claims.

(iii) must obtain the consent of the creditors to the reduction (s 136(4)).

If a creditor does not consent to the reduction the court may, if it thinks fit, dispense with the consent of that creditor on the company securing payment of this debt or claim by appropriating as the court may direct.

(i) the full amount of the debt or claim if the company admits it; or

(ii) an amount fixed by the Court if the company does not admit, or if the extent of the debt or claim is contingent or not ascertained (as if the company were being wound up by the court) (s 136(5)).

The court may, having regard to any special circumstances of the case, if it thinks proper dispense with these requirements as regards any class or any classes of creditors. Eg it may dispense with the advertisements and settling the list of creditors (s 136(6)).

APPROVAL AND REGISTRATION OF THE ORDER

If the court approves the reduction, it makes an order confirming the reduction. It may direct that the words 'and reduced' be added to the company's name for a specified time and that the reasons for the reduction be advertised to the general public (s 137). Such directions are rarely used.

The order confirming the reduction must be delivered to the Registrar together with a minute of the company's new capital structure. This minute, when registered, is deemed to be substituted for the previous corresponding part of the memorandum, and will be as valid and alterable as if it had been originally contained in the memorandum (s 138(1)(5)).

The Registrar then gives a certificate which is conclusive evidence that all the requirements of the Act in respect of the reduction of share capital have been complied with and that the share capital is such as is stated in the minute (s 138(4)).

### Re Walker & Smith Ltd (1903)

A court made an order confirming a reduction of capital and the Registrar issued a certificate of registration. It later appeared that there was no provision in the articles for the reduction of capital. Nevertheless it was held that the Registrar's certificate was conclusive evidence that the Act had been complied with. The reduction was therefore valid.

A public company may not reduce its capital below the statutory minimum under the provisions of s 135 unless the company first re-registers as a private Company.

## PURCHASE OF OWN SHARES

A limited company with a share capital may, if authorised by its articles (Article 35), purchase its own shares (s 162).

(a) Shares may only be purchased if fully paid.
(b) Shares may be purchased out of distributable profits or out of the proceeds of a fresh issue of shares made for the purpose of purchase.
(c) A company may not purchase its shares if as a result of the purchase of the shares there would no longer be any member holding shares other than redeemable shares.
(d) A public company must after the purchase satisfy the capital requirements of the Companies Act.

Shares may be purchased in

(a) A market purchase or
(b) An off market purchase

### MARKET PURCHASE

A market purchase is a purchase made on a recognised stock exchange (s 163). Generally only listed shares may be purchased in this way, but the Stock Exchange also has a market for certain unlisted shares ie Unlisted Securities Market (USM).

A company may only make an off market purchase of its own shares if authorised to do so by an ordinary resolution at a general meeting.

The authority may be general, or limited to the purchase of shares of a particular class or description and may be unconditional or subject to conditions (s 166). It must however.

(i) specify the maximum number of shares to be acquired.
(ii) determine both the maximum and minimum prices to be paid for those shares.

(iii) specify a date on which the authority is to expire. This date must not be more than 18 months after the date on which the resolution is passed (s 166).

A copy of the resolution authorising the purchase must be registered within 15 days.
The authority may be varied, revoked or renewed.

An off market purchase is a purchase of shares other than on a recognised stock exchange or, if the shares are purchased on a recognised stock exchange they are not subject to a marketing arrangement on that stock exchange (s 163).

(a) Authority for the purchase must be given in advance by a special resolution of the Company.
(b) The special resolution will only be effective if
   (i) a copy of the proposed contract (or if not in writing a memorandum of its terms) is made available for inspection by the members of the Company at its registered office for not less than 15 days before the meeting and at the meeting itself.
   (ii) The resolution is passed without casting the votes of the member whose shares are being purchased.
(c) In the case of a public company the authority given by the resolution must specify a date on which the authority is to expire. This must be no later than 18 months after the date on which the resolution is passed.
(d) The authority may be varied, revoked or renewed (s 164).

A company may enter into a contingent purchase contract ie in pursuance of a contract relating to any of its shares which does not amount to a contract to purchase these shares, but under which the company may (subject to any conditions) become entitled or obliged to purchase those shares eg on option.

The terms of the proposed contract must be approved in advance by a special resolution of the company. The authority must satisfy similar requirements to an off market purchase (s 165).

Any payment made by a company in consideration of acquiring an option of this kind must be made out of the company's distributable profits (s 168).

PURCHASE OUT OF CAPITAL

A private limited company with a share capital may purchase its shares other than out of its distributable profits or the proceeds of a fresh issue of shares. It may purchase its shares out of capital.

(a) It must be authorised to do so by its articles.
(b) The company must first exhaust available profits and the proceeds of any fresh issue of shares made for the purposes of purchase, before resorting to its capital. The sum required to purchase the shares therefore consists of the proceeds of any fresh issue of shares, and the required capital. This is called the permissible capital payment (s 171).

If the permissible capital payment is less than the nominal amount of the shares, the difference must be transferred to the capital redemption reserve.

If the permissible capital payment is greater than the nominal value of the shares, the amount of the difference may be deducted from the amount of any capital redemption reserve, or share premium account, or fully paid share capital, or revaluation reserve.

The directors of the company must make a statutory declaration specifying the amount of the permissible capital payment for the shares in question, and stating that having made full inquiry into the company's affairs and prospects they have formed the opinion that:

(i) immediately following the date of the proposed payment there will be no grounds on which the company will be unable to pay its debts.
(ii) in the year immediately following that date the company will be able to carry on business as a going concern and will accordingly be able to pay its debts as they fall due throughout that year (s 173(3)).

This declaration must be in the prescribed form and contain such information with respect to the nature of the company's business as may be prescribed. It must have annexed to it a report addressed to the directors by the auditors stating that

(i) they have inquired into the company's state of affairs; and
(ii) the amount specified in that declaration as the permissible capital payment for the shares is in their view properly determined; and
(iii) they are not aware of anything to indicate that the opinion

expressed by the directors in the statutory declaration is unreasonable in all the circumstances (s 173(5)).

Any director who makes a statutory declaration without reasonable grounds is liable to 2 years imprisonment or a fine, or both.

A special resolution approving the payment out of capital must be passed within a week of the directors making their statutory declaration.

A resolution will be invalid if a member who holds shares to which the resolution relates uses his voting rights on those shares to carry the resolutions (s 174(2)).

A resolution will not be effective unless the statutory declaration and auditor's report are available for inspection by members at the meeting at which the resolution is passed.

Within the week immediately following the date of the resolution the company must publish in the Gazette a notice:

(i) stating that the company has approved a payment out of capital for the purpose of acquiring its own shares,

(ii) specifying the amount of the permissible capital payment for the shares in question and the date of the resolution,

(iii) stating that the statutory declaration and the auditors' report are available for inspection at the company's registered office,

(iv) stating that any creditor may, within five weeks of the date of the resolution apply to the court for an order prohibiting the payment (s 175(1)).

The company must also publish this notice in an appropriate national newspaper or give notice in writing to each individual creditor (s 175(2)).

Payment out of capital must be made no earlier than five weeks, and no later than seven weeks from the date of the resolution.

Objections may be raised during this five week period, by;

(i) any member other than one who consented to or voted in favour of the resolution; and

(ii) any creditor of the company who may apply to the court for the resolution to be cancelled (s 176(1)).

If an application is made to the court the company must immediately notify this fact to the Registrar (s 176(3)).

On hearing the application the court may, if it thinks fit, adjourn the proceeding in order that an arrangement be made for the purchase of the interests of dissentient members or for the protection of dissentient creditors. It may give such directions, and make such orders, as it thinks necessary for carrying into effect any such arrangement.

The court may make an order on such terms and conditions as it thinks fit for either confirming or cancelling the resolution. It may in particular alter or extend any date or period of time specified in the resolution for the purchase of shares (s 177).

Within fifteen days of hearing the application (or such longer period as the court may direct), the company must deliver a copy of the court order to the Registrar (s 177).

If a company is wound up, within one year of making a payment out of capital, on the grounds that it is insolvent, the following are liable to contribute to the company's assets to enable it to meet its liabilities:

(i) the person from whom the shares were purchased (up to the amount of his share of the capital payment).
(ii) the directors who signed the statutory declaration (jointly and severally with the persons whose shares were purchased). A director who shows that he had reasonable grounds for making the statutory declaration is not liable (s 504).

A contributory may petition the Court for the winding up of the company on the grounds that

(i) the company is unable to pay its debts (s 517(4)); or
(ii) it is just and equitable that the company be wound up (s 517(g)).

# Chapter 9

# Shares

'A share is the interest of a shareholder in the company measured by a *sum of money* for the purpose of *liability* in the first place, and of *interest* in the second, but also consisting of a series of mutual covenants entered into by all the shareholders inter se.' (Farwell J in *Borland's Trustee v Steel Brothers & Co Ltd* (1901)).

A shareholder's interest is that of a proportionate owner of the company, and a share is an expression of this relationship. A shareholder does not own any of the company's assets as these belong to the company, a separate and independant legal entity.

(i) The '*sum of money*' is the nominal value of the share.
(ii) The shareholder's *liability* is to pay for the share and to contribute (if required) to the company's liabilities.
(iii) A shareholder's *interest* is the right to receive a proportion of the dividends, the right to vote, to attend meetings and to a return of capital.
(iv) The relationship between shareholders is subject to the Company's articles and memorandum, allied with the principle of majority rule. This is subject to certain safeguards in respect of minority rights.

Each share in a company having a share capital, must state in its memorandum 'the division of the share capital into shares of a fixed amount' (s 2(5)). A company may not therefore issue shares of no par value.

The rights which are attached to shares are usually stated in the Company's articles, although they may be found in a company's memorandum or the terms of issue of the shares, or in the resolution under which unissued shares are allotted. Article 2 provides that any share may be issued with:

'such rights or restrictions as the company may by ordinary resolution determine.'

If a company allots shares with rights which are not stated in its memorandum or articles, or in a resolution registered under s 380, it must (within 1 month) deliver a statement, in the prescribed form, to the Registrar, giving particulars of those rights unless the shares are similar to shares previously allotted (s 128). This ensures that information in respect of the rights attaching to any class of shares is always available at the Companies Registry.

There is a presumption that all shares rank equally with one another i e pari passu. This is rebutted if a company attaches different rights to different shares e g as regards dividends, return of capital.

Each share in a company having share capital must have a distinguishing number unless all the issued shares in a company, or all the issued shares of particular class are fully paid and rank pari passu of all purposes. In that case none of these shares need have a distinguishing number (s 182).

Shares are personal estate and are not 'in the nature of real estate'. They may therefore be bought and sold, subject to the provisions of the memorandum and articles.

## SHARE CERTIFICATE

A company must, within two months of allotment or lodging a valid transfer (not being a transfer which the company is entitled to refuse to register), complete and have ready for delivery share certificates in respect of these shares, unless the conditions of issue provide otherwise (s 185).

The form of the certificate is governed by the articles, but usually takes the following forms.

Certificate No. _____Number of shares_____

*This is to certify that_____of _____*
_____

*is/are the registered holder(s) of__ Shares of £_____each_____*
*paid in the above-named Company, subject to the Memorandum and Articles of Association of the Company.*

*The Common Seal of the Company was hereto affixed in the presence of:*

_____*Directors*

_____*Secretary*

*on_____ 19_____*

NO TRANSFER OF ANY OF THE ABOVE-MENTIONED
SHARES CAN BE REGISTERED UNTIL THIS
CERTIFICATE HAS BEEN DEPOSITED AT THE
REGISTERED OFFICE OF THE COMPANY.

Article 6 provides that every certificate must be under the seal or
under the official seal kept by the company by virtue of S 2 of the
Stock Exchange (Completion of Bargains) Act 1976, and must
specify the shares to which it relates and the amounts paid up on
those shares. A company seeking a Stock Exchange quotation must
also state in a footnote on the certificate that a transfer will not be
registered without the production of the share certificate. (A
preference share certificate must also state the conditions relating to
capital and dividends in respect of the share). The articles usually
provide that if a share certificate is defaced, lost or destroyed it will
be replaced by the company on such terms as to indemnity as the
directors think fit (Article 7).

Section 186 provides that a share certificate under the common
seal of the company, or its official seal under the Stock Exchange
(Completion of Bargains) Act 1976 specifying any shares held by
the member, shall be prima facie evidence of his title to the shares.

'The certificates . . . are the proper (and indeed the only) documentary
evidence of title in the possession of a shareholder' (per Lord Selbourne in
*Société Générale de Paris v Walker* (1885)).

'A share certificate is a declaration by the company to all the world that
the person in whose name the certificate is made out, and to whom it is
given, is a shareholder in the company, and it is given by the company with
the intention that it shall be so used by the person to whom it is given, and
acted upon in the sale and transfer of shares,' (per *Cockburn C J in Re
Bahia & San Francisco Railway* (1868)).

As a company makes a representation on the issue of a share
certificate, it must therefore exercise the utmost care in its issue.
The general rule is that a person who makes a representation of fact
with the intention that it should be acted upon will be estopped from
denying its truth as against a person who acts in good faith on such a
representation.

ESTOPPEL AS TO TITLE TO SHARES

A company may be estopped from denying to any person who has
relied in good faith on a share certificate that the person named on
the share certificate is the registered holder of that share.

A company recognises the validity of a transferor's title by registering or certifying a transfer to the transferee. It is therefore estopped from denying the transferee's title as it has held out to the transferee that the transferor had a title.

Although a transferee who has presented (in good faith) a forged transfer does not obtain a good title to the shares, the company must nevertheless indemnify him to the value of the shares if he has purchased the shares on the basis of a share certificate issued by the company of the transferor.

### Re Bahia and San Francisco Rly Co (1868)

Trittin, the holder of 5 shares in the company, left the shares with her broker. The broker submitted a forged transfer to the company for registration. The shares were transferred to S and G who were issued with share certificates and T's name was removed from the register. The shares were later transferred to B and F, who were issued with share certificates by the company. The forgery was subsequently discovered and the company was compelled to restore T's name to the register. The company was held liable in damages to B and F for wrongfully removing their names from the register ie the company was estopped from denying the validity of the certificates. The measure of the damages was the value of the shares at the time when the company refused to recognise B & F as the shareholders, with interest at 10 per cent from the date.

### Balkis Consolidated Company Ltd v Tomkinson (1893)

P, the owner of shares in a company, transferred them to persons who were registered in the company's books as owners of the shares. P afterwards fraudulently executed a transfer of the shares for value to T, who sent the transfer to the company, and received a share certificate stating that he was the proprietor of the shares. T, acting bona fide on the faith of the certificate, sold the shares. The company refused to register the purchaser as the new owner, on the ground that after granting the certificate to T they had discovered that he was not the real owner of the shares. T then, to fulfil his contract with the purchaser, bought other shares in the market and sued the company for the price. It was held that the company were estopped by their certificates from denying that it was the owner of the shares. He was entitled to recover from the company the damages which he had in fact sustained owing to their refusal to register the purchaser.

In exceptional cases a transferee may raise an estoppel against a company if he has been fraudulently induced to accept a duly executed transfer of shares from a transferee who had no title to the shares.

### Dixon v Kennaway & Co (1900)

Dixon applied to Liddell, a stockbroker and the Company's secretary for 300 shares in the company and paid for them. L's clerk who did not own shares in the company executed a transfer of 300 shares to Dixon. The Company registered the transfer without requiring the production of a certificate from L's clerk. It was held that the company was estopped from denying the validity of Dixon's certificate and was liable to Dixon in damages.

A company is not estopped from denying the title to shares as against a transferee who deposits a forged transfer with the company, even though the transferee may have acted in good faith in the belief that the transfer is genuine.

A company is entitled to be indemnified by the transferee for any loss caused by the forgery.

### Sheffield Corpn v Barclay (1905)

T and H were joint owners of Sheffield Corporation stock. T forged H's signature and transferred the stock to the defendant's bank as security for a loan. The bank sent the transfer to the corporation for registration and was registered as the stockholder. It later transferred the stock to a third party. On T's death H discovered the forgery and compelled the Corporation to buy equivalent stock and register it in his name. The corporation then sued the bank for indemnity. It was held that the action succeeded.

ESTOPPEL AS TO PAYMENT

A company may be estopped from denying that the shares are fully paid or paid up to the extent stated on the certificate.

### Bloomenthal v Ford (1897)

Bloomenthal lent £1,000 to the company and was given 10,000 shares as security for the loan. The share certificate described the shares as fully paid, but this was untrue. The company was wound up and the liquidator claimed from Bloomenthal the amount due on the shares. It was held that the liquidator and the company were estopped from denying that the shares were fully paid and the liquidator's claim must therefore fail.

In these circumstances the company may recover any unpaid share capital from the directors who issued the share certificate.

The doctrine will not operate in favour of a transferee who has knowledge or notice that the representation is not correct.

There is no estoppel if the certificate is forged or issued without authority.

### Ruben v Great Fingall Consolidated Co (1906)

A company secretary forged the signatures of directors to a share certificate and affixed the company's seal. It was held that the company was not estopped from denying that the certificate was worthless. The holder was not entitled to be placed on the register of members. (It is questionable whether the same decision would now be reached on these facts as a company secretary is now recognised as having a wide authority to enter into contracts on the company's behalf.)

### Re South London Greyhound Racecourses Ltd v Wake (1931)

A director and the company secretary signed a share certificate, in the mistaken belief that they had the authority to do so. It was held that the certificate was a forgery.

## CALLS ON SHARES

The majority of companies provide that the full nominal value of a share need not be paid on allotment. The terms of issue may provide that the balance may be paid by instalments at fixed times or by a call at some undetermined future time.

Public companies usually stipulate in the terms of issue that any sums owing shall be paid by fixed instalments within a relatively short time of the issue of the shares. This is financially advantageous to the company and also allows the shares to be converted into stock within a relatively short time, if the company so wishes. These instalments are not calls, although the articles usually provide that any sum payable at a fixed day shall be deemed to be a call duly made and payable on the date on which it became due (Article 16).

A call is therefore a demand by a company in respect of money unpaid on its shares where there is no stipulation as to the date of payment. A call, (and an instalment) is in the nature of a speciality debt i e the company may sue to recover the amounts outstanding at any time within twelve years from the date when payment was due. If payment is not forthcoming the directors may declare the shares forfeit. The articles generally provide that interest (at a rate not exceeding 5 per cent) may be charged on overdue calls (Article 18).

A call is made by the directors in the manner provided for by the articles. A resolution is passed at a board meeting and shareholders are then given notice of the call. The articles usually provide that the directors may from time to time make calls upon the members, but that no call shall exceed one quarter of the nominal value of the share; that at least one month must elapse between successive calls and that each member be given at least fourteen days notice of the call.

A call may be paid by instalments without the need for any express authority in the articles.

A call must be paid in cash, as otherwise a shareholder would be liable on the winding up of the company. If a shareholder is owed a sum of money by the company, which is due for payment at the time of the call, that amount may be set off against the call. The right of set off cannot be exercised after the commencement of a winding up.

The power to make a call is in the nature of a trust and must be exercised bona fide for the general benefit of the company.

### New Zealand Gold Extraction Co v Peacock (1894)

A company sold its undertaking to another company in exchange for shares in that company. Some of the first company's capital had not been called up, and it made a call on those shares so that it could pay this sum to the second company. It was held that such a call was valid.

### Alexander v Automatic Telephone Co (1900)

The directors made a call of 17½p(3/6) in respect of the company's shares, but paid nothing on their own shares. The shareholders were not informed of this fact. It was held that the directors actions amounted to a breach of trust and deprived the company of capital. The directors were ordered to pay a similar amount on each of their shares.

A call must be made in accordance with the manner set out in the articles and must specify the time and place of payment.

### Re Cawley & Co (1889)

A resolution was passed specifying the amount of the call, but omitted to fix the date of payment. It was held that the call was not valid until a subsequent resolution rectified the omission.

A minor irregularity will not invalidate a call.

### Dawson v African Consolidated Land & Trading Co (1898)

A company's articles contained a clause similar to that of Article 92 regularising the acts of directors, acting in good faith, who had not been properly appointed or who were not qualified to act. A call was made by the directors, one of whom was disqualified through having parted with his qualification shares for a few days. It was held that the call was valid.

A company may, if authorised by its articles, make arrangements on the issue of shares for a difference between the shareholders in the amounts and times of payment of calls on their shares (s 119(a)). Directors can only justify a call on selected members of a class in very exceptional circumstances, even though the articles may permit this.

### Galloway v Halle Concerts Society (1915)

Two members of the Society were in conflict with the ruling committee. The articles provided that any member should be liable to pay a sum not exceeding £100 (called the contribution) if and when demanded by the Society. The committee resolved to call up the whole contribution of the dissident members, but made no call on the other members. It was held that the call was invalid.

A shareholder is not bound to pay an invalid call. He may obtain an injunction to restrain the directors from forfeiting his shares, but he cannot obtain an injunction to restrain the directors from taking proceedings for the recovery of the call.

PAYMENT IN ADVANCE OF CALLS

Section 119(b) provides that a company, if authorised by its articles may accept from any member the whole or a part of the amount remaining unpaid on any shares held by him, although no part of that amount has been called.

Calls may be paid in advance if so authorised by the articles. A shareholder who has paid money in advance of calls is entitled to interest on the money advanced. The shareholder becomes a creditor of the company for the money due as interest. The company may pay such sums out of capital if there are no profits available.

Directors may only accept a payment in advance if the payment benefits the company i e if it can be used to the company's advantage.

### Re European Central Rly Co, Sykes' Case (1872)

The directors of an insolvent company paid into the company's bank account the amount which remained due on their partly paid shares. Later that day they paid this amount to themselves in payment of their fees. It was held that the payment was not for the company's benefit and the directors remained liable to pay the amount due on their shares.

A payment in advance is not regarded for dividend purposes as a sum paid on the shares, as a sum paid in advance would otherwise qualify for the payment of interest and dividend at the same time.

Capital paid in advance may not be repaid while the company is a going concern as this would amount to a reduction of capital. In a winding up it is repayable with interest after payment of the preferential and ordinary creditors, but before the repayment of capital not paid in advance.

## THE TRANSFER OF SHARES

Every shareholder has a right to transfer his shares in the manner provided by the articles. The transfer must be in writing and the company may not register a transfer unless a proper instrument of transfer has been delivered to it notwithstanding any provision to the contrary in the articles (s 183).

### Re Greene (1949)

The articles provided for the automatic transfer of shares to a director's widow on the death of a director. It was held that the articles were not a proper instrument of transfer and the purported transfer was invalid.

The articles usually provide for:

(a) the instrument of transfer in any usual or common form or any other form which the directors may approve (Article 23);
(b) 'the instrument of transfer' to be accompanied by the certificate of shares to which it relates (Article 24).

The Stock Transfer Act 1963 provides a form of transfer which is adopted by the majority of companies. The Act applies to the transfer of:

(a) Securities issued by any company within the meaning of the Companies Act, except a guarantee or an unlimited company.
(b) Securities issued by any body (other than a company as in (i)) in Great Britain by or under any enactment or by Royal Charter (other than a building society).
(c) Securities issued by the United Kingdom Government.
(d) Securities issued by any local authority.

The Act stipulates (s 1) that a transfer need only be signed by the transferor and must contain:

(i) particulars of the consideration,
(ii) a description of the number or amount of the securities,
(iii) particulars of the transferor,
(iv) the full name and address of the transferee.

The provisions may be followed, even if the articles specify additional requirements which must be followed. An instrument of transfer which is executed in the form laid down in the articles is valid as long as it complies with the provisions as to contents and execution of a stock transfer under the Act.

PROCEDURE ON TRANSFER

1. The transferor hands the share certificate and the executed form of transfer to the transferee.
2. The transferee completes the transfer and has it stamped. He then delivers the share transfer and the share certificate to the company for registration.
3. The board of directors approve the transfer and issue a new certificate to the transferee.
4. The transferee's name is entered on the register in place of the transferor.

The company must register the transfer within a reasonable time having regard to all the enquiries which it may deem necessary to make in respect of the transfer.

It must however have the share certificate complete and ready for delivery within 2 months of the transfer being lodged (s 185). Under The Stock Exchange Rules the share certificate must be issued within fourteen days, instead of two months.

If a company refuses to register a transfer it must, within 2 months of the transfer being lodged with the company, send a notice of its refusal to the transferee (s 183, Article 25).

If there is undue delay in registering the transfer, the transferee may be given all the rights he would have had if registration had taken place within a proper time.

### Re Sussex Brick Co (1904)

Transfers were submitted to the company for registration. The secretary sent a letter to the transferee stating that the transfers would be submitted for the board's approval at their next meeting. The company was wound up before that meeting. The liquidator refused to recognise the title of the transferees. It was held that the court would order registration nunc pro tunc i e as if the transfers had been registered when registration should have taken place.

The company usually retains the original certificate which it cancels on completion of the transfer. If a company negligently parts with the original share certificate eg by returning the certificate to the transferor and enabling him to pledge the same shares, the company does not owe a duty to the pledgee. It owes a duty to the transferee if he is damaged by the company's negligence, but to no one else.

### Longman v Bath Electric Tramways Ltd (1905)

B transferred shares to H & M. The company certified the transfer and returned the certified transfer to B. The Company later, in error, returned the original share certificates to B who deposited them with L as security for a loan. It was held that the company was not liable to L as L had not relied on the certified transfer.

#### PROCEDURE FOR STOCK EXCHANGE TRANSFER

Almost all transfers of shares and other securities listed on The Stock Exchange are handled by the Talisman system introduced under the Stock Exchange (Completion of Bargains) Act 1976.

By the use of computers all sales are effected by the seller transferring his shares under a Talisman Sold Transfer to Sepon Ltd (Stock Exchange Pool Nominees Ltd), a company owned by the Stock Exchange. The consideration for the sale is not stated on the transfer form and no stamp duty is chargeable.

Sepon then forwards details of the transaction to the company which records Sepon as the new holder of the shares, but does not issue Sepon with a share certificate.

A purchaser of shares will be allotted shares from the holdings of Sepon, who will then forward a Talisman Bought Transfer to the company. This transfer form will name the buyer and state the amount of the purchase price (stamp duty is therefore payable). A certificate will then be issued to the purchaser by the company.

#### CERTIFICATION OF TRANSFER

If a shareholder is (a) selling part only of his shareholding: or, (b) selling to more than one transferee, it would be unwise to give the transferee a share certificate for a greater number of shares than are comprised in the actual transfer.

1. The transferor lodges the share certificate and the transfer with the company.
2. The company retains the share certificate for cancellation, but returns the transfer to the transferor endorsed 'certificate lodged' or words to that effect.
3. The transferor delivers the transfer to the transferee, who will have the transfer stamped and present it to the company.
4. The company will issue a new certificate to each transferee, and a new certificate to the transferor for the balance of the shares which remain registered in his name.
5. This procedure is known as 'certification'.

Certification by a company is a representation to any person acting on the faith of the certification that there have been produced to the company such documents as on the face of them show a prima facie title to the shares in the transferor. It is not a representation that the transferor has any title to the shares (s 184(1)).

Where any person acts on the faith of a false certification made negligently by a company, it is under the same liability to that person as if the certification had been made fraudulently (s 184(2)).

EFFECT OF SHARE TRANSFER

A transferee does not become a member of the company or acquire a legal title to the shares until his name is placed on the register of members. From the time of entering into the contract for the sale of shares until his name is entered on the register he has an equitable title in respect of the shares.

The legal title in the shares is vested in the transferor during this interim period. He must do all that is necessary to give the transferee a valid transfer and enable the transferee to be registered as a member. The transferor nevertheless holds the shares in trust for the transferee until registration is effected.

The rights of the parties during the interim period are as follows:

(a) If dividends are declared and paid before registration of the transfer, the transferor is entitled to the dividends, unless there are provisions to the contrary in the articles.

As between transferor and transferee, the transferee is entitled to dividends, declared after the date of the transfer unless a contrary provision appears in the contract of sale.

Shares may be sold ex dividend (without the dividend) or cum dividend (with dividend).

**Re Wimbush** (1940)

Shares were sold privately to Wimbush in September 1935. A dividend for the year ending 31 December 1935, was declared in April 1936. It was held that as the sale was not governed by Stock Exchange rules, Wimbush was entitled to the dividend.

(b) The transferor is liable for calls made during this time, but he may recover the amount paid from the transferee (*Hardoon v Belilios* (1901)). The transferor is freed from any liability in respect of uncalled capital on the registration of the transfer, but if a winding up commences within one year after he ceased to be a member he may be placed on the B list of contributories as a past member.
(c) The transferor must vote in accordance with the dictates of the transferee, as the voting rights in the shares have passed to the transferee.


PRIORITIES

A transferee, who has an equitable title until the transfer is registered, may be affected by prior rights.

The general rule is that in the case of competing claimants the first to secure registration will be preferred, irrespective of the date when his claim arose.

**Peat v Clayton** (1906)

Clayton assigned his property, which included shares, to Peat as trustee for his creditors. As Peat was unable to obtain the share certificates from Clayton he gave notice of the assignment to the company. Clayton later sold the shares to a third party who applied for registration. It was held that Peat's equitable title had priority.

**Ireland v Hart** (1902)

A husband, who held shares in trust for his wife, mortgaged the shares with Hart as security for his debt. Hart lodged a transfer with the company. Before the registration was completed the wife claimed that her equitable title prevailed over that of the mortgage (Hart). It was held that the wife had the prior equity.

RESTRICTIONS ON THE TRANSFER OF SHARES

*The right of pre-emption*
The articles of most private companies contain a pre-emption clause which provides that any member who wishes to transfer his shares must first offer the shares to the other members of the company. The clause may further stipulate that a member may only transfer his shares to:

all the other shareholders rateably;
a certain class of shareholder;
the directors firstly, and then to the members;
the holder of a large block of shares and then to the members;
a shareholder whom he selects.

Such an article is strictly construed and each member is bound to observe its provisions.

### Lyle & Scott v Scott's Trustees (1959)

The articles of a private company provided that a shareholder who was 'desirous of trasnsferring' his shares must inform the company secretary and must sell the shares to any member who offers to buy them. A shareholder offered his shares to a third party without informing the company secretary. It was held that he must do so and comply with the article.

The articles may provide that holders of certain classes of shares (e g deferred shares) are under no obligation to offer their shares to the other shareholders, but are only subject to the general clause which gives the directors discretion to decline the registration of a transfer.

These clauses are generally supplemented by a clause which provides that where shares have been offered to members under a pre-emption clause and these members have declined to purchase the shares, the directors may nevertheless decline to register a transfer to another person.

A company's articles may also provide that on the death of a member, the surviving members or the directors are obliged to purchase the shares of the deceased member (*Rayfield v Hands* (1960) (see p 68) ).

The articles usually contain provisions for determining a fair value of the shares.

**Re Bird Precision Bellows** (1984)

Two directors of a company who alleged impropriety on the part of the majority were removed from office. They agreed that the majority should purchase their shares at a price to be determined by the Court. It was held that a fair price would be determined on a pro rata basis according to the value of the shares as a whole and not on a discount basis as a minority holding.

The articles usually stipulate that if the parties cannot agree on a valuation the value will be determined by the auditor. The auditor will be acting as an expert in this respect, and is not bound to give reasons for his valuation.

*The right of expropriation*
Power is sometimes given in the articles for the expropriation, in certain circumstances, of a member's shares ie the transfer of a member's shares irrespective of that member's consent at a price fixed in accordance with the provisions set out in the articles e g on the death or bankruptcy of a member. Such a power must be exercised in good faith and for the benefit of the company as a whole (*Dafen Tinplate v Llanelly Steel Co* (1920) (see p 65)).

*The right to refuse a transfer of shares*
The articles of most private companies give the directors power to refuse transfers of shares. Restrictions are rarely found in the articles of public companies as a company cannot have a stock exchange listing if such a restriction exists.
  The power of refusal may take various forms:

(a) An absolute discretion to refuse a transfer of shares without giving reasons for the refusal.

**Re Smith & Fawcett Ltd** (1942)

Smith & Fawcett were the directors of a company and each held half of the company's issued share capital, namely 4001 shares. The articles of the company provided that the directors 'may at any time in their absolute and uncontrolled discretion refuse to register any transfer of shares'. Fawcett died and his son, as executor, applied for the deceased's shares to be registered in his own name. Smith refused to register a transfer of the entire holding but offered to register 2001 shares, if 2000 shares were sold to him at an agreed price. It was held that Smith was entitled to refuse the transfer of shares. There was nothing to show that he had not exercised his powers in the company's interests.

The court will not interfere with this discretion unless it can be shown that the directors have not exercised a discretion in the matter, or that it was not exercised in good faith.

If the directors give reasons for their refusal, the court may consider whether those reasons are within the discretion conferred by the articles.

(b) A qualified discretion ie the directors may only refuse to register the transfer in circumstances specified by the articles e g if calls are in arrear, if the company has a lien on the shares (Article 24).

(c) Power to refuse to register a transfer to a person of whom they do not approve. Article 24 limits the refusal to register to a partly paid up share. In these circumstances the refusal must be personal to the transferee.

### Re Bede S S Co (1917)

A company's articles provided that the directors could refuse to register a transfer if 'in their opinion it is contrary to the interests of the company that the proposed transferee should be a member thereof'. The directors refused to register a transfer of single shares on the grounds that it was contrary to the company's interests to transfer small units to individuals who had no interest or knowledge of shipping. It was held that, as the refusal was not on personal grounds, the transfer must be registered.

(d) Power to refuse a transfer to an infant whose shares are not fully paid.

(e) If the directors have a power to refuse to register their transfer, they must act positively in rejecting the transfer.

### Re Hackney Pavilion (1924)

A transfer of shares was submitted to the company. The two directors held a board meeting but failed to agree as to whether the transfer should be registered. The company secretary wrote to the shareholder informing him that the directors refused to register the transfer. It was held that as a positive act was required for a refusal of a transfer the transfer must be registered, and the register was rectified accordingly.

(f) The power of refusal must be exercised within a reasonable time from the receipt of a transfer. As s 183 provides that a refusal must be notified to the transferee within 2 months it follows that the power of refusal must be exercised within that time, or the company must register the transfer.

## Re Swaledale Cleaners Ltd (1968)

Transfers of shares were submitted to a company on 3.8.67. The company's sole director refused to register the transfers in exercise of a power of refusal given in the articles. This power could only be exercised at a board meeting, where the quorum of 2 directors was necessary. On the 11.12.67 proceedings were commenced for rectification of the register, and a second director was appointed by the company on the 18.12.67. At a board meeting on that day the two directors refused to register the transfer. It was held that the refusal on the 18.12.67 was invalid as the company had not exercised its powers of refusal within a reasonable time ie the two month period.

If directors refuse to attend a meeting to consider transfer, the court may rectify the register and register the transfers.

## Re Copal Varnish Co (1917)

A company had two directors. The articles provided that a quorum at a board meeting was two and that the chairman had a casting vote. The other director deliberately refused to attend board meetings to consider transfers of shares so that a quorum was not present. It was held that the transfers should be registered.

Where a company transfers shares in breach of a pre-emption provision in the articles, the transfer is effective, although inchoate until registered. The transfer lawfully passes the property in the shares to a new shareholder who is entitled to be registered by the company as the holder of the shares (*Tett v Phoenix and Investment Co* (1984)).

## MORTGAGE OF SHARES

A shareholder may offer shares as security for a personal loan. He may mortgage his shares by granting.

(a) a legal mortgage; or
(b) an equitable mortgage.

### LEGAL MORTGAGE

A legal mortgage is created by a transfer of the shares from the borrower (the mortgagor) to the lender (the mortgagee). This transaction is subject to a separate agreement between the parties that on the redemption (re-payment) of the loan the shares will be re-transferred to the borrower. It is usual to include in the agreement a provision giving the lender the right to sell the shares if the borrower defaults on the loan.

Although the lender, as the registered holder, is entitled to vote and receive dividends it is usual to stipulate in the agreement that the dividends will be paid to the borrower and that the lender will exercise the voting powers attached to the shares in accordance with the wishes of the borrower.

A legal mortgage is an excellent form of security for the lender as he becomes the registered holder of the shares. His security cannot be defeated by a fraud on the part of the borrower. This form of mortgage does have certain disadvantages.

(i) it is not suitable for shares that are not fully paid,
(ii) stamp duty is payable twice on the transfer and re-transfer of its shares;
(iii) it is inappropriate for a mortgage of shares by a director who must retain a minimum shareholding as a share qualification.

EQUITABLE MORTGAGE

An equitable mortgage is usually created by the deposit of a share certificate with the lender. This is usually accompanied by a written agreement containing the terms of the loan and providing that on the repayment of the loan the share certificate will be returned to the borrower.

The borrower's name remains on the register of members and he is entitled to the dividends on the shares and to exercise the voting rights conferred by the shares. It is common practice for the borrower to sign a blank transfer ie a transfer signed by the borrower as the registered holder but with the transferee's name left blank. This gives the lender an implied power to insert his own name or that of a purchaser in the blank if the borrower defaults in foreclosure and transfers.

If the company's articles require the transfer of shares to be by deed, the blank transfer must be accompanied by a power of attorney under seal. If the lender does not take this precaution he will only be able to enforce his security by applying to the court for an order for sale, or foreclosure and transfer.

The weakness of an equitable mortgage is that the borrower remains a member of the company. A fraudulent borrower may inform the company that he has lost the share certificate. If the company issues him with a new certificate and he transfers those shares to a bona fide purchaser for value, the purchaser obtains a legal title to the shares which defeats the equitable interest of the lender. The company does not recognise the rights of the lender, as s 360 provides that a company cannot take notice of any trust or similar right over its shares.

The only safe course for the lender is to serve a stop notice on the company. The lender files a notice together with an affidavit setting out the nature of his interest in the shares in the Central Office of the High Court or in any district registry. He then serves an office copy of the affidavit and a duplicate of the notice on the company. The company may not then register a transfer of those shares or pay a dividend without giving eight days notice to the issuer of the notice i e the lender. He then has eight days to obtain an injunction to restrain the company from registering a transfer or paying a dividend. After this time the company will be at liberty to register a transfer or pay a dividend.

## LIEN

A lien is an equitable charge (mortgage) on the shares of a member to secure any debt or liability (including an unpaid call) owed by that member to the company.

Although a company does not have a lien over a member's share as a matter of right, the articles generally provide that company has a first and paramount lien on the shares for each member of his debts and liabilities to the company (Article 8). If the articles do not include a right of lien, they may be adopted by special resolution. Such a lien is valid, even if adopted after the death of the shareholder (*Allen v Gold Reefs of West Africa* (1900) (see p 66)).

A public company may only create a lien:-
on partly paid up shares; or
on full or partly paid up shares in the course of a moneylending business (s 150)

A lien may be enforced by the sale of the shares and the transfer of the shares into the purchaser's name, if such a provision is found in the company's articles (Articles 9, 10). If there is no such provision it may be necessary to apply to the court for a power of sale. If the company sells shares under a lien it may retain from the proceeds of sale the amount due, but must return the surplus (if any) to the member concerned (Article 11).

A company may not enforce its lien by forfeiture, as such a clause in an equitable mortgage is inoperative.

A company's articles usually contain a clause (known as an exemption clause) which relieves a company from an obligation to take notice of any equitable interests in relation to its shares (Article 5). Such a clause reinforces the rule in s 360 that a company may not enter an equitable interest on the register of members.

A company may therefore enforce its lien against a registered holder who is only a trustee.

### New London & Brazilian Bank v Brocklebank (1882)

The trustees of a marriage settlement invested part of the trust fund in the company's shares. The company's articles contained a paramount lien clause (similar to Article 8) and an exemption clause (similar to Article 5). One of the trustees was a partner in a firm which became indebted to the company. It was held that the company had a lien for the partnership debt over the shares, which prevailed over the interests of the beneficiaries.

A company cannot claim a lien for money owed by a beneficiary where the shares are registered in the name of the trustee.

A company's lien therefore has priority over other claims in respect of the shares unless the company has notice of some existing claim before the holder became indebted to the company.

### Bradford Banking Co v Briggs (1886)

The articles of a company gave the company a 'first paramount lien' over its shares. A shareholder deposited his share certificate with a bank to secure a loan. The bank gave notice to the company of the creation of the equitable mortgage. The shareholder later became indebted to the company who claimed that its lien had priority and that it was not bound to take notice of any trust. It was held that the bank had priority as the company's claim arose after receipt of the bank's notice, and that notice to the company was not notice of a trust.

As the charge created by a lien is a mortgage within the Law of Property Act 1925 (s 205) the shareholder or his transferee is entitled to require the company, on payment of the sum due, to assign the debt and lien on the shares to his nominee.

### Everitt v Automatic Weighing Machine Co (1892)

A company had a first and paramount lien over the shares of its members for any debt due to the company. Everitt, a shareholder, owed £4,670 to the company, which threatened to sell the shares in exercise of its lien. H agreed to pay the sum outstanding to the company on condition that the company transferred its lien on the shares to him, but the company refused. It was held that the company was bound to transfer its lien.

# FORFEITURE

A company's articles generally contain a provision for the forfeiture of shares, as a power of forfeiture is not inherent in a company.

Shares may only be forfeited for the non-payment of calls or instalments. A forfeiture on other grounds is invalid as an unauthorised reduction of capital.

A provision in the articles that the shares of any shareholder who commences or threatens an action against the company or the directors on payment to the shareholder of the full market value of his shares is invalid (*Hope v International Financial Society* (1876)). The usual procedure is for a company to serve a notice on the member requesting payment stating that if payment is not made by a certain date, the shares may be forfeited. The company may then declare the shares forfeit after that date and make the requisite entry in the register of members. The company usually requests the member to surrender the share certificate in his possession for cancellation. As this request is frequently ignored there will then be in existence two documents of title for the same shares if the company sells the forfeited shares, as it issues a new certificate for the purchaser.

Article 22 provides that a statutory declaration in writing by a director of the secretary that a share has been forfeited is conclusive evidence as against all persons claiming to be entitled to the share.

The power to declare shares forfeit is in the nature of a trust and must be exercised for the benefit of the company. It must not be used to benefit any individual shareholder e g to relieve him from liability.

## Re Esparto Trading Company (1879)

Finch & Goddard were given shares to qualify them as directors and paid nothing on the shares. At a later date they asked the company to cancel their shares and this was done by a board resolution. It was held that the forfeiture was invalid and they were liable to pay the nominal amount of the share.

The shareholder whose shares are forfeited, ceases to be a member of the company from the date on which the forfeiture becomes effective. (Article 21) His liability in respect of the shares depends upon the terms of the articles.

(i) If the articles do not contain a provision relating to the liability of the former member, he is discharged from liability in respect of the amounts unpaid, unless the company is wound up within a year of the forfeiture. In such a case he is liable to be placed on the B list of contributories, and may be called upon to pay any calls due at the date of the forfeiture, unless these have been paid by subsequent holders.

(ii) The articles may provide that the former holder continues to be liable to pay all calls (with interest) which were owed by him at the date of the forfeiture, unless the sum outstanding has been paid to the company by a subsequent holder. (Article 21) Such a provision creates a new obligation for which he may be sued as a debtor, not as a member.

The articles generally give power to the directors to re-issue forfeited shares (Article 20). The directors may sell the shares for less than the amount paid up prior to the forfeiture of the shares, but the shares remain unpaid, to the extent that they were unpaid at the date of the forfeiture. The purchaser is liable for calls on the amounts unpaid on the shares.

### Morrison v Trustees, Executors and Securities Insurance Corporation (1898)

A company forfeited several shares of £10 with £3 paid on the shares. It later converted these shares into £5.25 shares with £2.25 paid, and proposed to issue them at £1.50 per share. It was held that the sale was valid.

The articles may also provide that a purchaser of forfeited shares is not entitled to vote until all arrears of calls have been paid.

A public company must cancel the forfeited shares unless they are disposed of within 3 years. Neither the company nor a company's nominee may exercise any voting rights in respect of the shares during the interim period. If as a result of such a cancellation the company's authorised capital falls below the statutory minimum, it must re-register as a private company (s 146).

If the forfeiture is irregular, the shareholder may bring an action for the annulment of the forfeiture. He may also obtain an injunction to restrain the forfeiture pending the trial of the action. In such a case he will usually be required to pay the amount of the call into court.

### SURRENDER

A company's articles may give power to the directors to accept a surrender of shares. There is no provision in Table A but surrender is recognised as valid when used to avoid the formalities of forfeiture. A company could not otherwise accept a surrender of shares without the court's consent, as this would amount to a reduction of capital.

A surrender of partly paid shares can only be accepted where forfeiture is justified.

### Bellerby v Rowland & Marwood's SS Co Ltd (1902)

Three directors of a company agreed to surrender several of their shares to the company in order that the company could re-issue the shares and make good the loss of one of the company's ships, valued at £4,000. The shares were £11 shares of which £10 had been paid. The shares were not re-issued. It was held that the surrender was invalid as it amounted to a purchase by the company of its own shares.

The surrender of fully paid shares is not valid without the sanction of the court, but a company may accept a surrender where the company's shares are exchanged for new shares of the same nominal value.

Shares which have been surrendered may, if the articles provide, be re-issued in the same manner as shares which are forfeited.

Chapter 10

# Membership of a company

A person becomes a member of a company when he agrees to become a member and his name is entered in the register of members (s 22). A person may only be a member of a company limited by shares if he is also a shareholder.

A person may become a member in any one of the following ways:

1. By subscribing to the memorandum. The subscribers of the memorandum are deemed to have agreed to become members of the company and on the company's registration their names must be entered in the company's register of members. If their names are not entered they nevertheless become members of the company and are liable for calls on the shares for which they signed the memorandum (s 22). (The subscribers sign the form appointing the first directors and the secretary and fix the address of the company's registered office).
2. By signing and filing an undertaking as a director to take and pay for a qualification share.
3. By applying for share(s) in the company, being allotted the share(s) and being placed on the register of members.
4. By taking a transfer of shares from a previous member and being placed on the register of members.
5. By succeeding to the estate of a deceased or bankrupt member and being placed on the register of members.
6. By acquiring shares through an employees share scheme.
7. By holding himself out as a member and allowing his name to be entered on the register of members.

## A COMPANY

A registered company may be a member of another company if it is granted powers in its memorandum, or if it takes shares in payment of a debt by way of compromise.

The directors of a company may, by a resolution of the board of directors, authorise a person to represent its interests at meetings of a company of which it is a member. A duly authorised person is entitled to exercise the same powers on behalf of the company (e g speak, vote) as if he were an individual shareholder of that other company.

A subsidiary company cannot be a member of its holding company unless:

(i) The subsidiary was a member of its holding company before 1 July 1948. It may continue to be a member, but it has no power to vote at the meeting of the shareholders of the holding company.
(ii) The subsidiary is concerned as a personal representative or trustee and neither the subsidiary or holding company is beneficially interested under the trust other than in the ordinary course of business, which includes the lending of money (s 23).

This exception operates principally in favour of banks. A bank will frequently take a mortgage of shares as security for a loan, and as a mortgagee (a lender) would become a member of that company. Such shares are always held by a bank's subsidiary company or a nominee company which would be entitled to hold shares in its holding company (the bank's shares) if such shares were offered as security. A bank's subsidiary would also be entitled to hold the bank's shares under the terms of a trust or as a personal representative of a deceased individual.


## MINORS

A minor i e a person under the age of 18 may be a member unless forbidden to be so by the articles. A minor may repudiate a contract to take shares before or within a reasonable time of attaining his majority (the age of 18) i e the contract is voidable. The right to repudiate is lost when the company is wound up, unless the liquidator gives his consent. If a minor does repudiate, he is not liable to make any further payments on partly paid shares, but he cannot recover any money which he has already paid, unless there has been a total failure of consideration.

### Steinberg v Scala (Leeds) Ltd (1923)

An infant applied for and was allotted 500 £1 shares in a company. She paid 50p(10s) on each share. She repudiated the contract whilst an infant and claimed the recovery of the money she had paid and rectification of the register of members (removal of her name from the register) and so relieving her from liability on future calls. It was held that rectification would be granted, but she was not entitled to recover the money she had already paid, as there had not been a total failure of consideration. The shares always had a market value, even though they stood at a discount and she had been given rights as a member.

A company may also repudiate a contract if it subsequently discovers that the transferee is an infant and may restore the name of the transferor (the person who transferred the shares) to the register.

## PERSONAL REPRESENTATIVES

On the death of a member his shares vest in his personal representatives, either executors (if a will has been made) or administrators (in the absence of a will).

A company must recognise the rights of personal representatives to deal with the shares on production by an executor of a grant of probate, or a grant of letters of administration by an administrator. The company will make an entry to that effect in the register of members against the name of a deceased member. The personal representatives do not become members by the production of these documents and the deceased member's estate remains liable in certain cases e g for any calls on partly paid up shares.

A deceased member is not a member for the purpose of s 24 (the reduction of the number of members below the statutory minimum).

The rights and liabilities of personal representatives are usually set out in the articles. They are entitled to be registered as members unless the articles provide otherwise (Article 30).

An unregistered personal representative is however entitled to receive a dividend, a bonus, a rights offer, return of capital and notice of meetings (Article 31) but he cannot attend or vote at meetings.

A personal representative who registers as a member is entitled to vote at meetings. He becomes personally liable for any amounts unpaid on the shares, although he is entitled to an indemnity from the estate of the deceased member (or beneficiaries).

## TRUSTEES IN BANKRUPTCY

A shareholder does not cease to be a member on becoming bankrupt, unless the articles provide otherwise. The beneficial interest in his shares will be vested in his trustee, and the member must act in accordance with the dictates of the trustee. The articles usually provide that notice of meetings is to be sent to the trustee, and not to the bankrupt. The bankrupt will therefore vote in accordance with the trustee's directions.

A trustee in bankruptcy has similar rights and liabilities as a personal representative of a deceased member. He may apply for registration as a member in his own name or sell or transfer the shares. (Articles 30, 31 apply to a trustee in bankruptcy).

A personal representative or trustee in bankruptcy who does not elect to be registered as a member has various statutory rights e g to petition under s 459 on the grounds that the company's affairs have been conducted in a manner prejudicial to the minority; to petition as a contributory in a compulsory winding up (s 519).

## JOINT HOLDERS

A share may be owned jointly by two or more persons, and will be registered in all their names. A company's articles usually impose a limit on the number of joint holders who may be registered.

Article 6 provides that the company is not bound to issue more than one share certificate for each share owned by joint holders. Only the first named in the register is entitled to exercise the rights of membership i e issue of share certificate, payment of dividend, notice of meetings, the right to vote.

On the transfer of a share all the joint holders must join in the transfer, and on the death of a joint holder the shares are vested in the survivor(s).

## LENDER

A person who lends money to the company on a mortgage of the company's shares is liable as a member if the shares are registered in his name.

## Re Patent Paper Manufacturing Co, Addison's Case (1870)

Addison was given 100 × £5 shares as a security for a £500 loan to the company. The contract provided that the money was to be repaid on one month's notice and the shares should then be cancelled. Notice was later given and the money was repaid, but it was held that Addison was liable to pay £500 on the shares.

## TERMINATION OF MEMBERSHIP

A person ceases to be a member when his name is removed from the register of members in any of the following circumstances:

1. A transfer of his shares to another person. Membership does not cease until the transferee (person to whom the shares are transferred) is registered as a member.
2. The forfeiture or surrender of his shares.
3. The sale of his shares by a company under a provision in the articles e g to enforce a lien.
4. The expulsion of a member.
5. The death of a member. The estate of the deceased member remains liable until the shares are registered in the name of the transferee following a transfer by the executors or administrators.
6. The bankruptcy of a member and the registration of the shares in the name of the trustee or the disclaimer of the shares by the trustee.
7. Rescission of the contract of membership on the grounds of mistake or misrepresentation.
8. A minor repudiating his contract to take shares.
9. The issue of share warrants.
10. The redemption of redeemable shares.
11. The dissolution of the company.

## REGISTER OF MEMBERS

Every company is required under the Act to keep a register of members (s 352). The register may be in the form of a bound book or in any other form e g it may be computerised as long as adequate precautions are taken to prevent its falsification (s 722).

The register must contain the following particulars:

(i) The names and addresses of the members.

(ii) If a company has a share capital a statement of the shares held by each member. Each share must be distinguished by its number (if the share has a number) and where a company has different classes of shares, each class must be distinguished.

(iii) The amount paid or agreed to be considered as paid on the shares of each member.

(iv) The date at which each person was entered on the register as a member.

(v) The date at which any person ceased to be a member. Any entry relating to a former member may be removed from the register after the expiration of twenty years from the date on which he ceases to be a member (s 352).

Every company with more than fifty members must, unless the register itself constitutes an index, keep an index of the names of its members. It must make any necessary alterations within 14 days of the alteration of the register. The index must, at all times, be kept in the same place as the register (s 354).

The register is prima facie evidence of any matters directed or authorised by the Companies Act to be inserted in it (s 361).

If a company issues a share warrant it will remove the member's name from the register in respect of those shares and will record the issue of the share warrant.

The register must be kept at the company's registered office; unless: (a) the work of making it up is done at another office of the company when it may be kept at the office; or (b) the company arranges for the work of making it up to be undertaken on the company's behalf by another person, it may be kept at the other person's office.

If a company is registered in England the register must not be kept at a place outside England i e within the same country. Similar provisions apply to companies registered in Scotland (s 353).

Every company must notify the Registrar of the place where its register is kept, and of any change in that place.

The register and index must be open to the inspection of any member without charge, and of any other person on payment of 5 pence (or less) during business hours. The company must furnish, within ten days of being requested to do so, a copy of any part of the register on payment of 10p for every 100 words (s 356).

A company may, on giving notice by advertisement in a newspaper circulating in the district in which the registered office is situated, close the register for any time or times not exceeding 30 days in each year (s 358). This is to allow a company to prepare a list of members who are entitled to a dividend. Few companies take advantage of this provision, and the majority of companies declare a dividend which is payable to members whose names appear on the register at a given date.

The court has power to rectify a register:

(a) If a person's name is, without sufficient cause, entered in or omitted from the register of members;
(b) if default is made or there is unnecessary delay in entering on the register the fact that any person has ceased to be a member (s 359).

An application to the court for rectification of the register may be made by the person aggrieved, or any member of the company, or the company itself. The court may either:

(a) refuse the application, or
(b) order rectification of the register and payment by the company of any damages sustained by any party aggrieved (s 359).

The following are examples of situations where the court has made an order for rectification:

A shareholder made an ultra vires surrender of his shares to a company. (*Bellerby v Rowland and Marwood's Steamship Co* (1902)).

A shareholder's name had been removed from the register following a forged transfer (*Re Bahia and San Francisco Railway* (1868)).

A shareholder was induced to take shares by a misrepresentation (*Anderson's Case* (1881)).

A company neglected to register a transfer of shares (*Re Stranton Iron and Steel Co* (1873)).

The court's jurisdiction may be exercised even if the company is wound up.

**Re Sussex Brick Co** (1904) (see p 140).


OVERSEAS BRANCH REGISTER

A company which carries on business in some part of Her Majesty's dominions outside Great Britain, the Isle of Man and the Channel Islands may keep a branch register of members (overseas branch register) in any of those countries where it carries on business (s 362). Notice must be given to the Registrar, within 14 days, of the location of the company's office or of any change in the location. Notice must also be given if the register is discontinued. An overseas branch register is often required by stock exchanges in those countries as a condition of listing these shares for local dealings and transactions.

An overseas branch register is deemed to be part of the company's register of members (the principal register) and must be kept in the same manner as the principal register. A company must transmit to its registered office a copy of every entry in its branch register as soon as possible after it is made. It must also keep a duplicate of the branch register at the same place as its principal register. The branch may be rectified by applying to a competent court in the country or territory where the register is kept (Sch 14).

A transfer of a share registered in an overseas branch register is exempt from United Kingdom stamp duty.


NOTICE OF TRUSTS

No notice of a trust can be entered on the register of members, or be received by the Registrar in respect of companies registered in England and Wales (s 360).

A company is therefore entitled to treat every person whose name appears on the register as the beneficial owner of the shares, even though he may be holding the shares in trust for another person or persons.

> 'If a trustee is on the company's register as the holder of shares, the relations which he may have with some other person in respect of the shares are matters with which the company has nothing whatever to do; they can look only to the man whose name is on the register.' (Lord Coleridge C J in *Re Perkins, ex p Mexican Santa Barbara Mining Co* (1890).

A trustee of shares whose name is entered on the register as a member is personally liable for any calls on the shares. He is however entitled to be indemnified from the trust property, or (if this is insufficient) from the beneficiaries. He may vote at meetings, although he may be bound to vote in accordance with the directions of the beneficiaries.

A company does not incur any liability if it registers a transfer of shares held by a trustee, even if the trustee has acted fraudulently or in breach of trust.

## Simpson v Molsons' Bank (1895)

M's shares were, on his death, transferred by his executors to a third party in breach of the terms of the will. The company, which had a copy of the will, registered the transfer. One of the executors of the will was the president of the company. It was held that the company was not liable for registering the transfer, for although it was aware of the terms of the will and that the transfer was in breach of those terms, it was forbidden to take notice of any trust over its shares.

If the registered holder of shares is a nominee for another person, this fact does not appear on the register. The nominee is liable for calls on the shares, but is entitled to an indemnity from that other person for all calls paid, even if the calls exceed the amount of the property held by the nominee.

## Hardoon v Belilios (1901)

A broker's clerk held shares as a nominee for his employer. The shares were of no value, and the broker claimed that he was only liable to the extent of the value of the shares. It was held that he must indemnify the clerk for all calls paid by the clerk.

A company cannot go behind the nominee and enforce any claims against the beneficial owner of the shares.

## Re National Bank of Wales, Massey and Giffin's Case (1897)

A firm of stockbrokers purchased shares in a bank and registered the shares in the name of their clerk, who was an infant. Calls were made on the shares but were never paid and the company was wound up and the liquidator applied for rectification of the register ie to substitute the names of the stockbrokers for that of the clerk in the register and in the list of contributories. It was held that as there was no contractual relationship between the company and the stockbrokers, the application failed.

A company may however apply for rectification of the register if a person applies for shares in a fictitious name, or in the name of a person who had never agreed to accept the shares.

A company is not a trustee for persons claiming shares under an equitable title.

## Société Générale de Paris v Walker (1885)

W created two charges over shares in Tramway Union Ltd, the first on 9/3/1881, in favour of JW who took the certificates and a blank transfer; the second in favour of SG de P on 1/12/1882. SG de P claimed priority over JW as they notified Tramways Union Ltd first of their equitable interest. It was held that the company could not be treated as trustees for the purpose of notifying equitable interest, and the title to the shares was in the person who was eventually registered by the company i e JW.

The correct method of protecting a beneficiary's interest is to serve a stop notice on the company i e filing an affidavit (a sworn statement) setting out the nature of his interest in the shares and the appropriate notice in the Central Office of the Supreme Court (or in a district registry). Copies of the affidavit and the notice are then served on the company. The company may not register a transfer of those shares or pay a dividend on them, without giving written notice to the person who issued the notice. The company must then wait eight days before registering a transfer or paying a dividend. This will enable the issuer of the notice to obtain an injunction restraining the company from registering the shares or paying a dividend.

The company's articles usually provide that the company is not bound to recognise any equitable interest or any other right in a share except an absolute right in the registered holder (Article 5). This provision is wider than that found in s 360 and applies generally to the recognition of trusts, while s 360 deals only with entries on the register.

## DISCLOSURE OF SUBSTANTIAL SHAREHOLDINGS

In certain circumstances the register of members does not provide adequate information about the company's shareholders. A person may conceal his beneficial ownership of shares by registering the shares in the name of a nominee or a nominee company and in that way secretly build up a considerable shareholding in a company.

Various provisions have been included in a number of Companies Acts to secure disclosure of substantial shareholdings. These have proved extremely difficult to enforce, especially in dealing with nominee shareholders who are not resident in the United Kingdom. The relevant provisions are to be found in s 198 to 202.

The provisions apply to the voting shares of public companies, whether or not the company is quoted on a stock exchange. They do not apply to the ownership of shares in a private company or in a public company which does not carry an unrestricted right to vote at general meetings.

A person must inform a company when:

(i)  to his knowledge he acquires a 5 per cent interest in the share capital of a public company, or ceases to be interested in the shares, or

(ii) he becomes aware that he has acquired a 5 per cent interest in such shares or has ceased to be interested in any shares in which he was previously interested

This obligation arises where he becomes aware that:

(i) he has a notifiable interest in the shares comprised in the share capital which he did not previously have;
(ii) although he had an interest, he no longer has such an interest;
(iii) although both before and after the relevant time he had such an interest, the percentage levels of his interest immediately before and after that time are not the same.

A person is under a duty to notify the company when he becomes aware of the relevant facts, and not on the happening of an event of which he may be unaware. He must notify the company in writing within five days of becoming aware of the relevant circumstances. A notification must state:

(i) the identity of each registered holder of any shares to which the notification relates;
(ii) the number of these shares held by each registered holder;

so far as is known to the person making the notification at the date of the notification. Any known changes in these particulars (eg a change in the registered holder or a change in the number of shares held by a registered holder) must be notified to the company in writing within five days.

(i) A person is taken to have an interest in any shares in which his spouse, infant child or step child is interested.
(ii) Where any property is held in trust and any interest in shares is comprised in that trust, any beneficiary is taken to have an interest in those shares.
(iii) A person has interest in shares, if other than under an interest under a trust he has a right to call for delivery of the shares to himself or to his order or he has a right or obligation to acquire an interest in the shares.
(iv) A person has an interest in shares if he enters into a contract for the purchase of those shares, or not being a registered holder he is entitled to exercise any right which a registered holder would be entitled to exercise, or to control the exercise of such a right.
(v) A person has an interest in shares of a company if:

(a) that company or its directors are accustomed to act in accordance with his directions or instructions; or

(b) he is entitled to exercise or control one-third or more of the voting power at the company's general meetings.

A person who is entitled to exercise or control one-third of the voting power of a company at general meetings is regarded as having control of any other company which is controlled by the first company.

The disclosure provisions also apply to interests arising under a concert party i e an agreement to acquire an interest in the shares of a public company (s 204-206). The aim of these provisions is to prevent a build up of shares by persons acting in concert, who avoid the disclosure provisions by an agreement that each should acquire in person (or by the use of a nominee) less than the disclosure level (5 per cent). The combined interests of the parties would be used to gain control of the company ('the target company') or institute a takeover or pass a special resolution.

Every person who is involved in a concert party agreement is taken to be interested in all the shares in the target company in which any other party to the agreement is interested, even though some of the interests have been acquired before, or apart from the agreement. If the whole of his interests and those of the other parties exceed five per cent he must notify the company of his own interests and those of the other parties to the agreement.

If a party to a concert party agreement is a party to another separate concert party agreement in respect of shares in the same target company all the interests which he has under the concert party agreements will be attributed to him.

A person involved in a concert party agreement is under an obligation to inform every other party of all the facts relevant to his shareholding. He must inform the other parties of his existing interests, of any acquisition or disposal of shares, of any interest arising from family and corporate interest, or under any other agreement. He must notify the other parties in writing within five days of any acquisition or change. These provisions ensure that each and every member is aware of the interests which are attributable to him and of any changes in those interests.

REGISTER OF SUBSTANTIAL INTERESTS

Every public company must keep a register of interests in shares notified to it in accordance with these rules. The register must contain the name of the party, the information and date of the entry. It must be properly indexed and kept at the same place as the register of members and register of directors' interests. It is open to public inspection, and any person is entitled to a copy of the register or any part of it on payment of the appropriate fee. If a company ceases to be a public company it must nevertheless keep the register and associated index for a period of six years from the date on which it ceases to be a public company (s 211).

## INVESTIGATION BY A COMPANY OF INTERESTS IN ITS SHARES

Any public company may by notice in writing require any person whom the company knows, or has reasonable cause to believe has been, during the last three years, interested in the company's shares to confirm or deny that fact (s 212).

If he does confirm that he had such an interest he must supply the company with the following information:

(a) his own past and present interest in the company's shares during the last three years.
(b) any other past or present interest in the company shares during the last three years which is not referred to in the notice.
(c) where his interest is past, the identity of the person to whom his interest passed, if he is aware of the identity of that person.

The particulars in (a) and (b) include the identity of persons interested in the shares, family and corporate interests, options to subscribe for shares and the interests of members of a concert party.

This section is not confined to cases where a person holds a prescribed percentage of shares ie an interest in one share is sufficient. Neither is it confined to members of the company.

The company is required by s 213 to enter the information received in response to an inquiry under s 212 against the name of the registered holder of shares in a separate part of its register of interests in shares. The company is obliged to notify any person, within 15 days, that his name has been provided to the company as being interested in its shares and of the subsequent entry in the company's register of interests in shares. The company must at the same time inform him of his right to apply for the removal of the entry if the information on which the entry was based is incorrect.

Members of a company may requisition the company to investigate the ownership of shares. These members must hold not less than 10 per cent of the paid up equity capital at the date of the requisition (s 214).

The requisition must:

(a) state that the requisitionists are requiring the company to exercise its powers under section 212.
(b) specify the manner in which the company is to exercise these powers;
(c) give reasonable grounds for requiring the company to exercise those powers.

While the investigation continues the company must at three monthly intervals prepare interim reports on its findings to be made available at its registered office. It must within three days of making each report available notify the requisitionists of its availability.

If any person on whom the company serves notice fails to provide the information requested by the company, it may apply to the court for an order that the shares shall be subject to the restrictions imposed by s 212 (Restrictions may amount to a prohibition of the following – dealings in shares, voting at meetings, payment of dividends, return of capital). Although these restrictions may only be removed by the court, the company or any person aggrieved may apply to the court for such a restrictive order to be lifted.

Any person who refuses to supply information properly requested by the company, or who supplies false information is guilty of a criminal offence and may be punished by a fine or a term of imprisonment (s 216).

## ANNUAL RETURN

Every company having a share capital is required once at least in every year, to make a return to the Register ie the annual return (s 363). An annual return is not required in the year of its incorporation, or in the following year if it is not required by section 366 to hold an annual general meeting in that year.

The annual return must be in the form specified in the Fifteenth Schedule and contain the following:

1. The address of the registered office.
2. The address at which the registers of members and debenture holders are kept (if not at the registered office).
3. A summary distinguishing between shares issued for cash and

shares issued for a consideration other than cash specifying the following:

(i) the amount of share capital and the number of shares into which it is divided;

(ii) the number of shares taken up to the date of the return;

(iii) the amount called up on each share;

(iv) the total amount of calls received and calls unpaid;

(v) the total amount paid by way of commission in respect of shares or debentures;

(vi) the discount allowed on any shares issued at a discount or so much as has not been written off;

(vii) the total amount allowed by way of discount in respect of any debentures since the date of the last return;

(viii) the total number of shares forfeited;

(ix) the total amount of shares for which share warrants are outstanding, the share warrants issued and surrendered since the date of the last return and the number of shares comprised in each warrant.

4. The total amount of the company's indebtedness in respect of all mortgages and charges which are required to be registered with the Registrar.

5. A list of present and past members:

(i) who have ceased to be members since the date of the last return (or in the case of the first return since incorporation).

(ii) stating the number of shares held by each member at the date of the return, the shares transferred since the date of the last return by past and present members and the dates of registration of the transfers.

(iii) if the members' names are not arranged in alphabetical order, an index to enable any person's name to be easily found.

6. Particulars of the directors and secretary as at the date of the return.

The Annual return of a company not having share capital need only contain 1, 2, 4 and 6 (s 364).

The annual return must be completed to give particulars as at the fourteenth day after each annual general meeting and must be delivered to the Registrar within 42 days after the annual general meeting. If a company fails to comply with these provisions, the company and every officer of the company in default is liable to a fine.

# Chapter 11

# Meetings

Meetings of members of a company are of three kinds.

1. Annual general meetings
2. Extraordinary general meetings
3. Meetings of a particular class of members

## 1. ANNUAL GENERAL MEETING

Every company must in each calendar year hold a general meeting as its annual general meeting, in addition to any other meeting which it may hold. Not more than fifteen months may elapse between the date of one annual general meeting and that of the next. An exception is made for a newly formed company which may hold its first annual general meetings at any time within eighteen months of incorporation.

If default is made in holding an annual general meeting the Department of Trade and Industry may, on the application of any member, convene a meeting. It may give such directions as it thinks expedient including directions modifying or supplementing the operation of the companies articles in relation to the calling, holding and conduct of the meeting. It may also direct that one member of the company present in person or by proxy shall be deemed to consitute a meeting.

Any meeting convened and held by order of the Department of Trade and Industry shall, subject to any directions of the Department of Trade and Industry, be deemed to be an annual general meeting of the company. If such a meeting is not held in the year in which the default occurred, the meeting will only be treated as an annual general meeting if the meeting so resolves and a copy of the resolution must, within fifteen days of its passing, be forwarded to the Registrar.

If default is made in holding an annual general meeting the company and every officer in default is liable to a fine (s 366).

The nature of the business transacted to an annual general meeting depends upon the articles which usually specify business at a meeting as either 'ordinary' or 'special'.

Ordinary business is deemed to be:

declaring a dividend;
the consideration of the accounts, balance sheets;
the consideration of the directors and auditors reports;
the election of directors in place of those retiring;
the appointment of, and fixing of the remuneration of, the auditors.

Any other business at an annual general meeting and all business transacted at an extraordinary general meeting is special business.

## 2. EXTRAORDINARY GENERAL MEETING

Any general meeting other than the annual general meeting is an extraordinary general meeting. The directors are given the power to call an extraordinary general meeting whenever they think fit (Article 37).

The directors must convene an extraordinary general meeting of the company if required to do so by members holding not less than one tenth of the company's paid up capital or (if there is no share capital) at least one tenth of the voting rights. The requisition must state the objects of the meeting, and must be signed by the requisitionists and deposited at the company's registered office (s 368).

If the directors do not convene the meeting within 21 days, the requisitionists or any of them holding more than half the voting power of all of them, may themselves convene a meeting within 3 months of depositing the requisition.

Any reasonable expenses incurred by the requisitionists, by reason of the directors' failure to convene a meeting, may be recovered from the company which must then withhold these sums from the fees or other remuneration of the directors (s 368).

A public company must convene an extraordinary general meeting if there is a serious loss of capital to consider whether any, and if so what, measures should be taken to deal with the situation (s 142).

An auditor may requisition a meeting so that he may place before the meeting an explanation of the circumstances connected with his resignation (s 391).

## 3. MEETINGS OF CLASSES OF SHAREHOLDERS

The articles usually provide that the rights attaching to different classes of shares may be varied only with the consent in writing of the holders of three-quarters of the issued shares of that class, or by an extraordinary resolution at separate meetings of holders of shares of that class.

Only the members of a class may attend, vote and speak at that class meeting, unless this rule is waived by the meeting.

Class meetings are usually held to agree to variations of the rights of that class or to compromise or arrangements affecting the class.

The court may order a class meeting to be convened under s 425.

## NOTICE OF MEETING

A meeting is not properly convened unless notice has been given to every person entitled to receive notice. This rule is subject to the provisions in the articles, which invariably state that members with calls in arrear may not vote and that preference shareholders may only vote on certain well defined occasions e g if they are owed dividends or a resolution has been passed for winding up the company.

The articles may also provide that notice may be sent by post (Article 111); need not be given to members who do not have a registered address in the United Kingdom (Article 112); must be given to a personal representative of a deceased member or to a trustee in bankruptcy of bankrupt member (Article 116).

Failure to give notice of a meeting to any person entitled to such notice invalidates the meeting.

The articles usually provide that on accidental omission to give notice of a meeting or the non receipt of notice of a meeting, by any person entitled to receive notice, does not invalidate the proceedings at that meeting (Article 39).

### Re West Canadian Collieries Ltd (1962)

A company's articles contained a provision similar to that found in Article 39. Certain members did not receive notice of a meeting as certain address plates had, by mistake, been left out of the addressing machine used to prepare the envelopes in which the notices were sent. It was held that as the omission was accidental the meeting was validated by the article.

### Musselwhite v CH Musselwhite & Son Ltd (1962)

A company failed to give notice of a general meeting to certain members. The directors assumed that they were not entitled to notice as they had sold their shares. As the sale had not been concluded, the members remained on the register and were entitled to notice. The proceedings at the meeting were invalid as the error was one of law and could not be validated by Article 51 (now Article 39), or a similar article.

A company must give the following notice of a general meeting:

(a) 21 days for an annual general meeting (s 369) or for an extraordinary general meeting at which a special resolution is to be proposed (s 378).
(b) 14 days notice for any other meeting of a limited company (s 369).
(c) 7 days notice for any other meeting of an unlimited company (s 369).

A meeting may be called by shorter notice:

(a) An annual general meeting, if all the members entitled to attend and vote so agree.
(b) Any other meeting if a majority holding 95 per cent of the shares having the right to attend and vote (or 95 per cent of the total voting rights) so agree (s 369).

The notice must not only state the time, date and place of the meeting but also the nature of the business to be transacted.

Sufficient details of any special business to be transacted should be given.

### Baillie v Oriental Telephone Co (1915)

The directors of a company had between 1907 and 1914, received fees from a subsidiary company without disclosing this fact to the shareholders. They later sought approval of this remuneration and also for the alteration of the articles to allow payment to directors for serving on the boards of subsidiary companies. The notice to the shareholders merely stated that the fees would be a small percentage of the subsidiary's profits and did not disclose that the total amount of the director's fees was in the region of £45,000. It was held that as proper disclosure had not been made, the subsequent resolution approving the payments was invalid.

**Kaye v Croydon Tramways Co** (1898)

An agreement was made between the Croydon Tramways Company (CTC) and the British Electric Traction Co Ltd (BET) for the sale of the tramways to BET and for the payment of compensation to the directors of CTC. The notice of the meeting convened by CTC to consider the agreement merely referred to the sale of the undertaking. It was held that as proper disclosure had not been made, the meeting was not properly convened.

Certain business must be disclosed to shareholders and their approval signified e g

The payment of compensation by the company for loss of a director's office (s 312).
The payment of compensation to a director for loss of office resulting from a transfer of the company's property (s 313).
The payment of compensation to a director for loss of office resulting from a transfer of the company's shares (s 314).
Disclosure must be made to all the company's members.

**Re Duomatic Ltd** (1969)

The ordinary shareholders approved payment of compensation to a director for loss of his office. The payment was not disclosed to the holders of non voting preference shares. It was held that the payment was invalid and could be recovered.

## PROCEEDINGS AT A GENERAL MEETING

A meeting may only proceed to business if the following requirements are satisfied.

(a) It must be duly and properly convened.
(b) Notice must have been served in the prescribed manner on all persons entitled to receive notice of the meeting.
(c) A quorum of members must be present, either in person or by proxy.
(d) It must be presided over by a chairman.
(e) The business of the meeting must be properly transacted.
(f) Minutes of the proceedings must be kept.

## QUORUM

The quorum for meetings is generally fixed by the articles. (Article 40 fixes a quorum at two members present in person or by proxy).

The Act provides that two members personally present shall be a quorum unless the company's articles make some other provision.

Another company's representative is a member 'personally present' and would therefore count towards a quorum.

If a quorum is not present the meeting cannot proceed to business and any proceedings are therefore invalid. Most articles require that a quorum be present 'at the time when the meeting proceeds to business' so that a quorum is only required when the meeting commences.

### Re Hartley Baird Ltd (1955)

The minimum number of members necessary for a quorum was present at the start of a meeting. One member who disagreed with a resolution that had been proposed left the meeting before it was put to the vote. It was held that the resolution had been passed, as the articles only required a quorum at the start of the meeting.

If only one person remains present at the meeting, whether as a member or as a proxy, he may not pass valid resolutions as one person alone cannot constitute a meeting.

There are exceptions to this rule.

(i) If the Department of Trade and Industry calls or directs the calling of an annual general meeting it may direct that one member present in person or by proxy shall constitute a meeting (s 367).

(ii) The court may also direct that in circumstances where it is impracticable to call a meeting or conduct a meeting in the manner prescribed by the articles or the Act, one member present in person or by proxy shall be deemed to constitute a meeting. Such an order may be made by the Court on its own motion, or on the application of any director or member of the company (s 371).

### Re El Sombrero Ltd (1958)

A shareholder, who held 90 per cent of a company's shares, requisitioned an extraordinary general meeting to pass a resolution to remove the company's directors. The two directors, who each held 5 per cent of the company's shareholding did not attend the meeting, which could not proceed as there was no quorum present.

The court directed that a meeting be called and that one member present at that meeting should constitute a quorum.

(iii) If a class of shareholders consists of only 1 member, that member may be deemed to constitute a meeting.

A resolution signed by a member who held all the preference shares in a company was held to constitute the consent of a meeting of that class (*East v Bennett Bros* (1911)).

## Re XL Laundries (1969)

A special resolution to reduce a company capital was passed at a meeting at which only one member was present. As he was the only holder of the company's ordinary shares the resolution was held valid.

The articles usually provide that if a quorum is not present within half an hour from the time appointed for a meeting, the meeting is dissolved if convened on the requisition of members (Article 41). Any other meeting is adjourned to the following week at the same place and time (unless otherwise determined by the directors). If at the adjourned meeting a quorum is not present within half an hour, the members present shall constitute a quorum.

## THE CHAIRMAN

The articles generally provide that the chairman of the board shall preside as chairman at every general meeting. If however there is no chairman, or he is not present within 15 minutes of the appointed time for holding the meeting, or is unwilling to act, one of the directors present shall elect one of themselves to be chairman (Article 42). If there is no director present or willing to act the members present shall choose one of their number to be chairman of the meeting (Article 43).

If the articles do not contain any provision relating to this matter the members present at the meeting may elect any member to act as chairman (s 370).

The role of the chairman is to keep order and to ensure the proper conduct of the meeting. He must ensure that the meeting is properly constituted and that a quorum is present. He must deal with the agenda in a methodical manner, put resolutions to the meeting, count the votes and declare the result of all resolutions put to the meeting. He must decide questions of procedure and points of order.

He must only accept an amendment to a resolution which is within the limits of the notice convening the meeting.

Although the chairman must give a reasonable opportunity to members to discuss a proposed resolution, the members are not permitted an unlimited time for discussion. The chairman may, with the consent of the meeting, end the discussion and put the proposal to the vote.

### Wall v London and Northern Assets Corpn (1898)

At a meeting convened to discuss the proposed amalgamation of two companies, several shareholders wished to continue the discussion, even though the matter had been considered at length. The chairman moved that 'the question be now put' and a resolution was put to the vote. It was held that the resolution was valid and that the minority may not discuss a matter indefinitely so as to obstruct the business of a meeting.

The articles generally provide that the chairman's declaration that (unless a poll is demanded) a resolution has on a show of hands been carried, or carried unanimously, or by a particular majority and an entry to that effect is made in the minute book, is conclusive evidence of that fact. The Act provides that a declaration by a chairman that an extraordinary or special resolution is carried is conclusive evidence of the fact (s 378).

The chairman's declaration may nevertheless be challenged on the grounds of fraud or error on his part.

### Re Caratel (New) Mines Ltd (1902)

The chairman of a meeting put a special resolution to the vote on a show of hands. The resolution was lost on a show of hands by 23 to 6, but the chairman declared the resolution carried by counting 200 proxies held by him. It was held that the declaration was invalid as there was no majority on a show of hands, when proxies could not vote.

The articles usually grant the chairman a second or casting vote in the event of a tie (Article 50). This is in addition to his first vote as a member. In the absence of such an article he does not have this second vote.

A chairman has no general power to adjourn a meeting unless this is provided for by the articles. Otherwise his power of adjournment is limited to adjourning the meeting in case of disorder. If he prematurely closes or adjourns a meeting improperly, the meeting may elect another chairman in his absence and validly proceed with the business.

### VOTING

The articles usually contain provisions as to voting. Article 46 provides that a resolution should be decided on a show of hands unless a poll is demanded. Article 54 provides that each member present in person is entitled to one vote, subject to any rights or restrictions attaching to a class of shares.

If the articles are silent on this matter the Act provides that every member having a share capital is entitled to one vote in respect of each share, or one vote for every £10 of stock held by him (s 370). If a company does not have a share capital, each member is entitled, in the absence of any provision to the contrary in the articles, to one vote.

Voting on a resolution is usually taken in the first instance on a show of hands. Unless the articles otherwise provide, a proxy is not entitled to vote except on a poll (s 372).

The right to vote is vested in a registered member, and a company has no right to enquire into the beneficial ownership of shares and thereby deny a member his right to vote. In *Pender v Lushington* (1877), Jessel M R stated that 'the company has no right whatever to enter into the question of the beneficial ownership of the shares'.

The articles may provide that certain shares carry no votes, e g preference shares, or that shares carry special voting rights on certain occasions.

### Bushell v Faith (1970)

The articles of a company provided that 'in the event of a resolution being proposed at any general meeting for removal from office of any director any shares held by that director shall on a poll in respect of such resolution carry the right of three votes per share'. The company had an issued share capital of £300 fully paid £1 shares, which were held in equal shares by three members of a family. On a resolution for a removal of one member from office as a director it was held that his 100 shares carried 300 votes and the resolution was defeated.

The Act provides that a poll must be held if demanded by:

(i) five or more members
(ii) a member or members holding at least 10 per cent of the total voting rights at the meeting
(iii) a member or members holding at least 10 per cent of the paid up capital conferring the right to vote at the meeting.

The instrument appointing a proxy to vote at a meeting also confers authority on the proxy to demand or join in demanding a poll. A demand by a person as proxy for a member is the same as a demand by the member (s 373).

The articles may provide that a poll may be demanded by less than 5 members, or by members holding less than 10 per cent of the capital, but the articles cannot make it more difficult to demand a poll. Article 46 provides that the chairman or at least two members present in person or by proxy may demand a poll.

A poll may be demanded before or on the declaration of a show of hands. Article 51 provides that the time and place for taking a poll is at the discretion of the chairman, apart from a poll demanded on the election of a chairman or on the question of adjournment which must be taken forthwith. Any previous result or vote on a show of hands in respect of the matter in question is nullified by the demand. The chairman may direct that a poll be taken there and then, or defer holding a poll until a later date.

A member who was not present at a meeting at which a poll was demanded may still vote on a poll deferred to a later date.

On a poll each person voting signs a paper for or against the resolution and proxies are then counted.

A member who is entitled to more than one vote need not cast all his votes in the same way (s 374). This section meets the needs of the nominees who may vote in one way in respect of some shares and in another way, or not at all in respect of other shares.


## PROXIES

Every notice calling a meeting must include a statement that every member, who is entitled to attend and vote at a meeting of the company, is entitled to appoint another person as his proxy to attend and vote in his place. That person need not be a member (s 372).

A proxy's authority derives from the proxy paper (sometimes known as a 'proxy') which authorises another person to represent a member and vote on behalf of that member at a meeting.

There are two forms of proxy in use:

(i) A general proxy which enables a person to vote as he thinks fit on any matter at any meeting.
(ii) A special proxy which limits the proxy to a particular meeting or any adjournment.

Listed public companies are required by the Stock Exchange regulations to issue 'two-way proxy' cards, so that a vote may be cast 'for' or 'against' a resolution.

A proxy paper must be signed by or on behalf of the appointor or his attorney. If the appointer is a company it must be under seal or signed by an officer or attorney.

Although the articles may require the instrument appointing the proxy to be deposited with the company before the meeting, a requirement that it be received by the company more than 48 hours before the meeting is void.

If a company is a member of another company it may appoint a representative to act on its behalf at a meeting. Such a representative is not a proxy and may exercise the same powers as an individual member.

Unless the articles otherwise provide:

(i) a member of a company not having a share capital may not appoint a proxy.
(ii) a member of a private company may not appoint more than one proxy to attend on the same occasion.
(iii) a proxy may only vote on a poll, not on a show of hands (s 372).

A member of a public company may appoint more than one proxy, but a proxy at a meeting of a public comapny has no right to speak at the meeting, except to demand or join in demanding a poll. He may only vote on a poll. The articles of a public company may however extend these proxy rights.

A proxy appointed by a member of a private company may not only attend the meeting, but also speak at a meeting.

If a company's directors send invitations to members, at the company's expense, to appoint specified persons as proxies, invitations must be sent to all the members who are entitled to notice of the meeting (s 372). This is to prevent directors from selecting only those members who would grant them proxies of support.

The authority to vote by proxy may be revoked by informing the proxy of the fact. Notice must be given to the proxy before he has voted. A member who attends the meeting may vote in person, thus impliedly revoking the authority (*Cousins v International Brick Co* (1931)).

A proxy is also revoked by the death or insanity of the member unless the articles provide otherwise. Article 63 provides that a vote given in accordance with the terms of an instrument of proxy shall be valid notwithstanding the previous determination of the authority of the person voting or demanding a poll, unless the company has been notified of the facts before the commencement of the meeting at which the proxy is used.

## ADJOURNMENT OF A MEETING

The articles generally give the chairman power to adjourn a meeting. Power may be given to the chairman to adjourn a meeting of his own motion, but it is usual to provide that he may do so with the consent of the meeting, and must do so if directed by the meeting (Article 45).

An adjourned meeting is regarded for most purposes as a continuation of the original meeting.

No business may be transacted at the meeting except for business left unfinished at the original meeting. Any resolution passed at an adjourned meeting is deemed as passed on the date on which it was passed and not on the date of the original meeting (s 381).

Fresh notice of an adjourned meeting is only necessary if the meeting is adjourned for fourteen days or more (Article 45).

A chairman may adjourn a meeting for various reasons e g where there is no quorum present or where the business cannot be completed on that day. If there is disorder at a meeting a chairman may, without the passing of any resolution, adjourn the meeting.

CIRCUMSTANCES WHEN A MEETING IS UNNECESSARY

At a general meeting individual shareholders are given the opportunity of voting on the resolutions before the meeting. Protection is given to minority shareholders in that a meeting must be convened and conducted in a proper manner and the appropriate notice must be given of resolutions to be proposed at a meeting.

These formalities may be dispensed with if it can be shown that all the shareholders having the right to attend and vote at a general meeting endorse a particular course of action. Their unanimous decision is as binding as a formal resolution at a general meeting.

'I proceed on the basis that where it can be shown that all shareholders who have a right to attend and vote at a general meeting of the company assent to some matter which a general meeting of the company could carry into effect, that assent is as binding as a resolution in general meeting would be,' (per Buckley J in *Re Duomatic Ltd* (1969)).

### Re Duomatic Ltd (1969)

A liquidator sought to recover payment of directors' remuneration which had been made without approval of the shareholders in general meeting as required by the articles. The payments had however been made with the consent of the shareholders. It was held that the remuneration was properly paid as the assent of all the shareholders was binding on the company.

Article 53 provides that a resolution in writing signed by all the members entitled to receive notice of and to attend and vote at general meetings (or the representatives of a corporation) are as valid and effective as if the resolution had been passed at a general meeting.

If all the shareholders are present at a meeting and unanimously agree to a proposal, the agreement will be valid despite the fact that no formal resolution has been voted on.

'If you have all the shareholders present, then all the requirements in connection with a meeting of the company are observed,' (per Younger LJ in *Re Express Engineering Works Ltd* (1920)).

### Re Express Engineering Works Ltd (1920)

A company was formed by a syndicate of five people who were also the directors. At a *board* meeting they resolved to issue debentures. The company's articles provided that a director could not vote in respect of any contract or arrangement in which he was interested. The decision of the board was invalid, but it could be ratified by general meeting of the company. It was held that the decision was valid and the company was bound by the unanimous decision of its members.

The principle applies to an agreement to vary a provision in the articles, which would otherwise require the sanction of a special resolution.

### Cane v Jones (1981)

All the shares in a company were held by members of one family. They agreed that the articles should be altered so that the chairman no longer had a casting vote in the case of an equality of votes and that an independent chairman should be appointed where the votes were tied. Papers were signed to this effect but no meeting was held and the necessary special resolution giving effect to these proposals was not passed. Nevertheless it was held that the informal agreement was valid.

A resolution may be valid despite the fact that the meeting at which it was passed was not properly constituted.

### Re MJ Shanley Contracting Ltd (1979)

The three members of a company agreed that the company should be wound up. Only one member was present at the meeting called to pass a resolution for winding up. He purported to pass a resolution to wind up the company. It was held that although the meeting was not properly constituted, the resolution was nevertheless valid.

The principle of unanimity has also been invoked in situations where all the members have not expressed assent, but none have expressed dissent. Some members have merely abstained.

### Re Bailey Hay (1971)

The five members of a company attended a meeting called to wind up the company. Two members voted in favour of the resolution to wind up, while the other three abstained. One of the abstainers later discovered that insufficient notice had been given of the meeting. It was held that by not voting against the resolution, the members who had abstained must be taken to have assented to the resolution, which was therefore valid.

## MINUTES

A company must keep minutes of all general meetings, directors' meetings and (if applicable) managers' meetings (s 382). The minutes are generally kept in bound books, although they may be kept in some other way if adequate precautions are taken against falsification (s 722).

The minutes must be kept at the company's registered office and are open to inspection by any member, free of charge, for at least two hours per day. Any member is entitled to copies of the minutes at a charge not exceeding 2½p for every 100 words (s 383).

If inspection is refused or a copy is not sent within the proper time, the court may order an immediate inspection of the minutes or direct that copies be sent to the persons requiring them (s 383).

Any minutes signed by the chairman or by the chairman of the next succeeding meeting, is evidence of the procedure. Until the contrary is proved, the meeting is deemed to have been duly held and convened, all proceedings to have been properly conducted and all appointments of directors, managers and liquidators to have been valid (s 382).

## RESOLUTIONS

There are three types of resolutions passed at general meetings, namely: (1) ordinary, (2) special, (3) extraordinary.

The type of resolution used will depend upon the articles and the nature of the business to be transacted. The Act stipulates that certain resolutions be used for certain transactions. All other business may be approved of by ordinary resolution, unless the articles of the memorandum state otherwise.

ORDINARY RESOLUTIONS

An ordinary resolution is a resolution passed by a simple majority of those attending and voting at a meeting.

> 'An ordinary resolution is in the first place passed by a bare majority on a show of hands by the members entitled to vote who are present personally or by proxy and on such a vote each member has one vote regardless of his shareholding. If a poll is demanded then for an ordinary resolution still only a bare majority of votes is required. But whether a share or class of shares has any vote upon the matter and, if so, what is its voting power upon the resolution in question depends entirely upon the voting rights attached to that share or class of shares by the articles of association'.

Where the Act provides that a certain matter must be dealt with by the company in general meeting but does not specify the use of a particular type of resolution, an ordinary resolution will be sufficient.

Certain ordinary resolutions require special notice. These are resolutions for:

The removal of a director before the expiration of his period of office or the appointment of a person in place of the director removed from office at that meeting.
The appointment or reappointment of a director who is over seventy years of age.
The appointment as auditor of a person other than the retiring auditor.
The removal of an auditor before the expiration of his term of office.
Filling a casual vacancy in the office of an auditor.
The re-appointment of an auditor who was appointed to fill a casual vacancy.

Where a resolution requires special notice, notice of the intention to move it must be given to the company not less than 28 days before the meeting at which it is to be moved. The company must then give its members notice of any such resolution at the same time and in the same manner as it gives notice of the meeting.

If this is not practicable it must give them notice of it either by advertisement in a newspaper having an appropriate resolution, or in any other mode allowed by the articles not less than 21 days before the meeting. If a meeting is called within 28 days of the notice being given the notice is nevertheless deemed to have been properly given (s 379).

SPECIAL RESOLUTIONS

A special resolution is a resolution passed by not less than three-quarters of the members, voting in person or by proxy at a general meeting of which 21 days notice has been given specifying the intention to propose the resolution as a special resolution.

Shorter notice may be given if agreed upon by a majority of members holding not less than 95 per cent in nominal value of the shares giving the right to attend and vote at the meeting, or in the case of a company not having a share capital a majority representing not less than 95 per cent of the total voting rights at that meeting (s 378).

A special resolution is required for the following:
Alteration of the objects clause (s 4).
Alteration of the articles (s 9).
Alteration of the memorandum (s 17).
Creation of reserve capital (s 120).
Reduction of the company to share capital (s 135).
Making the liability of a director of a limited company unlimited (s 307).
Assignment of director's office (s 308).
Winding up by the court (s 517).
Initiating a member's voluntary winding up (s 572).
Sanctioning a sale to another company in consideration for the sale of the property of the company (s 582).
Substituting a memorandum and articles for a deed of settlement (s 690).
Re-registration of an unlimited company as limited (s 51).
Re-registration of a private company as a public company (s 43).
Re-registration of an unlimited company as a public company (s 48).
Re-registration of public company as a private company (s 53).
Change of company name (s 28).
Financial assistance for the acquisition of its own shares by a private company (s 155).
Off-market purchase by a company of its own shares (s 164).

Redemption or purchase of private company's own shares out of capital (s 173).

EXTRAORDINARY RESOLUTIONS

An extraordinary resolution is a resolution passed by three-quarters of the members voting in person or by proxy at a general meeting of which notice has been given specifying the intention to propose the resolution as an extraordinary resolution.

Extraordinary resolutions are required for:

Initiating a voluntary winding up on the grounds that the company cannot by reason of its liabilities continue its business (s 572).
Granting certain powers to a liquidator in a members voluntary winding up (s 598).
Sanctioning arrangements with creditors in a voluntary winding up (s 601).
Directing the disposal of the liquidator's books in a members voluntary winding up (s 640).
Varying class rights (s 125).

MEMBERS RESOLUTIONS

Members holding 5 per cent of the total voting rights of all the members having a right to vote at a meeting, or not less than 100 members holding shares on which there has been paid-up an average sum per member of not less than £100 may, at their own expense, require the company:

(a) to give to the members notice of any resolution it is intended to propose to move at the next annual general meeting;
(b) to circulate to members a statement of not more than 1,000 words with respect to the matter referred to in any proposed resolution or the business to be dealt with at that meeting (s 376).

A copy of the requisition signed by the requisitionists must be deposited at the company's registered office not less than 6 weeks before the meeting where the requisition requires notice of a resolution. Any other requisition must be deposited not less than one week before the meeting (s 377)(1)).

These provisions enable members opposed to a scheme or course of action to circulate their objections to the other members before the meeting.

The requisitionists must also deposit or tender with the requisition a reasonable sum to cover the company's expenses in giving effect to these provisions (s 377)(1)).

The company is not bound to circulate any statement if, on the application either of the company or of any other person who claims to be aggrieved, the court is satisfied that these rights are being abused to secure needless publicity for defamatory matter. The court may order that the company's costs on such an application be paid in whole or in part by the requisitionists (s 377)(3)).

REGISTRATION OF RESOLUTIONS

Printed copies of certain resolutions and agreements must be forwarded to the Registrar within 15 days of their being passed or made (s 380).

  (i) Special resolutions.
 (ii) Extraordinary resolutions.
(iii) Resolutions which have been agreed to by all the members which would not otherwise have been effective unless passed as special or extraordinary resolutions.
 (iv) Resolutions or agreements binding on all the members of a class of shareholders.
  (v) An ordinary resolution to wind up a company voluntarily on the effluxion of time.
 (vi) A resolution of the directors to re-register the company as a public company or private company.
(vii) A notice of increase of share capital. If a company increases its authorised share capital it must send a copy of the resolution to the Registrar.
(viii) A resolution conferring, varying, revoking or renewing the authority of a company to purchase its own shares on the stock exchange.

The Registrar may accept a copy of a resolution in a form other than a printed copy, but the documents must be durable and legible.

A copy of every such resolution or agreement must be embodied or annexed to every copy of the articles issued after the passing of the resolution or making the agreement (s 380).

Where a special resolution alters a company's memorandum or articles the company must send to the Registrar, with the copy of the resolution, a printed copy of the memorandum and articles as altered (s 18). The Registrar must also advertise in the London Gazette notice of the receipt (s 711).

# Chapter 12

# Directors

As a company is an artificial abstract legal entity it must exercise its powers through the medium of human agencies who are authorised to act on its behalf. These persons are called directors.

There is no comprehensive definition of the term director. Section 741 states that 'director includes any person occupying the position of director by whatever name called'. The articles of association of a company may provide that the company shall be managed by governors, managers, managing committee, council etc. Whatever term is used the test is functional i e participation and decision making at a properly convened meeting of the board of directors. The articles may also provide that the power of management shall be exercised by a life director or 'permanent director' who is not subject to election and re-election at general meetings. All directors may be removed from office at a general meeting by ordinary resolution of which special notice has been given (except a director of a private company holding office at 18/7/1945).

A person, who is not a director, will be regarded as a 'shadow director' if a company's directors are accustomed to act in accordance with his instructions or directions (s 741). He is not a 'shadow director' if the directors so act only on advice given by him in a professional capacity. Certain sections of the Act apply to shadow directors.

## THE NUMBER OF DIRECTORS

Every company must have at least one director while a public company must have at least two directors (s 282). Although the Act does not impose an upper limit on the number of directors, a company's articles may fix a minimum and maximum number of directors. If the number falls below the minimum figure set by the company the remaining directors cannot act, unless the articles give the board specific power to do so. Article 90 provides that if the number falls below the prescribed quorum, the continuing directors or director may act to increase the number to a quorum, or summon a general meeting of the company.

A company without directors may still operate, although it is in breach of section 282.

### Alexander Ward & Co Ltd v Samyang Navigation Co Ltd (1975)

A company which had no directors commenced an action to arrest a ship. The defendants claimed that as there were directors, the company could not authorise the action. It was held by the House of Lords that the company in general meeting could ratify the commencement of the action.

A person may be a director and company secretary, but a sole director cannot be secretary. Another company may act as secretary, but not if its sole director is also the sole director of the first company (s 283).

## APPOINTMENT OF DIRECTORS

A company's first directors are usually appointed by name in the articles, or in the manner provided for by the articles. If directors are not appointed by the articles, or if no articles are submitted, the names of the first directors will be determined in writing by the subscribers of the memorandum or a majority of them.

Section 10 provides that the statement submitted by the subscribers to the memorandum to the Registrar on the company's registration must contain, inter alia, the names of the first directors and their consent to act. This statement overrides any provision in the articles purporting to name other persons, making some other provision for the appointment of the first directors.

The appointment of subsequent directors in addition to or replacement of existing directors is determined by the provisions of the articles.

In the years following the first year, the articles usually provide that a fixed percentage of the board (usually one third) retires each year (Article 73). The directors retiring shall be those who have been longest in office since their last election (Article 74). A managing director and a director holding any other executive office are not subject to retirement by rotation (Article 84).

Where directors who were appointed on the same day fail to agree on who should submit for re-election, it shall be determined by lot (Article 74).

Although a retiring director is eligible for re-election another person may be elected to fill the vacant office. If the company does not elect another person, the retiring director will be automatically re-elected unless it is express resolved not to fill the vacated office or a resolution for his re-election is lost (Article 75).

If a person, other than a retiring director or a person recommended by the directors, seeks election as a director, a written notice must be left at the company's registered office at least 14 and not more than 35 clear days before the meeting. The notice must be signed by a member who is entitled to attend and vote and be accompanied by a notice signed by the person seeking election as to his willingness to be elected (Article 76).

The articles usually give the directors the power to appoint any person to fill a casual vacancy or to act as an additional director until the next annual general meeting (Article 79). The power of the company in general meeting to appoint directors is not affected by such an article.

## Barron v Potter (1914)

A company's articles provided that the directors had the power to appoint additional directors. There was a long standing dispute between the company's two directors, Barron and Potter (the chairman and managing director). Barron refused to attend meetings to appoint a new director, as he was aware that in the event of an equality of votes, the articles gave the chairman a casting vote. Potter met Barron at Paddington Station and purported to hold a board meeting on the platform, and gave his casting vote to a favoured candidate. Barron in the meantime had convened an extraordinary general meeting and at this meeting other directors were elected. It was held that the board meeting at Paddington Station was ineffective and the appointments made at the general meeting were valid.

A company may appoint a person as director for life. Such an appointment is illusory as a life director may be removed from office (s 303).

A director may, if the articles so provide, appoint an 'alternate director to act for him in his absence'. Such a director will have the same powers as the director that he represents. Such an appointment usually requires the approval of a majority of the directors, and may be terminated by the original director. In practice the alternate director will be a fellow director. On his appointment he will be able to cast two votes at board meetings.

The articles may give power to an outside body to appoint directors to the board of an independent company. A lender may, as a condition for granting a loan to a company, be given the power to appoint a certain number of directors to the board to safeguard his interests.

### British Murac Syndicate Ltd v Alperton Rubber Co Ltd (1915)

An agreement between a syndicate and a company provided that the syndicate could nominate two directors on the board of the company. Two persons were nominated but the company refused the nomination and proposed to alter the article which gave the syndicate this right. It was held that the company could not reject the appointees and a declaration was granted that both appointments were valid.

A director may assign his office (ie transfer his rights and liabilities as a director to another person) if permitted to by the articles or by agreement. An assignment of office is ineffective until approved by a special resolution of the company (s 308). A director of a private company who nominates his successor under a provision in the articles is not assigning his office and does not require the approval of a resolution in general meeting.

## QUALIFICATION SHARES

A company is not required by law to impose a share qualification for directors. The articles may however provide that each director must hold a fixed number of shares. The articles generally provide that the shareholding qualification for directors may be fixed in general meeting, and unless and until so fixed no qualification is required.

A director who is required to hold a share qualification must obtain the shares within two months of his appointment, or such shorter time as the articles specify. If he does not obtain his share qualification within the prescribed time he must vacate office and cannot seek re-appointment until he holds the requisite number of shares. A director who, by disposing of part of his holding, no longer holds sufficient shares to qualify is similarly disqualified until he re-acquires the prescribed share qualification.

If the articles provide that a person must hold the prescribed share qualification before his appointment as a director, the appointment of a person who lacks that qualification is defective. The acts of such a director may be validated by s 285.

The articles may provide that a director must hold qualification shares 'in his own right'. It was held in *Pulbrook v Richmond Consolidated Mining Co* (1878) that a director may be regarded as holding shares in his own right even though he is a trustee, for as between the company and the trustee he is the registered holder of the shares.

If it is shown on the register that a person is holding shares as a liquidator of another company (*Boschoek Proprietary Co Ltd v Fuke* (1906)) or as an executor, or as a trustee in bankruptcy (*Sutton v English and Colonial Produce Co* (1902)), that person is deemed not to hold shares in his own right.

'. . . A person holding shares in his own right' means holding in his own right as distinguished from holding in the right of somebody else. I do not think the test is beneficial interest, the test is being on or not being on the register as a member. ie with power to vote, and with these rights which are incidental to full membership. It means that a person shall hold shares in such a way that the company can safely deal with him in respect of his shares whatever his interest may be in the shares . . .' (Lindley LJ in *Bainbridge v Smith* (1889)).

Share warrants to bearer cannot be considered as qualification shares. Shares held jointly with another person may be treated as suitable qualification shares, unless the articles provide otherwise.

## DISQUALIFICATION OF DIRECTORS

Certain persons may not be appointed as directors while others may become disqualified under the articles or the various statutory provisions.

(1) A person may not be appointed a director of a public company if at the time of his appointment he has attained the age of 70 (s 293).

A director of a public company must vacate office at the conclusion of the annual general meeting commencing next after he attains the age of 70. This rule does not apply:

(i) To a director of private company, unless the company is a subsidiary of a public company.
(ii) If a resolution, (of which special notice has been given stating the actual age of the director), has been passed by the company in general meeting approving the appointment.
(iii) If modified or excluded by the articles.

(2) An undischarged bankrupt cannot act as a director (or liquidator) of or take part directly or indirectly in the management (promotion or formation) of any company except with the leave of

the court by which he was adjudged bankrupt (s 302).

(3) A court may make an order disqulifying a person from acting (without leave of the court) as a liquidator, receiver or manager of the company's property, or in any way (directly or indirectly) being concerned or taking part in the company's promotion, formation or management (s 295).

An order may be made on the following grounds:

(a) Where a person is convicted of an indictable offence in connection with the promotion, formation, management or liquidation of a company or with the receivership or management of the property of a company (s 296). (An application on these grounds may be made either to a court that has jurisdiction to wind up the company involved in the offence or the convicting court.)

(b) Where it appears to the court that a person has been persistently in default in relation to the relevant requirements i e any provision of the Companies Act which requires any return, account or other document to be filed with, delivered or sent, or notice of any matter to be given, to the Registrar. It is conclusive proof of persistent default to show that in the five years ending with the date of the application he has been adjudged guilty of three or more defaults (s 297). (An application on these grounds may be made either to a court that has jurisidiction to wind up any of the companies involved in the offence or to the convicting magistrates' court).

(c) If in the course of a winding up it appears that a person:

  (i) has been guilty of an offence under section 458 i e fraudulent trading. It is irrelevant whether he has been convicted of the offence, or

  (ii) has otherwise been guilty (while an officer or liquidator of the company's or receiver or manager of the property of the company) of any fraud in relation to the company or of any breach of his duty as an officer, liquidator, receiver or manager. (s 298).

(An application on these grounds may be made to a court that has the jurisidiction to wind up the company concerned).

(d) If he has been a director of two companies which have gone into liquidation within a five year period and that his conduct as a director of any of the companies makes him unfit to be concerned with the management of a company (s 300). (An application on these grounds may be made to the High Court by the Department of Trade and Industry).

An application for a disqualification order may be made to a court that has jurisdiction to wind up the company or companies concerned by:

(i) The Secretary of State;
(ii) The Official Receiver;
(iii) The Liquidator; or
(iv) Any past or present member or creditor of any company in relation to which the person has committed or is alleged to have committed an offence or other default.

The period of disqualification may vary from a maximum period of 15 years for an order made by a court having jurisdiction to wind up a company, to a maximum period of five years for an order made by a magistrates court.

A disqualification order takes effect from the date of the court order. A copy of the order must be forwarded to the Department of Trade. A register of disqualification orders is kept by the Department and is open to public inspection on payment of a fee (s 301).

OTHER GROUNDS FOR DISQUALIFICATION

A company's articles may specify other grounds of disqualification. The articles of the majority of companies include similar provisions to those found in Table A which provides the following additional grounds for disqualification (Article 81).

(i) If a director becomes bankrupt or makes any arrangement or composition with his creditors generally (This is far wider than the general bankruptcy provisions found in s 302).
(ii) If a director becomes of unsound mind.
(iii) If a director resigns his office by writing to the company.
(iv) If a director shall for more than 6 months have been absent without the permission of the directors from meetings of the directors held during that period.

The word 'absent' in this context includes an involuntary absence due to illness. If the article reads 'shall absent himself' or 'absenting himself' a director who is absent due to illness will not be disqualified.

### In Re London and Northern Bank, McConnell's Claim (1901)

A director was absent in the South of France to benefit his weak chest. It was held that he had absented himself.

### In Re London and Northern Bank, Mack's Claim (1900)

A director who lived in Belfast was unable to travel to attend board meetings as he was seriously ill. It was held that he was not disqualified.

Other grounds for disqualification which are occasionally found in a company's articles are those prohibiting a minor or an enemy alien or alien from holding office as a director, and disqualifying a director who has been convicted of a criminal offence.

The articles may also provide that a director must vacate office if requested to do so, by all his co-directors.

### Samuel Tak Lee v Chou Wen Hsien (1984)

A director of a company became suspicious about a sale of the company's holdings in certain associated and subsidiary companies, and asked the company secretary to convene a board meeting: Two days before the meeting he was given a notice signed by his fellow directors requesting him to resign. The notice was in accordance with an Article which provided that the office of a director was to be vacated if he was requested in writing by all his co-directors to resign. It was held that he must vacate office. If the request was made in breach of a fiduciary duty the remedy was not a personal action but a derivative action on the company's behalf to right a wrong done to the company.

## REMUNERATION OF DIRECTORS

A director is not entitled to remuneration unless provision is expressly made in the articles for payment, or the director has a service agreement with the company.

Article 82 provides that the remuneration of the directors shall be determined by the company in general meeting and be 'deemed to accrue from day to day'. Companies usually vote directors fees annually or stipulate a fixed sum to be paid every year. These are debts which are owed by the company and may be paid out of capital if insufficient profits have been made.

### Re Lundy Granite Co (1871)

The articles provided that the directors remuneration was to be one tenth of the profits, but no less than £100 a year. Although the company made no profits, it was held that the directors were entitled to £100 a year.

Article 83 further provides that directors may be paid 'all travelling, hotel and other expenses' properly incurred by them in attending and returning from meetings of the directors or any committee of the directors or general meetings of the company or in connection with the discharge of their duties'.

If a director vacates office during the currency of a year, due to death or resignation, the articles must be examined to determine his entitlement (if any) to a remuneration.

   (i) Article 82 provides that a director's remuneration shall 'be deemed to accrue from day to day'. A director is therefore entitled to a remuneration proportionate to the time he has served during that year. If there is no such article the position is unclear.
  (ii) If payment is deemed to be 'at the rate of £x per annum' he is entitled to be remunerated for the time served, as in (i).
 (iii) If payment is expressed to be '£x per annum' or '£x in a year' he is only entitled to payment if he served for the whole year.

### Inman v Ackroyd and Best Ltd (1901)

The remuneration of the directors was stated to be at 'the sum of £x per annum per director'. Inman who served on the board of directors for 19 months was held to be entitled to £x, the amount payable for one year.

  (iv) The Apportionments Act 1870 s 2 may apply to this situation. It provides that all rents, annuities, dividends and other periodical payments in the nature of income are deemed to accrue daily and are apportionable in respect of time. Annuities includes salaries and pensions. It is probable that a director's remuneration would be classified as salary and would be covered by this section.

It is not lawful for a company to pay a director remuneration free of income tax. Any provision for such a payment will have effect as if it provided for payment of the sum as a gross sum subject to income tax (s 311).

A director who is paid a sum in excess of that permitted by the articles or resolution is liable to repay the excess to the company.

A company's accounts must show the following in respect of the directors remuneration:

   (i) the aggregate amount of the directors emoluments,
  (ii) the aggregate amount of directors or past directors pensions,
 (iii) the aggregate amount of any compensation to directors or past directors in respect of loss of office,

(iv) the aggregate emoluments of directors if the sum is in excess of £60,000,
(v) the chairmans remunerations,
(vi) the remuneration of the highest paid director, if greater than that of the chairman,
(vii) a scale of directors' remuneration divided into bands of £5,000 with the number of directors in each band.

## BOARD MEETINGS

Management of a company is usually delegated by the shareholders to the board of directors. The articles of most companies include a provision similar to that found in Article 70, which provides that:

'The business of the company shall be managed by the directors, who may exercise all such powers of the company'.

The company in general meeting may not therefore override the directors discretion or direct the board how to act.

### Scott v Scott (1943)

A company's shareholders passed a resolution at a general meeting that certain payments in respect of dividends should be made to preference shareholders. It was held that the resolution was invalid as an attempt by the shareholders to usurp the directors' powers of control.

A general meeting may be able to act where the company has no directors (*Alexander Ward & Co Ltd v Samyang Navigation Co Ltd* (1975) (see p 188)) or where the directors are unable or unwilling to act (*Barron v Potter* (1914) (see p 189)).

If the articles confer on the directors the power to manage the company's affairs, this power must be exercised collectively by resolutions at board meetings. The articles usually provide that the board may delegate any of their powers to committees consisting of one or more directors and a managing director (Article 72). As it is often impossible for all matters to be dealt with at board meetings the articles usually provide that a document signed by all the directors shall be as valid and effectual as if it had passed at a duly convened meeting (Article 93). In practice, a minute is circulated amongst the directors and after each director has signed, it is inserted in the minute book.

The articles usually provide that 'the directors may regulate their proceedings as they think fit' (Article 88). The articles may provide for meetings at fixed intervals or allow directors a discretion as to when a board meeting should be convened. Directors are entitled to reasonable notice of meetings, unless there are regular meetings at fixed intervals. Unless the articles state otherwise the nature of the business to be transacted need not be specified in the notice of the meeting.

It is unnecessary to give notice of a meeting to any director who is temporarily absent from the United Kingdom (Article 88). If a company unadvertently fails to give proper notice to a director of a meeting, the resolutions passed at the meeting may be invalid. This is a technicality as the articles usually provide that a meeting is properly constituted despite an accidental omission to inform a director of the meeting. It may well be, that if there is no such provision, the director concerned has the right to convene another meeting to discuss the matters dealt with at the previous meeting.

The quorum is usually fixed by the articles or it may be left to the discretion of the directors. A quorum may be defined as the 'number of directors qualified to act who must be present at a meeting to enable them to act as a board'.

Article 89 provides that the quorum shall be fixed by the directors and unless so fixed shall be two. (This does not apply to a private company which has only one director). The quorum must, if the articles so provide, consist of directors who have no personal interest in the matter to be voted on at the meeting. Such directors are entitled to notice of the meeting, may attend and speak at the meeting, but may not vote, or be counted in a quorum.

### Re Greymouth Point Elizabeth Railway and Coal Co Ltd (1904)

The articles provided that a director must not vote in respect of a matter in which he had an interest. A company had three directors and the articles provided that two directors constituted a quorum. Two directors lent money to the company and the board issued debentures to secure the loan. It was held that the issue was void as only one director was qualified to vote, and did not therefore constitute a quorum.

Voting at a board meeting is by a simple majority with each director having a vote. The articles may provide that in the case of an equality of votes, the chairman may be given a second or casting vote. The articles may however give a director additional votes in certain specified circumstances (*Bushell v Faith* (1970) (see p 177)).

Every company must keep minutes of board meetings, on pain of a default fine. A minute signed by the chairman of the meeting or the next succeeding meeting is evidence of the proceedings, which are deemed to have been duly held and convened, until the contrary is proved (s 382).

## THE MANAGING DIRECTOR

A company may appoint a managing director or a number of managing directors to deal with various aspects of its business. As a managing director is an ordinary director with powers, provision must be made for such an appointment in the articles (Article 84), or a resolution must be passed to that effect at a general meeting.

A managing director may be appointed on such terms as the directors determine and they may remunerate any such director for his services as they think fit (Article 84). He has the apparent authority as an agent of the company to enter into business contracts with third parties. His actual authority derives from the articles which usually stipulate that the directors may confer on a managing director 'the powers exercisable by them upon such terms and conditions and with such restrictions as they may think fit.'

### Harold Holdsworth and Co (Wakefield) Ltd v Caddies (1955)

Caddies was appointed managing director of the company for five years under an agreement which provided that he should 'perform the duties and exercise the powers in relation to the business of the company and the businesses (howsoever) carried on of its existing subsidiary companies . . . which may from time to time be assigned to or vested in him by the board of directors of the company'. The company had three subsidiaries, and Caddies was also the full time managing director of one of these, a textile company, under a prior agreement. After differences had arisen between him and the board of Harold Holdsworth & Co Ltd, it was resolved that he should confine his activities to the affairs of the subsidiary company. He sued for damages for breach of contract. It was held that the directors had not been in breach of contract and that his duties could be confined to the management of a subsidiary company.

A managing director during his term of office, is not subject to retirement by rotation. His appointment may however be terminated by:

(i)  his fellow directors who may revoke such appointment. He then reverts to the position of an ordinary director.
(ii) the company in general meeting who may remove him from his office of director. He then ceases to be managing director as a

managing director's appointment will be automatically terminated if he ceases to be a director.

A company may be liable in damages for breach of contract if a director has a contract with the company, which is independent of the articles.

If his appointment was based solely on the basis of the articles he may not claim damages, as a company is permitted to alter its articles.

### Read v Astoria Garage (Streatham) Ltd (1952)

Read was appointed the managing director of a company. The articles provided that the appointment was to be 'for such term' as the directors might decide and that a managing director's appointment should automatically terminate if he ceased to be a director. Read was dismissed by the directors and the decision was ratified by the company in general meeting. Read sued for damages for wrongful dismissal on the ground that as there was a contract of an indefinite duration he was entitled to reasonable notice. It was held that as the appointment was on the terms of the articles he had no right to a period of notice.

He may not obtain an injunction to restrain the company from dismissing him. *Southern Foundries (1926) Ltd v Shirlaw* (1940)).

A managing director is entitled to such remuneration as his fellow directors may determine, and this may include not only his salary but commission or participation in profits.

A managing director who has a contract of service with the company is therefore entitled to the protection granted to employees under the Employment Protection (Consolidation Act 1978 and other relevant employment statutes.

## DIRECTORS SERVICE CONTRACTS

A company must keep a copy of the service contracts of its directors (including 'shadow directors,) and the directors of its subsidiaries at its registered office, or at the company's principal place of business in England or at the place where the register of members is kept (s 318).

If there is no written contract, a memorandum must be kept setting out the terms of the contract.

All copies and memorandums must be kept at the same place. If they are kept other than at the registered office, the company must inform the Registrar of that location.

Every copy and memorandum must be open to inspection to members without charge during business hours. If the company refuses to allow inspection, application may be made to the court which may order inspection.

This section does not apply to:

(1) A contract which has less than 12 months to run; or
(2) A contract which can be terminated by the company within the next 12 months without payment of compensation; or
(3) A contract with the company or with a subsidiary requiring a director to work wholly or mainly outside the United Kingdom (In this case a memorandum containing the director's name, the name and place of incorporation of the subsidiary (if any) and the duration of the contract is required).

## THE REGISTER OF DIRECTORS AND SECRETARIES

Every company must keep at its registered office a register of directors (including shadow directors) and secretaries (s 288). The following details must be entered on the register in respect of each director and secretary:

Name.
Address.
Business occupation (if any).
Nationality.
Particulars of any other directorship held currently or in the preceding five years (except for a directorship of a related company or dormant company incorporated in Great Britain).
Date of Birth (unless the company is a private company and is not a subsidiary of a public company).
For a director that is a corporation details of its corporate name and the location of its registered or principal office (s 289).

A company must, within 14 days of the initial appointment of a director (or secretary) or of any change in the particulars contained in the register, send to the Registrar a notification of the appointment or the change.

The register must be kept open during business hours for a minimum period of two hours per day, for inspection by members (free of charge) and by any other person on payment of 5p (or such smaller sum as the company may prescribe).

## PUBLICATION OF DIRECTORS' NAMES ON BUSINESS LETTERS

A company registered since 23 November 1916, under the Act and former Companies Act, and every company incorporated outside Great Britain since that date which has an established place of business within Great Britain must not state, in any form, the name of any of its directors (including shadow directors) on any business letter on which the company's name appears unless it states on the letter in legible characters the Christian name, or initials, and surname of every director of the company (s 305).

## COMPENSATION FOR LOSS OF OFFICE

It is unlawful for a company to make any payment to a director by way of compensation for loss of office, or in consideration for or in connection with his retirement from office, without disclosing particulars of the payment (including the amount) to the company and it being approved by the company (s 312).

Disclosure must be made to the members of the company before payment is made i e while the payment is still a proposed payment.

### Re Duomatic (1969)

A director was paid £4,000 for loss of office. The payment was not disclosed in the company's accounts, or to the non voting preference shareholders. It was held that the directors authorising the payment had misapplied the company's funds and were jointly and severally liable to repay the payment.

A director in receipt of an undisclosed payment holds the money in trust for the company.

Any payment made to a director as compensation for loss of office or in connection with his retirement from office, where there is a transfer of part or the whole of the company's undertaking is unlawful unless the payment is disclosed to the members and approved by them. Any payment received and not disclosed is deemed to be held on trust by the director on behalf of the company (s 313).

A director must disclose, in any notice of an offer made to the shareholders for the acquisition of their shares, any sums paid to him as compensation for loss of office or on his retirement. Such an offer may be made in any of the followng ways:

(a) An offer made to the general body of shareholders.
(b) An offer made by or on behalf of another company with a view to the company becoming its subsidiary.
(c) An offer made by or on behalf of an individual with a view to his obtaining the right to exercise or control the exercise of not less than one third of the voting power at any general meeting of the company.
(d) Any other offer which is conditional on acceptance to a given extent (s 314).

If disclosure is not made, or the payment is not approved before the transfer by a meeting of shareholders, the director holds the sum on trust for the shareholders who have sold their shares as a result of the offer. He is also liable to a fine (s 315).

If in connection with any transfer under the provisions of ss 313 and 315:

(i) the price to be paid to a director whose office is to be abolished or who is to retire from office for any shares in the company held by him is in excess of the price which could at the time have been obtained by other holders of similar shares; or
(ii) any valuable consideration is given to such director –
the excess of the money value of the consideration is deemed to have been a payment made to him as compensation for loss of office or a consideration for or in connection with his retirement from office (s 316).

Any bona fide payment of damages for breach of contract or by way of pension for past services will not be treated as compensation and does not require a disclosure to and approval by shareholders.

### Taupo Totara Timber Co Ltd v Rowe (1978)

Rowe entered into a contract with a company as managing director for a term of 5 years. The contract stipulated that in the event of the company being taken over he would have the option of resigning and receiving five years salary as compensation. The company was taken over and he subsequently resigned. The company refused to pay him the compensation unless it was approved by the members in general meeting. It was held that the requirements for the approval of the members applied only to voluntary payments. The provision could not be used to avoid contractual liability.

The aggregate amount of any compensation paid to directors for loss of office with the company or any of its subsidiaries must be disclosed, in the company's accounts. Compensation for loss of office includes sums paid as consideration for or in connection with a person's retirement from office (Sch 5).

## LIABILITY ON CONTRACTS

Directors are not generally liable to third parties on contracts made by them on behalf of the company. If they exceed their authority in making the contract, they are not personally liable on the contract. They may however be liable in damages for breach of an implied warranty of authority.

### Weeks v Probert (1873)

A company issued a prospectus inviting persons to lend money on the security of debentures. It issued a debenture to Weeks as security for a loan of £500. At the time of its issue the company had, unknown to Weeks, exceeded its borrowing powers. As the loan was ultra vires, the company could not be sued and the plaintiff brought an action against the directors for breach of warranty of authority. The action succeeded as the prospectus implied that the company had power to borrow.

A director may contract so as to incur personal liability. It may be that a creditor is unwilling to enter into a contract with a small company and will only supply goods if a director is willing to accept personal liability for their payment.

If a director contracts in his own name without disclosing the fact that he is acting for a company (ie an undisclosed principal) he is liable.

An action against a director will usually be undertaken by the company, unless a member takes action under the rules of minority protection.

### (a) *Damages*
A company may sue a director for breach of duty. If a director is dismissed due to incompetence the action is based on negligence, and the amount of damages will be calculated according to the general law of tort. If the director is sued for breach of fiduciary duty eg the misappropriation of company property, the company may seek compensation from the director.

### (b) *Injunction*
A company may obtain an injunction to restrain a director from committing a breach of duty.

## (c) *Rescission*

A company may rescind a contract with a director e g the sale of property to the company, where there has been no proper disclosure.

A company may not affirm such a contract and recover the profit from the director.

### Burland v Earle (1902)

Burland, a director of the American Bank Note Company purchased the plant and material of an insolvent company. He re-sold the plant and materials at a profit to the company. It was alleged that he had not made proper disclosure of the circumstances relating to the transaction to his fellow directors and that he acted as a trustee of the company when making the purchase. It was held that where a director purchased property and resold it to the company (in circumstances which did not make him a trustee for the company), that whether or not the company was entitled to a recission of the contract of resale, it could not both affirm it and at the same time treat the director as trustee of the profit made.

Rescission is only possible where the parties can be restored to their former position and the rights of third parties are not affected.

## (c) *Account of profits*

A director must account to the company for any profit that he makes from taking advantage of a corporate opportunity, whether in a contract with the company or with a third party (*Regal (Hastings) Ltd, v Gulliver* (1942) (see p 212); *Industrial Development Consultants Ltd v Cooley* (1972) (see p 212)).

## DIRECTORS DUTIES

Directors owe a duty to act honestly and in the best interests of the company. They must manage the company's affairs in accordance with the principles of the common law and statute and are bound by the provisions in a company's memorandum and articles of association.

Directors stand in a fiduciary relationship to the company in the performance of their duties. They have been described by the judiciary at various times as managing partners, trustees and agents.

'It does not much matter what you call them, so long as you understand what their true position is, which is that they are merely commercial men managing a trading concern for the benefit of themselves and all other shareholders in it' per *Jessel MR in Re Forest of Dean Coal Mining Co* (1878)

Directors owe the following duties:

### (1) TO ACT BONA FIDE IN THE BEST INTERESTS OF THE COMPANY

This duty is subjective and the directors may exercise their discretion in what they honestly consider to be the company's best interests. Their actions must not only be honest but in the company's interests.

### Re Roith Ltd (1967)

A company's memorandum and articles were altered so as to allow pensions to be paid to dependents of employees. A director, in poor health, was appointed general manager for life under a service agreement. One of the terms of the agreement stated that if he died in office the company would pay his widow a pension for the rest of her life. He died shortly after making his agreement. It was held that the agreement was not binding, as it was not reasonably incidental to carrying on the company's business and it was not bona fide for the company's benefit.

### (2) TO AVOID A CONFLICT OF INTEREST

A director must not allow his personal interest to conflict with his duty to the company.

> 'no one having such duties to discharge shall be allowed to enter into engagements in which he has or can have a personal interest conflicting or which possible may conflict with the interests of those whom he is bound to protect' (per Lord Cranworth LC in *Aberdeen Rly Co v Blaikie Bros* (1854))

The phrase '*possibly may conflict*' was interpreted a century later by Upjohn LJ in *Boardman v Phipps* (1967) as

> 'the reasonable man looking at the relevant facts and circumstances of the particular case would think that there was a real sensible possibility of conflict.'

### Aberdeen Rly Co v Blaikie Bros (1854)

A company entered into a contract with a firm for the supply of a certain manufactured articles. The company's chairman was at the time of making the contract, the managing partner of the firm. It was held that the company was not bound by the contract.

*Contracts made with the company*

The general rule is that a director may only enter into a contract or proposed contract with the company if the articles so permit or if the company in general meeting so approves. Otherwise the contract is voidable at the company's option.

### Parker v McKenna (1874)

The directors of the National Bank of Ireland issued 20,000 £5 shares. Any shares that were not taken up were to be disposed of by the directors at a premium of £30. Stock agreed to take 9,778 shares on terms by which he was to pay £5 deposit on each share and the balance by instalments. As he was unable to take all the shares the directors took over part of his bargain and later disposed of the shares at a profit. It was held that the directors must account to the bank for the profits made on the sale of the shares.

The rule applies even though the interest of the director is only that of a shareholder in another company which contracts with the company of which he is a director.

### Transvaal Lands Co v New Belgium (Transvaal) Co (1914)

A director of the Transvaal Lands Co. was also a shareholder of the New Belgium Co. The Transvaal Lands Co. bought shares in another company from the New Belgium Co. He voted at the meeting for the purchase, but did not disclose his shareholding in the New Belgium Co, as required by the articles which provided that a director could not vote in respect of any contract in which he was concerned. The contract was voidable at the option of the Transvaal Lands Co.

The articles generally provide that a director who is in any way interested, either directly or indirectly, in a contract or proposed contract with the company must declare 'the nature of his interest at a meeting of the directors'. A director may not vote in respect of any contract or arrangement in which he is interested, and if he does so, his vote will not be counted, nor will it count in the quorum present at the meeting. This does not apply to:

 (i) any arrangement for giving any director any security or indemnity in respect of any money lent by him to the company or obligation undertaken by him on behalf of the company
 (ii) any arrangement for giving a third party any security in respect of any debt or obligation of the company for which the director has assumed responsibility in whole or in part under a guarantee or indemnity or by the deposit of a security
(iii) any contract by a director to subscribe for shares or debentures of the company
(iv) any contract or arrangement with any other company in which

he is interested only as an officer of the company or as holder of shares (or other securities).

A director may hold any other office or profit under the company (other than the office of auditor) for such period and on such terms as the directors may determine, and may enter into contracts with the company. A director may be counted in the quorum present at any meeting where he or another director is appointed to hold any office of profit under the company, and may not vote on any such appointment other than his own appointment.

Any director may act by himself or his firm in a professional capacity for the company (other than as auditor) and he or his firm are entitled to be remunerated for his services as if he were not a director.

Section 317 provides that a director who is in any way interested in a contract or proposed contract must declare the nature of his interest at a board meeting.

In the case of a proposed contract the declaration must be made at the first meeting when the question of entering the contract is first considered. If at that time the director had no interest, but later becomes interested, he must disclose his interest at the first meeting held after he becomes interested.

This section applies to shadow directors and persons connected with directors. Any director who fails to comply with the provisions of the section is liable on conviction to a fine.

### (3) TO ACT FOR THE BENEFIT OF THE COMPANY

Directors must exercise their duties in good faith for the benefit of the company as a whole rather than to individual members.

### Percival v Wright (1902)

Percival, a shareholder in a company whose shares were not quoted on a stock exchange and were transferable only with the consent of the board, wrote to the company offering to sell his shares. The shares were later purchased by three of the directors at a price based on Percival's valuation. He later discovered that the directors were negotiating for the sale of the company's shares to a third party. If the negotiations had been successful, the price realised for each share would have been greater than that paid for Percival's shares. The negotiations proved abortive, but nevertheless Percival brought an action to set aside his sale to the directors. It was held that the directors were not under a duty to inform him of the negotiations as they did not owe a fiduciary duty to any individual shareholder.

A director owes a fiduciary duty to a shareholder if he acts as an agent for the sale of the shareholder's shares.

### Allen v Hyatt (1914)

The directors induced certain shareholders to grant them options to purchase their shares at par in order to effect an amalgamation with another company. The directors exercised the option to purchase the shares themselves and made a substantial profit. It was held that they must account for this profit to the shareholders.

(4) TO ACT FOR THE BENEFIT OF THE SHAREHOLDERS

The duty owed by a director to a company has been traditionally interpreted as a duty owed to the general body of shareholders.

In *Parke v Daily News* (1962) it was held that the interests of the company's employees should not be considered where their interests conflicted with the interests of the shareholders. In the case the directors proposed to distribute surplus assets amongst the employees of the company. It was held that the proposed distribution was void as it could not benefit the company's shareholders.

Section 309 now provides that the directors are to have regard to the interests of the company's employees in general as well as the interest of its members. This duty is enforceable in the same way as any other fiduciary duty owed to a company by its directors.

(5) ATTENTION AND DILIGENCE TO THE COMPANY'S BUSINESS

The degree of diligence required of a director is not defined by case law. Although a director owes a duty to be diligent and pay attention to the company's affairs the amount of time and attention given will vary according to the nature and complexity of the business.

A director whose attendance at meetings is such that he has a reasonable understanding of the company's affairs and the performance of the company's officers and directors, satisfies the requirements set out above.

He is not bound to attend all board meetings although he should attend whenever, in the circumstances, he is able to do so.

It is however doubtful if the general rule that a director does not incur liability for decisions taken at meetings which he did not attend still applies.

### Re Cardiff Savings Bank, Marquis of Bute's Case (1892)

A director, appointed to the board of the company at the age of six months, was held not liable for the negligent acts of the board even though he had only attended one board meeting in thirty eight years.

In certain circumstances failure to attend board meetings may amount to negligence on the part of the director concerned e g where the director had notice or knowledge that a specific duty that ought to have been performed at the meeting had not been performed.

A director may, in the absence of a breach of duty, rely on the acts of others and will not incur liability for their dishonesty, if he has no knowledge of such acts or if he has not acquiesced in them.

## (6) DUTY OF SKILL AND CARE

In *Re City Equitable Fire Insurance Co* (1925) three basic propositions were laid down:

(a) A director must show that degree of care and skill which might reasonably be expected from a person of his knowledge and experience.
(b) A director is not bound to give continuous attention to the affairs of the company. He is not bound to attend board meetings, but should do so.
(c) A director may in the absence of grounds for suspicion trust a company official to perform duties which may properly be delegated.

The standard laid down in the decided cases indicate that the duty is not onerous, as the degree of skill varies with the director's qualifications and the scope of the company. It was stated by Brett LJ in *Lagunas Nitrate v Lagunas Syndicate* (1899) that

'A director must be guilty of such negligence as would make him liable in any action. Mere imprudence is not negligence, want of judgement is not. It must be such negligence as would make a man liable in point of law'.

### Re New Mashonaland Exploration Co (1892)

The directors of a company lent money to Green on the security of a contract. The company was empowered to promote companies and lend money. The company's solicitor gave Green a cheque for £250 without obtaining security, and later the directors gave Green a cheque for £1,000 to promote a company. The liquidator sought to hold the directors liable for misfeasance in respect of the sums paid to Green. It was held that as the directors had exercised their judgement and discretion, they were not liable for misfeasance or breach of trust.

These are minimum standards and will not apply to an individual who is appointed as a full time director of a company. Such an appointment is usually under a service contract, and as an employee he is bound to give exclusive service to his employer. A director employed by a company who is professionally qualified and has expertise in a certain field is expected to show a high degree of competence.

Similar standards are imposed on a non-executive director who is also professionally qualified.

### Dorchester Finance Co v Stebbing (1980)

A company had three directors, only one of whom was a full time executive. The other two directors were qualified accountants, who rarely visited the company. The company, over a period of years, made loans which were unenforceable due to non compliance with the Moneylenders Acts 1900–1927. The company sued all three directors for negligence. It was held that the full time director had been negligent and was therefore liable for the misappropriation of the company's funds. The other two directors were also held liable in negligence as they had signed blank cheques without checking the full time director's work. Their claim to be excused as they were non-executive directors was rejected.

'For a chartered accountant . . . . . . to put forward the proposition that a non-executive director has no duties to perform I find quite alarming' (per Foster J).

### (7) TO EXERCISE THEIR POWERS FOR A PROPER PURPOSE

Directors must exercise their powers for the purposes for which those powers were conferred ie they must only use their powers for a proper purpose. If the directors use those powers for a collateral purpose the transaction will be invalid, unless the company ratifies the director's actions in general meeting (*Hogg v Cramphorn Ltd* (1967) (see p 211)).

If the directors exercise of a power is challenged the court must ascertain its nature and limits. It must then examine the substantial purpose for which the power was exercised to determine whether that purpose was proper or not. If the court concludes that the directors have acted improperly, the acts complained of will be set aside.

Problems frequently arise where directors have made an improper allotment of shares. The power to issue shares is in the nature of a trust to enable the directors to raise additional capital or obtain some advantage which will benefit the company. It may not be used to alter the balance of voting power within the company so as to oppress the minority (*Clemens v Clemens Bros Ltd* (1976)).

## Howard Smith Ltd v Ampol Petroleum Ltd (1974)

Ampol Petroleum Ltd and Bulkships Ltd held 55 per cent of the issued share capital of Millars Ltd. Ampol made an offer to buy all the issued shares in Millars at $2.27 per share. The directors of Millars were of the opinion that the company required additional capital which Howard Smith Ltd could provide if it obtained control of the company. They therefore allotted 4.5 ml $1 shares to Howard Smith Ltd at a premium of $1.30 per share, thereby destroying the majority holdings of Ampol Ltd and Bulkships Ltd. It was held that the allotment was void as the intention of the directors of Millars Ltd was to induce Howard Smith Ltd to proceed with a takeover bid by reducing the combined shareholding of Ampol Ltd and Bulkships Ltd.

'It must be unconstitutional for directors to use their fiduciary powers over the shares in the company purely for the purpose of destroying an existing majority or creating a new majority which did not previously exist' (per Lord Wilberforce).

If the directors have used their powers for an irregular purpose, they may nevertheless make full disclosure to the shareholders and obtain their approval. This is regarded as a proper case of majority control to which the minority must submit.

## Hogg v Cramphorn Ltd (1967)

The articles of the company gave the directors power to issue shares. The directors allotted shares to trustees of a pension fund for employees to forestall a takeover bid which they honestly believed would not be in the company's best interests. Each share carried 10 votes and this effectively meant that the directors and trustees had control of the company. It was held that the allotment was voidable, but could be ratified by the company in general meeting. However the shares could only carry the votes provided by the articles ie one vote per share.

## Bamford v Bamford (1970)

The directors of Bamford Ltd allotted 500,000 unissued shares to a third party to forestall a takeover bid. An extraordinary general meeting was later called and ratified the directors actions. (The holders of the newly issued shares did not vote). It was held that although there had been a breach of fidiciary duty, the act had been validated by the majority shareholders.

## (8) TO ACCOUNT FOR PROFIT

A director must account to the company for any profit that he has made by reason of the opportunities that have arisen by virtue of the fact that he is a director.

### Regal (Hastings) Ltd v Gulliver (1942)

The directors of the Regal company formed a subsidiary company to buy two other cinemas, so that the three cinemas could be sold together. As the Regal company was unable to provide all the necessary capital the directors purchased some of the shares in the subsidiary so as to enable the transaction to be effected. These shares were later sold at a profit. It was held that the directors were in a fiduciary relationship to the company and had to account to the company for the profit made.

The liability to account does not depend on proof of bad faith on the part of the director.

> 'The general rule of equity is that no one who has duties of a fiduciary nature to perform is allowed to enter into engagements on which he has or can have a personal interest conflicting with the interests of those whom he is bound to protect' per Viscount Sankey in *Regal (Hastings) Ltd v Gulliver* (1942)

The *Regal* case was followed in *Boardman v Phipps* (1967).

### Boardman v Phipps (1967)

Boardman, a solicitor, and Phipps were trustees of an estate, whose assets included shares in a private company. They concluded that the position of the company was unsatisfactory.

With the knowledge of the other trustees, they endeavoured to obtain control of the company by purchasing shares in their own names, as the trustees were not empowered to invest trust money in the company's shares, Boardman obtained information from the company as to the price at which shares had changed hands by purporting to act on behalf of the trustees. Both made a considerable profit from the capital distributions on the shares.

It was held that both were constructive trustees and had to account for the profit to the beneficiaries. The information relating to the shares and the opportunity for investment came as a result of their appointment as trustees.

A director is also liable if he resigns so that he may obtain a personal profit, even though the company could not have obtained the profit for itself.

### Industrial Development Consultants Ltd v Cooley (1972)

Cooley, an architect, was the managing director of IDC which provided consultancy services for gas boards. IDC failed to obtain a contract from the Eastern Gas Board for the construction of various depots, but Cooley was offered the contract in his private capacity. He therefore represented to IDC that he was ill and was released from the company's services. The Gas Board believed that Cooley had the company's permission to act as their architect and awarded him the contract. IDC successfully sued Cooley for the profit made on the contracts made with the Board, even though the Board would have at no time contracted with IDC.

It is possible that a director may retain a personal profit if the company has considered the proposition and bona fide rejected it. The opportunity therefore must arise in his personal capacity and not in his capacity as a director. This was the basis of the decision of the Supreme Court of Canada in *Peso Silver Mines v Cropper* (1966).

**Peso Silver Mines v Cropper** (1966)

The Peso company was offered claims near to its own property, and after due consideration declined the offer. A syndicate, Cross Bow Mines Ltd, was later formed by Peso's geologist to purchase the claims and a company was formed for the purpose. Cropper, a director of Peso, who had taken part in the earlier decision of the Peso board purchased shares in Cross Bow Mines Ltd. It was held that he was under no obligation to account to Peso for the shares that he had obtained. He had sound reasons, along with the other directors, to reject the original offer and was acting in his private capacity when he purchased the shares.

A director may retain a personal profit if the company in general meeting passes a resolution to this effect. Such a resolution may be regarded as a fraud or oppressive to the minority, and therefore of no effect, if the director concerned controls the voting in general meetings.

**Cook v Deeks** (1916)

The directors of the company entered into a contract on the company's behalf with the Canadian Pacific Railway for construction work. At a later date the directors used their votes as holders of three quarters of the issued share capital to pass a resolution at a general meeting to the effect that the company had no interest in the contract and subsequently obtained the contract for themselves. It was held that the contract belonged in equity to the company. The directors could not use their voting power to vest the contract in themselves and thereby perpetrate a fraud on the minority.

There are exceptions to the rule:-

(1) The articles may permit a director to enter into a contract or have an interest in a contract.
(2) The company in general meeting may approve such a contract.

(3)  A director must disclose the nature of his interest in a contract.

(4)  A director may agree to take up shares or debts in a company.


## DIRECTORS AS TRUSTEES

Directors are to some extent in the position of trustees, as they stand in a fiduciary relationship to the company in the performance of their duties. They are trustees for the company and not for the individual shareholder (*Percival v Wright* (1902)).

> 'The directors are the mere trustees or agents of the company – trustees of the company's money and property – agents in the transactions which they enter into on behalf of the company.' per Lord Selborne in *Great Eastern Rly Co v Turner* (1872).

> '. . . directors are called trustees. They are no doubt trustees of assets which have come into their hands, or which are under their control . . .' (per Sir George Jessel in *Re Forest of Dean Coal Mining Co* (1878)).

> 'Although directors are not properly speaking trustees, yet they have always been considered and treated as trustees of money which comes to their hands or which is actually under their control, and ever since joint stock companies were invented directors have been held liable to make good moneys which they have misapplied upon the same footing as if they were trustees . . .' (per Lindley LJ in *Re Lands Allotment Co* (1894)).

Although these statements indicate that the directors are in the position of trustees, yet they are not trustees in the legal sense e g the provisions of the Trustee Act 1925 does not apply to directors. They are best described as quasi trustees in that the company's property and money are not vested in them and their duties are not as onerous as those of trustees. They stand in a fiduciary relationship and in that way they are trustees of the powers entrusted to them.

The provisions of the Limitation Act 1980 applies to the acts of directors, as it applies to trustees. It bars any rights against a director for negligence or breach of trust, where the proceedings are commenced more than six years after the alleged wrong or ommission.


## DIRECTORS AS AGENTS

Directors are agents of the company for which they act. Cairns LJ stated in *Ferguson v Wilson* (1866) that –

'the company itself cannot act in its own person for it has no person, it can only act through directors and the case is, as regards those directors, merely the ordinary case of principal and agent. Wherever an agent is liable those directors would be liable, where the liability would attach to the principal and the principal only, the liability is the liability of the company'.

As long as the directors contract within the scope of the authority, they incur no personal liability for contracts made by them on behalf of the company unless they specifically undertake personal liability.

### Elkington and Co v Hürter (1892)

A company contracted to issue debentures for £600 to Elkington and Co as payment for the supply of goods. The debentures were not issued and the company was wound up at a later date. The chairman of the company was sued by Elkington and Co, but it was held that he was not personally liable, as the contract was made at a board meeting.

If the directors exceed their authority when entering into a contract on the company's behalf, they are liable for breach of warranty of authority ie they warrant that they have an authority that they do not possess. Their actions may be ratified by the company in general meeting as long as the act complained of is not outside the powers contained in memorandum ie the directors actions are ultra vires the board, but intra vires the company. (*Hogg v Cramphorn* (1967), *Bamford v Bamford* (1969) (see p 211)).

Directors who hold themselves out as agents to the shareholders in a transaction involving those shareholders, must account to them for any profit made in the course of the transaction (*Allen v Hyatt* (1914) (see p 208)).

If directors enter into a contract on the company's behalf, but in their own names, the company may be sued as an undisclosed principal by the other party on discovering that the company is the real principal.

## CONTRACTS MADE WITH OUTSIDERS

A director may have acted in excess of the powers conferred upon him when entering into a contract with a third party. It then becomes necessary to determine whether the outsider may hold the company liable for the director's actions.

The outsider may be able to rely on a company's articles (Articles 70, 71) or on other statutory or non-statutory rules.

(a) COMPANY CAPACITY

Section 35 provides that a person dealing with a company in good faith is deemed to be able to rely on a company's capacity to enter into a transaction decided upon by its directors. A party to such a transaction is not bound to enquire as to the company's capacity to enter into it or as to any limitation on the director's powers and is presumed to have acted in good faith unless the contrary is proved.

(b) THE RULE IN ROYAL BRITISH BANK V TURQUARD

A person dealing with a company may not have actual notice of the contents of a company's public documents, but is nevertheless deemed to have constructive notice of their contents. The memorandum of association, the articles of association, special resolutions, the register of charges, the register of directors are open to inspection at the Companies Registration Office.

The principle of constructive notice is qualified by the rule in *Royal British Bank v Turquand* (1856) which provides that –

'Persons dealing with the company are bound to read the public documents, and to see that the proposed dealing is not inconsistent therewith. But they are not bound to do more; they need not enquire into the regularity of the internal proceedings' (per Jervis J in *Royal British Bank v Turquand* (1856))

The principle was re-affirmed by Lord Hatherley in *Mahony v East Holyford Mining Co* (1875) who stated that –

'When there are persons conducting the affairs of the company in a manner which appears to be perfectly consonant with the Articles of association then those so dealing with them externally are not to be affected by any irregularities which may take place in the internal management of the company.'

An outsider contracting with a company is therefore entitled to assume that, in the absence of actual notice to the contrary, the internal procedures of the company have been complied with. He is not affected by an internal irregularity in the management of the company's affairs, as where the board of directors have acted in excess of their authority.

The rule also known as the 'indoor management rule' applies only to transactions which are intra vires the company but ultra vires the directors.

**Royal British Bank v Turquand** (1856)

A company's deed of settlement provided that the directors could only issue bonds if authorised by a general resolution of the company. The directors issued a bond to the Royal British Bank without a resolution having been passed. It was held that as the bank had no right to inspect the resolution it was entitled to assume that a resolution authorising the borrowing had been passed.

*The Rule does not apply in the following circumstances*
That is the company is not bound and the outsider is not protected:

1. If the transaction is ultra vires the company its agents cannot bind the company in that transaction.

2. If the memorandum or the articles prohibit a delegation of authority, the company is not bound to a third party as the third party has constructive notice of this prohibition.

However if delegation is allowed by the memorandum or the articles and the agent purports to exercise the authority which an agent in his position would usually have, the third party is bound by the agent's apparent authority.

3. If the agent purports to exercise an authority which is outside the scope of the usual authority of such an agent, the company will not be bound if the third party seeks to rely on the contents of the memorandum and the articles, without being aware of their contents at the time of making the contract. The doctrine of constructive notice operates in favour of a company, not against it, i e it operates against the person who has failed to inquire not in his favour.

### Rama Corpn Ltd v Proved Tin and General Investments Ltd (1952)

A company's articles provided that 'the directors may delegate any of their powers . . . to committees consisting of such members as they think fit.' A director of the company purported to make an agreement with the plaintiff company to participate in a joint venture to subscribe to a fund to be used for financing the sale of a telephone directory to be produced by a third party. The power to make such an agreement had not been delegated to that particular director and such a transaction was outside the scope of his usual authority. It was held that the plaintiff company could not rely on the articles, so as to hold the company as liable as the plaintiffs had not read the articles at the time of entering the transaction.

4. If there are suspicious circumstances which put the outsider on inquiry and he fails to do so.

### AL Underwood Ltd v Bank of Liverpool and Martins (1924)

A sole director and principal shareholder of a company paid cheques in favour of the company into his own account. The bank was unaware that the company had an account at a branch of another bank. It was held that the bank could not rely on the Rule as the payment of the company's cheques into a private account was unusual and the bank was put on inquiry as to whether the company had a separate account.

5. If the document on which the person seeks to rely is a forgery.

### Ruben v Great Fingall Consolidated (1906)

The secretary of a company forged a share certificate and then issued the share certificate to Ruben as security for a loan. The forgery was discovered and the company refused to register the shares. It was held that Ruben could not rely on the Rule as it did not apply where the document was forged.

It would appear that a company may be estopped from disclaiming a document as a forgery if it has been represented as genuine by an officer of the company acting within his actual or apparent authority (*Uxbridge Building Society v Pickard* (1939).

6. A person who deals with a company and who is aware of an irregularity in its internal management cannot rely on the Rule.

### Howard v Patent Ivory Co (1888)

The articles of a company provided that the directors could borrow up to £1,000 on the company's behalf without the approval of the shareholders. Any borrowing in excess of this amount required the approval of a resolution at a general meeting. The company borrowed £3,500 from its directors without a resolution being passed. It was held that the debentures for £3,500 issued to the directors as security for the loan were valid for £1,000 only as the directors knew that a resolution had not been passed.

7. A director of a company cannot rely on the Rule with regards to acts to which he is a party.

### Morris v Kanssen (1946)

A and B the first directors of a company quarrelled and A forged an entry in the board minutes appointing C as a director. A and C then purported to hold a board meeting and appointed M as a director. As no general meeting was held within the allotted time A and B ceased to be directors. M was aware that a dispute existed prior to his appointment as a director, but made no enquiries. At a later board meeting A and C purported to allot shares to M. It was held that M could not rely on the rule to validate the allotment of shares to him as he was in the position of a director at the time of allotment and could have discovered the true position had he made inquiries.

(c) ACTUAL AND APPARENT AUTHORITY

A company (the principal) is bound by a transaction entered into on its behalf by a director (the agent) if it can be shown that the director was acting within the scope of the authority which the company has conferred upon him.

The authority may be actual or apparent.

(i) *Actual authority*

This may be express or implied.

> 'It is express when it is given by express words, such as when a board of directors pass a resolution which authorised two of their number to sign cheques. It is implied when it is inferred from the conduct of the parties and the circumstances of the case, such as when the board of directors appoint one of their number to be managing director. They therefore impliedly authorise him to do all such things as fall within the scope of that office.' (per Lord Denning MR in *Hely Hutchinson v Brayhead Ltd* (1968)).

### Hely-Hutchinson v Brayhead Ltd (1968)

The chairman of B Ltd, although not appointed as the company's managing director acted in that capacity with the acquiescence of the board of directors. He purported to issue on the company's behalf, various gurantees and undertakings in connection with a take over. It was held that B Ltd was liable on the undertakings for although its chairman had no actual authority, arising from his position as chairman, to enter into such a transaction, as the company's de facto managing director he possessed that authority.

(ii) *Apparent authority*

An 'apparent' or 'ostensible' authority is a legal relationship between the principal and the contractor created by a representation made by the principal to the contractor, intended to be and in fact acted upon by the contractor, that the agent has authority to enter on behalf of the principal into a contract of a kind within the scope of the

> 'apparent authority so as to render the principal liable to perform any obligations imposed upon him by such contract. ... The representation, when acted upon by the contractor by entering into a contract with the agent, operates as an estoppel, preventing the principal from asserting that he is not bound by the contract. It is irrelevant whether the agent had actual authority to enter into the contract' (per Diplock LJ in *Freeman and Lockyer v Buckhurst Park Properties (Mangal) Ltd* (1964)).

A third party will therefore be able to enforce a contract against a company if the company holds out a director as having the apparent authority to enter into contracts on its behalf.

### Freeman and Lockyer v Buckhurst Park Properties (Mangal) Ltd (1964)

A company was formed to buy and resell Buckhurst Park. Its articles contained a power to appoint a managing director, but no such appointment was made. One of the directors, Kapoor, acted as the managing director, with the knowledge but without the express authority of the board of the directors. He entered into various contracts on the company's behalf, including engaging a firm of architects. It was held that the company was liable for the architects' fees as Kapoor had apparent authority to enter into transactions i e the company had by its acquiescence represented that Kapoor was a managing director with the usual authority of that office.

A company may ratify a contract made by a director who does not possess the actual authority to enter into contracts on its behalf.

A third party may only enforce the contract against the company under the principle of holding out if the following conditions are satisfied:–

(a) A representation was made to the third party that the director had the authority to enter on behalf of the company into a contract of the kind sought to be enforced.
(b) Such representation was made by a person or persons who had actual authority to manage the business of the company generally or in respect of those matters to which the contract relates.
(c) He was induced by the representation to enter into the contract i e he relied upon it.
(d) The company is not prevented by its memorandum or articles from entering into that kind of contract, or from delegating authority to an agent to enter into such a contract.

A representation may take the form of a positive statement that the agent has authority, or it may arise from the conduct of the directors or members in allowing the agent to act as such.

### Mahony v East Holyford Mining Co (1875)

The members of a company were entitled under the terms of the articles to appoint directors, but no such appointments were made. Certain members nevertheless acted as the company's directors. A document was sent to the bank in the form of a board resolution purporting to grant the bank a mandate to honour cheques if signed by two directors and the company's secretary. It was held that the bank was entitled to honour the cheques as those members had apparent authority to act in that capacity and their conduct was perfectly consistent with the company's articles.

(d) VALIDITY OF ACTS OF DIRECTORS

Section 285 provides that the acts of a director (or manager) are valid notwithstanding any defect afterwards discovered in his appointment or qualification. The articles generally contain a similar provision. (Article 92).

Certain conditions must be fulfilled before the section applies:–

(i) There must be an initial appointment which is later discovered to be defective eg an appointment at a meeting of which insufficient notice has been given. If there is no appointment the section does not apply (*Morris v Kanssen* (1946)).

(ii) The parties must have acted in good faith. If a party is put on inquiry he may be unable to obtain the benefit of the section.

In *Morris v Kanssen* (1946), Morris was aware that a dispute existed between the parties as to the legality of certain transactions prior to his becoming a 'director' (his appointment was invalid). He made no enquiries as to the allegation that the allotment of shares to him was invalid. It was held that he had not acted in good faith.

A person is not deemed to have acted in good faith if he is aware of the invalid nature of his appointment or has notice of some probable defect in his appointment.

(iii) The act must have taken place before the discovery of the defect.

The section applies both to dealings with outsiders and members.

### British Asbestos Co Ltd v Boyd (1903)

The articles provided that two directors were necessary to form a quorum, and that a director would be disqualified if he held any office of profit in the company. There were 3 directors, B, R, and M. M resigned and B became the company secretary. He was therefore disqualified from holding office. During that time B and R passed a resolution appointing D a director. It was held that D's appointment was valid and that the subsequent acts of B, R and D were validated by the section (then s 67 of the Companies Act 1862) and by an article similar to Article 92.

**Dawson v African Consolidated Land and Trading Co** (1898)

A company made a call, which was resisted by certain shareholders on the grounds that the directors were not de jure directors. One of the directors had, unknown to the other directors, parted with his qualification shares. Six days later he acquired a share qualification and continued to act as a director although technically he had vacated his office. It was held nevertheless that an article (similar to Article 92) validated the irregularities and the call was therefore valid.

Section 382 provides that until the contrary is proved, an appointment of a director at a duly minuted meeting shall be deemed to be valid.

## DIRECTORS' INTERESTS IN SHARES OR DEBENTURES

A director (including a shadow director) and a person who later becomes a director must disclose his holding in a company, in order that the members of the company and other interested parties may determine the degree of control exercised by that person over the company.

A director who is interested in the shares or debentures of the company, or its subsidiary, or its holding company, or a co-subsidiary must, within 5 days, notify the company in writing of his interest. He must specify the number of shares of each class and the amount of debentures of each class of the company and associated companies in which he has an interest. If he is unaware that he has acquired an interest in shares or debentures he must notify the company, in writing, within five days of becoming aware of the fact (s 324(1)).

A director must, within 5 days, notify the company in writing of the occurrence of any of the following:–

(i) If he becomes interested or ceases to be interested in shares and debentures of the company or related company.
(ii) If he enters into a contract to sell such shares or debentures.
(iii) If he assigns a right granted to him by the company to subscribe for shares or debentures of the company.
(iv) If he is granted a right by a related or associated company to subscribe for shares or debentures in that company, or he exercises or assigns such a right (s 324(2)).

The notice must also contain details of the price paid for or received for the shares or debentures.

These provisions also apply to the interests of the spouse and infant children of a director, which are regarded as the interests of the director (s 328).

If the shares or debentures are listed on the Stock Exchange, the company must notify the Stock Exchange of any matter which the director has notified to it in respect of these disclosure provisions and which affects those listed securities (s 329).

A director is deemed to have an interest where:–

1. He has an interest of any kind in shares or debentures, even though the exercise of the rights attached to the interest is subject to restraint or restriction.
2. He is a beneficiary of a trust, and the trust property includes shares or debentures.
3. He enters into a contract to purchase shares, or debentures, or not being the registered holder he is entitled to exercise or control the exercise of any right conferred by the holding of the shares e g the right to vote. (Other than being appointed proxy).
4. Another company is interested in the shares or debentures and
   (i) that company or its directors are accustomed to act in accordance with his instructions or directions; or
   (ii) he is entitled to exercise or control, the exercising of one third or more of the voting power at general meetings of that company. If he is entitled to exercise or control the voting power of a company which in turn can control the voting power of another company, he is deemed to be interested in the shares of that other company.
5. He has the right (other than by having an interest under a trust) to call for delivery of the shares or debentures to himself or to his order, or to acquire an interest in the shares of debentures, or he is under an obligation to take an interest in shares or debentures.
6. He is a joint holder of shares or debentures (s 324, Sch 13).

## REGISTER OF DIRECTORS' INTERESTS

Every company must keep a register of directors interested in the shares or debentures of the company or its related company (s 325(1)).

Whenever a company receives information from a director in respect of his interest under s 324 it is obliged to enter in the register, against the director's name, the information received and the date of the entry (s 325(2)).

Whenever a company grants a director a right to subscribe for shares or debentures of the company it must enter in the register against his name:

(i)　the date of the grant.
(ii)　the period during which, or time at which, it is exercisable.
(iii)　the consideration for the grant.
(iv)　the description of the shares or debentures involved their number or amount, and the price to be paid for them (s 325(3)).

Whenever the right is exercised the company must enter that fact in the register (s 325(4)).

The entries in the register must appear in chronological order. The register must be kept at the company's registered office or where the register of members is kept. It is open to inspection by members free of charge and to other persons on payment of 5p per inspection (Sch 13).

## DEALINGS IN OPTIONS

It is an offence for a director, or the spouse or infant children of a director to deal in options to buy or sell shares or debentures in the company, its holding company, subsidiary company or co-subsidiary, if the shares or debentures are listed on any Stock Exchange. The penalty for this offence is a fine and/or imprisonment for up to two years (s 323).

It is a defence for a person charged with the offence to prove that he had no reason to believe that his spouse or parent was a director of the company (or associated company) in which he was buying the option (s 327).

It is not an offence:–

(i)　to buy a right to subscribe for shares or debentures directly from the company; or
(ii)　to acquire an option to buy the unquoted securities of a public company; or
(iii)　to buy debentures which carry a right to subscribe for a convert into shares; or
(iv)　to acquire an option to purchase the shares or debentures of a private company (s 323).

This prohibition is aimed at preventing a director and his immediate family using inside information to speculate in the shares or debentures of a company with which he is closely associated. It differs from the prohibition on insider dealing, which applies to persons who are in possession of confidential price sensitive information, in that it is unnecessary to prove that a director (or spouse or infant child) who purchases an option was in possession of confidential information relating to the company.

If it appears that a director has been involved in prohibited option dealing, the Department of Trade may appoint an inspector to carry out an investigation and submit a report on the matter to the Department of Trade (s 446).

## PROPERTY TRANSACTIONS

Substantial property transactions involving a director or a person connected with a director are generally prohibited.

There are restrictions on an arrangement whereby:

(1) a director of the company or its holding company, or a person connected with such a director is to acquire one or more non-cash assets from the company (s 320); or
(2) the company acquires one or more non-cash assets of the requisite value from such a director or connected person (s 320);

These restrictions do not apply:–

(a) If the value of the non cash asset does not, at the time of the arrangement, exceed £1,000; or
(b) If more than £1,000 does not exceed in value £50,000 or 10% of the company's assets, whichever is the lower.

(Relevant assets – the value of the company's net assets as disclosed in its latest financial statements. If there are no such financial statements – the amount of the company's called up share capital (s 320).

(c) If the company is a wholly owned subsidiary of any company wherever incorporated (s 321(1)).

These restrictions do not apply if the director received the asset from the company in his capacity as a member or if the arrangement was entered into in the course of a winding up of an insolvent company.

If the value exceeds the specified limits the arrangements must be approved by a resolution of the company in general meeting. If the director is a director of the holding company or the connected person is connected with such a director the arrangement must also be approved by a general meeting of that company.

The arrangement is voidable at the company's option unless

(i) restitution of any money or property is no longer possible or the company has been indemnified by the director or any connected person for any loss or damage suffered by it.

(ii) any rights are acquired bona fide and for value and without actual notice of the contravention by any person who is not a party to the arrangement or transaction would be affected by its avoidance.

(iii) the arrangement is confirmed within a reasonable period, by the company in general meeting. If the arrangement is with a director of its holding company or a person connected with such a director, the arrangement must be confirmed by the holding company by a resolution in general meeting.

The director and any connected person is liable:

(i) to account to the company for any gain made directly or indirectly by the arrangement or transaction, and

(ii) jointly and severally, with any other person liable under this section, to indemnify the company for any loss or damage resulting from the arrangement or transaction (s 322).

Any other director who authorised the arrangement or any transaction entered into in pursuance of the arrangement is also liable. A director is not liable if he shows that he took all reasonable steps to ensure the company complied with this section, or he shows that at the time the arrangement was entered into he did not know the relevant circumstances which constituted the contravention.

## LOANS TO DIRECTORS

1) A company may not make a loan to a director, or to a director of its holding company or enter into any guarantee or provide any security in connection with a loan made by any person to a director of the company, or a director of its holding company (s 330(2)).

2) A relevant company (i e a public company or a company which is a member of a group which includes a public company) may not:
   i) make a quasi-loan to a director or to a director of its holding company.
   ii) make a loan or quasi- loan to a person connected with such a director.
   iii) enter into a guarantee or provide any security in connection with a loan or quasi-loan made by any other person for such a director or connected person (s 330(3)).

3) A relevant company may not enter into a credit transaction as

creditor for a director or a director of its holding company or a connected person, or enter into a guarantee or provide any security to any other person in connection with a credit transaction (s 330(4)).

4) A company may not arrange for the assignment to it of any rights obligations or liabilities which it could not have entered into without contravening (1), (2) or (3) above (s 330(6)).

5) A company may not take part in an arrangement whereby another person enters into a transaction which the company itself could not enter into and that other person obtains some benefit from the company or a related company (s 330(7)).

The following terms are used in connection with loans to directors:

*Quasi-loan*
A transaction under which a third party provides goods or services on credit for the first party and is reimbursed for these goods and services by the second party, which recovers the sum paid from the first party e g a company arranges for a director to use a credit card and pays the credit card company the sums owing. It then recovers those sums from the director.

*Credit transaction*
A transaction under which a *party* (the company) supplies goods or services, or sells, leases, or hires land.

*Connected person*
A person is connected with a director if:

(i) he or she is that director's spouse, child or step-child.
(ii) it is a company in which he and the persons connected with him have an interest in at least one-fifth of the share capital or control more than one fifth of its voting power.
(iii) if he is a trustee of any trust and the beneficiaries include the director, his spouse or a company with which he is associated
(iv) if he is partner in a firm in which the director or any other person connected with him is also a partner.

*Permitted loans*
(1) A relevant company which is a member of a group of companies may make a loan or a quasi-loan to another member of that group, or enter into a guarantee or provide security in connection with a loan or quasi-loan made by any person to

another member of that group in spite of the fact that a director of one member of the group is associated with another (s 333).

(2) A relevant company may make a quasi-loan to one of its directors, or to a director of its holding company if a term of the loan provides that aggregate amount owing does not exceed £1,000 and that the sum will be repaid within 2 months (s 332).

(3) A company may make a loan to a director or a director of its holding company if the aggregate amount owing does not exceed £2,500 (s 334).

(4) A company may enter into any credit transaction or provide security for a credit transaction for a director or a director of its holding company or a connected person if the aggregate amount does not exceed £5,000.

If the amount exceeds £5,000, the transaction will not be prohibited if:

(1) the company enters into the transaction in the ordinary course of business.

(2) the value of the transaction is no greater and the terms on which it is entered into are no more favourable than those offered to a person of similar financial standing (s 335).

(5) A company may make a loan or quasi-loan to its holding company, or enter into a guarantee or provide security in connection with a loan or quasi-loan made by any person to its holding company (s 336).

(6) A company may enter into a credit transaction as creditor for its holding company, or enter into a guarantee or provide security in connection with any credit transaction made by another person for its holding company (s 336).

(7) A company may provide funds to any of its directors:

(a) to meet any expenditure incurred or to be incurred by him for the purposes of the company; or

(b) to meet any expenditure incurred or to be incurred to enable him properly to perform his duties as an officer of the company; or

(c) to enable him to avoid incurring such expenditure.

The following conditions must be satisfied:

(i) The prior approval of the company must be given at a general meeting at which full disclosure of the expenditure is made; or

(ii) if the company's approval is not given at or before the next annual general meeting the loan must be repaid or any other liability arising under transaction must be discharged within six months of that meeting.

(iii) The aggregate of the relevant amounts must not exceed £10,000 (s 337).

(8) A money-lending company may enter into a loan, quasi-loan or a guarantee in connection with a loan or quasi-loan with a director or a director of a holding company if:

the terms and amount of the transaction are no more favourable than those which it is reasonable to expect that company to have offered to a person of similar financial standing, who is unconnected with the company. The aggregate of the relevant amounts must not exceed £50,000, with the exception of loans made by banks (s 338).

(9) A money – lending company or bank may lend a director up to £50,000 for the purchase or improvement of any dwelling house or land, which is the director's only or main residence. The terms of the loan must not be more favourable than those offered to a person of the same financial standing, who is not connected with the company (s 338).


## INSIDER DEALING

It is a criminal offence for an individual to deal in listed securities of a company if he has inside information relating to those securities which, if known, would be likely to affect the price of those securities.

The problems of insider dealing were considered in a government white paper in 1977.

'Insider dealing is understood broadly to cover situations where a person buys or sells securities when he, but not the other party to the transaction, is in possession of confidential information which affects the value to be placed on those securities. Furthermore the confidential information in question will generally be in his possession because of some connection which he has with the company whose securities are to be dealt in (e g, he may be a director, employee or professional adviser of that company) or because someone in such a position has provided him directly or indirectly, with the information. Public confidence in directors and others closely associated with companies requires that such people should not use inside information to further their own interests. Furthermore, if they were to do so, they would frequently be in breach of their obligations to the companies, and could be held to be taking an unfair advantage of the people with whom they were dealing.' (The Conduct of Company Directors Department of Trade White Paper, Cmnd 7037, 1977).

The Company Securities (Insider Dealing) Act 1985 contains a code of rules which prohibit certain aspects of inside dealing.
An individual who:

(a) at any time in the previous six months has been knowingly *connected* with a company (or who obtains information from an individual whom he knows to be so connected); and
(b) *has price sensitive information* which he holds by virtue of being connected with the company which he knows ought not to be disclosed except in the proper performance of the functions related to the company
(c) must not deal in securities of that company on a recognised stock exchange (s 1).

An individual is 'connected' with a company for these purposes only if:

1. He is a director of that company or a related company (ie subsidiary or holding company of the company in question or a company in the group); or
2. (a) He occupies a position as an officer (other than a director) or employee of that company or related company; or
   (b) He occupies a position involving a professional or business relationship between himself and the first company or a related company.

Such a position must reasonably be expected to give him access to unpublished price sensitive information, in relation to the securities of either company, which it would be reasonable to expect a person of his position not to disclose except for the proper performance of his functions (s 9).
Individuals comprised in this group would include the company secretary, the company auditor and its chief accountant.

*Price sensitive information*
Price sensitive information is defined as:–

(a) Information which relates to specific matters of concern (directly or indirectly) to the company in question eg a take-over bid. It does not include information of a general nature.
(b) Information which is not generally known to those persons who are accustomed or would be likely to deal in those securities but which would, if it were generally known to them, be likely to materially affect the price of those securities (s 10).

The general prohibition against insider dealings also applies to the following:

1. An individual who, by virtue of being connected with a company within the previous six months, has obtained unpublished price sensitive information relating to an actual or proposed transaction between that company and a second company (or to the fact that a transaction is no longer contemplated), may not deal in the securities of the second company (s 1(2)).

2. An individual who obtains information (either directly or indirectly) from another individual, who has in the preceding six months been connected with a company and who is in receipt of confidential information, may not deal in the securities of that company if he knows or has reasonable cause to believe that the information is unpublished price sensitive information (s 1(3)).

Neither may he deal in securities of any other company if he knows that such information is unpublished price sensitive information in regard to those securities, and it relates to a proposed transaction (or to the fact that transaction is no longer contemplated) between that company and the company with which he is connected (s 1(4)). No time limit is imposed on the second individual and he is prohibited from dealing until the information is no longer price sensitive or is published.

3. An individual who is contemplating or has contemplated a take-over for a company in a particular capacity (e g as a trustee) may not deal on a recognised stock exchange in securities of that company in another capacity (eg in his personal capacity) if he knows that information that the offer is contemplated or no longer contemplated is unpublished price sensitive information in relation to those securities (s 1(5)).

4. An individual who is for the time being prohibited from dealing on a recognised stock exchange in any securities must not:
   (i) counsel or procure any other person to deal in those securities, knowing or having reasonable cause to believe that that person would deal in them on a recognised stock exchange.
   (ii) communicate any unpublished price sensitive information to any other person if he knows or has reasonable cause to believe that that person or some other person will make use of such information for the purpose of dealing, or counselling or procuring any other person to deal in these securities on a recognised stock exchange (s 1(7)(8)).

5. A Crown servant who holds unpublished price sensitive information in relation to the securities of a particular company which it would be reasonable to expect him not to disclose except for the proper performance of his functions. The restriction also applies to an individual who knowingly obtains information from a Crown servant whom he knows or has reasonable cause to believe holds the information by virtue of his position (s 2(1)).

A Crown servant or an individual obtaining information may not:

(i) deal on recognised stock exchange in securities of the company in question.

(ii) counsel or procure any other individual to deal in any such securities knowing or having reasonable cause to believe that the other would deal in them on a recognised stock exchange.

(iii) communicate to any other individual the information held or obtained, if he knows or has reasonable cause to believe that that individual or some other person will make use of that information for the purpose of dealing, or counselling or procuring any other individual to deal on a recognised stock exchange, in these securities (s 2(3)).

A Crown servant is defined as an individual who holds office under, or is employed by, the Crown. No time limit is laid down in respect of such dealings.

OFF MARKET DEALS

An individual who is prohibited from dealing in the securities of a company or a recognised stock exchange may not circumvent the provisions of the Act by dealing 'off market' ie dealing through an off market dealer who is making a market in advertised securities.

Advertised securities are listed securities or securities in respect of which, not more than 6 months before the transaction in question, information indicating the prices at which persons have dealt or were willing to deal in those securities have been published for the purpose of facilitating deals in these securities (s 4).

Neither may such an individual counsel or procure any other individual to deal in these securities; or

Communicate that information to any other individual whom he knows or has reasonable cause to believe will deal in those securities; or

Communicate the information to any other individual who he

knows or has reasonable cause to believe would use it to counsel or procure other individuals to deal in these securities.

EXEMPTIONS

The prohibitions on insider dealing do not apply to the following:

(a) An individual who deals in securities other than with a view to the making of a profit or the avoidance of a loss, whether for himself or for another person e g where a person sells to meet a pressing debt.
(b) A liquidator, receiver or trustee in bankruptcy who enters into a transaction in good faith.
(c) A jobber who obtains information, in good faith, in the ordinary course of his business (A jobber is defined as an individual, partnership or company dealing in securities on a recognised stock exchange.)
(d) An individual who has information relating to a particular transaction. He is not prohibited from doing anything necessary to facilitate the completion or carrying out the transaction.
(e) A trustee or personal representative in any deal if advised to do so by an appropriate adviser who does not appear to be prohibited from dealing.
(f) An individual who is an issue manager may deal in connection with an international bond issue. (As may an officer, employer or agent of such an issue manager) (s 3 and 6).

GENERAL

1. The prohibition on insider dealing applies to individuals, not to companies.
2. The sanctions imposed for insider dealing are criminal, i e a fine and/or imprisonment for up to two years.
3. Any transaction which contravenes the provisions of the Act is not invalid i e it is neither void nor voidable.
4. The prohibition applies primarily to dealings in securities listed on a recognised stock exchange. (It does not apply to dealings in securities of a private company).
5. The prohibition applies to dealings in securities through an investment exchange.
   An investment exchange is an organisation maintaining a system where an offer to deal in securities made by a subscriber to the organisation is communicated without his identity being

revealed, to other subscribers to the organisation, and where any acceptance of that offer by any of those other subscribers is recorded and confirmed.

6. The provisions relating to insider dealing also apply to dealings on foreign stock exchanges. An individual who is precluded from dealing on a recognised stock exchange in Britain is also precluded from dealing in the securities of British and foreign companies on a foreign stock exchange (s 5).

# Chapter 13

# The company secretary

Every company must have a secretary, but a sole director may not also act as secretary. A company may not have as secretary a corporation the sole director of which is a sole director of the company, or have as sole director a corporation the sole director of which is secretary to the company (s 283).

A provision which requires or authorises a thing to be done by or to a director and the secretary cannot be satisfied by its being done by or to the same person acting in both capacities (s 284). A company may have joint secretaries (s 290(2)).

If the office of secretary is vacant or there is no secretary capable of acting, the functions of a secretary may be carried out by an assistant or deputy secretary. If there is no assistant or deputy secretary capable of exercising these functions, the directors may authorise an officer of the company to act in that capacity (s 283).

Every company must keep at its registered office a register of its directors and secretaries. The register must contain the following information in respect of the company secretary (or secretaries):–

if an individual, his name and address;
if a company or a Scottish firm, its corporate or firm name and its registered or principal office.

Any change in the person of the secretary must be notified to the Registrar within 14 days and must be accompanied by the signed consent of the person newly appointed (s 288(2)).

The secretary is usually appointed by the directors and his powers and salary are usually fixed by a written agreement. Otherwise they are provided for in the terms of the resolution appointing him and by the articles. Article 99 provides that:

'Subject to the provisions of the Acts, the secretary shall be appointed by the directors for such term, at such remuneration and upon such conditions as they may think fit; and any secretary so appointed may be removed by them.

Section 10 provides that a statement of the first director(s) and secretary of the company must be delivered to the Registrar on the company's application for registration. The statement must also contain a consent signed by the directors and secretary.

Section 286 imposes a duty on the directors of a public company to take all reasonable steps to secure that the secretary of the company is a person who appears to have the requisite knowledge and experience to discharge the functions of secretary. He must therefore be a person who:

(a) On the 22nd December 1980 held the office of secretary or assistant or deputy secretary of the company; or
(b) For at least three of the five years immediately preceding his appointment as secretary held the office of secretary of a company other than a private company; or
(c) Is a member of one of the following bodies: The Institute of Chartered Accountants in England and Wales; The Institute of Chartered Accountants of Scotland; The Association of Certified Accountants; The Institute of Chartered Accountants in Ireland; The Institute of Cost and Management Accountants; The Chartered Institute of Public Finance and Accountancy; or
(d) Is a barrister, advocate or solicitor called or admitted in any part of the United Kingdom; or
(e) Is a person who, by virtue of his holding or having held any other position or his being a member of any other body, appears to the directors to be capable of discharging those functions.

Although the Act does not define the general duties of a secretary it nevertheless imposes certain duties upon the company secretary:–

(i) In winding up by the court, the secretary must verify the statement of the company's affairs, submitted to the Official Receiver (s 528).
(ii) On the appointment of a receiver by the debenture holders, to verify the statement of the company's affairs, submitted to the receiver (s 496).
(iii) To sign the annual return (s 363).
(iv) To sign the form on a limited company's application to re-register as unlimited or on an unlimited company's application to re-register as limited (ss 49, 51).

In the ordinary course of events a company secretary's duties may include:–

Conducting the company's correspondence, especially with the shareholders on such matters as transfers, calls, forfeiture, dividends etc.

Attending board meetings and general meetings and taking proper minutes of those proceedings.

Maintaining the company's registers and books.

Making the necessary returns to the Registrar.

Being conversant with the requirements of the law relating to companies and seeing that they are observed.

Being conversant with the requirements of The Stock Exchange if the company's shares are listed.

A secretary's power and authority within a company is a matter of internal management and will vary according to the nature of the company's business and the size of the company.

A company secretary, by virtue of his position, is the chief administrative officer of a company. He is generally authorised by the board to enter into contracts of an administrative nature on behalf of the company e g the employment of staff, ordering office machinery and stationery, hiring of cars etc.

It was stated by Lord Denning MR in *Panorama Developments (Guildford) Ltd v Fidelis Furnishing Fabrics Ltd* (1971) that the company secretary

'. . . is an officer of the company with extensive duties and responsibilities. This appears not only in the modern Companies Act, but also by the role he plays in the day-to-day business of companies. . . . He regularly makes representations on behalf of the company and enters into contracts on its behalf which come within the day-to-day running of the company's business. So much so that he may be regarded as held out as having authority to do such things on behalf of the company. He is certainly entitled to sign contracts connected with the administrative side of a company's affairs, such as employing staff and ordering cars, and so forth. All such matters now come within the ostensible authority of a company secretary.'

Salmon LJ in the same case stated,

'I think there can be no doubt that the secretary is the chief administrative officer of the company. So far as matters concerned with administration, in my judgment, the secretary has ostensible authority to sign contracts on behalf of the company.'

## Panorama Developments (Guildford) Ltd v Fidelis Furnishing Fabrics Ltd (1971)

Bayne, the secretary of Fidelis Ltd ordered self drive cars from Panorama Developments representing that they were for use in the company's business i e driving customers from the airport to the company's factory at Leeds. This was untrue for no customers were met and the company did not have a factory at Leeds. The cars were ordered on specific dates by letter on Fidelis letterhead and were signed by Bayne as company secretary. It was held that as Bayne had ostensible authority to enter into contracts for the hire of the cars on the company's behalf, Fidelis Ltd were liable.

He may be given express authority to perform certain acts or enter into contracts or types of contract on behalf of the company. Such acts will bind the company.

He may be given implied authority to enter into contracts. As an agent he binds his principal (the company) in certain circumstances, e g following a course of dealing with a third party.

LIMITATIONS

There are limitations on a company secretary's authority and he may not:

1. *Borrow money on the company's behalf*

### Re Cleadon Trust Ltd (1939)

A director advanced a loan of £17,000 to a company at the request of the company secretary. The loan was confirmed at a board meeting at which the director concerned and another were present. The articles stipulated that two directors were a quorum, but that a director could not vote in respect of a contract in which he was interested. It was held that the company was not bound to repay the money as the secretary did not have the power to borrow on the company's behalf and the loan was not made or confirmed at a properly constituted meeting.

2. *Register a transfer of shares on behalf of the directors*

### Chida Mines Ltd v Anderson (1905)

A transfer of shares was lodged with the company secretary, who entered the transferee's name in the register. The directors refused to sanction the transfer and the transferee's name was removed from the register. It was held that as the transferor remained the registered holder of the shares, he was liable for calls on the shares.

3. *Alter the register without the approval of the board.*

### Re Indo-China Steam Navigation Co (1917)

The company secretary amended a share register, on discovering certain correspondence, by restoring the name of the former owner of the shares to the register. It was held that the alteration was a nullity.

4. *Summon a meeting without the board's authority.*

### Re State of Wyoming Syndicate (1901)

A company secretary, without the board's authority, summoned a meeting at which an extraordinary resolution to wind up the company voluntarily was passed. It was held that the resolution was invalid, as the meeting was improperly convened and that an order be made for the compulsory winding up of the company.

5. *Issue a notice without the board's authority.*

### Re Haycraft Gold Reduction and Mining Co (1900)

A company secretary issued notices summoning a meeting to press resolutions for the voluntary winding up of the company. It was held that as the notices had been issued without the authority of a board resolution, the subsequent extraordinary resolution to wind up the company was void.

6. *Issue writs in the company's name.*

### Daimler Co Ltd v Continental Tyre and Rubber Co Ltd (1916)

The majority shareholding in an English company was held by a German company. One share was held by the company secretary who was resident in England. He commenced an action on behalf of the company against the defendant company, who alleged that he did not have the authority to instigate proceedings. It was held that the action should be struck out as the secretary lacked such authority.

7. *Bind the company by contract.*

### Houghton and Co v Nothard, Lowe and Wills Ltd (1928)

A director of NLW Ltd, without the authority of the board, entered into a contract with H. The secretary of the company, by letter, purported to confirm the contract. It was held that as authority to make the contract had not been delegated by the board to the director and the secretary, they had no power to bind the company which was not liable on the contract.

A company secretary will usually be given the task of issuing share certificates and the company will be bound if he issues a share certificate without the authority of the board.

However if he has no express or implied authority to issue a share certificate he may incur personal liability for such an action.

### Bishop v Balkis Consolidated Co Ltd (1890)

A company secretary exceeded his authority and issued a share certificate which was relied upon by the transferee. It was held that the company was not liable and the secretary could be sued in his personal capacity as he had acted outside the scope of his authority.

A company will not incur liability if a secretary issues a forged certificate (*Ruben v Great Fingall Consolidated* (1906) (see p 136)).

Neither will a company be bound by a fraudulent representation on the secretary's part which induces a person to take shares in a company.

### Barnet, Hoares and Co v The South London Tramways (1887)

The secretary of a company, in answer to an inquiry represented that a sum of money retained by the company was payable after certain work had been completed. This statement was untrue and as the secretary had no authority to make such a representation, it was held that the company was not liable.

A company secretary is an officer of the company (s 735) and therefore any provision in the articles or in any contract exempting him from, or indemnifying him against, any liability is void (s 310). He may however be relieved from liability by the court, in certain circumstances (s 727).

In *Re Maidstone Buildings Provisions Ltd* (1971) it was held that a company secretary was not liable for fraudulent trading (s 630). His failure to advise the directors that the company was insolvent and should therefore cease trading was an omission and he could not therefore be held to be a party to carrying on the company's business.

'. . . a secretary, while merely performing the duties appropriate to the office of secretary, is not concerned in carrying on the business of the company.' (Pennycuick V-C in *Re Maidstone Buildings Provisions Ltd* (1971))

As an officer of the company he may be liable for certain offences committed in the course of a winding up e g

the fabrication of any books, papers or securities (s 627);
knowingly and wilfully making a material false statement in the balance sheet, reports, returns etc;
failure to keep proper accounting records (s 223).

A secretary, who is an employee, is entitled to the minimum period of notice of dismissal as set out in the Employment Protection (Consolidation) Act 1978. Certain events operate as a dismissal of the secretary e g

an order for the compulsory winding up of the company;
the appointment of a receiver and manager in a debenture holders action;
a voluntary winding up due to the company's insolvency.

# Chapter 14

# Majority rule, minority protection and investigations

Every member of a company is contractually bound by the articles to the company and to his fellow members. A member agrees to be bound by the decisions of the majority as expressed at a general meeting. He may express his wishes by voting for or against resolutions proposed at general meeting. If a resolution, to which he is opposed, is passed by the appropriate majority he is nevertheless bound ie the principle of majority rule.

## THE RULE IN FOSS v HARBOTTLE

The principle of majority rule was established in the case of *Foss v Harbottle* (1843) which provides that

(i)  the proper plaintiff in an action in respect of a wrong alleged to be done to a company is the company itself;
(ii) where the alleged wrong is a transaction which might be made binding on the company and on all its members by a simple majority of the members, no individual member is allowed to maintain an action in respect of that matter.

### Foss v Harbottle (1843)

Foss and others formed the Victoria Park Company which was to lay out various ornamental parks in Manchester. They became directors of the company and it was alleged that they:
(i)  procured the company to purchase land from themselves at an inflated price;
(ii) raised money by the company entering into a transaction to mortgage the land, which was ultra vires the powers in the Act of Incorporation. It was held that the first transaction was voidable

and could be ratified by the company in general meeting, while the second transaction was clearly outside the company's powers.

The following propositions were laid down in *Foss v Harbottle*.

(a) The company as a legal person is the proper plaintiff in proceedings.
(b) The rule does not apply to proceedings between shareholders concerning their rights among themselves.
(c) The rule is subject to exceptions.
(d) The rule applies, without exception, in cases where the general meeting has the power to and does permit the company to do the acts complained of.
(e) An individual shareholder can proceed on the company's behalf if the general meeting does not have power, or the general meeting cannot be effectively set in motion.

The reasons for the existence of the rule are:

(a) The right of the majority to determine how the company's affairs should be conducted.
(b) As the company is a legal person it is the company which has the right to bring an action, as it alone has suffered the injury.
(c) To prevent a multiplicity of actions, as otherwise each individual member might bring an action on similar grounds.
(d) It would be pointless commencing proceedings if the court order could be overruled by a majority who passed the appropriate resolution at a subsequent general meeting.

'If the thing complained of is a thing which in substance the majority of the company are entitled to do, or if something has been done irregularly which the majority of the company are entitled to do regularly, or if something has been done illegally which the majority of the company are entitled to do legally, there can be no use in having a litigation about it, the ultimate end of which is only that a meeting has to be called, and then ultimately the majority gets its wishes'. (per Mellish LJ in *MacDougall v Gardiner* (1875)).

EXCEPTIONS TO THE RULE

There are certain exceptions to the rule in *Foss v Harbottle* and the majority cannot confirm:

(a) An act which is ultra vires the company or illegal.
(b) An act which is a fraud on the minority and the wrong doers are in control of the company.
(c) A resolution passed by means of a trick.

(a) *An act which is ultra vires the company or illegal*
*In Parke v Daily News* (1962) a shareholder obtained a declaration that an ultra vires gift (i e compensation to redundant employees) could not be made from the assets of the company.

(b) *An act which is a fraud on the minority and the wrongdoers are in control of the company*
The majority, therefore would not allow an action to be brought in the company's name, and the minority would be unable to bring a minority shareholders action.

(i) The interests of justice dictate that the court will prevent the wrongdoers using their power to frustrate the minority from protecting themselves.

**Cook v Deeks** (1916)

A company's directors, who held 75 per cent of the company's share capital entered into a contract on their own behalf while ostensibly negotiating on the company's behalf. They subsequently passed a resolution declaring that the company had no interest in the contract. It was held that the benefit of the contract belonged to the company.

**Menier v Hooper's Telegraph Works** (1874)

The European and South American Telegraph Co was formed to lay a transatlantic cable from Portugal to Brazil. The cable was to be made by Hooper, a majority shareholder in the company. Hooper found that they could make a greater profit by selling the cable to another company, which did not have the concession to lay the cable. After much intrigue the Portuguese Government, trustee of the concession, agreed to transfer the concession to the other company which then bought the cable from Hooper. To prevent the first company from suing for loss of the concession, Hooper obtained the passing of a resolution to wind up the first company. A minority shareholder asked the court to compel Hooper to account to the first company for profits made on the sale of the cable to the second company.

It was held that this was a case of fraud and Hooper had to account to the first company for the profit.

(ii) A resolution constitutes a fraud on the minority if it is not passed for the benefit of the company as a whole i e for the benefit of the individual hypothetical member; or
it discriminates between the majority and minority shareholders so as to give the majority an advantage denied by the minority.

(iii) Questions relating to a 'fraud on the minority' have occurred in cases where companies have sought to alter their articles to compel the minority shareholders, at the request of the majority, to sell their shareholders to nominees of the majority ie the expropriation cases.

**Sidebottom v Kershaw, Leese & Co Ltd** (1920) (see p 63)

(iv) The controlling members are subject to equitable considerations and must not exercise their powers in a way that is unfair to a minority shareholder (*Clemens v Clemens Bros* (1976)).

(v) If the wrong alleged to be done to the company was negligent and not fraudulent in character an action will not lie under the rule in *Foss v Harbottle* (1843).

**Pavlides v Jensen** (1956)

A minority shareholder claimed that the directors of a company were negligent and in breach of their duty for selling a mine for £182,000 which was worth £1,000,000. It was held that the action was not maintainable as the sale was ultra vires, fraud was not alleged and the sale could be approved by a majority of the shareholders.

(vi) Recent cases have considerably widened the concept of fraud.

**Daniels v Daniels** (1978)

Three minority shareholders in Ideal Homes (Coventry) Ltd brought an action against the majority shareholders (who were also the directors) and the company alleging that the company had on the instructions of the majority shareholders sold land to one of the directors for £4,250, a figure well below its true value. The land was sold by the director some four years later for £120,000. It was held that the minority could bring an action for fraud. Although the transaction was not fraudulent in character, the directors use of their power was a fraud on the minority.

> 'If the minority shareholders can sue if there is fraud, I see no reason why they cannot sue where the action of the majority and the directors, though without fraud, confers some benefit on those directors and majority shareholders themselves'. (per *Templeman J*).

> The judge also distinguished the case from *Pavlides v Jensen* (1956) (where negligence was alleged) as the alleged negligence had resulted in a profit to one of the directors.

**Estmanco (Kilner House) Ltd v Greater London Council** (1982)

A minority shareholder brought an action on behalf of the plaintiff company to enforce a contract for the sale of a council flat belonging to the GLC, where the GLC (the only voting shareholder) had procured the company to seek to withdraw the action, following a change in political control. The plaintiff company had been formed for the management of the flats and for the purpose of facilitating the sale of the flats. It was held that the GLC would not be allowed to use its voting power to frustrate the purposes of the company, and that the rule in *Foss v Harbottle* did not apply as the GLC's behaviour constituted a fraud on the individual shareholder.

(vii) It must also be shown that those who appropriated the company's property are in effective control of the company.

### Prudential Assurance Co v Newman Industries (No 2) (1981 and 1982)

Two directors were the chairman and vice chairman of three companies. One company was in severe financial difficulty and the directors conceived a scheme whereby it would sell its assets to another of the companies (Newman Industries). The assets were over-valued and based on misleading information supplied by the two directors. Further 'tricky and misleading' information was included in a circular issued to shareholders who subsequently approved the transaction.

The Prudential Assurance Company, who held a 3.2% interest in Newman Industries, successfully brought a derivative action on its own behalf and on behalf of the other shareholders claiming damages from the two directors, as they had effective control of the company.

### (c) *A resolution passed by means of a trick*
A minority can prevent a company from taking advantage of a resolution passed by means of a trick

### Baillie v Oriental Telephone and Electric Co (1915) (see p 172)

### Kaye v Croydon Tramways (1898) (see p 173)

The rule in *Foss v Harbottle* (1843) cannot be invoked to over-ride the requirements of the Companies Acts or a company's articles that a special procedure be followed eg special or extraordinary resolutions. A company must therefore observe these procedures and a resolution passed by a simple majority would be ineffective in these circumstances.

A procedural irregularity in convening a meeting may not be sufficient to invalidate a resolution passed at a meeting.

### Bentley-Stevens v Jones (1974)

A director complained that he had been removed from office by a resolution of a general meeting which had been irregularly convened. The general meeting had been convened by two of the company's four directors, but not at a properly convened board meeting. In all other respects, the correct procedure had been followed i e the meeting had been properly convened and the resolution for his dismissal properly passed. It was held that the court could not intervene as the irregularities of the board meeting could be waived by the members in general meeting.

## ACTION BY SHAREHOLDERS

There are three forms of action which may be brought by shareholders:

(a) Personal action
(b) Representative action
(c) Derivative action

### (a) PERSONAL ACTION

This is an action brought by a shareholder in his own name to enforce a personal claim.

In *Pender v Lushington* (1877) a member sued the company as he had been denied the right to vote.

In *Wood v Odessa Waterworks* (1889) a member sued the company for the payment of a dividend in cash.

### (b) REPRESENTATIVE ACTION

This is an action brought by a shareholder on behalf of himself and all the other shareholders to enforce their collective rights and may be used where the shareholder seeks to enforce rights common to all shareholders or to that class which he represents.

It is permitted only where 'numerous persons have the same interest in any proceedings'. A shareholder may combine this form of action with a personal action if he can show that he has suffered actual loss.

### (c) DERIVATIVE ACTION

This is an action brought by a shareholder in his own name and in the names of the other shareholders on behalf of the company to enforce its right to recover its property. The company must be joined as a nominal defendent to the action and the directors are usually defendants. Judgement may therefore be given in the company's favour and it will be bound by the court's decision.

The form of the action (usually under RSC Ord 15, r 12) is;

> 'AB (a minority shareholder) on behalf of himself and all the other shareholders of the company against the wrongdoing directors and the company'. (per Lord Denning MR in *Wallersteiner v Moir (No 2)* (1975) ).

In deciding whether to allow a derivative action the court will usually have to decide whether the defendants' part in the transaction was such that they prevented the company, and/or the general meeting from taking a proper commercial decision which was bona fide in the company's interests. If the court decides that the defendants action were such, it will either:

(i) refer the matter back to the company in general meeting, with an interim injunction being granted to the plaintiff in the meanwhile; or

(ii) it will allow the action to proceed to judgment if the general meeting is unlikely to be free of improper pressure.

The minority shareholders may seek a declaration of rights under RSC Order 15 rule 16 to determine whether they may maintain an action against the majority.

The conduct of a minority shareholder may be examined to see if such a person is a proper person to bring an action on behalf of the company (*Nurcombe v Nurcombe* (1985) ).

The greatest obstacle in a minority shareholder's action is that of the cost involved, especially in cases dealing with the enforcement of corporate membership rights, as any money recovered will be paid to the company and not to the shareholder.

## Wallersteiner v Moir (No 2) (1975)

A shareholder took a series of actions against the controlling director of a group of companies for the misapplication of the company's money. The litigation dragged on for ten years, and although the shareholder obtained judgement he had exhausted his own and other shareholders finances. It was held that it was open to the court in a minority shareholder's action to order the company to indemnify a shareholder, whether or not the action is successful. The test is whether it is reasonable and in the company's interest for the shareholder to bring the action and whether it is brought by him in a good faith.

RATIFICATION

A wrongful act by directors may be ratified by the shareholders in general meeting if the act is not illegal, ultra vires or a fraud on the minority. The most recent cases heard by the courts have been concerned with the bonafide issue of shares by directors to prevent control of the company passing to an unwanted third party (*Hogg v Cramphorn* (1967); *Bamford v Bamford* (1970) (see p 211)).

## STATUTORY PROTECTION OF THE MINORITY

### RELIEF WHERE MEMBERS ARE UNFAIRLY PREJUDICED

A minority shareholder may always petition the court to wind up a company on the grounds that it is just and equitable that the company should be wound up. (ss 517, 519). It is often not in the shareholder's interest to take such a drastic step and an alternative remedy is provided under s 459.

Any member may petition the court for an order under s 459 on the grounds that either:

(a)  the affairs of the company are being or have been conducted in a manner which is unfairly prejudicial to the interest of some part of the members (including at least himself); or
(b)  any actual or proposed act or omission of the company (including an act or omission on its behalf) is or would be so prejudicial (s 459(1)).

The section applies to a person who is not a member of a company but to whom shares in the company have been transferred or transmitted by operation or law e g personal representatives, trustees in bankruptcy (s 459(2)).

A member may petition on the basis of a single act. It is no longer necessary to show a course of oppressive conduct.

Under previous legislation relief could only be claimed by a minority in respect of oppressive conduct. This was very much narrower in scope than a petition under s 459.

In only two reported cases between 1948 and 1980 were the petitioners successful in obtaining an order for relief in respect of oppressive conduct. The two cases in question were *Scottish Co-operative Wholesale Society Ltd v Meyer* (1959) and *Re Harmer Ltd* (1958).

### Scottish Co-operative Wholesale Society Ltd v Meyer (1959)

Meyers and the Scottish CWS entered into a joint venture and formed a subsidiary company to manufacture cloth and rayon. The Scottish CWS appointed three directors and held 4000 in £1 shares, while Meyer and his associates held 3900 £1 shares and appointed two directors. The Scottish CWS used its control of the company to run down the subsidiary, so that it could expand its own operations. The shares which were valued at one time at £6 became almost worthless. The minority petitioned the court, which held that the Scottish CWS must purchase their shares at a price related to their value before the Scottish CWS began to run down the company ie £3.75 per share.

### Re Harmer Ltd (1958)

Harmer, the founder of a philatelic business and his wife owned all the company's voting shares, although he had given his sons the majority of the company's non voting shares.

Harmer was the chairman of the board of directors and his two sons were the other directors. He consistently ignored the views of the directors and took several disastrous policy decisions on his own. The sons petitioned the court for relief. It was held that Harmer should be given the title of 'president' of the company and should not interfere in the company's affairs, except in accordance with the board's decisions.

The conduct complained of may be past, present or future conduct and must be unfairly prejudicial.

'Unfairly prejudicial' has not been judicially defined although it was considered by the Jenkins Committee to be:

> 'a visible departure from the standards of fair dealing and a violation of the conditions of fair play on which every shareholder who entrusts his money to a company is entitled to rely'.

It must therefore damage a member's interests and may also be discriminatory and/or unreasonable.

### Re Jermyn Street Turkish Baths Ltd (1971)

In 1954 P was the only living shareholder in the company which was in a poor financial condition. The remaining shares were held by the estate of L, who declined to inject further capital in the company. P over a period of years restored the company's financial stability and allotted additional equity shares to herself. She took the available profits as commission on the terms of a long standing directors resolution, so that no dividends were paid.

It was held that her conduct, as the company's dominant shareholder, was not oppressive, burdensome, harsh or wrongful to the other members of the company.

In *Re A Company (No 004475 of 1982)* (1983) it was argued that conduct could only be unfairly prejudicial if it resulted in affecting the value of a petitioner's shareholding.

**Re A Company (No 004475 of 1982)** (1983)

A minority shareholding in a private company passed on intestacy to two infant children. The shareholding represented the only assets available for their maintenance. The directors of the company proposed to establish a new business. The executors sought to sell the shares, but failed to reach agreement with the company on the value of the shares. The company's valuation of £112,000 was based on an open market valuation, while the executors valued the shares at £175,000. The executors sought to pressurise the company into purchasing the shares or formulating a scheme of reconstruction. When the company refused the executors sought relief under s 75 of the Companies Act 1980 (now s 459). It was held that an order would not be made as a shareholder needed to show an act or omission on the part which unfairly prejudiced him as a member, and this was not so in this case.

The section was not designed

> 'to enable a locked in minority shareholder to require the company to buy him out at a price which he considered adequately to reflect the value of the underlying assets referable to his shareholding' (per Lord Grant Chester).

If the court is satisfied that the petition is well founded it may make such an order as it thinks fit, for giving relief to the matters complained of.

In particular the court may make an order:

(a) regulating the conduct of the company's affairs in the future;
(b) requiring the company to refrain from doing or continuing an act or rectifying an omission;
(c) authorising civil proceedings to be brought in the company's name and on behalf of the company by such person or persons and on such terms as the court may direct;
(d) providing for the purchase of the shares of any members of the company by other members or by the company itself and, if appropriate, any consequent reduction in company's capital;
(e) an alteration in the company's memorandum or articles made under this section will be of the same effect as if made by a resolution of the company.

**Re Garage Door Associates Ltd** (1984)

A company was incorporated in 1976 with an authorised capital of £1000 divided into 1000 £1 shares. Of the 801 shares issued, B held 499 shares, his wife 300 shares and the petitioner one share. The petitioner sought a winding up order, and an alternative order under s 75 of the Companies Act 1980 (now s 459) setting aside the allotment of 799 shares as he alleged that the company was a joint venture between B and the petitioner. The petitioner, who was formerly a director, also sought an order that B and his wife should purchase the petitioner's shares.

It was held that the petition seeking relief under the Companies Act 1980, s 75 (now s 459) should be heard by the court to determine the question of the ownership of the shares. If appropriate the petitioner as a contributory could prosecute a winding up order.

## DEPARTMENT OF TRADE AND INDUSTRY INVESTIGATIONS

The Department of Trade and Industry is given powers to conduct various investigations and inspections.

### INVESTIGATION INTO A COMPANY'S AFFAIRS

(1) The Department of Trade and Industry *may* appoint an inspector or inspectors to investigate a company affairs and report on them:

(a) in the case of a company having a share capital, on the application of not less than 200 members or of members holding not less than one tenth of the shares issued.
(b) in the case of a company not having a share capital, on the application of not less than one fifth of the persons on the company's register of member.
(c) on the application of the company.

The application must be supported by evidence showing that the applicants have good reason for requiring the investigation. The Department of Trade and Industry may, before appointing an inspector, require the applicant to give securely to an amount not exceeding £5,000 for the payment of the costs of the investigation (s 431).

(2) The Department of Trade and Industry *must* appoint an inspector or inspectors to investigate a company's affairs and report on them if the court by order declares that its affairs ought to be investigated by an inspector appointed by the Department (s 432(1)).

(3) The Department of Trade and Industry may, at its own discretion, appoint inspectors to investigate a company's affairs if it appears that there are circumstances suggesting that:–

(i) a company's affairs are being or have been conducted with intent to defraud its creditors or the creditors of any other person or otherwise for a fraudulent or unlawful purpose or in a manner which is unfairly prejudicial to some part of its members, or that any actual or proposed act or omission of the company is or would be so prejudicial, or that it was formed for a fraudulent or unlawful purpose; or

(ii) the promoters or persons managing its affairs have been guilty of fraud, misfeasance or other misconduct towards the company or its members; or

(iii) the members have not been given all the information with respect to its affairs which they might reasonably expect (s 432(2)).

POWERS OF INSPECTORS

(1) An inspector may, if he thinks it necessary, investigate the affairs of any other company which is or has at any time been the company's subsidiary, or holding company, or a subsidiary of its holding company, or a holding company of its subsidiary (s 433).

(2) (i) He may call for the production of books and documents relating to the company from past and present officers of the company and agents e g auditors, bankers, solicitors. Such persons are under a duty to give the inspectors all reasonable assistance in connection with the investigation.

(ii) If the inspector considers that any other person is in possession of any information relating to the company's affairs he may require that person to produce any books or papers in his possession, to attend before him, and otherwise assist him with his inquiries (s 434).

(3) He may examine on oath the officers and agents of the company and any other company involved in relation to the company business. He may also examine on oath any other person mentioned in 2(ii) (s 434).

(4) If an officer or agent of the company or other company, or any person mentioned in 2(i) refuses to produce any book or document or refuses to answer any question relating to the affairs of the company or other company, the inspector may certify their refusal to the court. The court may then inquire into the case and may punish the person concerned as if he had been guilty of contempt of court (s 436).

(5) If an inspector has reasonable grounds for believing that a director or past director has maintained a bank account, whether in Great Britain or elsewhere into or out of which has been paid his undisclosed emoluments; or money used in financing any transaction which ought to have been disclosed; or used in any way as part of the misconduct (whether fraudulent or not) of that director, the inspector may require the director to produce all the documents in his possession or under his control relating to that bank account (s 435).

INSPECTOR'S REPORT

(1) The inspectors may and, if directed by the Department of Trade must, make interim reports, and on conclusion of the investigation must make a final report to the Department of Trade and Industry.
(2) The Secretary of State may if he thinks fit:

   (a) forward a copy of the inspector's report to the company's registered office;
   (b) furnish a copy on request and on payment of the appropriate fee to;
      (i) any member of the company or other company dealt with in the report,
      (ii) any person whose conduct is referred to in the report,
      (iii) the company's auditors,
      (iv) the applicants for the investigation,
      (v) any other person whose financial interests appear to be affected by matters dealt with in the report e g creditors.

   A copy of the report must be furnished to the court when the appointment was made under s 432 (in pursuance of a court order) (s 437).
(3) The expenses of the investigation must be defrayed in the first instance by the Department of Trade and Industry, but the following are liable to repay the Department:
   (i) any person convicted on a prosecution instituted as a result of the investigation,
   (ii) any company in whose name proceedings are brought is liable to the amount or value of any sums or property recovered by it as a result of the proceedings,
   (iii) any company dealt with by the report, where the inspector

was appointed other than by the Department's own motion, is liable except so far as the Department otherwise directs (except where the company was the applicant for the investigation),

(iv) the applicant for the investigation, where the inspector was appointed under s 431, is liable to such an extent (if any) as the Department may direct (s 439).

(4) A copy of any report of any inspector appointed under ss 431 or 432 of the Act is admissible in any legal proceedings as evidence of the opinion of the inspector in relation to any matter contained in the report (s 441).

INVESTIGATION OF THE OWNERSHIP OF A COMPANY

Where it appears to the Department of Trade and Industry that there is good reason to do so, they may appoint one or more inspectors to investigate and report on the company's membership to determine the identity of the persons who are, or have been financially interested in the company's success or failure, or able to control and materially influence its policy (s 442).

The inspector's appointment may define the scope of his investigation and may limit it to certain shares or debentures.

The Department of Trade and Industry must appoint inspectors if an application is made by members as in s 431 (Investigation of a company's affairs), unless it considers the request vexatious. The appointment must not exclude from the scope of the investigation any matter which the applicant seeks to include, unless the Department are satisfied that it is unreasonable for that matter to be investigated.

The inspector has power (subject to the terms of his appointment) to investigate any circumstances which suggest the existence of an arrangement or understanding which, not legally binding, is being or is likely be observed in practice and which is relevant to this investigation (s 442).

The general powers of the inspector are similar to those relating to an investigation under ss 433 and 435, i e the power to investigate the bank accounts of past and present directors.

An inspector may require all persons who are, or have been, or whom the inspector has reasonable cause to believe to be or have been financially interested in the success or failure of the company or related company, or able to control or materially influence the policy of the company or related company to produce documents and furnish information relevant to the investigation.

If the Secretary of State is of the opinion that there is a good reason for not divulging part of a report under this section he may deposit a complete or incomplete report with the Registrar.

## POWER TO REQUIRE INFORMATION AS TO PERSONS INTERESTED IN SHARES OR DEBENTURES

The Act gives the Department of Trade power to obtain information in circumstances where although it appears to the Department that there is a good reason to investigate the ownership of a company's shares or debentures, there is no need to appoint an inspector for this purpose.

The Department of Trade may therefore require any person whom they have reasonable cause to believe to have or to be able to obtain information as to the present and past interests in those shares or debentures, and the names and addresses of the persons interested and of any persons who act or have acted on their behalf in relation to the shares or debentures to give any such information to the Secretary of State. Any person who fails to give the required information or who makes a statement which he knows to be false in a material particular, or who recklessly makes a statement false in a material particular is liable to imprisonment and/or a fine (s 444).

## POWER TO IMPOSE RESTRICTIONS ON SHARES OR DEBENTURES

Where there has been an investigation under ss 442 or 444 and it appears to the Department of Trade and Industry that there is difficulty in finding out the relevant facts about any shares (issued or to be issued) the Department may by order direct that the shares shall, until further notice, be subject to the following restrictions.

  (i) Any transfer or issue of the shares is void.
 (ii) Voting rights may not be exercised in respect of the shares.
(iii) No rights issue may be made in respect of the shares.
(iv) Except in a liquidation no payment shall be made of any sums due from the company on the shares e g a dividend where shares are subject to the above restrictions, any agreement to transfer the shares or issue shares (in the case of unissued shares) (s 454).

Any person aggrieved by such an order may appeal to the court for the order to be lifted. The court may only remove the restrictions if:

(i) the court or the Secretary of State is satisfied that the relevant facts
have been disclosed and that no unfair advantage has accrued to
any person as a result of the earlier failure to make that disclosure;
or

(ii) the shares are to be sold and the court or the Secretary of State
approves the sale (s 456).

Where an order has been made by the Secretary of State, the
company may apply to the court for a further order relating to the sale
or to the transfer of shares. The proceeds of a compulsory sale, less the
costs of the sale must be paid into court for the benefit of the persons
who are beneficially interested in the shares.

A person who contravenes these restrictions will be liable on
conviction to a fine, although a prosecution may only be instituted with
the consent of the Department of Trade and Industry (s 455).

INVESTIGATION OF SHARE DEALINGS

Directors are prohibited from dealing in options to buy or sell quoted
shares in their companies (s 323), while directors of all companies are
required to notify their companies of their interest (and those of their
spouse and children) in the company's shares or debentures (ss 324,
328).

Section 446 provides that the Department of Trade may appoint one
or more competent inspectors to investigate any possible contravention
of these provisions, and report their findings to the Department.

An inspector is given powers, similar to those contained in section
434 to obtain documents relating to a company or related company and
examine its officers or agents on oath. The investigation may also apply
to:

(a) members of a recognised stock exchange or of a recognised
association of dealers in securities who are individuals and to
officers (past and present) of members who are companies.

(b) holders of licences granted under the Prevention of Fraud
(Investments) Act 1958 who are individuals and to officers (past
and present) of holders of licences who are companies.

(c) any individual who is an exempted dealer for the purposes of the
Prevention of Fraud (Investments Act) 1958, and to officers (past
and present) of any company declared to be such a dealer.

An inspector may, and if so directed must, make interim reports to
the Department, and on the conclusion of the investigation make a final
report to the Department. The report may be published if the

Department so decides. The expenses of such an investigation are defrayed by the Department of Trade out of moneys provided by Parliament.

INSPECTION OF A COMPANY'S BOOKS AND PAPERS

The Department of Trade and Industry may, if they think there is good reason to do so, require a company to produce specified books and papers. It may also require their production from any person who appears to the Department to be in possession of them.

If the books and papers are produced, the Department may;

(i)  take copies of them or extracts from them, and
(ii) require any past or present officer of the company to provide an explanation of any of them.

If the books or papers are not produced the Department may require the person who was required to produce them to state, to the best of his knowledge and belief, where they are (s 447).

If the requirement to produce books or papers or provide an explanation is not complied with, the company or person concerned is liable to a term of imprisonment or a fine or both. It is a defence for a person charged under this section to prove that they were not in his possession or under his control and that it was not reasonably practicable for him to comply with the requirement.

A statement made by a person in compliance with a requirement under this section may be used in evidence against him.

If a person provides an explanation or makes a statement which he knows to be false in a material particular, or recklessly provides a false explanation or statement he is guilty of an offence and is liable to a term of imprisonment and/or a fine (s 451).

ENTRY AND SEARCH OF PREMISES

If a justice of the peace is satisfied, on information on oath laid by an officer of the Department of Trade and Industry, that there are reasonable grounds for suspecting that there are on any premises any books or papers of which production has been required under s 447, and which have not been produced, he may issue a warrant authorising any constable to enter and search the premises and take possession of any books or papers appearing to be such.

Any books or papers which are taken may be retained for three months or (if criminal proceedings are commenced within that period) until the conclusion of the proceedings.

A person who obstructs the right of entry to search, or who obstructs a right to take possession of any books or papers may be subject to imprisonment or to a fine.

## PENALISATION OF DESTRUCTION, MUTILATION OF COMPANY DOCUMENTS

An officer of the company who destroys, mutilates or falsifies, or is a party to the destruction of a document affecting or relating to the company's property or affairs is guilty of an offence unless he proves that he did not intend to conceal the state of affairs of the company or defeat the law.

A person guilty of an offence under this section is liable to a term of imprisonment and/or a fine (s 450).

## PROVISION FOR SECURITY OF INFORMATION

Any information obtained under the provisions of s 447 may not, without the previous written consent of the company, be published or disclosed except to a competent authority, unless the publication or disclosure is required:

(a) to institute criminal proceedings
(b) to enable an inspector to examine any person; in the course of his investigation;
(c) to enable the Secretary of State to exercise his functions under the Companies Act, the Prevention of Fraud (Investments) Act 1958, the Insurance Companies Act 1982, and the Company Securities (Insider Dealing) Act 1985.

A person who publishes or discloses any information or document in contravention of this section is liable to a term of imprisonment and/or a fine (s 449).

# Chapter 15

# The Accounts

Every company must prepare and maintain two sets of accounts. It must –

(i) keep proper accounting records; and
(ii) prepare annual accounts.

The responsibility for preparing and maintaining both sets of accounts rests with the directors (ss 221(1), 227).

## 1. ACCOUNTING RECORDS

Every company must keep accounting records which are sufficient to show and explain the company's transactions. The accounting records shall be as such as to –

(i) disclose with reasonable accuracy, at any time, the financial position of the company at that time; and
(ii) enable the directors to ensure that any balance sheet or profit and loss account prepared by them gives a true and fair view of the company's state of affairs and profit and loss account as at the end of its financial year (s 221(2)).

In particular the accounting records must contain –

(i) entries from day to day of all money received and expended by the company and the matters in respect of which the receipt and expenditure take place;
(ii) a record of all the company's assets and liabilities.
(iii) where the company's business involves dealing in goods:
    (a) statements of stock held by the company at the end of each financial year;
    (b) statements of stocktaking;

(c) statements of all goods purchased and sold (except by way of ordinary retail trade) and the buyers and sellers of these goods (s 221(3), (4)).

These records must be kept at the company's registered office or at such other place as the company's directors think fit, and must be open to inspection at all times to the company's officers (s 222).

## 2. ANNUAL ACCOUNTS

The directors of every company must, in respect of each accounting reference period, prepare a profit and loss account and a balance sheet as at the date to which the profit and loss account is made up. A company not trading for profit must prepare an income and expenditure account in place of a profit and loss account (s 227).

Where a company has subsidiaries, copies of the group's accounts as well as holding company's accounts must be prepared.

## ACCOUNTING REFERENCE PERIODS

The directors must prepare annual accounts based on an accounting reference period which must coincide with the company's financial year.

A company may choose its own accounting reference period provided it gives notice to the Registrar within 6 months of its incorporation.

A company's first accounting reference period comences on the date of its incorporation to the next accounting reference period. The first accounting reference period must not exceed 18 months or be less than 6 months. The subsequent accounting reference periods are those successive periods of 12 months commencing after the end of the company's first accounting reference period and ending with the company's accounting reference date (s 224).

If a company does not notify the Registrar that it has selected its own accounting reference period, its accounting reference period will run from 1st April of each year to the 31st March of the following year (s 224(3)).

A company may alter its accounting reference date, and therefore its accounting reference period by giving notice of the fact to the Registrar. The notice must state whether the current or previous accounting reference period of the company is to be treated as shortened or extended because of the change in the accounting reference date. It must then draw up accounts for that shortened or extended period. A company may not extend its accounting reference period to longer than 18 months.

A company may only extend its accounting reference period if:

(i) no earlier accounting reference period has been extended by virtue of a previous notice given by the company.
(ii) at least five years have elapsed from the date on which any previously extended accounting reference period came to an end.
(iii) the company is a subsidiary or holding company of another company and the new accounting reference date coincides with the accounting reference date of that other company (s 225).

A profit and loss account prepared in respect of the first accounting reference period must cover the period beginning with the first day of an accounting reference period and end either on the date on which the period ends or within 7 days of the end of that period.

Each subsequent profit and loss account must begin on the day after the date to which the last preceding profit and loss account was made up and end either on the date on which the accounting reference period ends or within 7 days of that date.

The directors must lay before the company in general meeting, in respect of each financial year of the company, copies of the company's accounts for that year (s 241(1)).

A company's accounts for a financial year comprise the following documents:

(a) the profit and loss account and balance sheet;
(b) the directors' report;
(c) the auditors' report;
(d) where the company has subsidiaries (and if applicable) group accounts (s 239).

The profit and loss account must be annexed to the balance sheet and the auditors and directors' report must be attached to it.

Any accounts so annexed must be approved by the board of directors before the balance sheet is signed on their behalf (s 238(4)).

The directors must, in respect of each financial year, deliver to the Registrar, a copy of the accounts for that year, s 241(3).

The time allowed for laying and delivering a company's accounts for a financial year is determined by reference to its accounting reference period.

(a) A private company must lay and deliver its accounts within 10 months of the reference date.
(b) A public company must lay and deliver its accounts within 7 months of the reference date (s 242).

A copy of the accounts must be sent to every member, whether or not he is entitled to receive notices of general meetings, and to every debenture holder and other entitled person at least 21 days before the meeting (s 240).


## EXEMPTIONS AND MODIFIED ACCOUNTS

Various exemptions and concessions are granted to certain types of companies.

A company is not entitled to the benefit of any exemptions for individual accounts in respect of any accounting reference period if it is or was at any time during the financial year to which the accounts relate:

(i) a public company;
(ii) a banking insurance or shipping company;
(iii) a member of an ineligible group ie a holding company or a subsidiary company (s 247).

Certain banking, insurance and shipping companies may be permitted, by the Secretary of State, to file modified accounts e g a recognised bank may ask the Secretary of State for permission to file modified accounts.

An insurance company may prepare modified accounts for its members and for filing with the Registrar, unless otherwise directed by the Registrar.

A shipping company may prepare modified accounts for its members and for filing if it satisfies the Secretary of State that it ought in the national interest to be permitted to do so.

The main concessions are granted to small, medium sized and unlimited companies (s 247, 248).

(i) A small company need only file an abbreviated version of its balance sheet with the Registrar. It is not required to file a profit and loss account or the directors' report.
(ii) A medium sized company must file a full sheet and directors' report, but only a modified profit and loss account.
(iii) An unlimited company need not file its accounts, the directors' report or the auditor's report. It can only claim this exemption

if at no time during the accounting reference period has the company:

(a)   been a subsidiary of a limited company or have there been held by or on behalf of two or more companies, shares or powers which if they had been held or exercisable by one of them would have made the company its subsidiary.

(b)   been the holding company of a limited company.

(c)   been carrying on business as the promoter of a trading stamp scheme (s 241).

## THE BALANCE SHEET

The directors of every company must prepare a balance sheet as at the date to which any profit and loss account is made up (s 227). It must give a true and fair view of the state of affairs of the company as at the end of its financial year (s 228(2)). It must comply with the requirements of Sch 4 to the Act, so far as applicable.

The balance sheet and every copy of it which is laid before the company in general meeting or delivered to the Registrar must be signed on behalf of the board by two of the directors, or if there is only one director, by that one (s 238). Failure to comply with this section renders the company and every officer of the company liable to a fine.

Companies (other than banking, shipping and insurance companies) must adopt Format 1 or 2 in the presentation of their accounts.

Format 1 equates net assets to the aggregate of share capital and reserves and closely follows current United Kingdom practice.

Format 2 equates assets against claims and follows current European practice. The content of both formats is identical.

BALANCE SHEET FORMULA: *FORMAT 1*

A.   Called up share capital not paid

B.   Fixed assets

  I Intangible assets
    1.   Development costs
    2.   Concessions, patents, licences, trade marks and similar rights and assets

     3. Goodwill
     4. Payments on account

  II Tangible assets
     1. Land and buildings
     2. Plant and machinery
     3. Fixtures, fittings, tools and equipment
     4. Payments on account and assets in course of construction

  III Investments
     1. Shares in group companies
     2. Loans to group companies
     3. Shares in related companies
     4. Loans to related companies
     5. Other investments other than loans
     6. Other loans
     7. Own shares

C. Current assets

  I Stocks
     1. Raw materials and consumables
     2. Work in progress
     3. Finished goods and goods for resale
     4. Payments on account
  II Debtors
     1. Trade debtors
     2. Amounts owed by group companies
     3. Amounts owed by related companies
     4. Other debtors
     5. Called up share capital not paid
     6. Prepayments and accrued income

  III Investments
     1. Shares in group companies
     2. Own shares
     3. Other investments
  IV Cash at bank and in hand

D. Prepayments and accrued income

E. Creditors: amounts falling due within one year
     1. Debenture loans
     2. Bank loans and overdrafts
     3. Payments received on account

    4. Trade creditors
    5. Bills of exchange payable
    6. Amounts owed to group companies
    7. Amounts owed to related companies
    8. Other creditors including taxation and social security
    9. Accruals and deferred income

F.  Net current assets (liabilities)

G.  Total assets less current liabilities

H.  Creditors: amounts falling due after more than one year
    1. Debenture loans
    2. Bank loans and overdrafts
    3. Payments received on account
    4. Trade creditors
    5. Bills of exchange payable
    6. Amounts owed to group companies
    7. Amounts owed to related companies
    8. Other creditors including taxation and social security
    9. Accruals and deferred income

I.  Provisions for liabilities and charges
    1. Pensions and similar obligations
    2. Taxation, including deferred taxation
    3. Other provisions

J.  Accruals and deferred income

K.  Capital and reserves

    I Called up share capital

    II Share premium account

    III Revaluation reserve

    IV Other reserves
    1. Capital redemption reserve
    2. Reserve for own shares
    3. Reserves provided for by the articles of association
    4. Other reserves

V  Profit and loss account.

*FORMAT 2*

*Assets*

A.  Called up share capital not paid

B.  Fixed assets
  I  Intangible assets
    1.  Development costs
    2.  Concessions, patents, licences trade marks and similar rights and assets
    3.  Goodwill
    4.  Payments on account

  II  Tangible assets
    1.  Land and buildings
    2.  Plant and machinery
    3.  Fixtures, fittings, tools and equipment
    4.  Payments on account and assets in course of construction

  III  Investments
    1.  Shares in group companies
    2.  Loans to group companies
    3.  Shares in related companies
    4.  Loans to related companies
    5.  Other investments other than loans
    6.  Other loans
    7.  Own shares

C.  Current assets
  I  Stocks
    1.  Raw materials and consumables
    2.  Work in progress
    3.  Finished goods and goods for resale
    4.  Payments on account

  II  Debtors
    1.  Trade debtors
    2.  Amounts owed by group companies
    3.  Amounts owed by related companies
    4.  Other debtors

    5. Called up share capital not paid
    6. Prepayments and accrued income

III Investments
    1. Shares in group companies
    2. Own shares
    3. Other investments

IV Cash at bank and in hand

D.  Prepayments and accrued income

*Liabilities*

A.  Capital and reserves

   I Called up share capital

  II Share premium account

 III Revaluation reserve

 IV Other reserves
    1. Capital redemption reserve
    2. Reserve for own shares
    3. Reserves provided for by the articles of association
    4. Other reserves

  V. Profit and loss account

B.  Provisions for liabilities and charges
    1. Pensions and similar obligations
    2. Taxation including deferred taxation
    3. Other provisions

C.  Creditors
    1. Debenture loans
    2. Bank loans and overdrafts
    3. Payments received on account
    4. Trade creditors
    5. Bills of exchange payable
    6. Amounts owed to group companies
    7. Amounts owed to related companies
    8. Other creditors including taxation and social security
    9. Accruals and deferred income

D. Accruals and deferred income

The following details are required to supplement the information given in the balance sheet (Sch 4):

(1) The authorised share capital and where shares of one class have been allotted, the number and aggregate nominal value of shares of each class allotted.

(2) Where part of the allotted share capital consists of redeemable shares – the earliest and latest dates of redemption, whether the redemption is optional and details of any premium payable on redemption.

(3) Details of any allotment of shares during the financial year – the reason for the allotment, the class of shares, the number and aggregate nominal value of the shares, the consideration received for the allotment.

(4) Details relating to any contingent right to the allotment of shares ie any option to subscribe for shares and any other right to require the allotment of shares to any person whether arising on the conversion into shares of securities or otherwise.

(5) Details of any issue of debentures during the financial year – the reason for making the issue, the classes and amounts of debentures issued, the consideration received for the issue.

(6) Particulars of any redeemed debentures which the company has power to issue.

(7) The nominal amount and the amount at which they are stated in the accounting records of any debentures held by a nominee or trustee of the company.

(8) Details of valuations of fixed assets and the totals of any acquisitions, disposals, and transfer of assets during the financial year, along with details of revaluation and the cumulative amount of provisions for depreciation or diminution in the value of assets.

(9) Details of investments differentiating between listed investments and other investments. The aggregate market value and stock exchange value of an investment must be stated where the value differs from that shown in the balance sheet.

(10) The nature of the reserves and provisions for liabilities and charges during the financial year and the amounts (if any) transferred.

(11) Provisions for taxation.

(12) Details of indebtedness including:

any instalments and other amounts payable more than 5 years hence;

the terms of payment or repayment and the rate of interest payable;

the aggregate amount of any secured debts and the nature of the security given;

any arrears of fixed cumulative dividends.

(13) Details of any guarantees and other financial commitments entered into by the company on its own behalf or on behalf of its holding company or subsidiary. These include:

particulars of any charge on the company's assets to secure third party liabilities:

the amount and general nature of contingent liabilities;

the aggregate amount of capital expenditure insofar as not provided for or authorised by the directors and not contracted for;

pension commitments;

any other financial commitment not provided for but relevant to assessing the company's state of affairs.

THE FOLLOWING DOCUMENTS MUST BE ANNEXED TO THE BALANCE SHEET

The profit and loss account.

Group accounts (if applicable).

## THE PROFIT AND LOSS ACCOUNT

The directors of every company must in respect of each accounting reference period prepare a profit and loss account. The period in respect of which the account is prepared must be a financial year of the company (s 227(1)). Every profit and loss account must give a true and fair view of the profit or loss of the company for the financial year and show the items listed in any one of the profit and loss account formats set out in the Act.

Formats 1 and 2 are presented in a vertical form and are closest to current United Kingdom Practice. It is envisaged that the larger companies will adopt Format 1, while most small companies will adopt Format 2.

PROFIT AND LOSS ACCOUNT FORMATS *FORMAT 1*

1. Turnover
2. Cost of sales

3. Gross profit or loss
4. Distribution costs
5. Administrative expenses
6. Other operating income
7. Income from shares in group companies
8. Income from shares in related companies
9. Income from other fixed asset investments
10. Other interest receivable and similar income
11. Amounts written off investments
12. Interest payable and similar charges
13. Tax on profit or loss on ordinary activities
14. Profit or loss on ordinary activities after taxation
15. Extraordinary income
16. Extraordinary charges
17. Extraordinary profit or loss
18. Tax on extraordinary profit or loss
19. Other taxes not shown under the above items
20. Profit or loss for the financial year

FORMAT 2

1. Turnover
2. Change in stocks of finished goods and in work progress
3. Own work capitalised
4. Other operating income
5. (a) Raw materials and consumables
   (b) Other external charges
6. Staff costs:
   (a) wages and salaries
   (b) social security costs
   (c) other pension costs
7. (a) Depreciation and other amounts written off tangible and intangible fixed assets
   (b) Exceptional amounts written off current assets
8. Other operating charges
9. Income from shares in a group companies
10. Income from shares in related companies
11. Income from other fixed asset investments
12. Other interest receivable and similar income
13. Amounts written off investments
14. Interest payable and similar charges
15. Tax on profit or loss on ordinary activities
16. Profit or loss on ordinary activities after taxation

17. Extraordinary income
18. Extraordinary charges
19. Extraordinary profit or loss
20. Tax on extraordinary profit or loss
21. Other taxes not shown under the above items
22. Profit or loss for the financial year

*FORMAT 3*

A.  Charges
1. Cost of sales
2. Distribution costs
3. Administrative expenses
4. Amounts written off investments
5. Interest payable and similar charges
6. Tax on profit or loss on ordinary activities
7. Profit or loss on ordinary activities after taxation
8. Extraordinary charges
9. Tax on extraordinary profit or loss
10. Other taxes not shown under the above items
11. Profit or loss for the financial year

B.  Income
1. Turnover
2. Other operating income
3. Income from shares in group companies
4. Income from shares in related companies
5. Income from other fixed asset investments
6. Other interest receivable and similar income
7. Profit or loss on ordinary activities after taxation
8. Extraordinary income
9. Profit or loss for the financial year

*FORMAT 4*

A.  Charges
1. Reduction in stocks of finished goods and in work in progress
    (a) Raw materials and consumables
    (b) Other external charges
3. Staff costs:
    (a) wages and salaries
    (b) social security costs

    (c) other pension costs
4. (a) Depreciation and other amounts written off tangible and intangible fixed assets
    (b) Exceptional amounts written off current assets
5. Other operating charges
6. Amounts written off investments
7. Interest payable and similar charges
8. Tax on profit or loss on ordinary activities
9. Profit or loss on ordinary activities after taxation
10. Extraordinary charges
11. Tax on extraordinary profit or loss
12. Other taxes not shown under the above items
13. Profit or loss for the financial year

B. Income
1. Turnover
2. Increase in stocks of finished goods and in work in progress
3. Own work capitalised
4. Other operating income
5. Income from shares in group companies
6. Income from shares in related companies
7. Income from other fixed asset investments
8. Other interest receivable and similar income
9. Profit or loss on ordinary activities after taxation
10. Extraordinary income
11. Profit or loss for the financial year

In addition every profit and loss account must show the following items separately:

(i) the amount of the company's profit or loss on ordinary activities before taxation.
(ii) any amount set aside or proposed to be set aside to, or withdrawn or proposed to be withdrawn from, reserves;
(iii) the aggregate amounts of any dividends paid and proposed.

The following information is required either to supplement the information given with respect to any particular items shown in the profit and loss account or to provide particulars of income or expenditure or of circumstances affecting the items shown in the profit and loss account.

(1) The amount of the interest on bank loans, overdrafts and other loans made to the company which are repayable by instalments or otherwise before the end of a five year period.

(2) The amount set aside for redemption of share capital and loans.

(3) The amount of income from listed investments.

(4) The amount of rents from land (if a substantial part of the company's revenue).

(5) The amount paid for the hire of plant and machinery.

(6) The amount of remuneration of the auditors.

(7) The basis on which United Kingdom corporation tax and income tax is computed.

(8) If in the course of the financial year the company has carried on two or more classes of business which, in the opinion of the directors differ substantially from each other, a statement –
   (i) of the amount of turnover attributable to each class.
   (ii) the amount of profit or loss before taxation which is in the opinion of the directors attributable to class.

(9) Particulars of turnover where the company has supplied different markets during the course of the year and the amount of the turnover attributable to each market.

(10) The average number of persons employed by the company in the financial year; and the average number employed within each employment category.

(11) The aggregate amounts of wages and salaries paid to employees in respect of the financial year; along with social security costs and pension costs incurred on their behalf.

(12) Particulars of any extraordinary income or charges arising in the financial year.

(13) The effect of any transactions that are exceptional by virtue of their size or incidence, although falling within the company's ordinary activities.

## GROUP ACCOUNTS

Where at the end of its financial year a company has subsidiaries, it must include in its annual accounts group accounts dealing with the state of affairs and profit or loss of the company and its subsidiaries in respect of that accounting reference period (s 229(1)).

These accounts (together with any notes to those accounts) must give a true and fair view of the state of affairs and profit or loss of the company and the subsidiaries dealt with by those accounts as a whole, so far as it concerns members of the company.

Group accounts will normally be prepared as consolidated accounts, comprising a consolidated balance sheet and a consolidated profit and loss account of the company and its subsidiaries (s 229(5)). Where the group accounts are not prepared as consolidated accounts, they must give the same or equivalent information as consolidated accounts (s 229(6)). The financial year of each subsidiary should normally coincide with that of the holding company, but where it does not group accounts must deal with that subsidiary's state of affairs as at the end of the financial year, ending with the last before that of the holding company, and with the subsidiary's profit or loss for that financial year (s 230(5)–(7)).

Group accounts may be prepared in accordance with the exemptions granted to small and medium sized companies if the group as a whole satisfy these criteria.

A holding company must file its accounts in full if its group accounts do not qualify for exemption. If the holding company's accounts permit it to be treated as a small company, it must submit its accounts as a medium sized company.

Group accounts are not required if the holding company is a wholly owned subsidiary of another registered company (or any other corporation incorporated in Great Britain (s 229(2)).

Group accounts need not deal with a subsidiary if the company's directors are of the opinion that –

(i) such accounts would be impracticable, or of no real value in view of the insignificant amounts involved or expenses or delay to the members; or
(ii) the result would be misleading, or harmful to the business of the company or its subsidiaries; or
(iii) the business of the holding company and that of its subsidiaries are so different that they cannot reasonably be treated as a single undertaking (s 229(3)).

The approval of the Department of Trade and Industry is required for not dealing in group accounts on the grounds that the result would be harmful or on the ground of the difference between the business of the holding company and that of the subsidiary (s 229(4)).

## THE AUDITORS' REPORT

The auditors of a company must make a report to members on the accounts examined by them and on every balance sheet, every profit and loss account and all group accounts of which a copy is laid before the company in general meeting during their tenure of office (s 236(1)).

The report must be attached to the balance sheet, be read before the company in general meeting, and be open to inspection by any member.

The report must state whether, in the auditor's opinion:

(a) the balance sheet, profit and loss account and (if it is a holding company submitting group accounts) the group accounts have been properly prepared in accordance with the provisions of the Act;
(b) a true and fair view as given –
  (i) in the case of the balance sheet, of the state of the company's affairs as at the end of its financial year.
  (ii) in the case of the profit and loss account (if not framed as a consolidated profit and loss account), of the company's profit or loss for its financial year;
  (iii) in the case of group accounts submitted by a holding company, of the state of affairs and profit or loss of the company and its subsidiaries (s 236(2)).

It is the auditors' duty in preparing the report to carry out such investigations as will enable them to form an opinion as to whether:

 (i) Proper accounting records have been kept by the company and proper returns adequate for their audit have been received from branches not visited by them; and
(ii) The company's balance sheet and (if not framed as a consolidated profit and loss account) profit and loss accounts are in agreement with the accounting records and returns (s 237(1)).

If the auditors are of the opinion that (i) and (ii) above have not been complied with, they must state that fact in their report (s 237(2)).

If the auditors fail to obtain all the information and explanations which, to the best of their knowledge and belief, are necessary for their audit, they must also state that fact in their report (s 237(4)).

If disclosure is not made in the accounts of certain information relating to the emoluments of directors and certain employees; transactions involving directors and others; loans, quasi-loans, credit transactions or arrangements made between the directors and the company, the auditors are required to include the information in their report (s 237(5)).

# DIRECTORS' REPORT

A company must attach a report by the directors to every balance sheet which must give a fair view of the development of the business of the company and its subsidiaries during the financial year ending with the balance sheet date and of their position at the end of it and stating the amount, if any, which they propose to carry to reserves (s 235).

It must also give (Sch 7):

1. The names of the persons who at any time during the financial year were directors of the company.
2. The principal activities of the company and its subsidiaries in the course of the financial year, and any significant change in those activities.
3. Particulars of any significant changes in the fixed assets of the company or of any of its subsidiaries in that year. In respect of assets which consist of an interest in land, the difference between the market value and the amount at which they are included in the balance sheet if, in the opinion of the directors, the difference is of such significance that it should be drawn to the attention of the members or debenture holders.
4. The interest of a director in shares or debentures of the company or its subsidiary or holding company at the beginning and end of the financial year.
5. Particulars of any important event affecting the company or any of its subsidiaries which have occurred since the end of that year.
6. An indication of likely future developments in the business of the company and of its subsidiaries.
7. An indication of the activities (if any) of the company and its subsidiaries in the field of research and development.
8. Information regarding the arrangement in force for securing the health, safety and welfare of the employees of the company and its subsidiaries.
9. A statement of the company's policy in respect of disabled persons, including training, development and promotion of such persons.
10. If a company has on average more than 250 employees, a statement as to the company's policy for introducing, maintaining or developing arrangements aimed at furthering employee involvement.
11. Particulars of any charitable or political gift in excess of £200. In the case of political gifts: the name of each person to whom

more than £200 was given by way of donation or subscription to a political party, the identity of the party and the amount of the gift.

12. Particulars of the acquisition by a company (or its nominee) of its own shares where the shares are:
   (a) purchased by the company or acquired by forfeiture or surrender in lieu of forfeiture;
   (b) acquired by a company's nominee or by any other person with financial assistance from the company in circumstances in which the company has a beneficial interest in the shares;
   (c) made subject to a lien or other charge.

Details must be given of:

the number and nominal value of the shares;
the consideration paid and the reasons for the purchase;
the percentage of called up capital represented by the purchase;
the number and nominal value of shares disposed of by the company (or other person) or cancelled during the year;
the amount of any charge (if applicable);
the amount of value of the consideration where shares have been disposed of by the company (or other person) and the consideration received.

The auditors have a duty to consider whether the information given in the director's report is consistent with the accounts. If they are of the opinion that there is an inconsistency, they must state that fact in their report (s 237).

Every member of the company, every debenture holder and any other person who is entitled to receive notices of general meetings of a company, must be sent a copy of the directors' report (s 240).

The directors of a small company are not required to file a copy of the directors' report with the annual accounts.

If a company fails to take all reasonable steps to comply with the statutory requirements relating to the directors' report, every person who was a director in that relevant period is guilty of an offence and may be liable to a fine unless he proves that he took all reasonable steps to secure compliance with those requirements (s 235).

## ADDITIONAL INFORMATION TO BE GIVEN IN THE ACCOUNTS (SCHS 5, 6)

1. A statement of the aggregate amount of the following:

    (a) directors' emoluments;
    (b) directors' or past directors' pensions;
    (c) compensation paid to directors or past directors for loss of
        office.
2. The chairman's emoluments.
3. The emolument of the highest paid director, if greater than those of the chairman's.
4. The number of directors who received no emoluments.
5. A scale dividing directors' emoluments into bands of £5,000 showing the number of directors whose emoluments fell within each band.
    Items 2–5 need only be disclosed if item 1 exceeds £60,000. The number of directors who have waived the right to receive emoluments and the aggregate amount of those emoluments.
7. The number of employees (other than directors or employees working wholly or mainly outside the United Kingdom) who received salaries in excess of £30,000 divided into bands of £5,000, commencing at £30,000.
8. Where particulars of directors' emoluments or employees' salaries are shown, the corresponding amounts for the previous year.
9. (a) any loan, quasi-loan or credit transaction or arrangement, made by a public company with its directors, or directors of its holding company or persons connected with directors. Disclosure is not required if the aggregate amount does not exceed £5,000;
    (b) any agreement to enter into such a transaction or arrangement;
    (c) any other transaction or arrangement with the company and its subsidiary in which a director of the company or its holding company has a material interest, eg property transactions, consultancy agreements. Disclosure is not required if the aggregate amount does not exceed £1,000 or, if more, does not exceed £5,000 or 1 per cent of the value of the company's net assets at the end of the financial year (whichever is the less).
10. Any loans, quasi-loans, or credit transactions or arrangements made by a company with its officers (other than its directors) in excess of £2,500.
11. Where the company is a subsidiary, the name and country of incorporation of its holding company.
12. Where the company has subsidiaries, the names of the subsidiaries, the country of incorporation, particulars of the

shares of the subsidiary held by the company, the aggregate amount of the capital and reserves of the subsidiaries, and the amounts of their profit or loss.

13. Where the company holds 10 per cent of the allotted share capital of another company which is not a subsidiary, particulars of these shares and the identity and place of incorporation of such a company.

14. Where a company holds 20 per cent of the allotted share capital of another company, it must state the aggregate amount of the capital and reserves of that company and must provide the amount of the profit or loss of that company.

# Chapter 16

# Auditors

The first auditors of a newly created company may be appointed by the directors at any time before the first general meeting of the company at which accounts in respect of an accounting reference period are laid before the meeting. The auditors so appointed will hold office until the conclusion of the meeting. If the directors do not make an appointment, the company may do so in general meeting (s 384(3)).

Every company (with the exception of a dormant company) must, at each general meeting before which accounts are laid, appoint an auditor to hold office from the conclusion of that meeting until the conclusion of the next general meeting before which accounts are laid (s 384(2)).

An auditor may be re-appointed for another term on passing the appropriate resolution. If no such appointment or re-appointment is made the company must notify the fact within one week, to the Secretary of State who may appoint a person to fill the vacancy.

The directors or the company in general meeting may fill any casual vacancy in the office of auditor, but while the vacancy continues the surviving or continuing auditor(s) if any, may act (s 384(4)).

A company may by ordinary resolution remove an auditor before the expiration of his term of office notwithstanding anything in any agreement between it and him. Where a resolution removing an auditor is passed at a general meeting of a company, the company must within 14 days, give notice of the fact to the Registrar (s 386).

Special notice must be given of a resolution at a general meeting to:

(a) appoint as auditor a person other than a retiring auditor; or
(b) fill a casual vacancy in the office of auditor; or
(c) re-appoint as auditor a retiring auditor appointed by the directors to fill a casual vacancy; or

(d) remove an auditor before the expiration of his term of office (s 388).

On receipt of the notice the company must forwith send a copy to:

(a) the person proposed to be appointed or removed;
(b) the retiring auditor where it is proposed to appoint another person;
(c) the auditor who resigned if the casual vacancy was caused by his resignation.

Where notice is given of a resolution to appoint a person other than the retiring auditor or to remove an auditor from office, the retiring auditor or the auditor proposed to be removed may make written representations to the company and request that a copy be sent to every member of the company who is entitled to receive notice of the meeting. If a company does not send a copy of the representations to the members, the auditor may require that they be read out at the meeting. The court may waive these requirements if it is satisfied that these rights are being abused to secure needless publicity for defamatory matter (s 388).

An auditor who has been removed is entitled to attend and be heard at the general meeting at which his term of office would otherwise have expired and any general meeting at which it is proposed to fill the vacancy caused by his removal.

## QUALIFICATIONS

A person may only act as auditor if:

1. He is a member of a body of accountants recognised for this purpose by the Department of Trade and Industry. The following bodies are so recognised:
   The Institute of Chartered Accountants in England and Wales;
   The Institute of Chartered Accountants of Scotland;
   The Association of Certified Accountants;
   The Institute of Chartered Accountants in Ireland.
2. He is authorised by the Department of Trade to be appointed, as:
   (a) he has similar qualifications obtained outside the United Kingdom, or
   (b) he has obtained adequate knowledge and experience in the course of his employment by a member of a recognised body of accountants and was authorised before 19/4/1978.

    (c) he practised in Great Britain as an accountant before 6/8/1947 and applied to be authorised before 27/11/1968.

None of the following may be appointed auditor of a company:

(a) an officer or servant of the company.
(b) a person who is a partner of or in the employment of an officer or servant of the company.
(c) a body corporate.
(d) a person who for any of the above reasons is disqualified from acting as auditor of the company's holding company, subsidiary or co-subsidiary.

A person may not act as an auditor of a company at a time when he knows that he is disqualified for appointment. If to his knowledge he becomes disqualified he must vacate his office and give notice in writing to the company that he has vacated his office because of disqualification (s 389).

## RESIGNATION OF AUDITOR

An auditor may resign his office by depositing a notice in writing to that effect at the company's registered office. His resignation will take effect on that date or on such later date as the notice specifies.
    The notice is not effective unless it contains

(a) a statement that there are no circumstances connected with his resignation which he considers should be brought to the attention of the members or creditors; or
(b) a statement of any such circumstances.

A company must, within 14 days, send a copy of the notice to the Registrar.
    If the notice contains a statement that there are circumstances connected with the auditors resignation which he considers should be brought to the attention of the members or creditors, a copy of the notice must be sent to every member, every debenture holder and all persons entitled to receive notice of general meetings of the company (s 390).
    The company and any person who claims to be aggrieved may, within 14 days of the receipt of the notice by the company of such a notice, apply to the court. If the court is satisfied that the auditor is using the notice to secure needless publicity it may by order, direct that copies of the notice need not be sent out. It may further order

that the company's costs on the application be paid in whole or in part by the auditor, even though he is not a party to the application.

The company must, within 14 days of the court's decision, send to the Registrar and to all persons mentioned above:

a statement of the court order (if any order is made);
a copy of notice containing the statement (if the court does not make an order) (s 390).

Where an auditor's notice of resignation contains a statement that there are circumstances which should be brought to the attention of the members or creditors he may deposit with the notice a signed requisition that the directors forthwith convene an extraordinary general meeting to receive and consider an explanation of the circumstances connected with his resignation. He may also require the company to circulate to its members (before the general meeting at which his term of office would otherwise have expired or before the general meeting at which it is proposed to fill the vacancy caused by his resignation or convened on his requisition) a statement in writing (of reasonable length) of the circumstances connected with his resignation.

The auditor is entitled to attend such a meeting and receive all notices and communications relating to the meeting. He is entitled to be heard at any such meeting which he attends on any part of the business of the meeting which concerns him as former auditor of the company.

If the directors do not, within 21 days from the deposit of a requisition, proceed to convene a meeting on not more than 28 days notice, every director who failed to take all reasonable steps to secure that a meeting was convened is guilty of an offence and is liable on conviction to a fine. If the statement is not sent out as required, the auditor may, without prejudice to his right to speak at the meeting, require that the statement be read out at the meeting. The statement need not be sent out, or read out at the meeting if the court is satisfied that the rights are being abused to secure needless publicity for defamatory matter (s 391).

## THE REMUNERATION OF AUDITORS

An auditor's remuneration is fixed by:

(a) the directors when appointed by the directors; or
(b) the Secretary of State when appointed by the Secretary of State; or
(c) the company in general meeting (in other cases) or in such manner as the general meeting decides.

The amount of the auditor's remuneration (including expenses) must be shown under a separate heading in the profit and loss account.

## STATUS OF THE AUDITOR

Auditors are regarded as agents of the members to carry out certain duties for the audit, even when he has not been appointed by the members.

He is regarded as an agent of the company for the purpose of an investigation by the Department of Trade and Industry, (s 434(4)), but his signature on the auditor's report does not make him an agent of the company for the purpose of acknowledging a debt under the Limitation Act 1980.

### Re Transplanters (Holding Co) Ltd (1958)

A director lent money to the company and relied on two balance sheets, signed by two directors and certified by the auditors as evidence of the company's indebtedness. The liquidator rejected the director's proof on the ground that the debt was statute barred. It was held that the auditors were not agents of the company for the purpose of acknowledging such a debt and their signatures on the certificate of the balance sheet was not the signature of the agents within the Limitation Act 1939 (now the Limitation Act 1980).

The auditor has been held to an officer of the company in misfeasance proceedings (s 631) (*Re London and General Bank* (1895); *Re Kingston Cotton Mill Co (No 2)* (1896)).

The Companies Act 1985 does not include auditor in its definition of 'officer' of the company (s 744), but refers to an auditor in s 727 in the following terms – 'auditor (whether he is or is not an officer of the company').

An auditor who is appointed to fill an office as distinct from appointed for a particular audit, is an officer of the company.

### R v Shacter (1960)

An auditor appointed by a company in general meeting was held to be an officer of the company and was therefore liable for making false entries and default contrary to ss 330, 328 and 331 of the Companies Act 1948 and publishing fraudulent statements and falsifying books of accounts contrary to sections 83 and 84 of the Larceny Act 1916 (now Theft Act 1968).

An accountant appointed to carry out a private audit for the directors is not an officer of the company.

### Re Western Counties Steam Bakeries (1897)

Misfeasance proceedings were taken against persons as officers of the company in respect of a dividend declared at a general meeting. They had not been formally appointed as the company's auditors. It was held they were not officers of the company and therefore not subject to misfeasance proceedings.

Any provision to exempt an auditor from, or indemnify him against any liability for negligence, default, breach of duty or breach of trust is void (s 310). The court may however relieve him wholly, or in part, if having regard to all the circumstances it is of the opinion that he acted honestly and reasonably and ought fairly to be excused (s 727).

## RIGHTS OF AUDITORS

Auditors have the right of access at all times to the books and accounts and vouchers of the company and are entitled to require from the officers of the company such information and explanation as he thinks necessary for the performance of the duties of the auditors (s 237(3)).

If the auditors fail to obtain all the information and explanations which, to the best of their knowledge and belief, are necessary for the purposes of their audit, they shall state that fact in their report (s 237(4)).

Where a holding company has a subsidiary, which is incorporated in Great Britain, it is the duty of the subsidiary and its auditors to give the auditors of the holding company such information and explanation as those auditors may reasonably require for the purposes of their duties as auditors of the holding company. In any other case it is the duty of the holding company, if required by its auditors to do so, to take all such steps as are reasonably open to it to obtain from the subsidiary the required information and explanation (s 392).

The auditors are entitled to attend any general meeting of the company and to receive all notices of, and other communications relating to, any general meeting which any member of the company is entitled to receive, and to be heard at any general meeting which they attend on any part of the business of the meeting which concerns them as auditors (s 387).

# DUTIES OF AUDITORS

## 1. AUDITORS REPORT

The auditors must make a report to the members on the accounts examined by them, and on every balance sheet, profit and loss account and all group accounts laid before the company in general meeting during their tenure of office (s 236).

The report must expressly state whether in their opinion the company's balance sheet and profit and loss account and (if applicable) group accounts have been properly prepared in accordance with provisions of the Companies Act 1985.

The auditors must also state: whether proper accounting records have been kept by the company, and whether proper returns have been received from branches not visited by them; whether the balance sheet and profit and loss account are in agreement with the accounting records and returns, whether they have obtained all the information and explanations necessary for the purposes of the audit (s 237(1)(3)).

The auditors must consider whether the information given in the directors' report relating to the financial year in question is consistent with the company's accounts. If they are of the opinion that the information given in the directors' report is not consistent with the company's accounts for the financial year they must state that fact in their report (s 237(6)).

A company may not purchase its own shares out of capital or give financial assistance for the acquisition of its own shares unless the statutory declaration made by the directors have annexed to it a report by the auditors stating –

(a) they have inquired into the company's state of affairs.
(b) the amount specified as the permissible capital payment of the shares in question is in their view properly determined.
(c) they are not aware of any matter which would render the directors opinion unreasonable in the circumstances (s 173(5)).

If the auditors have qualified their report on the annual accounts, (where the accounts are the only relevant accounts for the purpose of determining whether a distribution may be made), they must state in writing whether in their opinion, their qualification is material for the purpose of determining whether a distribution can be made ie would such a distribution contravene ss 263-267 of the Companies Act 1985.

If a company's directors propose to deliver modified accounts in respect of small or medium sized companies, the auditor must provide the directors with a report stating whether in their opinion the requirements for exemptions are satisfied.

## 2. TO ASCERTAIN THE COMPANY'S TRUE FINANCIAL POSITION

Auditors are not responsible for matters that are concealed from them, but they should investigate matters if there are grounds for suspicion.

> 'If there is anything calculated to excite suspicion, he (the auditor) should probe it to the bottom but in the absence of anything of that kind he is only bound to be reasonable, cautious and careful' (per Lopes LJ in *Re Kingston Cotton Mill (No 2)* (1896))

### Re Thomas Gerrard and Son Ltd (1968)

The company's managing director falsified the accounts in three different ways. The auditors noticed that certain invoices had been altered but negligently failed to investigate the matter further. The auditors gave a favourable view of the company's profits. This resulted in the payment of dividends and tax on the payment of dividends.

It was held that the auditors must repay the dividends, the cost of recovering the tax and any tax not recoverable.

The auditors in that case claimed that they had not been given sufficient time to do their work. Pennycuick J stated in his judgment:

> 'The auditors of the company owe a statutory duty to make the members a report containing certain statements. If the directors do not allow auditors time to conduct such investigations as are necessary in order to make these statements, the auditors must, it seems to me, either refuse to make a report at all or make an appropriately qualified report. They cannot be justified in making a report containing a statement the truth of which they have not had an opportunity of ascertaining.'

### Re London and General Bank (No 2) (1895)

The greater part of the bank's capital was advanced on loan to companies upon securities which were insufficient and difficult to realise. The auditors drew attention to the situation in a confidential report to the directors which concluded with the words – 'we cannot conclude without expressing our opinion unhesitatingly, that no dividend should be paid this year'. This sentence was not included in the official report laid before the directors, which stated that 'the value of the assets as shown on the balance sheet is dependent on realisation'. The directors declared a dividend, which was in effect paid out of capital. It was held that the auditors had been guilty of misfeasance and they were ordered to repay one of the dividends.

## 3. DUTY OF CARE

The auditor must exercise reasonable care, for if he does not act in a reasonable and competent manner he may be sued for damages. (*Re Thomas Gerrard and Son Ltd* (1968))

He is not under a duty to take stock and may accept as honest, statements from the company's officers and employees provided he takes reasonable care.

### Re Kingston Cotton Mill Co (No 2) (1896)

The auditors accepted the certificate of the company's manager as to the value of the stock in trade. If the auditors had compared the amount of the stock at the commencement of the year with sales and purchases during the year, they would have been put on inquiry. They did not do so and as a result dividends were paid out of capital. It was held that the auditor was not liable.

> 'An auditor is not bound to be a dectective . . . or to approach his work with suspicion, or with a foregone conclusion that there is something wrong. He is a watchdog, not a bloodhound. He is justified in believing tried servants of the company in whom confidence is placed by the company. He is entitled to assume that they are honest and to rely upon their representation, provided he takes reasonable care' (per Lopes LJ).

The principles in the above case have been modified by in subsequent cases and higher standards of care and skill are required today, than in 1896.

In *Fomento (Sterling Area) Ltd v Selsdon Fountain Pen Co* (1958) Lord Denning observed that –

> 'An auditor is not to be confined to the mechanics of checking vouchers and making arithmetical computations. He is not to be written off as a professional "adder-upper and subtractor." His vital task is to take care to see that errors are not made, be they errors of computation, or errors of omission or commission, or downright untruths. To perform this task properly he must come to it with an inquiring mind – not suspicious of dishonesty, I agree – but suspecting that someone may have made a mistake somewhere and that a check must be made to ensure that there has been none.'

This higher duty of care was applied in *Re Thomas Gerrard and Son Ltd* (1968).

The auditors are not liable for 'not tracking out ingenious and carefully laid schemes of fraud when there is nothing to arouse their suspicion' per Lopes LJ in *Re Kingston Cotton Mill Co* (*No 2*) (1896).

### Re City Equitable Fire Insurance Co Ltd (1925)

In a winding up by the court an investigation of the company's affairs disclosed a deficiency of £1.2m due in part to the depreciation of investments, but mainly due to the deliberate fraud of the managing director. The auditors had been misled and deceived by the chairman of the company and large sums had been left in the hands of the company's stockbrokers, and lent to the company's general manager. They failed to discover that the company's stockbrokers, to reduce their indebtedness to the company for the purposes of the audit, purchased Treasury Bills before the close of the financial year and sold them immediately the new financial year opened. It was held that although the auditors had committed a breach of duty in not personally inspecting the securities in the hands of the stockbrokers, they had honestly and carefully discharged what they conceived to be the whole of their duty to the company and were not negligent.

### 4.   TO BE ACQUAINTED WITH THE ARTICLES AND THE COMPANIES ACT

'Auditors of a limited company are bound to know and make themselves acquainted with their duties under the Articles of the company whose accounts they are appointed to audit, and under the Companies Act for the time being in force; and when it is shown that audited balance sheets do not show the true financial condition of the company and that damage has resulted, the onus is on the auditors to show that this is not the result of any breach of duty on their part.' (per Astbury J in *Re Republic of Bolivia Exploration Syndicate Ltd* (1914).

The auditor is not expected to be a legal expert.

### Re Republic of Bolivia Exploration Syndicate Ltd (1914)

The company's memorandum provided for the payment of underwriting commission, but no provision for payment was made in the articles. The company paid underwriting commission to a director and the auditor passed these items in the balance sheet, relying on the power given in the memorandum and with the knowledge that the director concerned had not been appointed as such when the company was formed. The legality of the payment had been discussed at a meeting of the shareholders who had subsequently approved the balance sheet. It was held in the special circumstances of this case that the auditor was not liable.

## 5. THE VALUATION OF SHARES

The articles of many private companies contain a clause which provides that a member who wishes to sell his shares must offer them to the existing members at a price to be determined by the auditor.

An auditor is not bound to give the reasons for his valuation or the basis of his calculation. A 'non-speaking' certificate cannot be challenged unless it can be shown that the auditor was negligent in his valuation or there is evidence of fraud, collusion or error on the face of the certificate. If the auditor provides an explanation for his valuation i e a 'speaking certificate', the court may inquire into the valuation.

### Burgess v Purchase and Sons (Farms) Ltd (1983)

Executors sought to sell their shares in a private limited company and informed the company of their wishes. A valuation carried out by the company's auditors was said to be 'final, binding and conclusive.' The auditors valued the ordinary shares at £10.50 per share and the preference shares at 10p per share. The basis of the valuation was set out in the certificate. It was held that despite the provision as to final, binding and conclusive, the valuation could be challenged on the erroneous way in which the figures had been calculated.

The court will not interfere on matters of opinion.

### Dean v Prince (1954)

The articles of a private company provided that a deceased director's shares should be purchased by the surviving directors at a price to be certified by an auditor as a fair value. A director, who held a controlling interest in the company, died. The auditor having made a certified valuation, stated that for the purpose of his valuation he had not regarded the company as a going concern but that he had valued on a 'break up basis', as in his opinion the shares had no value on any other basis, having regard to the losses made by the company. It was held that the auditor was correct in not attributing a special value to the shares on account of their carrying control.

Minority shareholders must not be penalised and their shares must be valued on a similar basis to a major shareholding.

## Re A Company, 003420 of 1981 (1983)

A minority group of shareholders sought an order that the majority should purchase their shares. It was held that an order should be made and the shares should be valued pro rata according to the value of the company's shares as a whole. There would be no discount for the sale of a minority shareholding.

The auditors owe a duty of care to the vendor and purchaser when acting as arbitrators i e the valuation will determine the price to be paid under the contract of sale. An auditor is not acting as an arbitrator when exercising this function, as an arbitrator's function is to make an award after a difference has arisen between the parties, while a valuer seeks to determine a price so that a difference does not exist between the parties.

## Arenson v Casson, Beckman, Rutley and Co (1977)

The principal shareholder and chairman of a private company took his nephew into the business and gave him a parcel of shares in the company, on the understanding that in the event of the nephew terminating his employment he would sell his shares to his uncle at their 'fair value' i e to be determined by the auditors acting as experts not as arbitrators. He terminated his employment and transferred the shares to his uncle for £4,916, the value placed on the shares by the arbitrator. A few months later the company became a public company and the shares were seen to be worth around £30,000. It was held that the auditors had been negligent in their valuation in not taking account the flotation of the company.


## LIABILITY OF AUDITORS

Auditors may incur liability for:

(a) Misfeasance
(b) Negligence


(A) *MISFEASANCE*

Proceedings may be taken against the auditor as an officer of the company for misfeasance (s 631) (*Re London and General Bank* (1895)).

## (B) NEGLIGENCE

A company must prove that loss has been occasioned by the failure of the auditors to perform their duties with reasonable care and skill.

### London Oil Storage Co Ltd v Seear Hasluck and Co (1904)

An auditor was liable for damage sustained by the company when he failed to verify the existence of one of the assets in the balance sheet i e the petty cash.

### Leeds Estate Building and Investment Co v Shepherd (1887)

The company's articles provided that the directors should only receive remuneration if the dividends exceeded 5 per cent. A misleading balance sheet was prepared which permitted a dividend of over 5 per cent to be declared and remuneration to be paid to the directors. The auditor did not check the Articles but certified the accounts 'to be a true copy of those shown in the books of the company.' As a result dividends were paid out of capital. It was held that the auditor was liable.

### Pendleburys Ltd v Ellis Green and Co (1936)

The auditor of a private company reported to the directors, who were the sole shareholders of the company, that the company's system of book-keeping was unsatisfactory. The auditors were held not liable in an action for damages brought by the company.

> 'Where the interests of a small company are confined to a very few persons, and there are no outside people because all the interests in the company are held by the directors themselves, if the auditor has, in fact, reported to the directors, what more could he be expected to do?' (per Swift J).

The auditors may also be liable to third parties with whom they have no contractual relationship if they give advice or information to a third party.

> 'A reasonable man, knowing that he was being trusted or that his skill and judgment were being relied on, would I think, have three courses open to him. He could keep silent or decline to give the information or advice sought; or he could give an answer with a clear qualification that he accepted no responsibility for it or that it was given without the reflection or inquiry which a careful answer would require; or he could simply answer without any such qualification. If he chooses to adopt the

last course he must, I think, be held to have accepted some responsibility for his answer being given carefully, or to have accepted a relationship with the inquirer which requires him to exercise such care as the circumstances require.' (per Lord Reid in *Hedley Byrne and Co Ltd v Heller and Partners Ltd* (1964))

## JEB Fasteners Ltd v Marks Bloom & Co (1983)

Jeb Ltd who acquired the entire capital of F Ltd claimed damages from the auditors of F Ltd on the basis that they had suffered a loss as a result of relying on the accounts for 1974 which were negligently prepared. Sales and purchases had been omitted; there had been a failure to make a provision for interest due on the company's overdrawn account and the valuation of stock was incorrect. It was held the accounts were negligently prepared even though the auditor was unaware that a take-over bid was contemplated. He owed a duty of care to the plaintiff as he should have foreseen at the time of the audit that a person might rely on the accounts for the purpose of deciding whether or not to take over F Ltd and would suffer loss if the accounts were inaccurate. (It was held that defendants were not liable as the alleged negligence was not the cause of the loss).

## Twomax Ltd v Dickson, McFarlane and Robinson (1982)

T Ltd acquired a majority shareholding in a private company, Kintyre Knitwear Ltd. T Ltd asserted that in taking shares in the company it had relied on the accounts prepared by the defendant, which it was alleged had been negligently prepared. The accounts showed a profit of £20,000 in 1972 and a loss in the previous year of £12,318. The company made a loss of £87,000 in 1975 and subsequently went into liquidation. It was alleged that the loss incurred in 1975 could only be explained on the basis of undetected errors in previous years and that the profit in 1973 was seriously overstated. It was held that the audit was 'perfunctory and negligent'. The auditors should have foreseen that the accounts might have been relied upon by a potential investor for the purpose of deciding whether or not to invest in the company.

The rule in *Hedley Byrne* may apply to auditors, acting in their professional capacity, who give advice in the course of their business.

They may also owe a duty of care to potential shareholders who may have relied on their audit and their report to the shareholders. (This is a public document which is open to inspection).

# Chapter 17
# Dividends

A dividend is that part of the profits of trading which is distributed amongst the members of the company in proportion to their shareholding and in accordance with their rights as shareholders.

The provisions as to the declaration and payment of dividends are found in the articles.

(a) A company in general meeting may declare dividends, but no dividend may exceed the amount recommended by the directors (Article 102). If the directors do not recommend the payment of a dividend the members may not over-rule the directors by passing a resolution at general meeting declaring a dividend (*Scott v Scott* (1943)).

(b) The directors may from time to time pay such interim dividends as appear to the directors to be justified by the company's profits (Article 103). An interim dividend is usually declared part of the way through the financial year, and does not require the approval of the company in general meeting.

    (i) it does not create a debt payable by the company and if it is not paid, it cannot be sued for.

**Brookton Co-operative Society Ltd v Federal Commissioner of Taxation** (1979) (Australia)

A subsidiary company declared an interim dividend in favour of its holding company, the appellants. The subsidiary later withdrew the dividend when it became apparent that there were insufficient funds for the payment of the dividend. The Federal Commissioner claimed that the declaration of the interim dividend represented a debt which was owed to the appellants. It was held that as the dividend was not paid, and was not capable of giving rise to a debt before payment, it did not form part of the appellants income.

     (ii) Where the directors propose to pay an interim dividend, reference must be made to interim accounts which must be properly prepared (complying with the contents and form of accounts and signed by the directors) so as to allow a reasonable judgment to be made.

(c) The articles may give power to the directors, before recommending a dividend, to set aside out of the company's profits such sums as they think proper as a reserve. The directors may also be empowered to carry forward any profits which they think prudent not to divide.

(d) Dividends must be paid in cash, unless the articles provide otherwise.

### Wood v Odessa Waterworks Co (1889)

A company whose articles empowered the directors to declare a dividend (to be paid to its shareholders) passed a resolution to pay a dividend by distributing debenture bonds to its shareholders in lieu of cash. It was held that this was not a payment within the Act and the company could be prevented from acting on the resolution.

(e) The articles of the majority of companies that dividends may be paid otehwise than in cash eg by a distribution of paid up shares, debentures etc (Article 105). Such an article is necessary to avoid the difficulties encountered in *Wood v Odessa Waterworks* (1889).

(f) The articles may empower the directors to deduct from any dividend payable to any member all sums of money payable by him to the company on account of calls or otherwise in relation to the shares of the company.

(g) The articles usually provide that all dividends shall be paid to the shareholders in proportion to the amounts paid on the shares. Any amount paid or credited as paid in advance of calls should not be treated as a paid up amount in this context (Article 104).

(h) Any dividend may be paid by cheque or warrant sent through the post to the registered address of the holder, or in the case of joint holders to the first named joint holder on the register (Article 106).

(i) A shareholder is not entitled to a dividend until it is declared in accordance with the procedures laid down in the articles and the due date for payment has arrived. If, however, a company declares a dividend without any stipulation as to the date of payment, the declaration creates an immediate debt.

## PROFITS AVAILABLE FOR DISTRIBUTION

A company may not make a distribution eg pay a cash dividend, except out of the profits available for distribution (s 263(1)).

The profits available for distribution are accumulated realised profits (so far as not previously utilised by distribution or capitalisation) less its accumulated, realised losses (so far as not previously written off in a reduction or reorganisation of capital) (s 263(3)).

(a) Accumulated ie any losses of previous years must be made good before a distribution can be made.
(b) Realised ie any profit, income or capital which has actually been received by the comany.

 (i) A company may not apply an unrealised profit in paying up debentures or any amounts unpaid on any of its issued shares (s 263(4)).
 (ii) Any provision other than one in respect of any diminution in value of a fixed asset appearing on a revaluation of all the fixed assets, or of all the fixed assets other than the goodwill of the company shall be treated as a realised loss (s 275(1)).
 (iii) A revaluation of any of the fixed assets will be regarded as a revaluation of all the fixed assets if the directors are satisfied that the aggregate value of the assets which have not been revalued is not less than the aggregate amount at which they are stated in the company's accounts (s 275(4), (5)).
 (iv) Where on the revaluation of a fixed asset an unrealised profit is shown to have been made and, on or after the revaluation, a sum is written off or retained for depreciation of that asset, the surplus value over and above the amount which would have been written off or retained for depreciation may be treated as a realised profit made over that period (s 275(2)).
 (v) Where there is no record of the original cost of an asset, or the record cannot be obtained without unreasonable expense or delay, the company may use the earliest available record of its value to determine whether a profit or loss has been made in respect of that asset (s 275(3)).
 (vi) Where development costs are shown as an asset in a company's accounts any amount shown in respect of these costs shall be treated as a realised loss, unless there are special circumstances justifying the directors in not conforming to this rule. If the directors adopt this course of action they must disclose the expenditure in the accounts and explain the

circumstances upon which they rely to justify their decision (s 269).

(viii) The rules relating to distribution apply to all distributions except the following

    (a) An issue of fully or partly paid bonus shares;

    (b) The redemption of shares out of the proceeds of a fresh issue of shares and the payment of any premium payable on their redemption out of the share premium account;

    (c) The reduction of share capital by extinguishing or reducing liability in respect of share captial not paid up, or paying off paid up share capital;

    (d) The distribution of assets to the members on a winding up (s 263(2)).

## DISTRIBUTIONS BY PUBLIC COMPANIES

A public company must satisfy further conditions before it is permitted to make a distribution.

It may only make a distribution if at that time the amount of its net assets is not less than the aggregate of its called-up share capital and its undistributable reserves. It may only pay a dividend which will leave its net assets at not less than that aggregate amount (s 264(1)).

A public company must therefore maintain its capital, and take account of the changes in value of its fixed assets.

Its undistributable reserves are:

The share premium account.

The amount by which the accumulated unrealised profits exceed its current accumulated unrealised losses.

Any other reserve which a company is prevented from distributing (s 264).

## RELEVANT ACCOUNTS

The right of a company to pay a dividend is determined by reference to the relevant items in the relevant acounts.

The relevant items are any of the following:

profits, losses, assets, liabilities, provisions, share capital and reserves (including undistributable reserves) (s 270).

The relevant accounts are:–

(a) The company's latest annual accounts which were laid or filed in respect of the last preceding accounting reference period; or

(b) such (*interim*) accounts as are necessary to enable a reasonable judgment to be made as to the amounts of any reasonable item (this may be used where sole reliance on (a) would contravene the Act);
(c) such (*initial*) accounts as are necessary for a reasonable judgment to be made when a distribution is proposed during the company's first year before any annual accounts are prepared (s 271).

If the company latest annual accounts are taken as the relevant accounts:

(i) The accounts must have been properly prepared.
(ii) The company's auditors must have made a report in respect of those accounts.
(iii) If the report is not unqualified, the auditors must state in writing whether the subject matter of their qualification is material in determining whether a distribution should be made.
(iv) A copy of the auditor's statement must have been laid before the company in general meeting or delivered to the Registrar.

Interim and initial accounts prepared for a public company must conform with the forms and contents of accounts, and the balance sheet must be signed by two directors.

A copy of the interim accounts must be delivered to the Registrar (s 272).

Copies of the auditors report and of any statement made by the auditor must accompany the copy of initial accounts which must be delivered to the Registrar (s 273).

## UNLAWFUL DISTRIBUTIONS

Directors who pay a dividend out of capital, may be sued by the company for the whole of the amount of the dividend. The directors are jointly and severally liable to repay the amount to the company. They may however recover from each shareholder, who received a dividend, the amount paid if he knew that it had been paid out of capital.

A shareholder who knowingly receives a dividend paid out of capital cannot take proceedings against the directors to replace the amount of the dividend paid.

A shareholder may obtain an injunction to restrain the payment of dividend out of capital as such a payment is unlawful and ultra vires.

The Act further provides (s 277) that if a company makes a distribution to one of its members in contravention of the provisions of the Act, that member is liable to repay the distribution to the company if he knew or had reasonable grounds to believe that the distribution was so made.

## CAPITALISATION OF PROFITS

Capitalisation in relation to a company's profits means:

(a) applying the profits in wholly or partly paying up unissued shares in the company to be allotted to the members as fully or partly paid bonus shares; or
(b) transferring the profits to the capital redemption reserve (s 280).

A company may therefore make a bonus or capitalisation issue by issuing fully paid bonus shares to its members. This may be achieved by transferring to the share capital account an amount equal to the nominal value of the shares issued from any of the following:

(i) any profits not available for distribution,
(ii) any undivided profits not required for paying up preferential dividend,
(iii) share premium account,
(iv) capital redemption reserve (Article 110).

The issue of bonus shares involves an adjustment to a company's balance sheet, as the company does not part with cash. For example, a company having an authorised share capital of 20,000 £1 shares, has an issued share capital of 10,000 shares. It resolves to issue 10,000 shares as bonus shares by capitalising £10,000 from its reserves and issuing one bonus share for each share held. The adjustment is made by reducing the reserves of profit and loss account by £10,000 and adding £10,000 to its issued capital. As both items appear as a liability on the balance sheet, the company's liabilities remain the same

(a) A capitalisation of profits must be sanctioned by an ordinary resolution at a general meeting.
(b) The resolution must have the recommendation of the directors (as in the payment of a dividend).
(c) Provision for capitalisation must be found in the articles (Article

110) as othewise a shareholder would be entitled to the payment of a dividend in cash.

(d) A return of allotments and the contract between the members and the company (as the shares are allotted for a non-cash consideration) must be delivered to the Registrar within one month after allotment (s 88). Article 110(d) authorises the directors to appoint a peson to enter into an agreement on behalf of the members who have been allotted bonus shares, so as to avoid the necessity of making a contract with all those members.

(e) The number of bonus shares issued to each member must be in proportion to the number of shares held unless the articles or terms of issue provide otherwise.

(f) An issue of bonus shares may increase a company's authorised capital.

## INVESTMENT COMPANIES

An investment company is a public company which has given notice in the prescribed form to the Registrar of its intention to carry on business as an investment company i e its business consists of investing its funds mainly in securities with the aim of spreading investment risk and giving its members the benefit of the results of the management of its funds (s 266).

It may make a distribution out of its accumulated, realised revenue profits (so far as not previously utilised by distribution or capitalisation) less its accumulated revenue losses whether realised or unrealised so far as not previously written off in a reduction or re-organisation of capital. The company does not have to take account of any realised and unrealised capital losses in determining the amount available for distribution, but it may not distribute any realised capital profit.

At the time of making the distribution the value of the company's assets must be at least equal to one and a half times the aggregate of its liabilities, and the subsequent distribution must not reduce the value of the assets below that amount (s 265).

## INSURANCE COMPANIES

An insurance company that carries on a long term business may treat any amount properly transferred to its profit and loss account from a surplus or deficit in its business funds as a realised profit or a realised loss respectively (s 268).

# Chapter 18

# Debentures

There is no precise legal definition of the term 'debenture'. It was defined in *Levy v Abercorris Slate & Slab Co* (1887) as, 'a document which creates or acknowledges a debt'.

In modern commercial usage it is regarded as a document issued by a company, usually under seal, which sets out the terms of a loan and provides for its repayment at some future specified date. It also provides for the payment of interest to the debenture holder of a specified rate at fixed intervals during the interim period. The company usually creates a charge on its property by way of security for the loan.

The Act does not attempt a definition of the term but merely provides in its interpretative section that debenture includes debenture stock, bonds and other securities of a company whether constituting a charge and the assets of the company or not (s 744).

A variety of documents have been held to be debentures. In *Lemon v Austin Friars Investment Trust* (1926) a company issued 'income stock certificates' as an acknowledgement of a debt. There was no date fixed for repayment, no charge was created, and they were not issued under the company's seal, although a register of certificate holders was kept by the company. Three quarters of the company's profit were to be set aside for the redemption of the certificates. It was held that the certificates were debentures.

In *Knightsbridge Estates Trust Ltd v Byrne* (1940) a company mortgaged freehold property to secure a loan of £310,000 from an insurance company. The loan was to be repaid by half yearly instalments over 40 years. The company claimed that it was entitled to redeem the mortgage at an earlier date as postponing the date of redemption for 40 years was a clog on the equity of redemption i e preventing the mortgagor (borrower) from repaying the loan and interest and thereby extinguishing the mortgage. It was held that as the mortgage was a debenture, the doctrine of clogging the equity did not apply, as a debenture may be irredeemable.

A company may issue any of the following:

### 1. A SINGLE DEBENTURE

A company obtaining an overdraft or a secured loan from a bank or other lender may issue a single debenture as security for the loan.

### 2. DEBENTURES ISSUED IN A SERIES

These are usually registered and are expressed to rank pari passu i e equally. Each lender has an equal right to repayment in respect of his loan, as otherwise the loans would rank in priority according to the date of their creation.

### 3. DEBENTURE STOCK

Debenture stock is issued by a public company seeking to raise loan capital from the public at large. It may be transferred in fractional amounts although the articles generally prescribe that the stock may only be transferred in stipulated units e g £5 or multiples of £5.

Debenture stock is generally secured by a trust deed and a register of debenture stock holders is usually kept by the company. Each debenture stock holder is given a debenture stock certificate stating that he is the registered holder of £x of debenture stock. Where debenture stock is issued the debenture stock holders automatically rank pari passu in priority for repayment.

## KINDS OF DEBENTURE

There are several kinds of debentures.

## SECURED AND UNSECURED DEBENTURES

(a) Secured debenture i e a debenture secured by a charge on the company's assets.
(b) Unsecured debenture i e an unsecured promise by the company to pay the loan. The debenture holder ranks only as an ordinary creditor in a winding up.

## REDEEMABLE DEBENTURES

A debenture is usually redeemable and will provide that it may be redeemable on or before a certain date e g 1995-8. A company may therefore redeem the debenture within these years in any of the following ways:–

(a) By purchasing the debentures in the market. If purchased at a discount the profit made by the company is a revenue profit and is available for distribution, unless the articles otherwise provide.
(b) By drawing i e drawing lots and redeeming an agreed number of debentures.
(c) By financing the redemption out of a sinking fund (i e a sum set aside annually to provide for redemption) or out of a new issue of debentures. A new issue is attractive to a company when interest rates have fallen as the old debentures can be redeemed and the money borrowed at lower rates by a new issue.

A company may re-issue redeemed debentures (s 194(1)) unless the company has passed a resolution that they may not be re-issued, or the articles specify that they may not be re-issued, or the terms of issue of the debentures stipulate that they shall not be re-issued.

(i) A holder of a re-issued debenture has the same priorities as the original debenture holder (s 194(2)) i e he ranks pari passu with the holders of the original issue.
(ii) The rights of the debenture holder cannot be altered, cancelled or varied on re-issue e g the date of redemption must be the same as that of the original issue.
(iii) Where a company has deposited its debentures to secure advances made from time on current account or otherwise, the debentures are not deemed to have been redeemed by reason only that the account has ceased to be in debt (s 194(3)).
(iv) A company's balance sheet must contain particulars of any redeemed debentures which it has power to re-issue.

## PERPETUAL (OR IRREDEEMABLE) DEBENTURE

This debenture has no date fixed for its redemption. Such a debenture may only be redeemed by the holder in the event of a winding up or a breach of condition of its issue e g a failure to pay interest on the debenture. The company may nevertheless redeem the debenture at its option.

Such a debenture is not invalid by reason only that it is made irredeemable or redeemable only on the happening of a contingency, however remote, or on the expiration of a period, however long. (s 193). This section effectively removes any doubt as to whether an indefinite or long term postponement of the right of redemption might constitute a clog on the equity of redemption.

A company may therefore create a long term mortgage over its land or property by means of a debenture. Such a debenture is not invalid merely as it postpones the date of redemption to a remote period (*Knightsbridge Estates Trust Ltd v Byrne* (1940) (see p 302)).

The rule against clogging the equity is otherwise unaffected by this section and a mortgagor is entitled to redeem his mortgage free from any restriction.

### Bradley v Carritt (1903)

A loan agreement entered into by a shareholder who mortgaged his shares stipulated that the shareholder would use his endeavours to ensure that the mortgagee should thereafter be a broker for the company's products. It was held that such a condition amounted to a clog on the equity of redemption as the mortgagee still retained a right in the mortgagor's shares.

## CONVERTIBLE DEBENTURES

A company may issue debentures which grant the holder an option to convert his debenture, at stated times, into an ordinary or preference share at a stated rate of exchange. Although debentures may be issued at a discount they may not be exchanged during their currency for shares of equal value as this would amount to the issue of shares at a discount. (*Mosely v Koffyfontein Mines* (1904) (see p 106))

The directors may not issue convertible debentures unless authorised to do so by the company in general meeting or by the company's articles. A company may not make an allotment of convertible debentures unless it first offers them to existing debenture holders or members or employee shareholders on similar terms (s 89). A company may however:

(a) Exchange the debentures for shares at a rate not lower than par.
(b) Issue shares which are paid up to the value of the amount paid on the debentures.

(c) Secure an early discharge of the debentures by offering an immediate consideration (whether in cash or otherwise) which is in excess of the amount originally paid on the debentures.

## BEARER (OR UNREGISTERED) DEBENTURES

This is a negotiable instrument and is transferable by delivery without the payment of stamp duty. It has the following characteristics

(a) it is transferable by delivery;
(b) it is transferable free from equities;
(c) the delivery of the debenture and any interest coupon is a good discharge to the company;
(d) it enables the bearer to sue the company in his own name;
(e) it ensures that any person acquiring the debenture bona fide for valuable consideration has good title notwithstanding any defect in the title of the person from whom he acquires it.

Provision is made for the payment of interest by means of coupons attached to the debenture which are then presented to the company's bankers after a certain date. If repayment of the principal money is not to be made for a considerable time, or the debenture is a perpetual debenture it is usual for the company to make an initial issue of coupons providing for the payment of interest for ten or twenty years. Provision is also made for the issue of new coupons when the original coupons are exhausted by means of a talon which is presented to the company as a request for the issue of new coupons.

A company may issue a bearer debenture that may be exchanged for a registered debenture at the request of the holder.

## REGISTERED DEBENTURES

The lender is entered in the company's register of debenture holders. This simplifies dealings and meets the requirement of the money market. The registered debenture has several advantages;

(a) the title of the registered holder is recorded in the company's books;
(b) the registered holder is recognised by the company as being entitled to the debenture;

(c) the company may communicate with the registered holders more easily should it wish to do so e g in a compromise or reconstruction;

(d) it is a form of security recognised by stock exchanges and is popular with investors;

(e) it enables the company to make payments to an identifiable person whose receipt is a sufficient discharge.

*The usual form of a registered debenture* is under a common seal and contains the following clauses:

(a) A covenant to repay the registered holder the principal on a specified day or on such earlier day as it becomes payable.

(b) A covenant to pay interest half yearly on fixed days and at a fixed rate.

(c) A clause whereby the company charges its undertaking and all its property, present and future including its uncalled capital.

(d) A clause stating that the debenture is issued subject to certain conditions, which are deemed to be incorporated into the agreement;

    (i) All debentures of the series are to rank pari passu without any preference or priority over one another and the charge is to be a floating security (or charge). In the absence of this condition the debentures would rank in priority according to the dates of issue.

    (ii) Provision for keeping a register of debentures (s 190), the inspection of the register (s 191).

    (iii) The company will only recognise the registered holder or his legal personal representatives and is not bound to enter notice of any trust in the register or recognise any trust affecting the title of the debenture.

    (iv) Provision for the transfer of the debenture. Every transfer must be in writing and a proper instrument of transfer must be submitted to the company in respect of any proposed transfer. The company must have ready for delivery the debenture or certificate of debenture stock within two months of the transfer being lodged or within such time as the conditions of issue otherwise provide (s 185). If the company refuses to register the transfer it must give notice of refusal to the transferee within 2 months (s 183).

    (v) No transfer may be registered during the fourteen days immediately preceding the date fixed for the payment of interest. This is a matter of administrative convenience.

(vi)  A clause providing that the title of the registered holder is free from any equities between the company and any previous holder.

By excluding the company's claims, the debenture is more marketable, and future holders will not be saddled with a security which could depreciate in value as a result of a latent equity.

### Re Goy & Co Ltd (1900)

A company had embarked on a voluntary liquidation, and Chandler (a former director) transferred debentures of £600 to Robey as security for a loan. The conditions of the debenture contained a similar clause to that set out above. After the transfer it was discovered that Chandler had been guilty of misfeasance, and he was ordered to pay £300 to the liquidator. The liquidator declined to register the transfer of the debenture and claimed the right to deduct the £300 owed by Chandler. It was held that the right to transfer and to have the transfer registered was not affected by the winding up, and Robey was entitled to be paid the dividend on the debentures without deduction.

In the absence of such a clause the company can set up equities against an unregistered transferee of the debenture.

### Re Palmer's Decoration & Furnishing Co (1904)

A company issued debentures to B which contained a clause providing that 'the principal moneys secured became immediately payable in the event of a resolution for winding up being passed. A clause further provided that the principle moneys and interest hereby secured will be paid without regard to any equities between the company and the original or any intermediate holder thereof.' After a resolution for winding up the company had been passed, B transferred the debentures to C who took without notice of the defect in B's title. Notice of the transfer was given to the liquidator but no transfer was registered. It was held that as B had paid nothing for the debentures and had obtained them from the company by misrepresentation, the rights of the company prevailed over C's title.

(vii)  The power of the company to pay off the principal money after giving specified notice of its intention.

(viii) Immediate repayment of the principal money if any of the following circumstances occur:
  (a) If the company makes default (for a period of 3 months) in the payment of interest;
  (b) If an order or resolution is passed for winding up;
  (c) If a distress or execution is levied against the chattels or property of the company;
  (d) If a receiver is appointed;
  (e) If a company ceases or threatens to cease carrying on its business;
 (ix) The place at which interest is payable.
  (x) The power of a specified proportion of the debenture holders to appoint a receiver. The powers of such a receiver are also listed.
 (xi) The place of payment of principal moneys and interest e g a specified bank or the company's registered office.
(xii) Method of serving notice on debenture holders e g by post to a person at his registered address.

## NAKED DEBENTURES

These debentures have no charge on any of the company's assets and are mere acknowledgement of a debt owed by the company. The holder has the rights of an unsecured ordinary creditor.

## DEBENTURES SECURED BY A FIXED CHARGE

These debentures offer the best security and are particularly suitable for securing a charge on certain types of property e g land, building, interests in land or ships.

A company usually remains in possession of the property but may not dispose of it without the consent of the debenture holders.

A fixed charge may be created either by a legal or equitable morgage:

(a) The title in the property passes to the mortgagee (the lender) in a legal mortgage, subject to the company's right to redeem the property on payment of the principal sum and interest.
(b) An equitable mortgage may be created by a deposit of the title deeds as security for the loan, or by an agreement to grant a legal mortgage.

## DEBENTURE SECURED BY A FLOATING CHARGE

The characteristics of a floating charge were stated by Romer LJ in
*Re Yorkshire Woolcombers Association Ltd* (1903):

(a)  It is an equitable charge on a class of assets, present and future;
(b)  The class is one which, in the ordinary course of business, is
     changing from time to time;
(c)  Until some step is taken by or on behalf of those interested in
     the charge, the company may carry on its business in the
     ordinary way.

A floating charge is usually created by the use of express words,
but no particular words are necessary. If rights are given to a
creditor in respect of the company's assets, while allowing the
company to deal with its assets in the ordinary course of business,
this will constitute a floating charge.

It is an equitable charge which does not attach to any specific or
definite property and is constantly changing e g a charge on present
and future book debts. A company may therefore deal freely with
its assets until the charge crystallises, while the debenture holders
have a variety of assets available to satisfy the debenture debt on
crystallisation of the charge. It is therefore a general charge which
attaches to a class of assets and any one particular asset cannot be
identified until the charge crystallises.

A floating charge crystallises i e becomes a fixed charge on the
company's assets at a particular time on the occurrence of a
specified event:

(a)  when they company ceases to carry on in business;
(b)  when the company is wound up;
(c)  in the circumstances specified in the debenture or trust e g
     default in the payment of principal or interest;
(d)  the appointment of a receiver or manager for the debenture
     holders.

The effect of the appointment on the receiver was stated by
Mocatta J in *George Barker (Transport) Ltd v Eynon* (1974);

> 'The appointment of a receiver by the debenture holders does not end
> the legal life of the company; the company is so to speak anaesthetised,
> but the receiver may carry on business on its behalf. The legal persona of
> the company will continue to subsist until liquidation and the company
> in the case of the most successful receiverships may be restored to full
> conscious activity when the anaesthetic is no longer applied after the
> debts owing the debenture holders have been paid'.

A fixed charge is a far more satisfactory form of security as it confers rights over identifiable assets e g land and property. A holder of a floating charge will not know until a charge crystallises what assets will be comprised in his security. This may be advantageous in certain situations e g when the stock in trade of an insolvent company is more easily realised than factory premises.

DISADVANTAGES OF FLOATING CHARGE

A floating charge is postponed to the claims of the following creditors if they act before the debenture holders take steps to enforce their security i e by appointing a receiver;

1. (a) Value added tax and local rates which become payable within 12 months next.
   (b) Wages of a clerk or servant; or wages of a workman or labourer in respect of services rendered to the company during the 4 months next before the relevant date, not exceeding £800 per claimant.
   (c) Any one year's assessment of assessed taxes e g corporation tax, income tax, capital gains tax assessed on the company up to the 5 April next.
   (d) All accrued holiday remuneration payable to a clerk, servant, workman or labourer on the termination of his employment before or by the effect of the winding up order or resolution.
   (e) All the debts specified in s 153 (2) of the Social Security Pensions Act e g National Insurance contributions payable by the company as an employer, unless the company is being wound up voluntarily for the purposes of reconstruction or amalgamation (s 614, s 196, Sch 19).
2. A landord (who has distrained for rent) or a judgment creditor who has seized and sold the goods if the sale has been effected before the appointment of a receiver.
3. The owners of goods supplied to the company under a hire purchase agreement.
4. A seller of goods who has inserted a retention clause (a Romalpa clause) in a contract of sale. The seller thus retains the legal ownership in the goods until the buyer has paid for the goods. The buyer is given possession of the goods and may use them in the manufacture of goods which he then resells.

## Aluminium Industrie Vaassen BV v Romalpa (1976)

AIV sold aluminium foil to R on terms that the stock of foil should remain the property of the seller until the purchaser (R) had paid all sums owing to the seller. The contract also stipulated that if the foil was used to manufacture new objects, these objects should be stored separately and be owned by AIV as security for payment. R ran into financial difficulties and a receiver was appointed. It was held that the foil did not belong to R as the ownership of the goods had not passed to R ie R was a bailee of AIV's goods; and R was AIV's agent for the sale of the objects manufactured from the foil.

## AVOIDANCE OF A FLOATING CHARGE

A floating charge created within 12 months of the commencement of a winding up is void. There are two exceptions to this rule.

(a) If the chargee can prove that the company was solvent immediately after the creation of the charge.
(b) The charge is valid to the amount of any cash paid to the company at or after the time of creating the charge and on consideration of it, plus interest at 5 per cent (s 617).
  (i) Money advanced some days before the charge is created is nevertheless money paid 'at the time of' the creation of the charge if the advance was given in reliance on a promise to execute the charge.

### Re F & E Stanton Ltd (1928)

A loan was made to an insolvent company on the security of a floating charge. The loan was advanced in several instalments but the charge was not created until 5 days after the last instalment was paid. Five days after the creation of the charge the company went into liquidation. It was held that the charge was valid as the loan was made in consideration of the security in anticipation of its creation. The payments were therefore regarded as having been made at the time of the creation of the charge.

  (ii) Cash advanced after the creation of the charge which is used to pay some creditor will not be regarded as money advanced for a new loan. The charge will be void as it constitutes security for the later loan.
  (iii) The cash must be paid to the company to benefit the company and not some other party. The fact that the cash was paid into the company's account is not conclusive evidence of that fact.

## Re Destone Fabrics Ltd (1941)

A debenture was issued to Zimmerman as a floating charge on the assets and undertaking of an insolvent company to secure £900. The money was provided by Davis for whom Zimmerman was nominee, and later that day he paid £350 each to two directors as fees and £200 to Davis, the amount guaranteed by him in respect of the company overdraft. It was held that the payment did not benefit the company, as it was made for the benefit of certain creditors to the prejudice of other creditors. There was no bona fide payment to the company at the time of or subsequent to the creation of and in consideration for the charge. The charge was therefore invalid.

(iv) In certain cases payments made directly to the company's creditors have been held to be 'cash paid to the company' if such a loan is made in good faith to assist the company to carry on its business, and not merely to secure an existing debt.

## Re Matthew Ellis Ltd (1933)

A company owed £1,954 to the firm of Arthur Tipper for goods supplied on credit. The firm refused to supply any more goods until the debt was paid. Arthur D. Tipper who was the chairman of the company and a partner in the firm of Arthur Tipper advanced £3,000 to the company on the security of a floating charge, on condition that the money was to be used for the payment of the debt. The sum of £1,954 was paid directly to Arthur Tipper and the balance was paid to the company, which was insolvent at the time. Four months later the company went into liquidation. It was held that the charge was valid as it was a payment of £3,000 in cash to the company.

(v) Where a floating charge is created in favour of a bank as continuing security for 'all present or future indebtedness to the bank on current account', and further advances are made by the bank, the rule in *Clayton's* case applies

> ('. . . it is the sum first paid in that is first drawn out. It is the first item in the debit side of the account that is discharged or reduced by the first item on the credit side . . .' Sir William Grant in *Clayton's* case).

## Re Yeovil Glove Co Ltd (1965)

A company which had a bank overdraft of £68,000 created a floating charge in favour of a bank. Over the next few months it paid in cheques of £111,000 and drew cheques totalling £110,000. At the date of the commencement of the winding up the amount of the overdraft was £67,000 – similar to the amount at the date of the creation of the charge. It was held that the rule in *Clayton's* case applied. The payments in to the account operated to discharge the indebtedness to the bank existing at the date of the creation of the charge. The further advances were 'new money' and therefore the bank was a secured creditor in respect of those payments.

AVOIDANCE OF A CHARGE

Any charge created by a company which was insolvent at the time and within 6 months of the commencement of winding up is void if it is a fraudulent preference ie voluntarily preferring one creditor at the expense another (s 615).

## PRIORITY OF CHARGES

1. A fixed charge as a legal mortgage ranks before an equitable floating charge.

If the floating charge is created first, the fixed charge nevertheless ranks before it, unless at the time of the creation of the fixed charge, notice of the existing floating charge is given to the holder of the fixed charge. Registration of the floating charge merely gives notice of the existence of the charge.

It is usual to insert a clause in the instrument creating the floating charge that 'the charge hereby created is to be a floating security but . . . the corporation is not to be at liberty to create any mortgage or charge ranking pari passu with or in priority to the said debentures.' This clause ('negative pledge clause) is effective against a person who has notice of the floating charge and the provision, but not against a person who obtains a legal charge (mortgage) of the property and who can show that:

(a) he was not aware of the existence of the floating charge; or
(b) although he was aware of the charge he was not aware of the restriction.

The legal mortgage will be entitled to priority by virtue of the legal estate, which will rank before the equitable charge.

### Wilson v Kelland (1910)

A company issued debentures secured by a floating charge which prohibited the creation of any charge ranking in priority to or pari passu with this particular charge. A fixed charge was later created by the company in favour of Kelland who was unaware of the existence of the debenture and had made no inquiry or search in respect of the company's title. It was held that although K had constructive notice of the existence of the floating charge (as it was registered) he did not have constructive notice of the prohibition.

2. Legal charges rank according to the order of creation.

3. Floating charges rank according to the order of creation.
A floating charge on a specific asset e g book debts will however rank over the whole of the company's undertaking.

4. A company which has created a floating charge may create a further floating charge over the same assets, which ranks in priority to the earlier floating charge. This must be expressly provided for in the original charge.

### Re Automatic Bottle Makers Ltd (1926)

A company reserved the right in a trust deed secured by a floating charge to create further charges which would rank in priority to the first floating charge. The company created a second floating charge on its documents, materials and stock to rank in priority to the floating charge. It was held that such a charge was valid and had priority over the first floating charge.

5. If a company deposits title deeds with a lender as security for an equitable mortgage, the specific charge will rank prior to the floating charge if the lender was unaware, at the time of the creation of the charge of the existence of the floating charge.

## DEBENTURE TRUST DEED

A company which invites the public to subscribe for its debentures will usually enter into a trust deed with a number of trustees or a trustee company.
  The creation of a trust deed has various advantages for the company and for the debenture holders.

1. The trustees can act promptly to protect the interests of the debenture holders if the company makes default e g by appointing a receiver.
2. The legal estate is vested in the trustee and where necessary a

legal mortgage or charge is registered which gives priority over any subsequent charges created by the company.

3. The trustees have possession of the title deeds, thus ensuring that no subsequent charge may be created which has priority over an existing charge.
4. The trustees are in a position to ensure that the company fulfills its obligations under the trust deed e g covenants by the company to insure, repair.
5. The company is entitled to use the property for the purpose of its business and transfer the property with the consent of the trustees.
6. The trust deed usually gives the trustees the power to sell the property without the aid of the court.
7. The trust deed usually sets out the terms and conditions of the debenture in more detail than the conditions printed on a debenture.
8. A mortgage of ships, patents, foreign property is best achieved by a mortgage to trustees, rather than by giving a charge in the debentures.

CONTENTS OF TRUST DEED

A trust deed usually contains the following provisions.

1. The amount and terms of issue of the debentures.
2. A legal charge of the company's property (both freehold and leasehold) or a registered charge in the case of registered title.
3. A floating charge on all other assets.
4. The company to retain possession until default is made in payment of interest of interest etc.
5. The circumstances in which the securities can be enforced e g default in repayment of principal, payment of interest, breach of condition, the manner of enforcement e g entry into possession, sale, appointment of receiver.
6. The power of the trustees to sell or exchange the property of the company at the request of the company.
7. Meetings of debenture holders.
8. Covenants by the company to repair and insure the property.
9. Remuneration of trustees.
10. The exemption of trustees from liability.

Any provision in a trust deed exempting a trustee from, or indemnifying him against liability for breach of trust where he fails to show the degree of care and diligence required of him as a trustee, is void except for:

(a) a release given in respect of anything done or omitted to be
done;
(b) a provision enabling a release to be given by ¾ in value of the
debenture holders voting at a meeting summoned for the
purpose with regard to specific acts or omissions or on the
trustee dying or ceasing to act.
(c) a provision in force on 1 July 1948 that as long as one trustee
remains (who was appointed before that date) the benefit of the
provision extends to other trustees, present and future, by a
resolution approved of by ¾ in value of the debenture holders
(s 192).

## ISSUE OF DEBENTURES

The power to issue debentures is usually set out in a company's
memorandum of association.

In general similar prospectus rules apply to the issue of
debentures to the public, as are applicable to shares. A prospectus
deals with the offer 'to the public for subscription or purchase any
shares or debentures of a company' (s 744).

Debentures may not be offered for sale to the public by a private
company (s 81). Debentures may, unlike shares, be issued at a
discount or on terms that a premium be paid on their redemption.
The share Premium account may be used to provide such a
premium. Debentures may also be issued at a premium and there is
no restriction on the company's use of this premium.

If money is advanced to a company under an agreement that
debentures shall be issued, the lender becomes (in equity) the
debenture holder, as equity looks upon that as done which ought to
be done.

### Pegge v Neath and District Tramways Co Ltd (1898)

The company undertook to issue second mortgage debentures to Pegge as
security for a loan. The first and same second mortgage debenture holders
successfully brought an action against the company to enforce their security
and obtained judgment. Pegge then brought an action for the issue of the
debentures. It was held that he was in equity a holder of the debentures to
the amount of his loan.

An agreement to issue debentures must be registered within 21
days (s 395). However an agreement to create a charge in the future

does not require registration until the charge comes into existence.

An agreement with a company to issue debentures may be enforced by an order for specific performance. A company may enforce an agreement to take debentures (s 195).

## REGISTRATION OF CHARGES

Charges must be registered in the company's register of charges while certain charges must be registered with the Register of Companies.

### REGISTRATION IN THE COMPANY'S REGISTER OF CHARGES

Every limited company must keep at its registered office a register of all charges specifically affecting the property of the company and all floating charges on the undertaking or any property of the company. The register must contain:

(a) a short description of the property charged;
(b) the amount of the charge;
(c) the names of the persons entitled to it (except in the case of bearer securities) (s 407).

Every company must keep at its registered office a copy of every instrument creating a charge, which is required to be registered. Where there is a series of uniform debentures, a copy of one of the debentures of the series is sufficient.

Any creditor or member of the company may inspect, free of charge, the register of charges and the instruments creating the charges. A member of the public may inspect the register of charges on payment of a fee, not exceeding 5p.

If a company refuses to permit inspection of the register or of the copies every officer of the company in default is liable to a fine and a further default fine for every day during which refusal continues. The court may however order an immediate inspection of the copies or register (s 408).

Failure to register a charge in the company's register does not invalidate the charge. (Failure to register at the Companies Registry affects the validity of a charge). Any officer of the company who wilfully authorises or permits the ommission of any entry required to be made under the Act is liable to a fine (s 407).

REGISTRATION WITH THE REGISTRAR OF COMPANIES

Section 395 provides for the registration of certain specified charges created by companies over their assets. Prescribed particulars of the charge together with the instrument (if any) by which the charge is created must be delivered to the Registrar within 21 days after the date of its creation.

This section applies to the following charges.

(a) a charge for the purpose of securing any issue of debentures;
(b) a charge on uncalled share capital of the company;
(c) a charge created or evidenced by an instrument which, if executed by an individual, would require registration as a bill of sale;
(d) a charge on land, wherever situated, or any interest therein, but not including a charge for any rent or other periodical sum issuing out land;
(e) a charge on calls made but not paid;
(f) a floating charge on the undertaking or property of the company;
(g) a charge on calls made but not paid;
(h) a charge on a ship or any share in a ship;
(i) a charge on goodwill, on a patent or a licence under a patent, on a trademark or a copyright or a licence under a copyright.

If a company acquires any property which is already subject to any of the charges listed above, it must register the prescribed particulars of the charge (with a copy of the instrument creating the charge) with the Registrar within 21 days of the acquisition of the property. If the property is situated outside Great Britain, registration must be effected within 21 days of the date of the receipt in the United Kingdom of a copy of the instrument (if despatched by post with due diligence.) If default is made, the company and every officer of the company in default is liable to a fine, but the validity of the charge is unaffected (s 400).

The Registrar will then issue a certificate that the charge has been duly registered, and a copy is endorsed on every debenture certificate issued.

## Re C L Nye Ltd (1971)

A Company negotiated a loan from a bank, together with an overdraft on the security of the premises.

A charge was created in favour of the bank in February. The charge was sealed by the company but the transfer and charge were left undated and were handed over to the bank's solicitor. By an oversight the charge was not registered at the time and the oversight was not noticed until 18th June.

On the 3rd July the solicitor applied for registration and included 18th June as the date on which the charge was created or evidenced. A certificate of registration was issued under s 98 of the Companies Act 1948. The company later went into liquidation and the liquidator challenged the validity of the charge. It was held that the certificate issued by the Registrar was conclusive evidence that the charge was valid and that it had been registered within 21 days of its creation, even though the date was incorrectly stated.

When the debt for which the charge was given has been paid or satisfied in whole or in part; or that part of the property or undertaking charged has been released from the charge or has ceased to form part of the company's property or undertaking the Registrar may enter on the register a memorandum of satisfaction. The company is entitled to a copy of the memorandum (s 403).

EFFECT OF NON-REGISTRATION

If a charge is not registered within 21 days of its creation:

(i) It is void against the liquidator and other creditors of the company. The debenture holder becomes an unsecured creditor in the company's winding up.

(ii) The charge is not void against the company while it is a going concern, so that prior to liquidation a person seeking to enforce a charge has all the remedies of a mortgagee, e g power of sale, foreclosure which a liquidator in a subsequent winding up cannot set aside. Any subsequent creditor who obtains rights over the same asset, before the first charge is registered obtains priority.

### Re Monolithic Co (1915)

Two charges were created over the company's property but were not registered. The company created a third charge in favour of the managing director, who was aware of the existence of the existing charges. The third charge was duly registered within the prescribed time. It was held that the two unregistered charges were void against the holder of the third charge. The court allowed the late registration of these charges on condition that the third charge should retain its existing priority.

(iii) The money secured becomes immediately repayable.
(iv) The company and every officer who is knowingly a party to the default is liable to a default fine.

The court is given power under s 404 to

(a) extend the time for registration;
(b) rectify the register in respect of errors in the registration of the charge.

It must be satisfied that the omission to register a charge or mortgage within the prescribed time or the omission or mis-statement with regard to the charge or mortgage was 'accidental or due to inadvertence or to some other sufficient cause, or is not of a nature to prejudice the position of creditors or shareholders of the company, or that, on other grounds, it is just and equitable to grant relief (per Russell LJ. In *Re C L Nye Ltd* (1971)).

The court may therefore extend the time for registration on such terms and conditions as it thinks fit. The following clause is usually inserted in an order permitting late registration.

'This order to be without prejudice to the rights of parties acquired prior to the time when such debentures shall be actually registered.'

This proviso protects rights acquired against the company's property between the 21 days allowed for registration and the extended time allowed by the order. It does not give priority to any rights acquired in the original 21 day period e g

(i) Debenture A created on 1/1/85
   Debenture B created 20/1/85
   Debenture B registered on 24/1/85
   Late registration of Debenture A on 1/4/85
   Debenture A ranks before debenture B
(ii) Debenture B created on 23/1/85
   Debenture B ranks before Debenture A

### Watson v Duff Morgan and Vermont Holdings (1974)

A company created debentures in favour of the plaintiff and defendant on the 22 January 1971. The second debenture in favour of the defendant was expressed to rank after that of the plaintiff. The defendant registered his charge within 21 day period (on 28 January 1971), but the plaintiff did not. On 20 October the plaintiff applied for and was granted an order for late registration.

The company was wound up in November 1971. It was held that the plaintiff's charge ranked before that of the defendant whose rights were acquired at the date of the execution of the charge (22 January 1971) and not at the expiration of the 21 day period allowed for the registration of the first debenture (12 February 1971).

## Re R M Arnold & Co Ltd (1984)

In January 1982 T lent money to a company (C) to enable them to purchase a parcel of land. A bank (L) already had a debenture covering any land that C might acquire. L expressly consented to T having a fixed charge on the parcel of land and T advanced monies under a debenture and a mortgage dated 18/1/1982. The land was conveyed in March 1983 and a mortgage by way of legal charge was created on 18/3/1983 which was never registered due to inadvertance. It was held than an order for registration out of time would be made to ensure the correct order for the agreed priority as between the bank (L) and T, but as regards unsecured creditors T could always fall back on its fixed equitable charge of January 1982. There was no creditor apart from L (other than the unlikely but possible case of a person who had obtained a legal interest in the land between its acquisition and the registration of the March 1983 mortgage) who could possibly be adversely affected by a registration out of time. Only a proviso to protect such a person would be inserted in the order.

The unregistered charge, if subsequently registered while the company is a going concern, has priority over the unsecured creditors. If a winding up has commenced before the charge is registered, the unregistered charge no longer has the priority and only in exceptional cases will the court allow late registration or rectification after the commencement of a winding up.

## REMEDIES OF DEBENTURE HOLDERS

If a debenture is not secured by a charge the remedies available to the debenture holder are:

1. to sue the company on its promise to repay the principal and/or interest and obtain judgement from the court;
2. to levy execution against the company if judgement has been obtained;
3. to petition as a creditor, for winding up of the company, on the grounds that the company is unable to pay its debts;
4. to prove in a winding up (if the company is already being wound up) for the debt that is owed him.

Where the debenture is secured by a charge the debenture holder has far more satisfactory remedies than an unsecured debenture holder. The deed creating the charge ie the debenture or the trust deed usually contains remedies (e g sale, appointment of a receiver) for enforcing the security without the need to seek the aid of the court.

The following additional remedies are available to the secured debenture holder.

### 1. SALE

The power of sale is usually contained in the debenture or the trust deed, and may be exercised without the court's consent. If a debenture is a single debenture, with a charge over the company's assets it will usually contain an express power of sale, but even in the absence of an express power an implied power of sale may be given under s 103 of the Law of Property Act 1925.

This arises if the debenture is under seal and either;

(a) notice requiring repayment has been served on the company and default has been made for three months; or
(b) interest has been in arrears for two months; or
(c) there has been a breach of the major condition of the debenture (other than payment of principal or interest).

The proceeds of a sale will be applied in paying costs, expenses and the payment of principal and interest. Any surplus will be returned to the company.

### 2. FORECLOSURE

He may apply to the court for an order of foreclosure. This order is rarely applied for as every debenture holder must be a party to the action. Its effect is to extinquish the borrower's interests in the assets charged, and vest the title in the assets in the lender (the debenture holder) free from the company's equity of redemption i e the company's right to redeem the loan and recover its property free from the charge.

### 3. DEBENTURE HOLDERS ACTION

He may bring an action against the company for default in payment of interest or repayment of capital. If the debenture is one of a series he sues on behalf of himself and the other debenture holders for

(a) a declaration that the debentures are a charge on the assets;
(b) an account and inquiry to show the amount owed to the debenture holder, the assets available, the existence of prior claims;
(c) the appointment of a receiver and manager;
(d) an order of sale or foreclosure.

### 4. APPOINTMENT OF A RECEIVER

The debenture or trust deed usually give the debenture holder(s) the power to appoint a receiver.

If no such power is given the debenture holder may apply to the court in a debenture holders' action for such an appointment.

### 5. WINDING UP PETITION

He can present a petition for winding up the company if the company is indebted to him for the payment of principal and interest. He may present a petition even though he has obtained the appointment of a receiver.

### 6. VALUATION OF SECURITY

If a company is being wound up, he may value his security and prove for the balance of his debt or surrender his security and prove for the whole debt.

The amount recovered by enforcing his security may be applied to pay his costs, principal and interest up to the date of payment.

## RECEIVER

A receiver may be appointed under the express power in the debentures; or by the court.

### APPOINTMENT UNDER A POWER IN THE DEBENTURES

(a) The debenture (or debenture trust deed) usually gives power to the debenture holders (or the trustees for the debenture holders) to appoint a receiver in circumstances specified in the debenture (or debenture trust deed) e g default in the payment of principal or interest, winding up of the company.

A receiver appointed under a fixed charge does not have the power to manage the business, and will usually sell the asset charged for the benefit of the debenture holders. It is usual to appoint a 'receiver and manager' under a floating charge if there is a provision to this effect in the debenture.

(b) A receiver appointed by the debenture holders is the agent of the debenture holders, unless the debenture states that he is to be the agent of the company. This may be expressly stated in the debenture or it may be incorporated by reference to the provisions of s 109 (2) of the Law of Property Act (which provides that a receiver shall be the agent of the mortgagor.)

(c) The company therefore becomes responsible for the contracts entered into by the receiver, and for his remuneration, his acts and defaults.

(d) A receiver appointed under the terms of a debenture is personally liable on all contracts entered into by him, unless liability is excluded by the contract. He is therefore entitled to an indemnity out of the company's assets if he acts within his authority (s 492).

A receiver usually requires an express indemnity from the debenture holders as a pre-requisite of appointment.

He is entitled in certain circumstances to repudiate a contract, without legal liability.

### Airlines Airspares Ltd v Handley Page Ltd (1970)

The plaintiff company were the assignees of the benefit of an agreement under which the defendant company agreed to pay a commission of £500 in respect of every 'Jetstream' aircraft sold by them. A receiver was appointed by a bank in respect of a debenture issued by the defendant company.

He formed a subsidiary company and transferred part of the defendant company's assets to the subsidiary. The receiver then entered into negotiations for the sale of the subsidary's shares and informed the plaintiff company that he could no longer comply with the agreement to pay commission.

It was held that the receiver could not be restrained from selling the shares. The repudiation would not adversely affect the realisation of the assets or the company's future trading prospects.

The receiver could therefore frustrate the contract in circumstances where the company itself would not be entitled to do so.

(e) His power to borrow without the court's approval depends upon the terms of the debenture or trust deed. If the debenture or trust deed gives him the power to carry on the business, he has an implied power to borrow for that purpose. Such a loan will rank in priority to the existing debentures.

The receiver will not be personally liable for loans made as a result of the court giving him leave to borrow money, unless he has exceeded the authorised amount of the loan or has undertaken personal liability by the terms of the loan.

(f) A receiver appointed by the debenture holders may apply to the court for directions in relation to any matter connected with the exercise of his functions (s 492).

(g) His remuneration is determined by agreement with the debenture holders.

(h) On the commencement of a winding up, the receiver ceases to be the company's agent and no longer has authority to bind the company. As the company is unable to trade, he is personally liable as a principal for any contracts entered into on its behalf.

His rights in regard to company's property comprised in the debenture are unaffected and he may hold and dispose of the property without restriction and may use the company's name for that purpose.

## APPOINTMENT BY THE COURT

A receiver may be appointed by the Court in a debenture holders action if the debenture does not contain the power to appoint a receiver.

The court will only make an appointment

(a) if the principal or interest is in arrears; or
(b) if the company is being wound-up; or
(c) if the security is in jeopardy.

The security may be regarded as being in jeopardy even if there is no default in payment of interest or a winding up, if the company's assets are diminishing in value or if the company disposes of its assets. There is no jeopardy if the assets charged are found to be of less value than the amount of the debt secured by the charge.

The following are examples of situations where the court has regarded the security as being in jeopardy.

1. Where a creditor had obtained judgment against the company and was in a position to issue execution against the company (even though there was no default in payment of principal and interest): *Re London Pressed Hinge Co Ltd* (1905).

2. Where the company's works had closed and the creditors were threatening action (even though no case had arisen under the

debenture for the appointment of a receiver): *McMahon v North Kent Ironworks* (1891)

3. Where a company proposed to distribute its reserve fund (its only asset) among its members as a dividend, thereby leaving the debentures insufficiently secured: *Re Tilt Cove Copper Co Ltd* (1913).
4. Where a winding up petition had been presented (even though the charge had not yet crystallised): *Re Victoria Steamboats Ltd* (1897).
5. Where a company's funds and credit were exhausted and creditors were threatening action: *Re Braunstein and Marjolaine* (1914).

A receiver appointed by the court is not an agent of the debenture holders or the company, but is an officer of the court, and any interference with him is a contempt of court. No proceedings may be taken against him except with the leave of the court.

Although his remuneration is fixed by the court it *is paid by the company*.

(a) He is personally liable on the contracts entered into by him but is entitled to be indemnified out of the company's assets in priority to the debenture holders.
(b) Contracts made by the company and current at the date of the appointment are not binding on him personally, unless they become binding by novation. The contracts continue to bind the company so that in the event of a breach, the company will be liable for damage.
(c) A receiver who is also appointed manager is under a duty to preserve the goodwill as well as the assets of the company.

A receiver and manager was not permitted to repudiate a company's forward contracts for the supply of coal, despite the fact that the price of coal had risen since the contracts were made. Such repudiation would have damaged the company's goodwill: *Re Newdigate Colliery Ltd* (1912).
(d) He must obtain the court's approval to borrow money. The court in granting approval may authorise the receiver to borrow money in priority to the existing debentures.

He may apply to the court for directions in relation to any matter connected with the performance of his duties.
(e) He may be removed by the court.

The Registrar must be informed within 7 days of the appointment of a receiver by the person making the appointment or obtaining the order. The receiver must notify the Registrar on ceasing to act (s 405).

The following may not be appointed to act as receiver:

(a)  any corporate body (s 489),
(b)  an undischarged bankrupt (s 490),
(c)  a person disqualified by a court under s 296,
(d)  a person disqualified under s 299.

The court may appoint the Official Receiver to act as receiver for debenture holders or creditors if the company is being wound up by the court.

The court may also appoint a liquidator to act in place of a receiver in order to avoid unnecessary expenditure and conflict.

APPOINTMENT OF A MANAGER

A manager will be appointed if it is necessary to carry on a trade and business or if it is proposed to sell the business as a going concern. The same person is usually appointed receiver and manager. Although a manager is usually appointed to sell the business as a going concern, this rule is not inflexible.

### Re Victoria Steamboats Ltd (1897)

A company was formed to carry passengers and operate a ferry service, under contract with the Great Eastern Railway. The company was wound up and stopped the passenger service. The debenture holders applied for the appointment of a manager of the ferry service on the grounds that if the contract were broken, the debenture holders would suffer a heavy loss. It was held that a manager would be appointed for although there was no immediate prospect of a sale, the property would be realised at some future date.

A manager is usually appointed to act for a fixed time eg 3 months. If he acts beyond the decreed time, without obtaining an order from the court extending the time, he will be disallowed his expenditure.

THE EFFECT OF AN APPOINTMENT

On the appointment of a receiver or manager

1.  He takes all the company's property and assets into his custody and control. The company's power to deal with its assets and property is therefore suspended.
2.  The directors' power to control the company are also suspended. The directors may however take steps to wind up the company.

The directors may however exercise certain powers as long as they do not prejudice the receiver or threaten the debenture holders interests. They may therefore sue on behalf of the company if the receiver does not wish to pursue such an action.

### Newhart Developments Ltd v Co-operative Commercial Bank Ltd (1978)

The plaintiffs were property developers and in 1973 entered into a scheme with the defendant bank for a development in North Wales, where the bank would provided finance for the plaintiffs. A Company owned jointly by both parties was formed to carry out the development. In 1974 the scheme ran into difficulties and the bank withdrew its financial support. It later appointed a receiver under a charge created in 1973. In 1976 it appeared to plaintiffs that they had a claim for breach of contract arising out of the withdrawal of financial support, but the receiver refused to bring proceedings against the bank. It was held that directors had the power to institute proceedings for the benefit of the company and the receiver's consent was unnecessary.

3. The directors remuneration ceases. The directors however are entitled to claim any arrears from the company.
4. The floating charges crystallize and become fixed. A company may not then deal with the assets charged, without the receiver's consent.
5. Every invoice, order for goods or business letter issued by the company or on behalf of the company or receiver, and any document on which the company's name appear must contain a statement that a receiver or manager has been appointed (s 493).
6. The company's employees are automatically dismissed if a receiver is appointed by the Court (*Reid v Explosives Co* (1887)). Any employees who continue to work for him do so under new contracts of employment. (The receiver in such a case is not the agent of the company).
   The appointment by the debenture holders of a receiver who is the agent of the company will not usually operate as a dismissal of the company's employees, except in the following circumstances.
   (i) Where the receiver sells the company's business.
   (ii) Where the receiver enters into a new contract with an employee which is inconsistent with the previous contract.
   (iii) Where the continued employment of a particular

employee (e g managing director) is inconsistent with the position of the receiver.

7. He must send notice to the company of his appointment.

8. The company must, within 14 days of receipt of this notice (or such longer period as may be allowed by the court or the receiver) submit to the receiver a statement of affairs showing the following at the date of this appointment:
   (a) the assets debts and liabilities of the company;
   (b) the names, residence and occupations of its creditors;
   (c) the securities held by the creditors and the dates in which the securities were given.

   The statement of affairs must be submitted by and be verified by affidavit by one or more directors and by the company's secretary.

   The receiver, subject to the direction of the court, may require any of the following to submit and verify the statement:
   (a) past and present officers of the company;
   (b) persons who have taken part in the company's formation at any time within one year before the date of the receiver's appointment;
   (c) employees or ex-employees of the company who were in the company's employment at any time within the year prior to the receiver's appointment if in the receiver's opinion they are capable of giving the required information;
   (d) officers or ex-officers of the company which is, or within the said year was, an officer of the company to which the statement relates (s 496).

9. Within 2 months of receiving the statement of affairs, the receiver must forward to
   (a) The Registrar and the Court a copy of the statement and of any comment he sees fit to make on the statement.
   (b) The Registrar a summary of the statement and his comments (if any).
   (c) The company a copy of any comments made by him or if he does not see fit to make any comment, a notice to that effect.
   (d) Any trustees for the debenture holders, and to all debenture holders (so far as he is aware of their addresses) a copy of the summary.

10. Where a receiver or manager of the whole or substantially the whole of the company's property is appointed on behalf of debenture holders secured by floating charge, he must each year prepare an abstract showing his receipts and payments

during that year. He must also prepare a final account covering the period from the date of the last annual account to the date of his ceasing to act, together with the aggregate amount of his receipts and payments since his appointment.

A receiver appointed other than above must deliver to the Registrar every six months and on ceasing to act, an abstract of his receipts and payments (s 498).

DISTRIBUTION OF ASSETS

A receiver must apply the proceeds of the sale of a company's assets in the correct order if the assets are insufficient to meet the company's debts. The order is as follows:

(a) Payment of expenses incurred in the sale or realisation of the property.
(b) Payment of the receiver's expenses and remuneration (including any claims against the company under his indemnity).
(c) Payment of the expenses of the trustees of the debenture holders (if provided for by the trust deed)
(d) Payment of any costs incurred by the debenture holder or other person in bringing an action for the appointment of the receiver.
(e) Payment of the debenture debt with interest to the date of payment.
(f) Payment of the preferential debts (s 614).
(g) Payment of the trustees' remuneration (if they are not yet given special priority in the trust deed.)

THE RECEIVER AND WINDING UP

If a winding up is initiated while a receiver is in possession of the company's property, the position of the receiver is as follows:

(a) He can no longer act as the agent of the company, if appointed in that capacity, as the company can no longer trade.
(b) He continues to have the standard powers of a receiver and may dispose of the property in his possession. If any surplus remains after payment of the secured creditors he must account for it to the liquidator.
(c) If he enters into contracts he is personally liable on these contracts, but may be indemnified from the company's assets (s 492).

(d) The receiver's charge may be affected in the following way.

    (i) It may be void against the liquidator if not registered within the prescribed time (s 395).

    (ii) It may be void as a fraudulent preference (s 615).

    (iii) It may be void if created in the previous 12 months if the company was insolvent at the time of the creation of the charge (s 617).

# Chapter 19

# Winding up – I

A company may be dissolved and its name removed from the Register of Companies if the procedure laid down in the Act is followed.

Although a company may be struck off the register as a defunct company (s 652) or its immediate dissolution ordered by the court on the approval of a scheme of arrangement (s 427), in other circumstances a company must be wound up.

This process is carried out by a liquidator, whose functions are to realise the company's assets, apply them in payment of its debts and distribute any surplus among its members according to their rights. The various stages in a liquidation are governed by Part X of the Act and the Companies (Winding-Up) Rules 1949 (as amended).

There are 4 methods of winding up.

(a) Compulsory winding up by the court.
(b) Members voluntary winding up.
(c) Creditors voluntary winding up.
(d) Winding up under the supervision of the court.

## WINDING UP BY THE COURT

The High Court has jurisdiction to wind up any company registered in England and Wales. Where the amount of the share capital paid up or credited as paid up does not exceed £120,000 the county court of the district in which the registered office of the company is situated has concurrent jurisdiction with the High Court to wind up the company.

The court has jurisdiction if it can be shown that that company has assets within the jurisdiction and there are persons within the jurisdiction who are directly concerned with the distribution of those assets. The company need not have a place of business in the country or have carried on business in the country.

### Banque Des Marchands de Moscou (Koupetschesky) v Kindersley (1951)

A company formed in Russia in 1800 was dissolved by the Russian Government in 1918. Although it was doubtful whether business had been carried on in England, the Court had a discretion to wind up the company as the company had substantial assets in this country.

An application for winding up must be by way of petition which is supported by affidavit. It must be advertised in the London Gazette and one other local or London paper seven days before the hearing. If there are several petitions, the order will usually be made on the basis of the first petition presented.

GROUNDS FOR WINDING UP (s 517)

A company may be wound up by the court if:

1. The company has passed a special resolution to be wound up by the court.
2. It has not been issued with a s 117 certificate. This only applies to a public company.
3. The company does not commence business within a year from its incorporation or suspends its business for a whole year.
4. The number of members is reduced below two.
5. The company is unable to pay its debts.
6. The court is of the opinion that it is just and equitable that the company be wound up.

### 1. *Special resolution*
This is rarely used. It is far easier to initiate a voluntary winding up.

### 2. *Section 117 certificate*
A public company that has not obtained a s 117 certificate, issued by the Registrar on being satisfied that the minimum share capital has been subscribed, may be wound up by the court if more than 1 year has elapsed since the company's registration.

### 3. *Failure to carry on business*
An order may be made if a company has not carried on business for a year. The power of the court is discretionary and it must be

satisfied that the company has no intention to carry on in business or is unable to carry on the main objects of the company.

'. . . the court has power to wind up a company which has not commenced its business within a year, . . . if it thinks the fact it has not commenced business within a year is, in the circumstances of the case, a fair indication that the company has no intention of carrying on business and is not likely to do so' per Lord Cairns in *Re Metropolitan Railway Warehousing Co Ltd* (1867).

### Re Metropolitan Railway Warehousing Co Ltd (1867)

Work on building a railway warehouse had not been commenced within a year of the company's incorporation, due to difficulties in acquiring a satisfactory site. The site was later acquired but the price was subject to arbitration. The erection of the warehouse was one of the company's principal objects. It was held that a petition for winding up should be dismissed as there was no evidence that the company had no intention of carrying on business.

### Re Capital Fire Insurance Association (1883)

An insurance company which had created a lucrative market in France within the year of its incorporation intended to commence business in England as soon as sufficient capital had been subscribed. It was held that a petition to wind up the company would be dismissed.

A company will not be wound up if it abandons one or more of its businesses unless that business is the main object of the company.

The court will not grant an order if there are prospects of commencing business in the future and a majority of members do not wish the company to be wound up.

### Re Middlesborough Assembly Rooms Co (1880)

A company's shareholders passed a resolution to suspend building operations during a trade recession but to resume operations as soon as trading prospects improved. A petition for winding up was dismissed as it was opposed by 80 per cent of the shareholders who claimed that the company's future prospects were bright.

The Registrar may strike the name of a company which is not carrying on business (ie a defunct company) off the register (s 652).

### 4. *Reduction of members*

A petition is rarely applied for on this ground as the court will leave the company to wind up voluntarily.

### 5. *Inability to pay debts*
A company is deemed to be unable to pay its debts if:

(a) a creditor to whom the company owes £750 or more has served on the company, by leaving it at the company's registered office, a written demand requiring the company to pay the sum due and the company has for 3 weeks thereafter neglected to pay the sum due or secure or compound it to the reasonable satisfaction of the creditor;

(b) an execution or other process issued on a judgment, decree or other order of any court in favour of a creditor is returned unsatisfied in whole or in part;

(c) it is proved to the satisfaction of the court that the company is unable to pay its debts, taking into account its contingent and prospective liabilities, as well as the debts which are immediately payable; (s 518)

Examples of contingent debts are claims for unliquidated damages (ie the amount is unascertained) rents not yet due etc.

### 6. *Just and equitable*
The words 'just and equitable' are widely interpreted and need not be construed 'ejusdem generis' as the other grounds under this section. . . . The words are general and therefore permit the courts to subject legal rights to equitable considerations.

Examples of situations where companies have been wound up under this section:

(i) Where the company's main object could not be achieved ie the disappearance of the company's substratum.

**Re German Date Coffee Co** (1882) (see p 50).

(ii) Where a company was formed for an illegal or fraudulent purpose.

**Re TE Brinsmead and Sons** (1897)

TE Brinsmead and his sons had been employed by John Brinsmead and Sons (JEB) piano manufacturers. They formed a company TE Brinsmead and Sons (TEB) to carry on a similar business and issued a prospectus to raise capital. An injunction was obtained by JEB restraining TEB from using the name 'Brinsmead'. Numerous actions were brought against the company for fraud in the prospectus. It was held that the company should be wound up as it was formed to trade on the goodwill of the name 'Brinsmead'.

(iii) Where a company carried on its business at a loss.

### Re Factage Parisien Ltd (1865)

A company carried on its business at a loss and paid its debts by making calls on its members. It was held that the company should be wound up.

(iv) Where there was complete deadlock in the management of the company's affairs.

### Re Yenidje Tobacco Co (1916)

A company's two directors were the sole shareholders, and held an equal number of shares in the company. As a result they were not on speaking terms. They communicated with one another and conducted board meetings by passing notes to each other via the company secretary. One of the directors petitioned for winding up. It was held that the company should be wound up.

### Ebrahimi v Westbourne Galleries (1973)

Ebrahimi and Nozer carried on business as partners from 1945 to 1958. In 1958 they formed a private company to take over the existing business. Both were appointed directors and each held 500 £1 shares. No dividends were paid by the company and all profits were distributed as directors' remuneration. The articles provided that the company's shares could not be transferred without the consent of the directors. E and N later transferred 100 shares each to GN, N's son, and GN was appointed a director. After a dispute between E and N, N and GN at a general meeting removed E from his directorship under the power of removal given by s 184 (now s 303). E then petitioned for an order under s 222 (now s 517) that the company be wound up. It was held that although in law E could be removed from his office of director, the past relationship of the parties made it inequitable, as E and N had formed the company on the basis that the character of the association would as a matter of faith and trust remain the same. E was also unable to dispose of his interest in the company without the consent of N N and GN.

### Re A and BC Chewing Gum Ltd (1975)

The petitioners, Topps Chewing Gum, held one third of the company's ordinary shares on the basis that they should have equal control with the two brothers who held the remaining two thirds holding. A set of new articles was adopted by the company which allowed Topps to appoint and remove a director representing them, and for board decisions to be unanimous. Topps appointed a director to represent their interests and later removed him. They then appointed another director but the company's other two directors refused to accept the change. The petitioners were thus prevented from participating in the company's management. It was held that the company should be wound up.

(v) Where the directors deliberately withheld information from the shareholders and mismanaged the company's affairs.

### Loch v John Blackwood Ltd (1924)

A company was formed to carry on John Blackwood's business. The directors failed to hold general meetings, submit accounts or recommend a dividend in order to keep the shareholders in ignorance of the company's affairs. The directors object was to acquire shares at an undervaluation. It was held that in the circumstances it was just and equitable that the company should be wound up.

## THE PETITIONERS

The following may petition for the winding up of a company:

1. The company itself.
2. A creditor.
3. A contributory
4. The Department of Trade and Industry.
5. The Official Receiver.
6. The Attorney General.

### 1. *The company itself*

The company may present a petition if a special resolution has been passed, but the directors do not have the power to petition on the company's behalf (*Smith v Duke of Manchester* (1883)). Such a petition is rarely presented as a voluntary liquidation is a speedier and less expensive method of liquidation.

### 2. *A creditor*

A creditor is a person who is owed money by a company and who may enforce his claim by an action at law.

A claim in contract must be for a liquidated sum i e ascertained and certain, or he must obtain a judgment fixing the amount of the debt. In practice a creditor obtains a judgment on a debt before presenting a petition, as the company cannot then deny the existence of the debt or that it is an unliquidated sum.

The creditor's debt need not amount to £750 but an order will only be made in special circumstances if the debt is less than this amount (s 518). In these circumstances a creditor will join with other creditors in order that the total amount of the debts exceeds £750.

A creditor whose debt is disputed on substantial grounds will not generally obtain a winding up order.

### Re Lympne Investments Ltd (1972)

On the 4 November 1971 a petitioner served a demand on the company for the payment of a debt of £3,500. The debt was not repaid on the 24 November 1971 and a petition was served for the compulsory winding up of the company on the grounds that it was unable to pay its debts. The company denied the existence of the debt and contended that the sum was a payment for shares in another company, which were to be held in trust for the petitioner. It was held that as there was a substantial dispute as to the existence of the debt the petitioner was not a 'creditor' within the meaning of the Act who had locus standi to present a petition, the company had not neglected to pay the debt.

### Re A Company No 003729 of 1982 (1984)

A petitioner rendered an invoice to a company for work done. The sum claimed was £12,435. The company disputed the amount and suggested that the true figure should be £2234. The petitioner served a demand on the company under section 518 and then sought a winding up order on the ground that the company was unable to pay its debts due to its neglect to pay the sum demanded. The company applied to have the petition dismissed and paid the petitioner £2234. It was held that since the company in good faith and on substantial grounds disputed its liability to pay the outstanding balance it had not neglected to pay within 21 days, a sum which was in dispute.

The court has a discretion under s 645 to have regard to the wishes of the creditors (and contributories) and may refuse a winding up order even though the above requirements have been fulfilled.

### Re ABC Coupler and Engineering Co Ltd (No 2) (1962)

A judgment creditor of £17,540 petitioned for winding up. Other creditors who were owed £18,328 opposed the petition as the company's assets exceeded its liabilities by £7 million. It was held that the petition would be refused and the wishes of the majority would be respected.

The court may restrain a creditor by injunction from bringing a petition.

### Niger Merchants Co v Capper (1877)

A creditor claimed that he was owed £500 by a company. The company stated that the amount owed was £260 and that it had a set off for this amount. The creditor then threatened to wind up the company if he was not paid. It was held that an injunction would be granted to restrain him from presenting the petition.

If the majority of the creditors favour a voluntary winding up, but a creditor petitions for a compulsory winding up he must show some special reason why the wishes of the majority should be over ruled. The fact that a voluntary winding up has commenced is no bar to a creditor obtaining a winding up order (s 605).

The following have been held to be creditors for the purpose of this section:–

a. An assignee of a debt or the assignee of part of a debt.
b. A secured creditor.
c. An executor of a creditor, as long as probate has been granted prior to the hearing.
d. A debenture holder if the principal sum is payable to him directly, but not if the sum is to be paid to trustees of a debenture trust deed.
e. A contingent creditor ie 'a person towards whom under an existing obligation the company may or will become subject to a present liability on the happening of some future event or at some future date.' per Pennycuick J in *Re William Hockley Ltd* (1962)).

CONTRIBUTORIES

A contributory is defined by s 507 as every person liable to contribute to the assets of a company in the event of its being wound up.

A contributory is not entitled to present a petition unless:–

(a) The number of members is reduced below two; or
(b) The shares in respect of which he is a contributory, or some of them –
    (i) were originally allotted to him; or
    (ii) have been held by him and registered in his name for at

least 6 months during the 18 months before the commencement of the winding up; or

(iii) have devolved on him through the death of a former holder (s 519).

## Re Gattopardo (1969)

The petitioner purchased 50 shares in a company in June 1967 and a share transfer was executed, stamped and dated in that month. The company did not however register the transfer until October 1968, when the shares were delivered to her. In December she presented a petition for winding up the company. It was held that as the shares had not been held and registered in her name for at least 6 months during the 18 months before the commencement of the winding up the petition could not be heard.

A contributory includes:–

(a) a holder of partly paid shares;
(b) a person who held partly paid shares in the previous twelve months;
(c) a holder of fully paid shares;
(d) a person who ceased to be a member more than a year before the commencement of the winding up.
(e) one of the joint shareholders.
(f) the trustee in bankruptcy of a contributory.
(g) the personal representative of a deceased contributory.

All of these have an interest in preventing a company from incurring further debts towards which they would have to contribute.

The court may have regard to the wishes of the contributories and may call meetings to ascertain these wishes. It must have regard to the voting rights of each contributory under the Act or the articles and is not bound to make a winding up order on a contributory's petition.

A petition may be brought by a contributory (or creditor) to have the company wound up by the court, even though a voluntary winding up is in progress. In the case of an application by a contributory, the court must be satisfied that the rights of the contributory will be prejudiced by a voluntary winding up.

A contributory cannot petition unless it can be shown that there will be surplus assets for distribution.

## Re Expanded Plugs Ltd (1966)

One of the two directors of a company presented a winding up petition. The company had made a small profit in that year, but heavy losses in previous years and was insolvent. It was held that the petition must be dismissed as there was no likelihood of any surplus assets being available for distribution.

## THE OFFICIAL RECEIVER

The Official Receiver may petition for a winding up order where the company is being wound up voluntarily or under the supervision of the court. A winding up order will only be made if the court is satisfied that the voluntary winding up cannot be continued with due regard to the interests of the creditors or contributories (s 519).

### Re Ryder Installations (1966)

Default proceedings were taken against a liquidator who on numerous occasions failed to submit reports to the Registrar and facts and documents to an investigating officer appointed by the Department of Trade and Industry to investigate the company's affairs. It was held that the application of the Official Receiver for a winding up by the court would be granted.

## THE DEPARTMENT OF TRADE AND INDUSTRY

The Department of Trade and Industry may petition for a winding up if it appears, as a result of investigations, that it is in the public interest that the company should be wound up.

## THE ATTORNEY GENERAL

The Attorney General may petition for the winding up of a company which has been formed for a charitable purpose.

## THE PETITION

The petition must be in one of the forms specified in the Companies (Winding-Up) Rules 1949.
   It sets out:

the date of the company's incorporation,
the address of the company's registered office,
the capital of the company,
the company's objects,
the grounds on which an order is sought.

Every petition must be verified by an affidavit of the petitioner. The affidavit must be filed within 7 days after the presentation of the petition and is prima facie evidence of the statements in the petition.

The petition is presented at the office or chambers of the Registrar. It must be advertised in the London Gazette not less than 7 clear days after it has been served on the company and not less than 7 clear days before the day fixed for the hearing.

Every petition must, unless presented by the company be served on the company at its registered office, or if there is no registered office at its principal or last known place of business. Where a company is being wound up voluntarily the petition must also be served on the liquidator (if any) appointed to wind up the company's affairs. After a petition has been presented the petitioner must attend before the Registrar and satisfy him that the petition has been duly advertised, and that all formalities, relating to the petition and to its service have been complied with.

An application may be made to the court, after the presentation of the petition or before a winding up order is made, for the appointment of a provisional liquidator, who is usually the Official Receiver.

A provisional liquidator is usually appointed if the company's assets are in jeopardy, or the company is insolvent, or if it is thought to be in the public interest that such an appointment be made.

(a) He takes into his custody or under his control all the company's property (s 537)
(b) He may appoint a special manager if he is satisfied that the nature of the estate or business of the company or interests of the contributories generally require such an appointment (s 556)
(c) Although the powers of the board of directors are assumed by the liquidator, the directors nevertheless retain some residuary powers e g they may instruct solicitors and counsel to oppose the petition and if a winding up order is made, to appeal against the order.

The company, any creditor or any contributory may attend the hearing of the petition. Any person who wishes to appear must give notice to the petitioner of his intention to appear and must state whether he intends to support or oppose the petition. The evidence consists of affidavits filed in support or against the petition, unless the court allows the presentation of oral evidence.

The court may:

(a) dismiss the petition,
(b) adjourn the hearing conditionally or unconditionally,
(c) make any interim order,
(d) make any other order that it thinks fit.

The court may not refuse to make a winding up order on the ground only that the company's assets have been mortgaged to an amount equal to or in excess of those assets or that the company has no assets (s 520).

THE WINDING UP ORDER

1. If a winding up order is made, the Official Receiver becomes, by virtue of his office, the provisional liquidator and continues to act in that capacity until he or another person is appointed liquidator (s 533).
2. The winding up dates from the presentation of the petition.
3. A copy of the order is forwarded to the Registrar (s 525).
4. No action or proceedings may be proceeded with or commenced against the company except by leave of the court (s 525).
5. Any disposition of the company's property, any transfer of shares or alteration in the status of the members made after the commencement of the winding up is void, unless the court orders otherwise (s 522).
6. Any attachment, sequestration, distress or execution put in force against the estate or effects of the company after the commencement of the winding up is void (s 523).
7. Most of the powers of the directors cease.
8. The company's employees are dismissed. The liquidator may however re-engage certain employees. In these circumstances the employees have been held to have been continuously employed from the date of the commencement of their employment with the company.
9. If a company has passed a resolution for voluntary winding up before the presentation of a petition for winding up by the court, all proceedings taken in the voluntary winding up will be deemed valid unless the court directs otherwise. The winding up in these circumstances, will be deemed to have commenced at the time of passing the resolution (s 524).

THE STATEMENT OF AFFAIRS

Within 14 days of the appointment of a provisional liquidator or making a winding up order a statement of affairs must be submitted to the Official Receiver.

The statement must be in the prescribed form, and show particulars of the company's assets, debts and liabilities; the names addresses and occupations of its creditors, the securities held by them and the dates on which those securities were given and such further information as may be prescribed or the Official Receiver may require (s 528).

The statement must be verified by affidavit by one or more of the directors and the company's secretary.

When a company is being wound up every invoice, order for goods or business letter issued by or on behalf of the company or the liquidator of the company on which the name of the company appears, must contain a statement that the company is being wound up (s 637).

The Official Receiver may, subject to the courts directions, require any of the following to submit and verify the statement:

(i) present or past officers of the company;
(ii) persons who have taken part in the company's formation at any time within one year before the relevant date;
(iii) employees or persons who were in the company's employment within that year and are, in the opinion of the Official Receiver, capable of giving the required information;
(iv) persons who, within that year, were officers of or in the employment of a company which was an officer of the company to which the statement relates eg a company which was the secretary of the company in question (s 528).

As soon as practicable after receipt of the statement of affairs the Official Receiver must submit a preliminary report to the court:

(i) as to the amount of capital issued, subscribed and paid up; and the estimated amount of assets and liabilities.
(ii) if the company has failed, the causes of failure;
(iii) whether in his opinion further enquiry is desirable into the promotion, formation or failure of the company or the conduct of its business (s 530).

The Official Receiver may make a further report, if he thinks fit, and is of the opinion that fraud has been committed in a company's promotion or formation or by any officer of the company since its formation or any other matter which he considers should be brought to the notice of the court (s 530).

If a report is made by the Official Receiver under s 530 the court may order the public examination of that person or officer of the company against whom the allegation of fraud has been made. The Official Receiver must take part in the examination and the liquidator or any creditor or contributory may take part. Evidence is given on oath. Notes of the examination are taken down in writing, read over to the person examined and signed by him. It may be used in evidence against him.

The Official Receiver must summon separate meetings of the creditors and contributories within one month after the date of the winding up order (or 6 weeks if a special manager is appointed), unless the court directs otherwise (s 533).

At least seven days notice of the meetings must be given:

in the London Gazette and a local paper;
to each creditor and contributory by post.

The Official Receiver must also send to each creditor and contributory a summary of the company's statement of affairs, including the causes of its failure and any observations which he sees fit to make. He may also give seven days notice to all the officers of the company who, in his opinion, ought to attend the meetings. It then becomes their duty to attend and give such information as the meeting may require.

The proceedings at a meeting are not invalidated by reason of any summary or notice not having been sent or received before the meeting.

Apart from considering the statement of affairs and examining the company's officers, the object of the meeting is to determine whether or not application is to be made to the court:

(a)  to appoint a liquidator in place of the Official Receiver;
(b)  to appoint a committee of inspection.

If the meetings cannot agree, the court will decide.

## THE LIQUIDATOR

APPOINTMENT

In the majority of cases the Official Receiver, who is automatically appointed provisional liquidator, will continue as liquidator.

If the meetings of creditors and contributories resolve that a person other than the Official Receiver be appointed liquidator, the court may make any order it thinks fit to give effect to their wishes. If the meetings nominate different persons the court will decide on the appointment (s 533). If more than one person is appointed liquidator, the Court may determine their respective functions and the amount of remuneration to be paid to each (s 536).

The liquidator must give notice of his appointment to the Department of Trade (for publication in the Gazette) and to the Registrar.

He must give security to the satisfaction of the Department of Trade and Industry. This usually takes the form of a policy or bond with a guarantee company.

The Official Receiver hands the company's property and books to the liquidator, on payment of any fees costs or charges due to him.

A liquidator is generally an accountant of not less than five years standing.

A corporation cannot be appointed liquidator (s 634).

REMUNERATION

The remuneration of the liquidator, unless the court otherwise orders, is fixed by the committee of inspection. It consists of a commission or percentage on the amount realised (less the amounts paid to secured creditors other than debenture holders) and on the dividend distributed. If the Department of Trade considers the remuneration of the liquidator to be excessive they may apply to the court to reduce the remuneration. If there is no committee the scale of fees payable on realisation and distribution, will be similar to that received by the Official Receiver.

RESIGNATION

If a liquidator wishes to resign he must summon separate meetings of creditors and contributories who must agree to accept his resignation. If both meetings, by ordinary resolution accept his resignation he files a memorandum of registration with the Registrar of the court and sends a notice to the Official Receiver. The resignation then takes effect.

If one or both of the meetings do not accept his resignation he must report the result of the meetings to the court and the Official Receiver.

The court will then determine whether his resignation should be accepted, and on what terms.

The liquidator must hand over to the new liquidator all books, documents, papers and accounts relating to the liquidation before his release becomes effective.

REMOVAL

(a) A liquidator may be removed by the court on 'cause shown' (s 536). Examples of removal under this heading include:–

failure to keep proper accounting records or banking receipts; acting in the interests of the shareholders only, when the company was insolvent; ignoring the wishes of the majority of creditors, when the company is insolvent.

Being so closely connected with a creditor or director that his impartiality may be brought into question.

(b) A liquidator may be removed from office by the Department of Trade for:–
  (i) not faithfully performing his duties and observing all the statutory requirements of the post.
  (ii) for retaining a balance in excess of £100 for more than 10 days. (All money received by a liquidator must be paid promptly into the Insolvency Services Account at the Bank of England) (s 542).

(c) A liquidator is removed from office if a receiving order in bankruptcy is made against him.

Vacancies are filled by the court, and an appointment of a new liquidator made in the same manner as the first appointment. If one tenth in value of the creditors or contributories so request the Official Receiver must summon meetings to determine whether or not the vacancy should be filled. Otherwise the Official Receiver becomes the liquidator.

RELEASE

A liquidator may apply for his release when he:

  (i) has realised all the property of the company or so much as can, in his opinion, be realised without needlessly protracting the liquidation; has distributed a final dividend to the creditors;

  adjusted the rights of the contributors among themselves; and
  made a final return.
 (ii) has resigned; or
(iii) been removed from office.

The Department of Trade and Industry must prepare a report on
the liquidator's accounts. Before granting release it will take into
consideration the report and any objections lodged by any creditor
or contributory. The Department may grant or withhold a release
as it thinks fit, subject to a right of appeal to the court. The court
may subsequently charge the liquidator with the consequence of
any default on his part.

The release discharges the liquidator from all liability in respect
of any act, or default in the administration of the company's affairs
or his conduct as liquidator. It may only be revoked on proof that it
was obtained by fraud, suppression or concealment of any material
fact (s 545).

COMMITTEE OF INSPECTION

A committee of inspection may be appointed to assist the liquidator
and supervise his actions and activities. It consists of creditors and
contributories or persons holding general powers of attorney from
creditors (or contributories) in such proportions as may be
determined by agreement, or by the court.

The committee must meet at least once a month, at such times as
they from time to time appoint. The liquidator or any member of
the committee may summon a meeting as and when he thinks
necessary.

The committee acts by a majority of those present and a quorum
is a majority of the committee. A person's membership of the
committee ceases if he:

  (i) submits his resignation to the liquidator;
 (ii) becomes bankrupt or compounds with creditors;
(iii) is absent from five consecutive committee meetings without
       leave;
(iv) is removed by ordinary resolution at a meeting of the creditors
       (or contributories) (s 546, Sch 17).

When a vacancy occurs the liquidator summons a meeting of
creditors (or contributories) to fill the vacancy. If the liquidator is of
the opinion that it is unnecessary to fill the vacancy he may apply to
the court for an order that the vacancy shall not be filled.

Every member of the committee is in a fiduciary position. He may not purchase any of the company's property without leave of the court, and may not profit from any transaction arising out of the winding up.

## THE POWERS OF THE LIQUIDATOR

The liquidator's power in a winding up may be divided into two categories:–
1. those requiring the sanction of the court or committee of inspection.
2. those which do not require any such authorisation.

The liquidator's exercise of these powers is subject to the control of the court and any creditor or contributory may apply to the court in respect of the exercise or proposed exercise of any of these powers.

### With the sanction of the court or committee of inspection
1. Bring or defend any action or other legal proceedings in the name and on behalf of the company.
2. Carry on the company's business so far as is necessary for its beneficial winding up.
3. Pay any class of creditors in full.
4. Make any compromise or arrangement with creditors, debtors and contributories.
5. Compromise all calls and liabilities to calls debts and liabilities.
6. Compromise any questions relating to or affecting the assets of the company,or the winding up of the company, on such terms as are agreed.
7. Appoint a solicitor to assist him in the performance of his duties.

### Without such sanction or authorisation
1. Sell and transfer the real and personal property of the company by public auction or private contract.
2. Execute and seal deeds, receipts and documents on behalf of the company.
3. Prove in the bankruptcy, insolvency or sequestration of any contributory.
4. Draw, accept, make and endorse any bill of exchange or promissory note. These will have the same effect as if drawn by the company in the course of its business.
5. Raise money on the security of the assets.

6. Take out in his own official name, letters of administration to any deceased contributory.
7. Appoint an agent to do any business which he is unable to do himself.
8. Do all such other things as are necessary for winding up the affairs of the company and distributing its property (s 539).

The liquidator must, in administering and distributing the property, have regard to any resolutions of creditors and contributories at any general meeting or by the committee of inspection. In the case of conflict any directions given by the creditors for contributories over-ride those of the committee (s 540).

He may summon meetings of the creditors and contributories to ascertain their wishes. He must summon meetings:

(i) when requested in writing by one-tenth in value of the creditors and contributories, as the case may be.
(ii) to fill a vacancy occurring in the committee of inspection. A liquidator may apply to the court for an order that the vacancy be not filled if he is of the opinion that it is unnecessary to fill the vacancy (s 540, Sch 17).

DUTIES OF THE LIQUIDATOR

*1. Duty to take the company's property into his custody*
Where a winding-up order has made (or where a provisional liquidator has been appointed) the liquidator (or provisional liquidator) must take into his custody or under his control all the property and choses in action to which the company is or appears to be entitled (s 537).

Although the property does not vest in the liquidator on his appointment he may apply to the court for a vesting order. He may then bring or defend in his official name any action or other legal proceedings relating to that property or which is necessary for winding up the company and recovering its property (s 538).

The court may at any time after making a winding up order:

(i) require any contributory, trustee receiver, banker, agent or officer of the company to pay any money, convey, deliver, surrender, or transfer any property or books or papers to the liquidator, to which the company is prima facie entitled (s 551).
(ii) make an order on any contributory to pay any money due from

him to the company, exclusive of any money payable by him by virtue of an call (s 552).

(iii) issue a warrant for the arrest of a contributory whom it believes is about to abscond or remove or conceal any property in order to avoid payment of calls. It may also seize his books, papers and moveable property (s 565).

(iv) summon before it for examination on oath any officer of the company, or person known or suspected to have the company's property or to owe it money, or any person who may be able to give information about the company's promotion, formation, trade dealings or property (s 561).

Moneys received by the liquidator must be paid into the Insolvency Services Account at the Bank of England. It may not be paid into his private account. If he retains sums over £100 for more than 10 days, (unless authorised by the Department of Trade and Industry to retain a larger sum) he is liable to:

(i) pay interest on the amount retained at 20 per cent per annum;
(ii) dismissal by the Department of Trade and Industry;
(iii) refund the expenses occasioned by reason of his default (s 542).

The court may order moneys due to the company to be paid directly into the liquidator's account at the Bank of England (s 554). All moneys representing unclaimed or undistributed assets which have remained unclaimed or undistributed for 6 months and any money held in trust for dividends must be paid into this account (s 642).

### Other property to which the liquidator is entitled
A liquidator may set aside certain transactions and so recover property for the benefit of unsecured creditors.

### (a) Floating charges
A floating charge created by a company within 12 months of the commencement of winding up is invalid, unless the company was solvent immediately after the creation of the charge, except as to the amount of any money paid to the company at or after the time of creating the charge and in consideration of it (s. 617).

### (b) Execution creditors
A creditor who has issued execution against a company's goods and land (or has attached any debt due to the company) is not entitled to

retain the benefit of the execution (or attachment) against the liquidator unless he has completed the execution (or attachment) before:

(i) the commencement of the winding up; or
(ii) he had notice of a meeting called for the purpose of passing a resolution for voluntary winding up (s 621).

### (c) *Fraudulent preference*

Any conveyance, mortgage, delivery of goods, payment of money, execution or other act relating to property made or done by or against a company which was insolvent at the time and within 6 months before the commencement of its winding up is void if made with the intention of fraudulently preferring one creditor to the detriment of the other creditors (s 615).

### Re Kushler Ltd (1943)

Kushler and his wife were the directors and shareholders of a company. Kushler personally guaranteed the company's overdraft with a bank. On realising on 12 May that the company was insolvent he made payments between 12-21 May which extinguished the company's overdraft and his personal liability. A winding up resolution was passed on 23 May. No trade creditors were paid during this time. It was held to be a fraudulent preference. The money had to be surrendered to the liquidator by the bank.

### Re F P and C H Matthews (1982)

Mathews and his wife were the sole directors and shareholders of a company and personally guaranteed the company's overdraft. They extinguished the company's overdraft without the bank exerting any pressure on them. The company went into liquidation. Mathews believed at the time of the payment that although the company's debts could not be paid as they became due, the debts would be paid in due course. It was held nevertheless that the payment to the bank was a fraudulent preference.

### Re Eric Holmes (Property) Ltd (1965)

A creditor made an advance and received a promise from the debtor to execute formal mortgages on demand. It was held to be a right to be preferred on request and therefore void.

The following have been held *not* to constitute a fraudulent preference:–

the threat of criminal proceedings;
payment to a bank in the hope of obtaining future banking facilities;
executing a legal charge in favour of a bank to honour pre-existing obligation under memorandum of title deeds.

Any conveyance or assignment of the company's property to trustees for the benefit of all its creditors is also a fraudulent preference as this would only benefit the company's creditors and would be detrimental to the interests of other parties.

### (d)  *Unauthorised profits of directors*
A liquidator may recover any unauthorised profits made by directors by virtue of their position: *Regal (Hastings) Ltd v Gulliver* (1942); *Industrial Development Consultants Ltd v Cooley* (1972) (see p 212).

This would include the payment of directors salaries not authorised by the general meeting.

### (e)  *Misfeasance*
The Official Receiver, a liquidator, a creditor or contributory may apply to the court if it appears that any director, promoter, liquidator or officer of the company has been guilty of misfeasance or breach of trust in relation to the company's property.

Examples of misfeasance are:–

directors selling their own property to the company without disclosing the fact to the members;
directors using the company's property to make profits for themselves;
an auditor sanctioning the payments of dividends out of capital;
a liquidator's failure to make provision for the payment of preferential debts.

The court may compel such a person to repay or restore the money or property or to contribute to the assets of the company by way of compensation as the court thinks just (s 631).

#### FRAUDULENT TRADING

If in the course of a winding up it appears that any business of the company has been carried on with the intent to defraud creditors, or for any fraudulent purpose, the court, on the application of the Official Receiver, or the liquidator or any creditor or contributory may declare that any pesons who were knowingly parties to the carrying on of the business in this way shall be personally liable, without limit, for such of the company's debts as it may direct (s 630).

Carrying on a business requires some positive act on the part of the person concerned. If a person's role in a company's activities are ministerial and advisory, this does not constitute carrying on in business.

## Re Maidstone Buildings Provisions Ltd (1971)

The secretary of a company was also a partner in a firm, who were the company's auditors and financial advisers. The company carried on trading when it was hopelessly insolvent. The liquidator brought an action against P on the grounds that as the company's secretary and financial adviser he should have advised the directors that the company should cease trading and that he was therefore a party to the company carrying on business in a fraudulent manner. It was held that P was not concerned in carrying on the company's business as his failure to give proper advice to the company did not make him a party to the carrying on of the company's business.

> 'If a company continues to carry on a business when there is to the knowledge of the directors no reasonable prospect of the creditors ever receiving payment of their debts, it is in general, a proper inference that the company is carrying on business with intent to defraud' per Maughan J in *Re William C Leitch Brothers Ltd* (1932).

## Re William C Leitch Brothers Ltd (1932)

A manufacturer sold his business to a newly formed company for £5,000 payment to be made by the issue of 1,000 £5 shares and a debenture of £4,000. He was also appointed the company's managing director at a salary of £1,000 per annum. Three years later when the company was insolvent, he ordered goods for a further £6,000 which became subject to the debenture. A receiver was appointed and the company was later wound up. It was held that Leitch should pay £3,000 to the liquidator.

A creditor who accepts a payment knowing it to be obtained by carrying on a business with intent to defraud creditors is, for the purpose of making the payment, a party to carrying on a business with intent to defraud creditors.

The court has a discretion in respect of the disposition of money recovered from any party guilty of fraudulent trading. When an application is made by a liquidator, the court generally orders that the sum be paid in discharge of the debt of a particular creditor or class of creditors.

A person guilty of fraudulent trading may not, without leave of the Court be a director or concerned in the management of a company for up to 15 years. Such a person is also liable to imprisonment and/or a fine.

DISCLAIMER OF ONEROUS PROPERTY

A liquidator may, with leave of the court, disclaim property which is more of a liability than an asset e g land burdened with onerous covenants, unprofitable contracts, stocks and shares in other companies, property not readily saleable as money has to be spent on it. He must disclaim in writing, within twelve months from the commencement of the winding up, or from his becoming aware of the existence of the property, or within such extended time as the court may allow (s 618).

The liquidator may not disclaim any property where an application has been made in writing to him by any person interested in the property requiring him to decide whether he will or will not disclaim and the liquidator has not, within 28 days after the receipt of the application or such further period as may be allowed by the court, given notice to the applicant that he intends to apply to the court for leave to disclaim (s 619).

In the case of a contract if the liquidator after such an application does not within 28 days, or further period as allowed by the court, disclaim the contract, the company is deemed to have adopted it (s 619).

The effect of the disclaimer is to determine the rights, interest and liabilities of the company in the property disclaimed, but not the rights or liabilities of any other person (s 618) eg if a liquidator disclaims a lease held by a company the company's rights and liabilities under the lease are terminated, but not the rights of other parties e g an under-leasee, the landlord.

Any person who is entitled to the benefit or subject to the burden of a contract may apply to the court for rescission of the contract on such terms as to payment by or to the other party of damages for the non-performance of the contract, or otherwise as the court thinks just. Any damages payable under this order may be proved as a debt in the winding up (s 619).

Any person injured by the operation of a disclaimer is deemed to be a creditor of the company for the amount of the damage and may prove the amount as a debt in the winding up (s 619).

## 2. *Duty to settle the list of contributories*

As soon as possible after making a winding up the Court must settle a list of contributories, and collect the assets of the company and apply them in discharge of its liabilities (s 550).

The liquidator appoints a time and place for settling the list and gives notice of this, in writing, to every person whom he intends to include in the list. On that day the liquidator hears from any person who objects to being put on the list, and settles the list. A person whose name appears on the list may apply to the court within 21 days for variation of the list.

A person who is wrongly placed on the list of contributories may apply to the court for rectification of the list.

There are two lists of contributories.

(i) The 'A' list comprising all those who were members of the company at the date of the commencement of the winding up.
(ii) The 'B' list comprising all those who were members within one year of the commencement of the winding up.

The list must also distinguish between those who are contributories in their own right and those who are liable as representatives of, or liable for the debts of others.

'A' list contributories are liable for the amounts unpaid on their shares.

'B' list contributories are liable for the amounts unpaid on their shares by the 'A' list contributories. They are not liable to contribute in respect of any debt or liability contracted after they ceased to be members.

The court may dispose with the list of contributories where it appears that it will not be necessary to make calls on or adjust the rights of contributories (s 550).

3. *Duty to make calls*
The liability of a contributory is enforced by means of calls. The amount to be called up is the amount of money which the court considers necessary to satisfy the debts and liabilities of the company and the costs, charges and expenses of winding up, and for the adjustment of the rights of the contributories among themselves. In making a call the court may take into consideration the probability that some of the contributories may partly or wholly fail to pay the call (s 553).

The liquidator must summon a meeting of the committee of inspection to obtain their sanction to the intended call. If there is no committee of inspection he may not make a call without obtaining the leave of the court. Seven days clear notice of the meeting must be sent to each member of the committee of inspection and must state the proposed amount of the call and the purpose for which it is intended.

Notice of the intended call and meeting must be advertised in a London or local newspaper.

Any statements or representation made by contributories to the liquidator or to the committee of inspection must be considered before the call is made.

The majority of the committee may sanction the call. A copy of the resolution is then served on each contributory with a notice stating the amount or balance due from him in respect of the call.

Payment of the call may be enforced by order of the court, to be made in chambers on summons by the liquidator.

### 4. *Duty to establish proof of debts*

The debts which may be proved include 'all debts payable on a contingency, and all claims against the company present or future, certain or contingent ascertained or sounding only in damages'. A just estimate must be made, as far as possible of the value of such debts or claims' (s 611). (This assumes that the company is insolvent.)

Debts which cannot be proved include:

unliquidated damages in tort;
unliquidated damages arising other than by reason of a contract; promise or breach of trust;
statute barred debts;
foreign taxation claims;
those debts which the court by order declares to be incapable of being fairly estimated.

In winding up of an insolvent company the same rules apply as under the law of bankruptcy to

(i) the respective rights of secured and unsecured creditors.
(ii) debts provable.
(iii) the valuation of annuities and future and contingent liabilities (s 612).

### SECURED CREDITORS

A secured creditor holds some security for the debt owed to him by the company e g mortgage, charge or lien. He must give credit for the realised or estimated value of his security, unless he is prepared to surrender it to the liquidator and prove for the whole amount of the debt.

He has four options open to him. He may –

(i) rely on his security and not prove in the winding up;
(ii) realise his security and prove, as an unsecured creditor, for the balance due to him after deducting the sum realised;

(iii) value his security and prove, as an unsecured creditor, for the balance due to him after deducting the value of the security;
(iv) surrender the security and prove, as an unsecured creditor for the whole debt.

Where a secured creditor has security, the liquidator may:

(i) redeem the security at the value placed on it for dividend purposes; or
(ii) insist on the sale of the security. If the sale is by public auction both the liquidator and the creditor may bid.

A creditor may serve notice on a liquidator requiring him to elect whether or not he will exercise either of the above powers. If the liquidator does not signify his intention to elect within 6 months he will lose the right to do so and the security vests in the creditor at its estimated value.

A creditor who has made a bona fide mistake in valuing his security may amend his valuation by making an application to the court (Bankruptcy Act 1914, Sch 2).

If a secured creditor votes in respect of his whole debt at a creditor's meeting he will be deemed to have surrendered his security, unless the court is satisfied that the omission to value the security arose from inadvertence.

Where a creditor has estimated the value of the security and used the proof in voting at a meeting the liquidator may, within 28 days, require the creditor to give up the security for the benefit of the creditors generally on payment of the estimated value, plus 20 per cent.

Where there have been mutual debts, natural credits or other mutual dealings between a creditor and a company, an account must be taken of what is due from one to the other and the creditor may only prove for the balance (Bankruptcy Act 1914, s 31).

A contributory who is owed money by a company may not set off the amount against his liability to pay a call, on the principle that a person who owes a contribution to a fund that is available for creditors must contribute in full before participating rateably with other creditors from that fund.

There are certain exceptions to this rule:

(i) where all the creditors have been paid in full (s 552);
(ii) the trustee of a bankrupt may claim set off as he is acting in a dual capacity, as a creditor and as a member's representative.

360 *Winding up – I*

PROCEDURE FOR PROOF OF DEBTS

   (i) The liquidator must fix a date, not less than 14 days from the date of the notice on or before which the creditors must prove their debts or be excluded.

  (ii) The date must be advertised and notice given to any creditor whose claim has not been admitted.

 (iii) The debts must be proved by delivering or by posting an affidavit to the liquidator.

 (iv) The liquidator must, within 28 days of its receipt, admit or reject every proof tendered. He may also require further evidence.

  (v) A creditor may appeal to the court within 21 days, against rejection of a proof.

 (vi) On the first day of every month the liquidator must file a list of proofs received during the preceding month. He must distinguish between those accepted, rejected or held over until further enquiry.

 (vii) He may also apply to the court to expunge or reduce a proof if he considers that a proof has been wrongly admitted. (An application may also be made by a creditor or contributory).

(viii) Not more than 2 months before declaring a dividend the liquidator must give notice to the creditors mentioned in the statement of affairs who have not proved their debts. Such proofs must be lodged, not less than 14 days from the date of the notice.

 (ix) A creditor must bear the costs of proving his debt, unless the court determines otherwise. The cost is added to the amount of the debt.

## 5. *Duty to pay the company's debts*
If the company is solvent all its debts will be paid in full.

If the company is insolvent the order of payment will be as follows:

Costs incurred in winding up.

   (i) Fees and expenses incurred in preserving, realising or getting in the assets.

  (ii) Costs of the petition.

 (iii) Remuneration of the special manager (if any)

 (iv) Costs of making the company's statement of affairs.

  (v) Costs of any shorthand writer appointed to take an examination.

 (vi) Other disbursements of the liquidator.

(vii) Costs of any person properly employed by the liquidator.
(viii) Remuneration of the liquidator.
 (ix) The actual out of pocket expenses of the committee of inspection.

Following the payment of the costs of the liquidation the liquidator must then pay the debts of the company in the following order:–

(a) preferential debts.
(b) ordinary debts.
(c) deferred debts.

*Preferential debts*
All these rank equally and must be paid in full unless the assets are insufficient in which case they abate in equal proportions, s 614 (see p 311).

The relevant date when a company is being wound up compulsorily is the date of the appointment of a provisional liquidator. If no appointment is made, the date of the winding up order. If any person (eg a bank) has advanced money to a company to enable the wages, salaries or accrued holiday remuneration of employees to be paid, that person shall have the same right of priority in the money advanced as those employees who are paid out of the money advanced. A bank may obtain maximum benefit under this provision by operating a separate wages account out of which advances are made for the payment of wages. The company undertakes to make regular transfers to that account from its current account to discharge the earliest withdrawals from the wages account. (The rule in *Claytons Case* provides that payments made into an account discharge the earliest debits in the account).

### Re James Rutherford and Sons Ltd (1964)

A company had a current account at a bank which became overdrawn. The company, at the insistance of the bank opened a separate wages account to ensure that the company's indebtedness to the bank in respect of sums advanced for wages, should rank as preferential debts in the event of the company being wound up. The company went into voluntary liquidation and it was held that the bank ranked as a preferential creditor in respect of the amount transferred from current to wages account. The rule in *Clayton's Case* applied to the sums credited to the current account so as to discharge the earliest in date of the debits on that account.

## Re Rampgill Mill Ltd (1967)

A bank granted overdraft facilities to a company and agreed that cheques could be drawn at a bank at another town. This arrangment was made with the payment of wages in mind. The company was wound up. It was held that the bank was a preferential creditor as its intention in advancing money to the company was to allow it to meet its commitments.

Preferential debts have a priority, over a landlord or other person who have distrained on the company's goods within 3 months before the date of the winding up order. The preferential debts are at first charge on the goods distrained or the proceeds of sale. The landlord or other person has the same priority as the person paid out of the proceeds (s 614).

Preferential debts also have priority over claims for principal or interest in respect of debentures secured by a floating charge (s 196). If the charge crystallises prior to the winding up, the priority no longer exists in respect of property subject to the charge.

Ordinary debts are paid after the payment of the preferential debts in full. These debts also rank equal and if there are insufficient assets to meet their claims in full, they will abate equally.

Deferred debts are paid after payment of preferential and ordinary debts in full.

### 6. *Duty to keep books and papers*
A liquidator must keep the following books:–

(1) A record book of minutes, resolutions passed at meetings of creditors and contributories, and all matters necessary to give a correct view of his administration.
(2) A cash book in a form directed by the Department of Trade and Industry in which are entered receipts and payments.

The liquidator must submit these books for audit to the committee of inspection (if any) when required, and not less than at three monthly intervals.

### 7. *Duty to keep accounts*
The liquidator must at such times as may be prescribed, but not less than twice a year, send to the Department of Trade and Industry an account of his receipts and payments.

The account must be in a prescribed form, in duplicate and must be verified by a statutory declaration. It must be audited by the Department of Trade and Industry. One copy must be filed and retained by the Department and another copy must be delivered to the court for filing and may be open to inspection by any person on payment of a fee. A copy of the account as audited (or a summary) must be sent to every creditor and contributory by the liquidator.

The liquidator must submit, with the first account, a summary of the company's affairs showing the amounts realised. He must also submit every 6 months a report on the position of the liquidation.

If the balance at the credit of any company account exceeds £2,000, the liquidator may give notice to the Department of Trade and Industry that it is not required. The company then becomes entitled to interest at the rate of 2 per cent per annum or such other rate as may for the time being be prescribed by order of the Treasury (s 660).

If the liquidator carries on the company's business he must keep a trading account which must be submitted for examination and verification to the committee of inspection.

If the liquidation is not concluded within one year of its commencement the liquidator must send to the Registrar, within 30 days after the expiration of the first year of the liquidation a statement as to the proceedings and position of the liquidation. He must send subsequent statements at 6 monthly intervals.

8. *Duty to distribute the balance*
Where capital is returned to contributories the liquidator must prepare a list of persons to whom it must be paid and the amount payable to each. If the assets are sufficient to pay the contributories, the surplus is divided into the number of shares held, not the amounts paid on the shares. If the assets are insufficient and a similar amount has not been paid in respect of each share, an adjustment must be made by making a call on these shareholders whose shares are only partly paid.

The court must adjust the rights of the contributories among themselves and distribute any surplus among those entitled (s 558).

## DISSOLUTION OF THE COMPANY

When the company's affairs have been fully wound-up the liquidator makes an application to the court and the court will make an order for the dissolution of the company. The liquidator must, within 14 days, forward a copy of the order to the Registrar of

Companies, who will make an entry on the Register dissolving the company from the date of the court order (s 568).

The Registrar must also publish in the Gazette notice of the receipt by him of the order dissolving the company (s 711).

# Chapter 20

# Winding up – II

## VOLUNTARY WINDING UP

A company may be wound up voluntarily when:–

(i) the period, if any, fixed for the duration of the company has expired, or an event has occurred on which under the articles the company is to be dissolved and the company has passed a resolution to wind up voluntarily.

(ii) the company has passed a special resolution to wind up voluntarily.

(iii) the company has passed an extraordinary resolution that it cannot by reason of its liabilities continue its business and that it is advisable to wind up (s 572).

When a company has passed a resolution for voluntary winding up it must advertise the fact in the London Gazette within 14 days.

### CONSEQUENCES OF WINDING UP

1. A voluntary winding up is deemed to commence at the time of the passing of the resolution which authorises it (s 574).
2. The company ceases to carry on its business except as required for its beneficial winding up (s 575).
3. A liquidator must be appointed to take the necessary steps to wind up the company.
4. Any transfer of shares, without the sanction of the liquidator, is void (s 576).
5. Any alteration in the status of the members is void (s 576).

### Castello's Case (1869)

A company passed a resolution to wind up on the 7 August and the resolution was confirmed on 23 August. Shares were transferred to a minor on 14 August and he confirmed the transfer on reaching full age in October. It was held that the transfer was void as the individual was a minor at the date of the winding up and could not change his status so as to be capable of ratifying after the winding up.

6. The directors' powers cease on the appointment of a liquidator except in so far as the company in general meeting or the liquidator or committee of inspection or creditors sanction their continuance (s 580).
7. The company's employees are not discharged unless the company is insolvent, e g a winding up to effect an amalgamation does not operate as a discharge. A liquidator who, after the commencement of the winding up, continues to employ the employees to wind up the company, will so do as the manager of the company.
8. A resolution for voluntary winding up does not prevent proceedings being taken against a company. A liquidator may, however, apply to the court for a stay (s 602).

## THE TYPES OF VOLUNTARY WINDING UP

There are 2 types of voluntary winding up.

(a) A members voluntary winding up where the company is solvent. The liquidator is appointed by the company in general meeting and is accountable to the members.
(b) A creditors voluntary winding up where the creditors, to a great extent, control the course of the liquidation.

### MEMBERS VOLUNTARY WINDING UP

The directors (or if there are more than two, the majority of the directors) make a statutory declaration –

a. that they have made a full inquiry into the company's affairs; and
b. having done so have formed the opinion that the company will be able to pay its debts in full within 12 months.

This declaration of solvency must be –

made within 5 weeks preceding the resolution to wind up;
filed with the Registrar before the resolution is passed;
contain a statement of the company's assets and liabilities (s 577).

If a director makes a declaration, without having reasonable grounds for the opinion that the company will be able to pay its debts in full within the time specified in the declaration, he is liable to a term of imprisonment and/or a fine (s 577(4)).

The company may then appoint a liquidator in general meeting and also fix his remuneration (s 580).

The liquidator must give notice of his appointment to the Registrar and publish it in the London Gazette. He is not an officer of the court, but an agent of the company.

A vacancy in the office of liquidator by death, resignation or otherwise may be filled by an appointment by the company in general meeting (s 581). If there is no liquidator acting the court may make an appointment, and may, on cause being shown, remove a liquidator and appoint another liquidator (s 599).

The powers of the directors cease on such an appointment except in so far as the company in general meeting or the liquidator sanctions their continuance (s 580(2)).

If the winding up continues for more than one year the liquidator must summon a general meeting of the company at the end of the first year and each successive year and lay before the meeting an account of his acts and dealings and the conduct of the winding up during the preceding year (s 584).

As soon as the company's affairs are wound up the liquidator must call a general meeting of the company which must be advertised in the London Gazette at least one month before the meeting. The liquidator presents an account of the winding up, showing how the winding up has been conducted and how the company's property has been disposed of. Within a week after the meeting the liquidator must send to the Registrar a copy of the accounts and a return of the holding of the meeting. If a quorum was not present at the meeting the liquidator makes a return that the meeting was duly summoned and that no quorum was present. The provisions as to the making of the return will be deemed to have been complied with. The Registrar registers the accounts and returns and on the expiration of 3 months from the registration of the return the company is deemed to be dissolved (s 585).

If in a members' voluntary winding up the liquidator is at any time of the opinion that the company will not be able to pay its debts in full within the period stated he must summon a meeting of the creditors and lay before the meeting a statement of the company's assets and liabilities. The winding up then proceeds as in a creditors voluntary winding up (s 583).

CREDITORS VOLUNTARY WINDING UP

If the directors are unable to make a declaration of solvency, the winding up proceeds as a creditors voluntary winding up (s 578). The company must call a meeting of its creditors for the same day as, or on the next day after, the meeting at which the resolution for voluntary winding up is to be proposed. Notice of the creditors meeting must be sent to each creditor at the same time as notices convening a general meeting. At least seven days notice must be given of the meeting (s 588).

Notice of the creditors meeting must be advertised in the London Gazette and two local newspapers. The directors must lay before the meeting a full statement of the company's affairs, together with a list of creditors and the estimated amount of their claims. The meeting is presided over by a director nominated for that purpose by his fellow director(s).

The company and the creditors may at their respective meetings each nominate a liquidator. Should different persons be nominated, the nomination of the creditors will prevail, subject to the right of any director member or creditor to apply to the court for an order that the company's nominee be appointed. If no person is nominated by the creditors, the company's nominee (if any) will act as liquidator (s 589).

The creditors at their meeting may appoint a committee of inspection of not more than five persons. The company may then nominate not more than five persons to serve on the committee, subject to the power of the creditors to disapprove of any of the persons appointed (s 590).

## THE LIQUIDATOR

The role and function of the liquidator in a voluntary winding up is very similar to that in a winding up by the court.

There are however certain differences.

APPOINTMENT

In a members' voluntary winding up the appointment is made by the company in general meeting. A contributory may convene a general meeting to fill a vacancy in the office of liquidator.

In a creditors voluntary winding up the meeting of creditors and members may each nominate a liquidator.

REMUNERATION

This may be determined by the company in general meeting in a member's voluntary winding up. In a creditors voluntary winding up it may be fixed by the committee of inspection, or creditors if there is no committee. It may also be fixed by the court.

REMOVAL

If a vacancy occurs by death, resignation or otherwise in a members' voluntary winding up the company in general meeting may, subject to any arrangement with its creditors, fill the vacancy (s 581). The words 'or otherwise' include where a liquidator is removed by the court for due cause. The court may appoint another liquidator in place of the liquidator removed in a creditors' voluntary winding up and may also appoint an additional liquidator (s 599).

POWERS OF THE LIQUIDATOR

A liquidator is entitled to exercise any of the powers given to a liquidator appointed by the court in a compulsory winding up.

1. He may, with the sanction of a special resolution sell the whole or part of the company's business or property to another company on a reconstruction under s 582.
2. He may, with the sanction of (a) an extraordinary resolution in a members voluntary winding up, or (b) the court or committee of inspection, or (if no committee) a meeting of the creditors in a creditors' voluntary winding up, exercise the following powers:
   (i) pay any class of creditors in full;
   (ii) make any compromise or arrangement with creditors;
   (iii) compromise all calls, debts and liabilities.
3. Without sanction or authorisation he may –
   (a) Exercise any of the other powers given to the liquidator in a winding up by the court.
   (b) Settle a list of contributories.
   (c) Make calls.
   (d) Summon meetings of the company to obtain the sanction of a special or extraordinary resolution or for any other purpose he may think fit (598(3)).

DUTIES OF THE LIQUIDATOR

The duties of the liquidator in a voluntary winding up are, with certain exceptions, the same as those for a liquidator in a compulsory winding up.

## (1) *Duty to take the company's property into his custody*
As in a compulsory winding up, except that –

(a) A liquidator is not required to pay all his money into the Insolvency Services Account at the Bank of England, unless he holds unclaimed or undistributed assets in his hands for 6 months.

(b) A liquidator may recover the sum received from the sale of goods seized to satisfy a judgment debt, if he notifies the sheriff within 14 days of the sale that a meeting has been called to propose a resolution for the voluntary winding up of the company, and a resolution is subsequently passed (s 622(4)).

## (2) *Duty to settle the list of contributories*
As in compulsory winding up except that the list of contributories settled by the liquidator is only prima facie evidence of liability (s 598).

## (3) *Duty to make calls*
A liquidator may make the call upon his own authority i e he does not require the sanction of the court or committee of inspection.

The liquidator or any contributory or creditor may apply to the court to determine any question in respect of enforcing calls, which the court might exercise as if the company were being wound-up by the court (s 602).

## (4) *Duty to establish proof of debts*
As in a compulsory winding up, except that formal proof of debts is not necessary.

## (5) *Duty to pay the company's debts*
All costs, charges and expenses properly incurred in the winding up, including the remuneration of the liquidator are payable out of the company's assets in priority to all other claims (s 604). The company's property must then be applied in satisfaction of its liabilities pari passu and, unless the articles provide otherwise among the members according to their rights (s 597).

The debts of a solvent company are paid in full in the same manner as if the company was being wound up by the court.

If the company is insolvent, the debts must be paid in the same order as if the company was being wound up by the court.

## (6) *Duty to keep books and papers*

There are no rules laid down for keeping books and papers in a members voluntary winding up.

In a creditors voluntary winding up, the liquidator must keep such books as the committee of inspection or (if there is no committee) the creditors direct and must produce them and any other books and papers to the committee or creditors or company as and when the committee or creditors direct.

## (7) *Duty to keep accounts*

The duties imposed on a liquidator in a voluntary winding up are not as stringent as those imposed on a liquidator in a winding up by the court. He is bound to give details to the Department of Trade and Industry of accounts and money held by him if directed to do so by the Department. The Department may also audit his accounts.

## (8) *Duty to call meetings*

In the event of a members voluntary winding up continuing for more than one year, the liquidator must summon a general meeting of the company at the end of the first year and each successive year and lay before the meeting an account of his acts and dealings and the conduct of the winding up during the preceding year (s 584).

In a creditors voluntary winding up, the liquidator must summon a meeting of creditors (as well as members) and lay the same information before the creditors (s 594).

As soon as the company's affairs are fully wound up the liquidator makes a final account, (showing how the winding up has been conducted and the company's property disposed of) and calls a general meeting to lay before it his accounts. The meeting must be advertised in the Gazette.


DISSOLUTION OF THE COMPANY

Within one week after the meeting the liquidator must send the Registrar a copy of the accounts and make a return to him of the holding of the meeting. The Registrar registers the account and the return. Three months from the registration of the return the company is deemed to be dissolved (s 585).

The same procedure is followed in a creditors voluntary winding up with the liquidator calling a final meeting of the creditors. The information laid before the meeting is similar to that in a members voluntary winding up, as are the steps to the dissolution of the company (s 595).

The Registrar must in both cases publish in the Gazette notice of the receipt by him of the return by the liquidator of the final meeting of the company (s 711).

The Court may on the application of the liquidator or any other interested person make an order deferring the date of dissolution of the company until such time as the court thinks fit (ss 585, 595).

## WINDING UP UNDER THE SUPERVISION OF THE COURT

When a company has passed a resolution for voluntary winding up, the court may make an order that the voluntary winding up shall continue, but subject to such supervision of the court and on such terms and conditions as the court thinks just (s 606).

An application for a supervision order may be made by a creditor, contributory, the liquidator or the company. Such orders are rarely applied for as s 602 enables a creditor, contributory or liquidator to apply to the court to determine any question arising in the winding up of a company and to exercise all or any power which the court could exercise in a compulsory winding up.

A petition for winding up subject to the supervision of the court is, for the purpose of giving jurisdiction to the court over actions, deemed to be a petition for winding up by the court (s 607). The petition is presented in the same way as an application for winding up by the court and must set out the resolutions for a voluntary winding up and show that the requirements for a voluntary winding up have been met. The petition must be served on the company and the voluntary liquidator, unless the petition is presented by the company. It must be advertised in the London Gazette within 12 days.

The court may appoint an additional liquidator who has the powers and obligations as if he had been appointed by the company. The court may remove any liquidator so appointed, or any other liquidator and, fill any vacancy (s 609).

The supervision order directs the liquidator to submit to the Registrar every 3 months a report of the position and progress made in the winding up and realization of the assets. It also directs all costs to be taxed by the court.

The effect of the order is that any disposal of the company's property, transfer of shares or alteration in the status of members since the commencement is void (s 522). Any attachment, sequestration, distress or execution put in force against the effects of the company after the commencement of the winding up is void (s 525).

The liquidator may, subject to any restrictions imposed by the court, exercise all his powers as if the company were being wound up voluntarily, with certain exceptions.

He requires the sanction of the court where the winding up was previously a creditors' voluntary winding up, or the committee of inspection (if any), otherwise the creditors to –

(i) pay any classes of creditors in full.
(ii) make any compromise or arrangement with creditors and or persons claiming to be creditors.
(iii) to compromise calls and liabilities to calls, debts and liabilities capable of resulting in debts subsisting or supposed to subsist between the company and contributories or alleged contributories, on such terms as may be agreed and give a complete discharge in respect of these calls, debts and liabilities (s 610).

A supervision order is for all purposes deemed to be an order for winding up by the Court except for the provisions listed in Sch 18 to the Act (which are appropriate to a compulsory liquidation).

Supervision orders are rarely sought today and the Jenkins Committee (para 503) recommended their repeal as it was felt they served no useful purpose.


## DEFUNCT COMPANIES

Where the Registrar has reason to believe that a company is not carrying on business or is not in operation he may send a letter to the company inquiring whether it is carrying on business or is in operation.

If no reply is received within one month he may send a registered letter to the company referring to the first letter and stating that if an answer is not received to the second letter within one month, a notice will be pubished in the Gazette with a view to striking the company's name off the register.

If he either receives an answer to the effect that the company is not carrying on business or in operation, or does not receive an answer within one month of sending the second letter he may publish in the Gazette and send to the company by post a notice that, unless cause is shown to the contrary, the company will be struck off the register and dissolved within three months.

A similar procedure is followed by the Registrar where a company is being wound up and he has reasonable cause to believe either that no liquidator is acting or that the company's affairs are fully wound up and the returns required to be made by the liquidator have not been made for a period of six consecutive months.

The Registrar may, unless cause to the contrary is shown by the company, at the expiration of the time stipulated in the notice strike the company's name off the register and publish notice of this fact in the Gazette. The company is dissolved on publication of the notice (s 652).

This method of dissolution deprives the creditors and members of the various safeguards provided for by the normal winding up procedures. The section therefore provides that the liability of every director, managing officer and member shall continue as if the company had not been dissolved and the court can wind up a company whose name has been struck of the register.

Any of the company's property remaining after its dissolution is deemed to be bona vacantia and belongs to the Crown or to the Duchy of Lancaster or to the Duke of Cornwall (s 654).

The court may at any time, within 2 years of the dissolution of a company, declare the dissolution void on the application of the liquidator or any other person appearing to the court to be interested. The court may make an order on such terms as it thinks fit, and any proceedings may be taken as if the company had not been dissolved (s 651). (This makes possible the distribution of any asset which was overlooked on the dissolution of the company).

An application may be made to the court by the company or any member or creditor, within 20 years of the dissolution, for the company's name to be restored to the register. If the court is satisfied that the company was at the time of striking off carrying on business or in operation, or that it is just that the company be restored to the register, order the company's name to be restored. An office copy is then sent to the Registrar for registration. The company is then deemed to have continued in existence as if its name had never been struck off (s 653).

# RECEIVERS AND LIQUIDATORS

A receiver is appointed by the secured creditors (or by the court on their behalf) to enforce their security. This is achieved by realising sufficient of the company's assets as are necessary to pay off the debenture holder(s). On payment of the debt, the receiver vacates office and control of the company reverts to the directors.

A liquidator is either appointed by the Court (in a compulsory winding up) or by the members (in a members' voluntary winding up) or by the members and creditors (in a creditors' voluntary winding up). His function is to provide for an orderly winding up of the company for the benefit of the creditors and members. This is achieved by realising the company's assets, paying its debts and distributing the surplus (if any) to the members. On conclusion of the liquidation the company is dissolved ie its name is removed from the register.

The powers of a receiver are derived from the provisions of the debenture under which he is appointed while a liquidator has numerous powers derived from statute (s 359). The liquidator may however be controlled by meetings of creditors and contributories. A liquidator appointed by the court is an officer of the court.

A receiver appointed under a floating charge is also receiver and manager and is empowered to carry on company's business. It may be sold as a going concern or carried on throughout the receivership and returned to the control of the directors on termination of the receivership.

A liquidator may, with the court's sanction, carry on the company's business, usually for the purpose of selling it as a going concern, as a liquidator's function is to sell an asset at the best price obtainable.

A receiver appointed under a floating charge, and a liquidator in a compulsory liquidation must be supplied with a statement of affairs by the directors.

A receiver is personally liable on the contracts made by him for the company but a liquidator has no such liability.

# Chapter 21

# Reconstruction, amalgamations and take-overs

The words reconstruction and amalgamation are commercial terms and are not defined in the Act.

A reconstruction consists of either:

(i) a transfer by a company of its assets to a new company; or
(ii) an alteration to the capital structure of a single company or group of companies.

An amalgamation takes place when the undertakings of two or more companies are united under single control. The simplest method, is a take over bid where one company acquires the issued share capital of another and exercises control over that company.

There are various ways in which an amalgamation or reconstruction may be accomplished. A company will select the most appropriate and convenient method to effect the change.

## SALE OF THE UNDERTAKING UNDER A POWER IN THE MEMORANDUM

A company's objects clause generally gives a company a power to sell the whole of its undertaking and property to another company in return for shares in that company. The old company is then wound up and the shares in the new company are distributed amongst the members of the old company in accordance with their rights.

The sale must be authorised by special resolution and the procedure laid down in s 582 must be followed (including the provisions for the protection of dissentient shareholders and creditors) as the company is considered to be in the course of a voluntary winding up.

**Bisgood v Henderson's Transvaal Estates (1908)**

A company proposed to sell its undertakings for shares in a newly formed company. The new company was to issue £1 shares credited as only paid up to 87½p (17/6). The scheme provided that each member should exchange each share in the old company for one share in the new company. Any dissenting shareholder who did not take up the shares was to receive the price received by the liquidator on a sale of the shares unapplied for. It was held that the scheme was ultra vires, as the dissenting shareholders should have had their interests in the company valued and purchased according to the terms of s 287 (now s 582).

# RECONSTRUCTION OR AMALAGAMATION UNDER S 582

A company which is proposed to be, or is in the course of being, wound up voluntarily (ie a members voluntary winding up) may effect a reconstruction or amalgamation by transferring all or part of its business or property to another company for a consideration consisting of cash, or shares, policies or other like interests in that other company to be distributed among its members (s 582(1)).

The procedure is as follows:

1. If the company is not already in liquidation it must circulate details of the scheme to its members and convene a general meeting.
2. At the general meeting resolutions are passed for winding up, for the appointment of a liquidator and giving authority to the liquidator to enter into an agreement on terms already agreed in principle with the transferee company.
3. The liquidator enters into the agreement and transfers the whole or part of the company's assets to the transferee company, while retaining a sufficient sum to meet the transferor company's liabilities.
4. Money or shares, policies or other interests in the transferee company will then be distributed amongst the members of the transferor company in accordance with their rights. In this way the shareholders of the transferor company become the holders of shares or other securities in the transferee company.

The transferor company may well retain certain assets which will be distributed amongst its shareholders.

The liquidator will invariably seek the approval of the court in a members voluntary winding up, for without its approval the special resolution for the sale of the company's assets will be void if a winding up or supervision order is made within a year of the resolution being passed (s 582(7)).

Although s 582 is limited to a members' voluntary winding up it may also be applied in a creditors' voluntary winding up. The liquidator must, in that case, obtain the sanction of the court or the committee of inspection to the scheme (s 593).

The section may be used in the following ways:

(a) Company A sells all its undertaking and property (except for money in a bank account) to a newly formed company, Company B, in exchange for shares in Company B credited as fully paid. The shares in Company B along with the money retained are divided rateably amongst the shareholders of Company A.

(b) Company A sells all its undertaking and property to a newly formed company, Company B, in exchange for shares in the new company which are distributed to the shareholders in Company A pro rata to their holdings. The amount unpaid on the new shares is then called up to provide additional capital. As the shareholders have the right of dissent or refusal, it is usual to arrange the underwriting of the new capital.

(c) Company A sells the whole of its undertaking to Company B, an existing company, for fully paid up shares in Company B. The business of both companies is thus amalgamated.

(d) Companies A and B sell the whole of their undertakings to a newly formed company Company B (Holdings) in exchange for fully paid up shares in that company. Companies A and B are then dissolved and to complete the amalgamation B (holdings) assumes the name of one of the companies and becomes Company B.

If the assets received by the new company as consideration for the sale exceed the nominal value of the shares, it must transfer the excess to a share premium account: *Henry Head and Co v Ropner Holdings* (1952) (see p 107).

PROTECTION OF DISSENTIENT MEMBERS

Any sale or arrangement is binding on the members of the transferor company.

Any member who did not vote in favour of the special resolution may express his dissent by serving a written notice on the liquidator, at the company's registered office, within 7 days of passing the resolution, requiring him either:

(i) to abstain from carrying the resolution into effect; or
(ii) to purchase his interest at a price to be determined by agreement or arbitration (s 582(5)).

If the liquidator elects to purchase the member's interests, the purchase money must be paid before the dissolution of the company (s 582(6)).

A provision in the articles which deprives a member of his right to dissent is void.

### Payne v The Cork Co Ltd (1900)

A company's articles provided that in a voluntary winding up no member could require a liquidator to abstain from carrying out a scheme to sell the company's undertaking and assets. A dissentient member was only given the right to request the liquidator to sell his shares. On receipt of this request the liquidator might sell his shares and pay over to them the proceeds of sale. It was held that the articles were ultra vires as they purported to deprive shareholders of their rights under the Act.

PROTECTION OF CREDITORS

Creditors of the transferor company are usually safe-guarded by the transferee company giving an indemnity that it will meet the liabilities of the transferor company or by the transferor company retaining sufficient assets to meet its liabilities. If the creditors are of the opinion that they will be prejudiced by the transfer of the company's assets to the transferee company they may petition for a compulsory winding up order or a supervision order. The special resolution for winding up the company will be void if either of these petitions is granted within a year of its passing, unless the court sanctions the resolution (s 582(7)).

## COMPROMISE OR SCHEME OF ARRANGEMENT UNDER SS 425–427

The procedure laid down in section 425 may be followed where a company wishes to enter into a scheme of arrangement or composition with its creditors. It can be used where a company, in financial difficulties, is unable to make an arrangement or compromise which is acceptable to the creditors and other interested parties. The company need not be wound up to carry out a scheme or compromise.

It thus differs from s 582 and the other provisions in the Act which deal with compromises or arrangements with creditors, which require a company to be in liquidation before the provisions can be carried out.

Under s 539(1) a liquidator in a compulsory liquidation may make any compromise or arrangement with creditors if he obtains the sanction of the court or committee of inspection, while under s 425, a liquidator may enter into a compromise or arrangement with its creditors where a company is being or is about to be wound up voluntarily.

Section 615 forbids a company, not in liquidation, to make a conveyance or assignment of all its property to trustees for the benefit of all its creditors.

Section 425 provides a method where a compromise or arrangement may be made between:

a company and its creditors (or any *class* of creditors); or
a company and its members (or any *class* of members); or
a company and its creditors and members (or any *class* of them).

A scheme under this section requires the approval of a specified majority of creditors and/or members and the sanction of the court.

The procedure is as follows:

1. Application is made to the court by the company, any creditor, any member, or liquidator (if the company is being wound up) for an order that a meeting of the creditors and/or members shall be held.
2. Details are submitted to the court of the terms of the scheme of arrangement. If the court is satisfied that the scheme is generally suitable for consideration it will order that a meeting or meetings be held to consider the scheme.
3. The scheme must be approved by a majority –
   (i) in number
   (ii) representing three quarters in value of those present and voting either in person or proxy at the meeting(s) (s 425(2)).
   The scheme must disclose the effect of the compromise or arrangement upon the interests of the directors, especially where it involves the retirement of any director(s) and/or compensation for loss of office. Similar information must be given in respect of the trustees of a debenture trust deed if the compromise or arrangement affects the rights of debenture holders (s 426).

It is the duty of any director or trustee for the debenture holders to give notice to the company of any matters relating to himself as are necessary for the purposes of the above disclosures.

4.  If the scheme is approved at the meeting(s) an application is then made to the court for an order sanctioning the scheme. In particular the court will satisfy itself that creditors are not being prejudiced by the proposed scheme.
5.  Once the scheme is approved by the court it binds the company, the members and the creditors who were parties to the scheme. If the company is being wound up, it binds the liquidator and the contributories. The scheme becomes binding when an office copy of the order is delivered to the Registrar for registration.

Section 425 refers to a *class* of members or creditors ie

'confined to those persons whose rights are not so dissimilar as to make it impossible for them to consult together with a view to their common interest' per Lord Esher MR in *Sovereign Life Assurance Co v Dodd* (1892).

### Re Hellenic and General Trust (1975)

A scheme was proposed between Hambros and Hellenic Trust by which 15,000,000 issued and fully paid ordinary shares were to be cancelled and the shareholders paid 58p per share by Hambros for the loss of their shares. Hambros would then receive 15,000,000 new shares in Hellenic. The scheme was approved by a numerical majority (84.67%) holding three quarters in the value of the shares. A wholly owned subsidiary of Hambros (MIT) held 53% of the ordinary shares and voted in favour of the scheme. A Greek Bank holding 13.95% in value opposed the scheme, as it would be liable to capital gains tax in Greece for the cash received for its shares. It was held that as the interests of the wholly owned subsidiary were different from those of the other shareholders and separate meetings should have been convened.

The court may, and usually does, require dissentient shareholders to be given the same rights as they would have received under s 582.

Examples of schemes approved by the court include:

Debenture holders giving an extension of time for the payment of loan capital.
Debenture holders accepting shares in exchange for their debentures.

Debenture holders accepting a cash payment less than the par value of their debentures.

Debenture holders agreeing to forego their right to interest for a period of time.

Preference shareholders giving up their right to arrears of dividend.

Creditors accepting shares in full or part payment of their debts.

## THE PROVISIONS OF S 427

The reconstruction of a company or the amalgamation of two or more companies may be facilitated by the provision of s 427. This section provides that when an application is made to the court under s 425 to sanction a compromise or arrangement in connection with a reconstruction or amalgamation, and the scheme requires the transfer of the whole or part of the undertaking of one company (the transferor company) to another company (the transferee company), the court may make an order for all, or any of, the following matters:

(a) The transfer to the transferee company of the whole or part of the undertaking and of the property or liabilities of any transferor company.

(b) The allotment of shares, debentures or other similar interests by the transferee company to the persons concerned.

(c) The continuation of any legal proceedings by or against the transferor company to be brought in the name of the transferee company.

(d) The dissolution of the transferor company without winding up.

(e) Provision for persons who dissent from the scheme.

(f) Such incidental matters as are necessary to ensure that the scheme is fully and effectively carried out.

An office copy of an order made under this section must be delivered to the Registrar within 7 days of making the order.

## TAKE-OVERS

A take-over takes place when a company acquires the whole or a significant proportion of the share capital of another company from its shareholders. The consideration for the acquisition may be the issue of shares or debentures in the acquiring (transferee) company, a cash payment, or a combination of both.

There are several methods in which a take-over may be achieved.

1. The purchase of shares from the individual members of the transfer or (target) company.

2. The purchase of shares on the Stock Exchange or by private treaty or both. This is usually a gradual process of building up a substantial shareholding.
3. An offer to all or a significant number of the shareholders in the target company to purchase all or a large proportion of their shareholding at a fixed price within a stipulated time, with a proviso that the offer is conditional on acceptance by a certain percentage of the shareholders. The offer is made by means of an offer document which is circulated to all the shareholders to whom the offer is made. It is not a prospectus, and therefore does not have to comply with the rules relating to disclosure in prospectuses (*Governments Stock and Other Securities Investment Co Ltd v Christopher* (1956) (see p 80).

The offer document usually stipulates that shareholders who accept the offer are bound to sell their shares, but the transferee company is only bound to purchase their shares when there is an acceptance by a stipulated percentage (usually 90%). The offer price is usually higher than the market price quoted for the shares on the Stock Exchange and payment for the shares may be in cash or in kind e g £3 per share or 2 shares in the transferee company for every share in the target company.

There are various reasons for a company becoming the object of a take-over bid.

The transferee company may seek to acquire a particular asset, or acquire an asset and use it in a different and more profitable way. The transferee company may seek to eliminate competition or diversify its interests.

The shares of the target company may be quoted at a price below the actual or potential value of the business.

The company may have pursued a conservative dividend policy, or it may have not revalued its fixed assets, or the transferee company may feel that the management of the target company is inefficient or ineffective.

## SECTIONS 428 AND 429

The interests of both the majority and minority shareholders are served by s 428. A small minority who have rejected an offer to purchase their shares in a take-over situation may prove to be a bar to the effective operation of the company if a take-over bid is

384 Reconstruction, amalgamations and take-overs

successful. The minority may also prefer to be bought out than remain as shareholders of a subsidiary company. It has been stated that the section is designed to prevent the oppression of the majority by the minority (Greene Committee 1926).

Section 428 provides that the transferee company may acquire the shares of a dissentient minority if the following conditions are fulfilled:

1. There is a scheme or contract for the transfer of shares or any class of shares in the transferor company to the transferee company, whether it is a registered company or not.
2. The scheme is approved by the holders of 90 per cent of the shares involved, within 4 months of the date of the offer. Any shares already held by the transferee company or a nominee for the company or its subsidiary is disregarded in this calculation.
3. The transferee company may within two months after the expiration of four months give notice to any dissenting shareholder that it desires to acquire his shares.
4. The dissenting shareholders must be offered similar terms as the assenting shareholders.

### Re Carlton Holdings Ltd (1971)

A transferee company made an offer to acquire the shares of Carlton Holdings Ltd for either an exchange of shares or a cash alternative. Over 90% of the shareholders accepted the offer and the majority opted for the cash alternative. A minority shareholder did nothing and after his death his personal representatives sought to compel the transferee company to purchase his shares on the basis of the cash alternative. It was held that the minority were entitled to similar treatment as that given to the assenting shareholders.

5. A dissenting shareholder may, within one month of the receipt of a notice (in 3), apply to the court for a declaration that the transferee company is not entitled to acquire his shares.

   The court will generally give its approval to a scheme if it considers it fair to the body of shareholders as a whole. the burden of proving that it is unfair rests on the dissenting shareholder. The procedure must not be abused, and the court will not approve a scheme which enables the majority to expropriate the shares of the minority.

### Re Bugle Press (1961)

Two shareholders who held ninety per cent of the shares in a company offered to buy the third shareholder's ten per cent holding, but he refused the offer. They then formed a new company in which they held all the issued share capital. This company then made an offer to buy the first company's shares. Ninety per cent of the shareholders accepted the offer and the second company sought to acquire the third shareholder's shares under the provisions of s 209. It was held that the provisions of s 209 (now s 428) could not be used to evade the rule forbidding the expropriation of a minority.

6. After notice has been given to a dissentient shareholder the transferee company must send a copy of the notice to the transferor company with an instrument of transfer executed by the transferee company and, on behalf of the shareholder, by a person appointed by the transferee company.
7. The transferee company must pay or transfer the money, or other consideration representing the price payable for the shares, to the transferor company. It is then entitled to be registered as the holder of the shares. The money received by the transferor company must be transferred into a separate bank account, and must (together with any other consideration received) be held on trust for the persons entitled to the shares.
8. Where, at the date of the offer, the transferee company (or its nominee or its subsidiary) holds more than 10 per cent of the shares subject to the offer s 428 does not apply unless:
   (i) the offer is made to all the holders of the shares (other than those held by the transferee company).
   (ii) the assenting shareholders hold ninety per cent in value of the shares involved and are not less than three quarters in number of the holders of the shares.
9. If as a result of a scheme or contract under s 428 the transferee company acquires ninety per cent in value of the shares of the transferor company it must within one month give notice of this fact to every dissenting shareholder (s 429).
10. A dissenting shareholder may, within three months of receiving this notice, require the transferee company to acquire his shares on the same terms as in the offer, or on terms agreed upon by the parties, or in default on such terms as the court may direct (s 429).

### Re Grierson, Oldham and Adams Ltd (1968)

An offer made to the ordinary shareholders of a company to purchase their ordinary shares at 30p per share was accepted by 99 per cent of the shareholders. The two shareholders who held 1 per cent of the shares applied to the Court for a declaration that they were not bound to sell their shares. As the majority had accepted the offer the price stipulated was fair and above the market price. The declaration was refused.

It is not sufficient for a dissentient to show that the scheme is open to criticism or is capable of improvement.

## THE CITY CODE ON TAKE-OVERS AND MERGERS

The main control in regard to the take-over and merger of listed companies is the City Code on Take-overs and Mergers which is administered by the City Panel, which has its own permanent secretariat. Companies or individuals who act in breach of the Code may be reprimanded, publicly censured or face withdrawal of Stock Exchange facilities. The Panel may refer certain aspects of a case to the Department of Trade, the Stock Exchange or other appropriate body. There is a right of appeal to an Appeal Committee where the Panel proposes to take disciplinary action, or where it is alleged that the Panel has acted outside its jurisdiction.

> 'The Code represents the collective opinion of those professionally concerned in the field of take-overs and mergers on a range of business standards. It is not concerned with the evaluation of the financial or commercial advantages or disadvantages of a take-over or merger, which are matters for the company and its shareholders and in certain circumstances for the Government, advised by the Monopolies and Mergers Commission.
>
> The Code has not, and does not seek to have, the force of law; but those who wish to take advantage of the facilities of the securities markets in the United Kingdom should conduct themselves in matters relating to take-overs and mergers according to the Code.' (City Code on Take-overs and Mergers 5th edition)

The provisions of the code fall into 2 categories –

(a) *General principles* of conduct which are a codification of good standards of commercial behaviour; and
(b) *Rules* which consist of examples of the application of general principles and rules of procedure governing take-over and merger transactions.

### GENERAL PRINCIPLES

There are 14 general principles in the City Code which have to be observed in a take-over or merger transaction.

1. The spirit as well as the precise wording of the Code must be observed and is applicable in areas or circumstances not explicitly covered by a rule.

2. Although the boards of companies have a duty to act in the best interests of their members the General Principles and Rules will impinge on the freedom of action of boards and persons involved in take-over and merger situations.
3. Shareholders should be provided with sufficient time, evidence, facts and opinions upon which to reach an adequate judgement and decision. No relevant information should be withheld from them.
4. Where a bone fide offer has been made or is imminent, the board of the offeree company may not take any action to frustrate the offer, without the approval of the shareholders in general meeting.
5. It must be the object of all parties to a take-over or merger transaction to use every endeavour to prevent the creation of a false market in the shares of an offeror or offeree company.
6. A board which receives an offer should in the interests of its shareholders seek competent independent advice.
7. Rights of control must be exercised in good faith and the oppression of a minority is wholly unacceptable.
8. All shareholders of the same class of an offeree company shall be treated similarly by an offeror.
9. If after a take-over or merger is reasonably in contemplation and an offer has been made to, or shares purchased from one or more shareholders, any subsequent general offer to the shareholders of the same class must not be on less favourable terms.
10. During the course of a take-over or merger or when a take-over or merger is contemplated, neither company must furnish information to some shareholder which is not available to all shareholders.
11. Directors of companies must always act only in their capacity as directors in advising their shareholders. They must not have regard to their personal or family shareholdings or their personal relationships with the companies.
12. Any document or advertisement sent out to shareholders by a board must be treated with the same standard of care as if it were a prospectus within the Companies Act 1985. Especial care must be take over profit forecasts.
13. If control of a company is acquired by a person or persons acting in concert a general offer to all the other shareholders is normally required.
14. An offer should only be announced after the most careful and responsible consideration. It should only be made when

an offeror has every reason to believe he will be able to implement the offer.

There are 42 rules dealing with the standards of conduct required from the parties in a take-over and merger transaction and setting out the procedures to be followed.

The following are some of the more important rules found in the City Code.

### The general approach

The offer should be put forward in the first instance to the board of the offeree company and its advisors. If the offer is not made by the ultimate or potential offeror the identity of that person must be disclosed at the outset.

The board of the offeree company is entitled to be satisfied that the offeror is or will be in a position to implement the offer in full. It must also obtain competent independent advice on any offer and make known that advice to its shareholders.

### The announcement of the offer

When any firm intention to make an offer is notified to a board from a serious source, it must publicise that fact, by press notice, without delay. It must also send a copy of the press notice, or a circular setting out the contents of that notice to its shareholders.

The terms of an offer and the identity of the offerer must be disclosed. He must also disclose any existing shareholding in the offeree company.

If the offer comes within the statutory provisions for possible reference to the Monopolies and Mergers Commission it must contain a term stating that it will lapse if the offer is referred to the Commission before the closing date for the offer, or on the date on which it is declared unconditional.

Absolute secrecy before an announcement must be maintained.

### The consideration of an offer by the board

The offer document should be posted within 28 days of the announcement of a firm intention to make an offer. At the same time, or as soon as practicable, the board of the offeree company should circulate its views on the offer.

When there has been an announcement of a firm intention to make an offer, it cannot be withdrawn without the Panel's consent, unless the offer has been expressed as being subject to the prior fulfilment of a specific condition, which has not been met.

Any information given to a preferred suitor must be furnished to all bona fide potential offerors.

## The offer document

Every offer document must contain information relating to arrangements by the offeror company in connection with the offer e g that the consideration for the offer will be implemented in full without any lien, set off, counterclaim or other claim.

It must also include confirmation by an appropriate third party that resources are available to satisfy the full acceptance of an offer made for cash. Documents sent to shareholders of the offeree company recommending acceptance or rejection of an offer must contain particulars of all service contracts of directors.

Any document relating to an offer must be prepared with the same standard of care as if it were a prospectus.

It must contain details of:

(i) the offeror's shareholding in the offeree company.
(ii) any shareholding in the offeror and offeree company in which the directors of the offeror company are interested.

Details must also be given of shareholdings owned or controlled by persons acting in concert with the offeror, and of shareholdings controlled by persons who, prior to the posting of the offer document, have irrevocably committed themselves to accepting the offer. Information must also be given as to the interests of the directors and advisers of the offeree company.

## The offer

No offer may be made which would result in the offeror having control of the company unless it is on terms that it will be made unconditional only if the offeror acquires more than 50 per cent of the voting shares.

An offer must initially be open for at least 21 days. If revised it must be open for at least 14 days from the date of the revised offer.

No offer (whether revised or not) is capable of being declared unconditional after 3.30 pm on the 60th day after the date the offer is initially posted.

The consent of the panel is required for any partial offer. In the case of an offer which would result in the offeror holding shares carrying less than 30% of the voting rights of a company consent will normally be granted. Where an offer is for between 30% and 100%, consent will not normally be granted if the offeror or persons acting in concert have acquired shares in the offeree company during the previous 12 months.

If a partial offer could result in the offeror holding over 50% (but less than 100%) of the voting rights of the offeree company, the offer document must contain a prominent statement advising shareholders that, if the offer succeeds, statutory control will pass to the offeror who will be free to exercise that control and acquire further shares without incurring any mandatory obligation under the Code.

## Dealings

All persons in possession of price sensitive information relating to an offer or contemplated offer must treat that information as secret and must not pass it to any other person unless it is necessary to do so.

It is considered undesirable to fetter the market and all parties to a take-over or merger transaction and their associates are free to deal, subject to daily disclosure to the Stock Exchange, the panel and the press.

If the offeror acquires 15% of the shares under offer for cash, the offer must include a cash alternative at not less than the highest price for shares of that class during the offer period and in the previous 12 months.

During the course of an offer, or if an offer is imminent the board of the offeree company must not (except in accordance with a pre-existing contract or with the approval of shareholders in general meeting) issue any shares or grant any options or dispose of any material assets, during the course of an actual or imminent offer.

Neither may an offeror enter into arrangements to deal or make purchases and sales of shares in the offeree company on more favourable terms than those extended to all shareholders.

## Mandatory bids and substantial acquisitions

A purchaser of shares who has acquired (on his own account or in concert with others) shares carrying 30% or more of the voting rights of a company must make a general offer for the remainder of the shares. The rule also applies when a purchaser (on his own or in concert with others) holding between 30% and 50% of a company's voting rights acquires more than 2% of the voting rights in any 12 month period.

A purchaser (on his own or with others) who does *not* hold 30% of the voting rights of a company may not, prior to the announcement by him of a firm intention to make an offer, acquire any shares carrying voting rights in that company which would increase his holding to 30% more.

A purchaser who holds between 30% and 50% of a company's voting rights is also prevented, prior to such an announcement, from acquiring any shares which when aggregated with his acquisitions in the previous 12 months would carry more than 2% of the company's voting rights. (These restrictions do not apply to purchases from a single shareholder, or when the purchases precede and are conditional on the board recommending acceptance of the offer).

After the announcement of the offer the offeror may not for 7 days purchase any shares carrying voting rights in the offeree company (or any rights over such shares) unless it already holds shares carrying 50% of the voting rights or its offer has been declared unconditional in all respects, whether or not the bid is recommended by the board of the offeree company. (Apart from these exceptions control cannot pass to the offeree in less than 21 days as an offer must be kept open for that length of time).

## OTHER CONTROLS ON TAKE-OVERS AND MERGERS

Other legal and extra-legal controls to be considered when a take-over or merger is contemplated include the following:

1. The Code of Conduct for dealers in securities which aims to establish standards of ethical behaviour so as to promote the effective functioning of the securities, markets and to safeguard the public interest.
2. The Model Code for securities transactions by directors of listed companies, published by the Stock Exchange.
3. The Stock Exchange Listing Agreement which requires listed companies to furnish certain information relating to a take-over or merger.
4. The Licensed Dealers (Conduct of Business Rules) 1960 laid down certain requirements relating to the conduct of a take-over and the contents of take-over circulars. Although it only applies to licensed dealers, it is observed generally.
5. The Fair Trading Act 1973 (as amended by the Competition Act 1980) empowers the Secretary of State to refer large scale mergers and proposed mergers to the Monopolies and Mergers Commission for its consideration. The Fair Trading Act is concerned with mergers or proposed mergers of economic

significance i e if the value of the assets taken (or to be taken) over exceeds £30 million or a situation is produced where at least one quarter of all the goods or services of a particular description supplied in the United Kingdom or a substantial part of the United Kingdom will be supplied by or to the same person or group of persons.

The Commission is asked to investigate and report on the merger, or proposed merger, usually within 6 months. It must take into account all matters which appear relevant including:
the maintenance and promotion of effective competition in the United Kingdom;
the reduction of costs by competition and development;
the maintenance of a balanced industry and employment in the United Kingdom; and
the maintenance of a competitive market outside the United Kingdom.

If the Commission's report finds that the merger is not contrary to the public interest it may proceed. If it is found to be against the public interest, the Secretary of State is given various powers under the Fair Trading Act. He may:-
prohibit the merger;
cancel an existing merger;
allow the merger to proceed but subject the new entity to various regulations;
provide for the division of any business or the sale of an undertaking.

It is the duty of the Director General of Fair Trading to be acquainted with actual or proposed mergers and to make recommendations in respect of such mergers to the Secretary of State.

6. Article 86 of the European Communities Treaty may be applied, in certain circumstances, to a merger situation. It prohibits any abuse by one or more undertakings of a dominant position within the Common Market, or a substantial part of it, if this would affect trade between member states. The Article does not specifically refer to mergers.

**Europeamballage Corporation and Continental Can Co Inc v E C Commission** (1973)

A subsidiary of an American company obtained control of a German company which had a substantial share of the German market in metal tins and containers. Two years later the American company obtained control of a Dutch company which was the largest manufacturer of metal containers in the Benelux countries. The Commission contended that as control of the German company gave the American company a dominant position in the German market, its subsequent acquisition of the Dutch company was an abuse of that dominant position. It would eliminate future competition between the two companies and thus affect trade between member states. The European Court upheld this interpretation of the Article, but allowed the company's appeal on other grounds.

7. Under the Transfer of Undertakings (Protection of Employment) Regulations 1981, provision is made for consultation with Trade Union representatives prior to a take-over or merger, and for the automatic transfer of contracts of employment from the transferor to the transferee company.

# Appendices

# Appendix A
# Table A

*Companies (Alteration of Table A etc) Regulations 1984, SI 1984/1717*

## REGULATIONS FOR MANAGEMENT OF A COMPANY LIMITED BY SHARES

### INTERPRETATION

**1.** In these regulations –

'the Acts' means the Companies Acts 1948 to 1983 including any statutory modification or re-enactment thereof for the time being in force.

'the articles' means the articles of the company.

'clear days' in relation to the period of a notice means that period excluding the day when the notice is given or deemed to be given and the day for which it is given or on which it is to take effect.

'executed' includes any mode of execution.

'office' means the registered office of the company.

'the holder' in relation to shares means the member whose name is entered in the register of members as the holder of the shares.

'the seal' means the common seal of the company.

'secretary' means the secretary of the company or any other person appointed to perform the duties of the secretary of the company, including a joint, assistant or deputy secretary.

'the United Kingdom' means Great Britain and Northern Ireland.

Unless the context otherwise requires, words or expressions contained in these regulations bear the same meaning as in the Acts but excluding any statutory modification thereof not in force when these regulations become binding on the company.

SHARE CAPITAL

**2.** Subject to the provisions of the Acts and without prejudice to any rights attached to any existing shares, any share may be issued with such rights or restrictions as the company may by ordinary resolution determine.

**3.** Subject to the provisions of the Acts, shares may be issued which are to be redeemed or are to be liable to be redeemed at the option of the company or the holder on such terms and in such manner as may be provided by the articles.

**4.** The company may exercise the powers of paying commissions conferred by the Acts. Subject to the provisions of the Acts, any such commission may be satisfied by the payment of cash or by the allotment of fully or partly paid shares or partly in one way and partly in the other.

**5.** Except as required by law, no person shall be recognised by the company as holding any share upon any trust and (except as otherwise provided by the articles or by law) the company shall not be bound by or recognise any interest in any share except an absolute right to the entirety thereof in the holder.

SHARE CERTIFICATES

**6.** Every member, upon becoming the holder of any shares, shall be entitled without payment to one certificate for all the shares of each class held by him (and, upon transferring a part of his holding of shares of any class, to a certificate for the balance of such holding) or several certificates each for one or more of his shares upon payment for every certificate after the first of such reasonable sum as the directors may determine. Every certificate shall be sealed with the seal and shall specify the number, class and distinguishing numbers (if any) of the shares to which it relates and the amount or respective amounts paid up thereon. The company shall not be bound to issue more than one certificate for shares held jointly by several persons and delivery of a certificate to one joint holder shall be a sufficient delivery to all of them.

**7.** If a share certificate is defaced, worn-out, lost or destroyed, it may be renewed on such terms (if any) as to evidence and indemnity and payment of the expenses reasonably incurred by the company in investigating evidence as the directors may determine but otherwise free of charge, and (in the case of defacement or wearing-out) on delivery up of the old certificate.

LIEN

**8.** The company shall have a first and paramount lien on every share (not being a fully paid share) for all moneys (whether presently payable or not) payable at a fixed time or called in respect of that share. The directors may at any time declare any share to be wholly or in part exempt from the provisions of this regulation. The company's lien on a share shall extend to any amount payable in respect of it.

**9.** The company may sell in such manner as the directors determine any shares on which the company has a lien if a sum in respect of which the lien exists is presently payable and is not paid within fourteen clear days after notice has been given to the holder of the share or to the person entitled to it in consequence of the death or bankruptcy of the holder, demanding payment and stating that if the notice is not complied with the shares may be sold.

**10.** To give effect to a sale the directors may authorise some person to execute an instrument of transfer of the shares sold to, or in accordance with the directions of, the purchaser. The title of the transferee to the shares shall not be affected by any irregularity in or invalidity of the proceedings in reference to the sale.

**11.** The net proceeds of the sale, after payment of the costs, shall be applied in payment of so much of the sum for which the lien exists as is presently payable, and any residue shall (upon surrender to the company for cancellation of the certificate for the shares sold and subject to a like lien for any moneys not presently payable as existed upon the shares before the sale) be paid to the person entitled to the shares at the date of the sale.

CALLS ON SHARES AND FORFEITURE

**12.** Subject to the terms of allotment, the directors may make calls upon the members in respect of any moneys unpaid on their shares (whether in respect of nominal value or premium) and each member shall (subject to receiving at least fourteen clear days' notice specifying when and where payment is to be made) pay to the company as required by the notice the amount called on his shares. A call may be required to be paid by instalments. A call may, before receipt by the company of any sum due thereunder, be revoked in whole or part and payment of a call may be postponed in whole or part. A person upon whom a call is made shall remain liable for calls made upon him notwithstanding the subsequent transfer of the shares in respect whereof the call was made.

**13.** A call shall be deemed to have been made at the time when the resolutions of the directors authorising the call was passed.

**14.** The joint holders of a share shall be jointly and severally liable to pay all calls in respect thereof.

**15.** If a call remains unpaid after it has become due and payable the person from whom it is due and payable shall pay interest on the amount unpaid from the day it became due and payable until it is paid at the rate fixed by the terms of allotment of the share or in the notice of the call or, if no rate is fixed, at the appropriate rate (as defined by the Acts) but the directors may waive payment of the interest wholly or in part.

**16.**   An amount payable in respect of a share on allotment or at any fixed date, whether in respect of nominal value or premium or as an instalment of a call, shall be deemed to be a call and if it is not paid the provisions of the articles shall apply as if that amount had become due and payable by virtue of a call.

**17.**   Subject to the terms of allotment, the directors may make arrangements on the issue of shares for a difference between the holders in the amounts and times of payment of calls on their shares.

**18.**   If a call remains unpaid after it has become due and payable the directors may give to the person from whom it is due not less than fourteen clear days' notice requiring payment of the amount unpaid together with any interest which may have accrued. The notice shall name the place where payment is to be made and shall state that if the notice is not complied with the shares in respect of which the call was made will be liable to be forfeited.

**19.**   If the notice is not complied with any share in respect of which it was given may, before the payment required by the notice has been made, be forfeited by a resolution of the directors and the forfeiture shall include all dividends or other moneys payable in respect of the forfeited shares and not paid before the forfeiture.

**20.**   Subject to the provisions of the Acts, a forfeited share may be sold, re-allotted or otherwise disposed of on such terms and in such manner as the directors determine either to the person who was before the forfeiture the holder or to any other person and at any time before sale, re-allotment or other disposition, the forfeiture may be cancelled on such terms as the directors think fit. Where for the purposes of its disposal a forfeited share is to be transferred to any person the directors may authorise some person to execute an instrument of transfer of the share to that person.

**21.**   A person any of whose shares have been forfeited shall cease to be a member in respect of them and shall surrender to the company for cancellation the certificate for the shares forfeited but shall remain liable to the company for all moneys which at the date of forfeiture were presently payable by him to the company in respect of those shares with interest at the rate at which interest was payable on those moneys before the forfeiture or, if no interest was so payable, at the appropriate rate (as defined in the Acts) from the date of forfeiture until payment but the directors may waive payment wholly or in part or enforce payment without any allowance for the value of the shares at the time of forfeiture or for any consideration received on their disposal.

**22.** A statutory declaration by a director or the secretary that a share has been forfeited on a specified date shall be conclusive evidence of the facts stated in it as against all persons claiming to be entitled to the share and the declaration shall (subject to the execution of an instrument of transfer if necessary) constitute a good title to the share and the person to whom the share is disposed of shall not be bound to see to the application of the consideration, if any, nor shall his title to the share be affected by any irregularity in or invalidity of the proceedings in reference to the forfeiture or disposal of the share.

TRANSFER OF SHARES

**23.** The instrument of transfer of a share may be in any usual form or in any other form which the directors may approve and shall be executed by or on behalf of the transferor and, unless the share is fully paid, by or on behalf of the transferee.

**24.** The directors may refuse to register the transfer of a share which is not fully paid to a person of whom they do not approve and they may refuse to register the transfer of a share on which the company has a lien. They may also refuse to register a transfer unless –

   *(a)* It is lodged at the office or at such other place as the directors may appoint and is accompanied by the certificate for the shares to which it relates and such other evidence as the directors may reasonably require to show the right of the transferor to make the transfer;

   *(b)* it is in respect of only one class of shares; and

   *(c)* it is in favour of not more than four transferees.

**25.** If the directors refuse to register a transfer of a share, they shall within two months after the date on which the transfer was lodged with the company send to the transferee notice of the refusal.

**26.** The registration of transfers of shares or of transfers of any class of shares may be suspended at such times and for such periods (not exceeding thirty days in any year) as the directors may determine.

**27.** No fee shall be charged for the registration of any instrument of transfer or other document relating to or affecting the title to any share.

**28.** The company shall be entitled to retain any instrument of transfer which is registered, but any instrument of transfer which the directors refuse to register shall be returned to the person lodging it when notice of the refusal is given.

TRANSMISSION OF SHARES

**29.** If a member dies the survivor or survivors where he was a joint holder, and his personal representatives where he was a sole holder or the only survivor of joint holders, shall be the only persons recognised by the company as having any title to his interest; but nothing herein contained shall release the estate of a deceased member from any liability in respect of any share which had been jointly held by him.

**30.** A person becoming entitled to a share in consequence of the death or bankruptcy of a member may, upon such evidence being produced as the directors may properly require, elect either to become the holder of the share or have some person nominated by him registered as the transferee. If he elects to become the holder he shall give notice to the company to that effect. If he elects to have another person registered he shall execute an instrument of transfer of the share to that person. All the articles relating to the transfer of shares shall apply to the notice or instrument of transfer as if it were an instrument of transfer executed by the member and the death or bankruptcy of the member had not occurred.

**31.** A person becoming entitled to a share in consequence of the death or bankruptcy of a member shall have the rights to which he would be entitled if he were the holder of the share, except that he shall not, before being registered as the holder of the share, be entitled in respect of it to attend or vote at any meeting of the company or at any separate meeting of the holders of any class of shares in the company.

ALTERATION OF SHARE CAPITAL

**32.** The company may by ordinary resolution –

*(a)* increase its share capital by new shares of such amount as the resolution prescribes;

*(b)* consolidate and divide all or any of its share capital into shares of larger amount than its existing shares;

*(c)* subject to the provisions of the Acts, sub-divide its shares, or any of them, into shares of smaller amount and the resolution may determine that, as between the shares resulting from the sub-division, any of them may have any preference or advantage as compared with the others; and

*(d)* cancel shares which, at the date of the passing of the resolution, have not been taken or agreed to be taken by any person and diminish the amount of its share capital by the amount of the shares so cancelled.

**33.** Whenever as a result of a consolidation of shares any members would become entitled to fractions of a share, the directors may, on behalf of those members, sell the shares representing the fractions for the best price reasonably obtainable to any person (including the company) and distribute the net proceeds of sale in due proportion among those members, and the directors may authorise some person to execute an instrument of transfer of the shares to, or in accordance with the directions of, the purchaser. The transferee shall not be bound to see to the application of the purchase money nor shall his title to the shares be affected by any irregularity in or invalidity of the proceedings in reference to the sale.

**34.** Subject to the provisions of the Acts, the company may by special resolution reduce its share capital, any capital redemption reserve and any share premium account in any way.

PURCHASE OF OWN SHARES

**35.** Subject to the provisions of the Acts, the company may purchase its own shares (including any redeemable shares) and, if it is a private company, make a payment in respect of the redemption or purchase of its own shares otherwise than out of distributable profits of the company or the proceeds of a fresh issue of shares.

GENERAL MEETINGS

**36.** All general meetings other than annual general meetings shall be called extraordinary general meetings.

**37.** The directors may call general meetings and, on the requisition of members pursuant to the provisions of the Acts, shall forthwith proceed to convene an extraordinary general meeting for a date not later than eight weeks after receipt of the requisition. If there are not within the United Kingdom sufficient directors to call a general meeting, any director or any member of the company may call a general meeting.

NOTICE OF GENERAL MEETINGS

**38.** An annual general meeting and an extraordinary general meeting called for the passing of a special resolution or a resolution appointing a person as a director shall be called by at least twenty-one clear days' notice. All other extraordinary general meetings shall be called by at least fourteen clear days' notice but a general meeting may be called by shorter notice if it is so agreed –

(a) in the case of an annual general meeting, by all the members entitled to attend and vote thereat; and

(b) in the case of any other meeting by a majority in number of the members having a right to attend and vote being a majority together holding not less than ninety-five per cent in nominal value of the shares giving that right.

The notice shall specify the time and place of the meeting and the general nature of the business to be transacted and, in the case of an annual general meeting, shall specify the meeting as such.

Subject to the provisions of the articles and to any restrictions imposed on any shares, the notice shall be given to all the members, to all persons entitled to a share in consequence of the death or bankruptcy of a member and to the directors and auditors.

**39.** The accidental omission to give notice of a meeting to, or the non-receipt of notice of a meeting by, any person entitled to receive notice shall not invalidate the proceedings at that meeting.

PROCEEDINGS AT GENERAL MEETINGS

**40.** No business shall be transacted at any meeting unless a quorum is present. Two persons entitled to vote upon the business to be transacted, each being a member or a proxy for a member or a duly authorised representative of a corporation, shall be a quorum.

**41.** If such a quorum is not present within half an hour from the time appointed for the meeting, or if during a meeting such a quorum ceases to be present, the meeting shall stand adjourned to the same day in the next week at the same time and place or to such time and place as the directors may determine.

**42.** The chairman, if any, of the board of directors or in his absence some other director nominated by the directors shall preside as chairman of the meeting, but if neither the chairman nor such other director (if any) be present within fifteen minutes after the time appointed for holding the meeting and willing to act, the directors present shall elect one of their number to be chairman and, if there is only one director present and willing to act, he shall be chairman.

**43.** If no director is willing to act as chairman, or if no director is present within fifteen minutes after the time appointed for holding the meeting, the members present and entitled to vote shall choose one of their number to be chairman.

**44.** A director shall, notwithstanding that he is not a member, be entitled to attend and speak at any general meeting and at any separate meeting of the holders of any class of shares in the company.

**45.** The chairman may, with the consent of a meeting at which a quorum is present (and shall if so directed by the meeting), adjourn the meeting from time to time and from place to place, but no business shall be transacted at an adjourned meeting other than business which might properly have been transacted at the meeting had the adjournment not taken place. When a meeting is adjourned for fourteen days or more, at least seven clear days' notice shall be given specifying the time and place of the adjourned meeting and the general nature of the business to be transacted. Otherwise it shall not be necessary to give any such notice.

**46.** A resolution put to the vote of a meeting shall be decided on a show of hands unless before, or on the declaration of the result of, the show of hands a poll is duly demanded. Subject to the provisions of the Acts, a poll may be demanded –

*(a)* by the chairman; or

*(b)* by at least two members having the right to vote at the meeting; or

*(c)* by a member or members representing not less than one-tenth of the total voting rights of all the members having the right to vote at the meeting; or

*(d)* by a member or members holding shares conferring a right to vote at the meeting being shares on which an aggregate sum has been paid up equal to not less than one-tenth of the total sum paid up on all the shares conferring that right;

and a demand by a person as proxy for a member shall be the same as a demand by the member.

**47.** Unless a poll is duly demanded a declaration by the chairman that a resolution has been carried or carried unanimously, or by a particular majority, or lost, or not carried by a particular majority and an entry to that effect in the minutes of the meeting shall be conclusive evidence of the fact without proof of the number or proportion of the votes recorded in favour of or against the resolution.

**48.** The demand for a poll may, before the poll is taken, be withdrawn but only with the consent of the chairman and a demand so withdrawn shall not be taken to have invalidated the result of a show of hands declared before the demand was made.

**49.** A poll shall be taken as the chairman directs and he may appoint scrutineers (who need not be members) and fix a time and place for declaring the result of the poll. The result of the poll shall be deemed to be the resolution of the meeting at which the poll was demanded.

**50.** In the case of an equality of votes, whether on a show of hands or on a poll, the chairman shall be entitled to a casting vote in addition to any other vote he may have.

**51.** A poll demanded on the election of a chairman or on a question of adjournment shall be taken forthwith. A poll demanded on any other question shall be taken either forthwith or at such time and place as the chairman directs not being more than thirty days after the poll is demanded. The demand for a poll shall not prevent the continuance of a meeting for the transaction of any business other than the question on which the poll was demanded. If a poll is demanded before the declaration of the result of a show of hands and the demand is duly withdrawn, the meeting shall continue as if the demand had not been made.

**52.**   No notice need be given of a poll not taken forthwith if the time and place at which it is to be taken are announced at the meeting at which it is demanded. In any other case at least seven clear days' notice shall be given specifying the time and place at which the poll is to be taken.

**53.**   A resolution in writing executed by or on behalf of each member who would have been entitled to vote upon it if it had been proposed at a general meeting at which he was present shall be as effectual as if it had been passed at a general meeting duly convened and held and may consist of several instruments in the like form each executed by or on behalf of one or more members.

VOTES OF MEMBERS

**54.**   Subject to any rights or restrictions attached to any shares, on a show of hands every member who (being an individual) is present in person or (being a corporation) is present by a duly authorised representative, not being himself a member entitled to vote, shall have one vote and on a poll every member shall have one vote for every share of which he is the holder.

**55.**   In the case of joint holders the vote of the senior who tenders a vote, whether in person or by proxy, shall be accepted to the exclusion of the votes of the other joint holders; and seniority shall be determined by the order in which the names of the holders stand in the register of members.

**56.**   A member in respect of whom an order has been made by any court having jurisdiction (whether in the United Kingdom or elsewhere) in matters concerning mental disorder may vote, whether on a show of hands or on a poll, by his receiver, curator bonis or other person authorised in that behalf appointed by that court, and any such receiver, curator bonis or other person may, on a poll, vote by proxy. Evidence to the satisfaction of the directors of the authority of the person claiming to exercise the right to vote shall be deposited at the office, or at such other place as is specified in accordance with the articles for the deposit of instruments of proxy, not less than 48 hours before the time appointed for holding the meeting or adjourned meeting at which the right to vote is to be exercised and in default the right to vote shall not be exercisable.

**57.**   No member shall vote at any general meeting or at any separate meeting of the holders of any class of shares in the company, either in person or by proxy, in respect of any share held by him unless all moneys presently payable by him in respect of that share have been paid.

**58.**   No objection shall be raised to the qualification of any voter except at the meeting or adjourned meeting at which the vote objected to is tendered, and every vote not disallowed at the meeting shall be valid. Any objection made in due time shall be referred to the chairman whose decision shall be final and conclusive.

**59.** On a poll votes may be given either personally or by proxy. A member may appoint more than one proxy to attend on the same occasion.

**60.** An instrument appointing a proxy shall be in writing, executed by or on behalf of the appointor and shall be in the following form (or in a form as near thereto as circumstances allow or in any other form which is usual or which the directors may approve)–

'                               PLC/Limited
                   I/We,                        , of
                                                    , being a
member/members of the above-named company, hereby appoint
                               of
                   , or failing him,
of                        , as my/our proxy to vote in my/our name[s]
and on my/our behalf at the annual/extraordinary general meeting of the
company, to be held on                           19        ,
and at any adjournment thereof.
Signed on                          19            .'

**61.** Where it is desired to afford members an opportunity of instructing the proxy how he shall act the instrument appointing a proxy shall be in the following form (or in a form as near thereto as circumstances allow or in any form which is usual or which the directors may approve) –

'                               PLC/Limited
                   I/We,                        , of
                                                    , being a
member/members of the above-named company, hereby appoint
                               of
                   , or failing him,
of                        , as my/our proxy to vote in my/our name[s]
and on my/our behalf at the annual/extraordinary general meeting of the
company, to be held on                           19        ,
and at any adjournment thereof.'

This form is to be used in respect of the resolutions mentioned below as follows:

> Resolution No. 1 *for *against
> Resolution No. 2 *for *against.

*Strike out whichever is not desired.

Unless otherwise instructed, the proxy may vote as he thinks fit or abstain from voting.

Signed this            day of                  19        .'

**62.** The instrument appointing a proxy and any authority under which it is executed or a copy of such authority certified notarially or in some other way approved by the directors may –

    *(a)* be deposited at the office at such other place within the United Kingdom as is specified in the notice convening the meeting or in any instrument of proxy sent out by the company in relation to the meeting not less than 48 hours before the time for holding the meeting or adjourned meeting at which the person named in the instrument proposes to vote; or

    *(b)* in the case of a poll taken more than 48 hours after it is demanded, be deposited as aforesaid after the poll has been demanded and not less than 24 hours before the time appointed for the taking of the poll; or

    *(c)* where the poll is not taken forthwith but is taken not more than 48 hours after it was demanded, be delivered at the meeting at which the poll was demanded to the chairman or to the secretary or to any director;

and an instrument of proxy which is not deposited or delivered in a manner so permitted shall be invalid.

    **63.**   A vote given or poll demanded by proxy or by the duly authorised representative of a corporation shall be valid notwithstanding the previous determination of the authority of the person voting or demanding a poll unless notice of the determination was received by the company at the office or at such other place at which the instrument of proxy was duly deposited before the commencement of the meeting or adjourned meeting at which the vote is given or the poll demanded or (in the case of a poll taken otherwise than on the same day as the meeting or adjourned meeting) the time appointed for taking the poll.

NUMBER OF DIRECTORS

    **64.**   Unless otherwise determined by ordinary resolution, the number of directors (other than alternate directors) shall not be subject to any maximum but shall be not less than two.

ALTERNATE DIRECTORS

    **65.**   Any director (other than an alternate director) may appoint any other director, or any other person approved by the directors and willing to act, to be an alternate director and may remove from office an alternate director so appointed by him.

    **66.**   An alternate director shall be entitled to receive notice of all meetings of directors and of all meetings of committees of directors of which his appointor is a member, to attend and vote at any such meeting at which the director appointing him is not personally present, and generally to perform all the functions of his appointor as a director in his absence but shall not be entitled to receive any remuneration from the company for his services as an alternate director. But it shall not be necessary to give notice of such a meeting to an alternate director who is absent from the United Kingdom.

**67.** An alternate director shall cease to be an alternate director if his appointor ceases to be a director; but, if a director retires by rotation or otherwise but is reappointed or deemed to have been reappointed at the meeting at which he retires, any appointment of an alternate director made by him which was in force immediately prior to his retirement shall continue after his reappointment.

**68.** Any appointment or removal of an alternate director shall be by notice to the company signed by the director making or revoking the appointment or in any other manner approved by the directors.

**69.** Save as otherwise provided in the articles, an alternate director shall be deemed for all purposes to be a director and shall alone be responsible for his own acts and defaults and he shall not be deemed to be the agent of the director appointing him.

POWERS OF DIRECTORS

**70.** Subject to the provisions of the Acts, the memorandum and the articles and to any directions given by special resolution, the business of the company shall be managed by the directors who may exercise all the powers of the company. No alteration of the memorandum or articles and no such direction shall invalidate any prior act of the directors which would have been valid if that alteration had not been made or that direction had not been given. The powers given by this regulation shall not be limited by any special power given to the directors by the articles and a meeting of directors at which a quorum is present may exercise all powers exercisable by the directors.

**71.** The directors may, by power of attorney or otherwise, appoint any person to be the agent of the company for such purposes and on such conditions as they determine, including authority for the agent to delegate all or any of his powers.

DELEGATION OF DIRECTORS' POWERS

**72.** The directors may delegate any of their powers to any committee consisting of one or more directors. They may also delegate to any managing director or any director holding any other executive office such of their powers as they consider desirable to be exercised by him. Any such delegation may be made subject to any conditions the directors may impose, and either collaterally with or to the exclusion of their own powers and may be revoked or altered. Subject to any such conditions, the proceedings of a committee with two or more members shall be governed

410   *Table A*

by the articles regulating the proceedings of directors so far as they are capable of applying.

**73.** At the first annual general meeting all the directors shall retire from office, and at every subsequent annual general meeting one-third of the directors who are subject to retirement by rotation or, if their number is not three or a multiple of three, the number nearest to one-third shall retire from office; but, if there is only one director who is subject to retirement by rotation, he shall retire.

**74.** Subject to the provisions of the Acts, the directors to retire by rotation shall be those who have been longest in office since their last appointment or reappointment, but as between persons who became or were last reappointed directors on the same day those to retire shall (unless they otherwise agree among themselves) be determined by lot.

**75.** If the company, at the meeting at which a director retires by rotation, does not fill the vacancy the retiring director shall, if willing to act, be deemed to have been reappointed unless at the meeting it is resolved not to fill the vacancy or unless a resolution for the reappointment of the director is put to the meeting and lost.

**76.** No person other than a director retiring by rotation shall be appointed or reappointed a director at any general meeting unless –

*(a)* he is recommended by the directors; or

*(b)* not less than fourteen nor more than thirty-five clear days before the date appointed for the meeting, notice executed by a member qualified to vote at the meeting has been given to the company of the intention to propose that person for appointment or reappointment stating the particulars which would, if he were so appointed or reappointed, be required to be included in the company's register of directors together with notice executed by that person of his willingness to be appointed or reappointed.

**77.** Not less than seven nor more than twenty-eight clear days before the date appointed for holding a general meeting, notice shall be given to all who are entitled to receive notice of the meeting of any person (other than a director retiring by rotation at the meeting) who is recommended by the directors for appointment or reappointment as a director at the meeting, or in respect of whom notice has been duly given to the company of the intention to propose him at the meeting for appointment or reappointment as a director. The notice shall give the particulars of that person which would, if he were so appointed or reappointed, be required to be included in the company's register of directors.

**78.** Subject as aforesaid, the company may by ordinary resolution appoint a person who is willing to act to be a director either to fill a vacancy or as an additional director and may also determine the rotation in which any additional directors are to retire.

**79.** The directors may appoint a person who is willing to act to be a director, either to fill a vacancy or as an additional director, provided that the appointment does not cause the number of directors to exceed any number fixed by or in accordance with the articles as the maximum number of directors. A director so appointed shall hold office only until the next following annual general meeting and shall not be taken into account in determining the directors who are to retire by rotation at the meeting. If not reappointed at such annual general meeting, he shall vacate office at the conclusion thereof.

**80.** Subject as aforesaid, a director who retires at an annual general meeting may, if willing to act, be reappointed. If he is not reappointed, he shall retain office until the meeting appoints someone in his place, or if it does not do so, until the end of the meeting.

DISQUALIFICATION AND REMOVAL OF DIRECTORS

**81.** The office of a director shall be vacated if –

*(a)* he ceases to be a director by virtue of any provision of the Acts or he becomes prohibited by law from being a director; or

*(b)* he becomes bankrupt or makes any arrangement or composition with his creditors generally; or

*(c)* he is, or may be, suffering from mental disorder and either –

(i) he is admitted to hospital in pursuance of an application for admission for treatment under the Mental Health Act 1983 or, in Scotland, an application for admission under the Mental Health (Scotland) Act 1960, or

(ii) an order is made by a court having jurisdiction (whether in the United Kingdom or elsewhere) in matters concerning mental disorder for his detention or for the appointment of a receiver, curator bonis or other person to exercise powers with respect to his property or affairs; or

*(d)* he resigns his office by notice to the company; or

*(e)* he shall for more than six consecutive months have been absent without permission of the directors from meetings of directors held during that period and the directors resolve that his office be vacated.

REMUNERATION OF DIRECTORS

**82.**   The directors shall be entitled to such remuneration as the company may by ordinary resolution determine and, unless the resolution provides otherwise, the remuneration shall be deemed to accrue from day to day.

DIRECTORS' EXPENSES

**83.**   The directors may be paid all travelling, hotel, and other expenses properly incurred by them in connection with their attendance at meetings of directors or committees of directors or general meetings or separate meetings of the holders of any class of shares or of debentures of the company or otherwise in connection with the discharge of their duties.

DIRECTORS' APPOINTMENTS AND INTERESTS

**84.**   Subject to the provisions of the Acts, the directors may appoint one or more of their number to the office of managing director or to any other executive office under the company and may enter into an agreement or arrangement with any director for his employment by the company or for the provision by him of any services outside the scope of the ordinary duties of a director. Any such appointment, agreement or arrangement may be made upon such terms as the directors determine and they may remunerate any such director for his services as they think fit. Any appointment of a director to an executive office shall terminate if he ceases to be a director but without prejudice to any claim to damages for breach of the contract of service between the director and the company. A managing director and a director holding any other executive office shall not be subject to retirement by rotation.

**85.**   Subject to the provisions of the Acts, and provided that he has disclosed to the directors the nature and extent of any material interest of his, a director notwithstanding his office –

   *(a)* may be party to, or otherwise interested in, any transaction or arrangement with the company or in which the company is otherwise interested;

   *(b)* may be a director or other officer of, or employed by, or a party to any transaction or arrangement with, or otherwise interested in, any body corporate promoted by the company or in which the company is otherwise interested; and

   *(c)* shall not, by reason of his office, be accountable to the company for any benefit which he derives from any such office or employment or from any such transaction or arrangement or from any interest in any such body corporate and no such transaction or arrangement shall be liable to be avoided on the ground of any such interest or benefit.

**86.** For the purposes of regulation 85 –

*(a)* a general notice given to the directors that a director is to be regarded as having an interest of the nature and extent specified in the notice, in any transaction or arrangement in which a specified person or class of persons is interested, shall be deemed to be a disclosure that the director has an interest in any such transaction of the nature and extent so specified; and

*(b)* an interest of which a director has no knowledge and of which it is unreasonable to expect him to have knowledge shall not be treated as an interest of his.

DIRECTORS' GRATUITIES AND PENSIONS

**87.** The company may provide benefits, whether by the payment of gratuities or pensions or by insurance or otherwise, for any director who has held but no longer holds any executive office or employment with the company or with any body corporate which is or has been a subsidiary of the company or a predecessor in business of the company or of any such subsidiary, and for any member of his family (including a spouse and a former spouse) or any person who is or was dependent on him, and may (as well before as after he ceases to hold such office or employment) contribute to any fund and pay premiums for the purchase or provision of any such benefit.

**88.** Subject to the provisions of the articles, the directors may regulate their proceedings as they think fit. A director may, and the secretary at the request of a director shall, call a meeting of the directors. It shall not be necessary to give notice of a meeting to a director who is absent from the United Kingdom. Questions arising at a meeting shall be decided by a majority of votes. In the case of an equality of votes, the chairman shall have a second or casting vote. A director who is also an alternate director shall be entitled in the absence of his appointor to a separate vote on behalf of his appointor in addition to his own vote.

**89.** The quorum for the transaction of the business of the directors may be fixed by the directors and unless so fixed at any other number shall be two. A person who holds office only as an alternate director shall, if his appointor is not present, be counted in the quorum.

**90.** The continuing directors or a sole continuing director may act notwithstanding any vacancies in their number, but, if the number of directors is less than the number fixed as the quorum, they may act only for the purpose of filling vacancies or of calling a general meeting.

**91.** The directors may appoint one of their number to be the chairman of the board of directors and may at any time remove him from that office. Unless he is unwilling to do so, the director so appointed shall preside at every meeting of directors at which he is present. But if there is no director holding that office, or if the director holding it is unwilling to preside or is not present within five minutes after the time appointed for the meeting, the directors present may appoint one of their number to be chairman of the meeting.

**92.** All acts done by a meeting of directors, or of a committee of directors, or by a person acting as a director shall, notwithstanding that it be afterwards discovered that there was a defect in the appointment of any director or that any of them were disqualified from holding office, or had vacated office, or were not entitled to vote, be as valid as if every such person had been duly appointed and was qualified and had continued to be a director and had been entitled to vote.

**93.** A resolution in writing signed by all the directors entitled to receive notice of a meeting of directors or of a committee of directors shall be as valid and effectual as if it had been passed at a meeting of directors or (as the case may be) a committee of directors duly convened and held and may consist of several documents in the like form each signed by one or more directors; but a resolution signed by an alternate director need not also be signed by his appointor and, if it is signed by a director who has appointed an alternate director, it need not be signed by the alternate director in that capacity.

**94.** Save as otherwise provided by the articles, a director shall not vote at a meeting of directors or of a committee of directors on any resolution concerning a matter in which he has, directly or indirectly, an interest or duty which is material and which conflicts or may conflict with the interests of the company unless his interest or duty arises only because the case falls within one or more of the following paragraphs –

 (a) the resolution relates to the giving to him of a guarantee, security, or indemnity in respect of money lent to, or an obligation incurred by him for the benefit of, the company or any of its subsidiaries.

 (b) the resolution relates to the giving to a third party of a guarantee, security, or indemnity in respect of an obligation of the company or any of its subsidiaries for which the director has assumed responsibility in whole or part and whether alone or jointly with others under a guarantee of indemnity or by the giving of security;

 (c) his interest arises by virtue of his subscribing or agreeing to subscribe for any shares, debentures or other securities of the company or any of its subsidiaries, or by virture of his being, or intending to become, a participant in the underwriting or sub-underwriting of an offer of any such shares, debentures, or other securities by the company or any of its subsidiaries for subscription, purchase or exchange;

 (d) the resolution relates in any way to a retirement benefits scheme which has been approved, or is conditional upon approval, by the Board of Inland Revenue for taxation purposes.

For the purposes of this regulation, an interest of a person who is, for any purpose of the Acts (excluding any statutory modification thereof not in force when this regulation becomes binding on the company), connected with a director shall be treated as an interest of the director and, in relation to an alternate director, an interest of his appointor shall be treated as an interest of the alternate director without prejudice to any interest which the alternate director has otherwise.

**95.** A director shall not be counted in the quorum present at a meeting in relation to a resolution on which he is not entitled to vote.

**96.** The company may by ordinary resolution suspend or relax to any extent, either generally or in respect of any particular matter, any provision of the articles prohibiting a director from voting at a meeting of directors or of a committee of directors.

**97.** Where proposals are under consideration concerning the appointment of two or more directors to offices of employment with the company or any body corporate in which the company is interested the proposals may be divided and considered in relation to each director separately and (provided he is not for another reason precluded from voting) each of the directors concerned shall be entitled to vote and be counted in the quorum in respect of each resolution except that concerning his own appointment.

**98.** If a question arises at a meeting of directors or of a committee of directors as to the right of a director to vote, the question may, before the conclusion of the meeting, be referred to the chairman of the meeting and his ruling in relation to any director other than himself shall be final and conclusive.

SECRETARY

**99.** Subject to the provisions of the Acts, the secretary shall be appointed by the directors for such term, at such remuneration and upon such conditions as they may think fit; and any secretary so appointed may be removed by them.

MINUTES

**100.** The directors shall cause minutes to be made in books kept for the purpose –

(a) of all appointments of officers made by the directors; and
(b) of all proceedings at meetings of the company, of the holders of any class of shares in the company, and of the directors, and of committees of directors, including the names of the directors present at each such meeting.

416   *Table A*

THE SEAL

**101.**   The seal shall only be used by the authority of the directors or of a committee of directors authorised by the directors. The directors may determine who shall sign any instrument to which the seal is affixed and unless otherwise so determined it shall be signed by a director and by the secretary or by a second director.

DIVIDENDS

**102.**   Subject to the provisions of the Acts, the company may by ordinary resolution declare dividends in accordance with the respective rights of the members, but no dividend shall exceed the amount recommended by the directors.

**103.**   Subject to the provisions of the Acts, the directors may pay interim dividends if it appears to them that they are justified by the profits of the company available for distribution. If the share capital is divided into different classes, the directors may pay interim dividends on shares which confer deferred or non-preferred rights with regard to dividend as well as on shares which confer preferential rights with regard to dividend, but no interim dividend shall be paid on shares carrying deferred or non-preferred rights if, at the time of payment, any preferential dividend is in arrear. The directors may also pay at intervals settled by them any dividend payable at a fixed rate if it appears to them that the profits available for distribution justify the payment. Provided the directors act in good faith they shall not incur any liability to the holders of shares conferring preferred rights for any loss they may suffer by the lawful payment of an interim dividend on any shares having deferred or non-preferred rights.

**104.**   Except as otherwise provided by the rights attached to shares, all dividends shall be declared and paid according to the amounts paid up on the shares on which the dividend is paid. All dividends shall be apportioned and paid proportionately to the amounts paid up on the shares during any portion or portions of the period in respect of which the dividend is paid; but, if any share is issued on terms providing that it shall rank for dividend as from a particular date, that share shall rank for dividend accordingly.

**105.**   A general meeting declaring a dividend may, upon the recommendation of the directors, direct that it shall be satisfied wholly or partly by the distribution of assets and, where any difficulty arises in regard to the distribution, the directors may settle the same and in particular may issue fractional certificates and fix the value for distribution of any assets and may determine that cash shall be paid to any member upon the footing of the value so fixed in order to adjust the rights of members and may vest any assets in trustees.

**106.** Any dividend or other moneys payable in respect of a share may be paid by cheque sent by post to the registered address of the person entitled or, if two or more persons are the holders of the share or are jointly entitled to it by reason of the death or bankruptcy of the holder, to the registered address of that one of those persons who is first named in the register of members or to such person and to such address as the person or persons entitled may in writing direct. Every cheque shall be made payable to the order of the person or persons entitled or to such other person as the person or persons entitled may in writing direct and payment of the cheque shall be a good discharge to the company. Any joint holder or other person jointly entitled to a share as aforesaid may give receipts for any dividend or other moneys payable in respect of the share.

**107.** No dividend or other moneys payable in respect of a share shall bear interest against the company unless otherwise provided by the rights attached to the share.

**108.** Any dividend which has remained unclaimed for twelve years from the date when it became due for payment shall, if the directors so resolve, be forfeited and cease to remain owing by the company.

ACCOUNTS

**109.** No member shall (as such) have any right of inspecting any accounting records or other book or document of the company except as conferred by statute or authorised by the directors or by ordinary resolution of the company.

CAPITALISATION OF PROFITS

**110.** The directors may with the authority of an ordinary resolution of the company –

(a) subject as hereinafter provided, resolve to capitalise any undivided profits of the company not required for paying any preferential dividend (whether or not they are available for distribution) or any sum standing to the credit of the company's share premium account or capital redemption reserve;

(b) appropriate the sum resolved to be capitalised to the members who would have been entitled to it if it were distributed by way of dividend and in the same proportions and apply such sum on their behalf either in or towards paying up the amounts, if any, for the time being unpaid on any shares held by them respectively, or in paying up in full unissued shares or debentures of the company of a nominal amount equal to that sum, and allot the shares or debentures credited as fully paid to those members, or as they may direct, in those proportions, or partly in one way and partly in the other: but the share premium account, the capital redemption reserve, and any profits which are not available for distribution may, for the purposes of this regulation, only be applied in paying up unissued shares to be allotted to members credited as fully paid;

*(c)* make such provision by the issue of fractional certificates or by payment in cash or otherwise as they determine in the case of shares or debentures becoming distributable under this regulation in fractions; and

*(d)* authorise any person to enter on behalf of all the members concerned into an agreement with the company providing for the allotment to them respectively, credited as fully paid, of any shares or debentures to which they are entitled upon such capitalisation, any agreement made under such authority being binding on all such members.

NOTICES

**111.** Any notice to be given pursuant to the articles shall be in writing and the company may give any such notice to a member either personally or by sending it by post in a prepaid envelope addressed to the member at his registered address or by leaving it at that address. In the case of joint holders of a share, all notices shall be given to the joint holder whose name stands first in the register of members in respect of the joint holding and notice so given shall be sufficient notice to all the joint holders.

**112.** A member whose registered address is not within the United Kingdom and who gives to the company an address within the United Kingdom at which notices may be given to him shall be entitled to have notices given to him at that address, but otherwise no such member shall be entitled to receive any notice from the company.

**113.** A member present, either in person or by proxy, at any meeting of the company or of the holders of any class of shares in the company shall be deemed to have received notice of the meeting and, where requisite, of the purposes for which it was called.

**114.** Every person who becomes entitled to a share shall be bound by any notice in respect of that share, which, before his name is entered in the register of members, has been duly given to a person from whom he derives his title.

**115.** Proof that an envelope containing a notice was properly addressed, prepaid and posted shall be conclusive evidence that the notice was given. A notice shall, unless the contrary is proved, be deemed to be given at the expiration of 48 hours after the envelope containing it was posted.

**116.** A notice may be given by the company to the persons entitled to a share in consequence of the death or bankruptcy of a member by sending or delivering it, in any manner authorised by the articles for the giving of notice to a member, addressed to them by name, or by the title of representatives of the deceased, or trustee of the bankrupt or by any like description at the address, if any, within the United Kingdom supplied by them for that purpose by the persons claiming to be so entitled. Until such an address has been supplied, a notice may be given in any manner in which it might have been given if the death or bankruptcy had not occurred.

WINDING UP

**117.** If the company is wound up, the liquidator may, with the sanction of an extraordinary resolution of the company and any other sanction required by the Acts, divide among the members in specie the whole or any part of the assets of the company and may, for that purpose, value any assets and determine how the division shall be carried out as between the members or different classes of members. The liquidator may, with the like sanction, vest the whole or any part of the assets in trustees upon such trusts for the benefit of the members as he with the like sanction determines, but no member shall be compelled to accept any assets upon which there is a liability.

INDEMNITY

**118.** Subject to the provisions of the Acts but without prejudice to any indemnity to which a director may otherwise be entitled, every director or other officer or auditor of the company shall be indemnified out of the assets of the company against any liability incurred by him in defending any proceedings, whether civil or criminal, in which judgment is given in his favour or in which he is acquitted or in connection with any application in which relief is granted to him by the court from liability for negligence, default, breach of duty or breach of trust in relation to the affairs of the company.

## Appendix B

# Memorandum of Association

The Memorandum of Association printed below is that of Marks and Spencer plc and is reproduced with their kind permission.

*Companies Acts 1908 to 1917*

COMPANY LIMITED BY SHARES

MEMORANDUM OF ASSOCIATION OF MARKS AND SPENCER LIMITED

1. The name of the Company is 'MARKS AND SPENCER LIMITED.'

2. The Registered Office of the Company will be situate in England.

3. The objects for which the Company is established are:–

   (A) To enter into and carry into effect, with such modifications (if any) as may be agreed upon, the agreement with Marks and Spencer Limited and the Liquidator thereof mentioned in Clause 3 of the Company's Articles of Association.

   (B) To carry on, either in connection with each other or as distinct and separate businesses, the business or businesses of bazaar and general stores proprietors, building contractors, general merchants, storekeepers, co-operative stores, general supply society, universal providers, importers, exporters, furnishing and general warehouse-men, warehouse keepers, publishers, booksellers, cabinet makers, silk mercers, milliners, drapers, dressmakers, furriers, costumiers, haberdashers, hosiers, tailors, hatters, clothiers, gloves and general outfitters, embroiderers, dyers, cleaners, house furnishers, upholsterers, binders, decorators, furniture dealers and removers, depositories, contractors, gas fitters, plumbers, electrical, sanitary, motor and general engineers, brokers, auctioneers, valuers, surveyors, advertising agents, grocers, bakers, pastrycooks, confectioners, butchers, provision merchants, farmers, dairymen, market gardeners, nuserymen, florists, greengrocers, tobacconists, hairdressers, manicurists and chiropodists, caterers, refreshment contractors, entertainment purveyors and agents, theatre and box office keepers and agents, tourist agents, money changers, financiers, passenger, railway and steamship agents, packing and forwarding agents, restaurant and hotel keepers, licensed victuallers, printers, publishers, book and music sellers, bookbinders, die sinkers, engravers, picture and print dealers and framers, newsagents, gold and silversmiths, jewellers, proprietors of circulating libraries, carriers, owners and letters of all kinds of goods, houses and dwellings, naturalists, manufacturers and merchants of and dealers in household furniture, ironmongery, turnery, cutlery and other household fittings, utensils and goods, ornaments, pictures, works of art, books, novels, stationery, oriental and fancy goods, boots and shoes, indiarubber and electrical goods, articles and commodities of personal and household use, fabrics, wares, toys, sports goods, games, tools, hardware, earthenware and enamel ware, safes, clocks, watches, jewellery, plate, plated goods, toilet requisites, glass, china, carpets, leather goods, artists' materials, artificial flowers and other goods, gramophones, gramophone records, musical instruments and articles required or adapted for personal, domestic, or general use, ornament, recreation or amusement stores, provisions, perfumery, soaps, chemicals, drugs, proprietary articles, garden and household requisites, agricultural implements, cycles, cars, scientific, optical, wireless and photographic apparatus, appliances, instruments, requisites and goods, component parts, trunks, boxes, portmanteaux, bags, baskets, aerated and mineral waters, liquors, beers, wines, spirits, coal, wood and other fuel, corn, seeds, hay, straw, forage, saddlery, stable requisites, and generally as manufacturers, planters, growers, cultivators, importers, merchants and dealers of and in all manufactured goods, materials, provisions and produce.

(c) To buy, sell, manufacture, repair, alter and exchange, let on hire, export, and deal in all kinds of articles and things which the Company is empowered to deal in or may be required for the purposes of any of the said business or are usually supplied or dealt in by persons engaged in any such businesses or which may seem capable of being profitably dealt with in connection with any of the said businesses.

(d) To provide, manage and conduct refreshment rooms, newspaper rooms, clubs, reading and writing rooms and other conveniences for the use of customers and others.

(e) To carry on any other business which may seem to the Company capable of being conveniently carried on in connection with any business which the Company is authorised to carry on, or may seem to the Company calculated directly or indirectly to benefit the Company, or to enhance the value of or render profitable any of the Company's properties or rights.

(F) To acquire and carry on all or any part of the business or property and to undertake any liabilities of any person, firm, association or company possessed of property suitable for any of the purposes of the Company, or carrying on any business which the Company is authorised to carry on, and as the consideration for the same to pay cash or to issue any shares, stocks or obligations of the Company.

(G) To enter into partnership or into any arrangement for sharing profits, union of interest, joint adventure, reciprocal concessions or co-operation with any person or company carrying on, engaged in, or about to carry on or engage in, any business or transaction which the Company is authorised to carry on or engage in, or any business or transaction capable of being conducted so as directly or indirectly to benefit the Company, and to take or otherwise acquire and hold, sell, re-issue or otherwise deal with shares or stock in or securities or obligations of, and to subsidise or otherwise assist any such company.

(H) To guarantee the payment of money secured by or payable under or in respect of bonds, debentures, debenture stock, shares, contracts, mortgages, charges, obligations and securities of any company, whether British, Colonial or Foreign, or of any authority, supreme, municipal, local or otherwise, or of any person whomsoever, whether corporate or unincorporate.

(I) To purchase, take on lease or in exchange, hire, or otherwise acquire any real or personal property, rights or privileges which the Company may think suitable or convenient for any purposes of its business; and to erect and construct buildings and works of all kinds.

(J) To apply for, purchase or otherwise acquire any patents, licences and like rights, conferring an exclusive or non-exclusive or limited right to use, or any secret or other information as to any invention which may seem capable of being used for any of the purposes of the Company, or the acquisition of which may seem calculated directly or indirectly to benefit the Company, and to use, exercise, develop, grant licences in respect of, or otherwise turn to account the rights and information so acquired.

(K) To purchase, subscribe for or otherwise acquire, and to hold the shares, stocks or obligations of any company, in the United Kingdom or elsewhere, and upon a distribution of assets or division of profits to distribute any such shares, stocks or obligations amongst the Members of the Company in kind.

(L) To borrow or raise or secure the payment of money, and for those or other purposes to mortgage or charge the undertaking and all or any part of the property and rights and the Company, present or after acquired, including uncalled capital,and to create, issue, make, draw, accept and negotiate perpetual or redeemable debentures or debenture stock, bonds or other obligations, bills of exchange, promissory notes or other negotiable instruments.

(M) To lend money to such persons, upon such terms and subject to such conditions, as may seem expedient.

(N) To sell, let, develop, dispose of or otherwise deal with the undertaking, or all or any part of the property of the Company, upon any terms, with power to accept as the consideration any shares, stocks or obligations of or interest in any other company.

(O) To pay out of the funds of the Company all expenses which the Company may lawfully pay of or incident to the formation, registration and advertising of or raising money for the Company and the issue of its capital, including brokerage and commissions for obtaining applications for or taking, placing or underwriting shares, debentures or debenture stock, and to apply at the cost of the Company to Parliament for any extension of the Company's powers.

(P) To enter into any arrangements with any governments or authority, supreme, municipal, local or otherwise, and to obtain from any such government or authority any rights, concessions and privileges that may seem conducive to the Company's objects or any of them.

(Q) To establish and support, or aid in the establishment and support of associations, institutions and conveniences calculated to benefit any of the employees or ex-employees of the Company, or the dependants or connections of such persons, and to grant pensions and allowances, and to make payments towards insurance, and to subscribe or guarantee money for charitable or benevolent objects, or for any exhibition, or for any public, general or useful object.

(R) To promote any company or companies for the purpose of its or their acquiring all or any of the property, rights and liabilities of the Company, or for any other purpose which may seen directly or indirectly calculated to benefit this Company, and to pay all the expenses of or incidental to such promotion.

(s) To carry out all or any of the foregoing objects as principals or agents, or in partnership or conjunction with any other person, firm, association or company, or by means of any subsidiary or auxiliary company, and in any part of the world.

(t) To do all such other things as the Company may deem incidental or conducive to the attainment of any of the aforesaid objects of the Company.

And it is hereby declared that the word 'Company', save where used in reference to this Company in this clause, shall be deemed to include any partnership or other body of persons, whether incorporated or not incorporated, and whether domiciled in the United Kingdom or elsewhere, and the intention is that the objects specified in any paragraph of this clause shall, except where otherwise expressed in such paragraph, be in nowise limited or restricted by reference to or inference from the terms of any other paragraph: provided that nothing herein contained shall empower the Company to carry on the business of assurance or to grant annuities within the meaning of the Assurance Companies Act, 1909, as extended by the Industrial Assurance Act, 1923, or to reinsure any risks under any class of assurance business to which those Acts apply.

4.   The liability of the Members is limited.

5.   The share capital of the Company is £850,000*, divided into 350,000 shares at £1 each and 1,000,000 shares of 10s. each, with power to increase and with power from time to time to issue any shares of the original or new capital with any preference or priority in the payment of dividends or the distribution of assets, or otherwise, over any other shares, whether ordinary or preference, and whether issued or not, and to vary the regulations of the Company as far as necessary to give effect to any such preference or priority, and upon the subdivision of a share to apportion the right to participate in profits or surplus assets, or the right to vote in any manner as between the shares resulting from such subdivision.

---

NOTES
1. *Capital increased by Resolution passed 11th June, 1928 from £850,000 to £950,000.*
2. *Capital increased by Resolution passed 11th June, 1929 from £950,000 to £1,200,000.*
3. *Capital increased by Resolution passed 17th June, 1930 from £1,200,000 to £2,200,000.*
4. *Capital increased by Resolution passed 10th May, 1932 from £2,200,000 to £2,500,000.*
5. *Capital increased by Resolution passed 14th December, 1934 from £2,500,000 to £3,050,000.*
6. *Capital increased by Resolution passed 28th May, 1937 from £3,050,000 to £3,300,000.*
7. *Capital increased by Resolution passed 9th May, 1939 from £3,300,000 to £3,950,000.*
8. *Capital increased by Resolution passed 12th June, 1952 from £3,950,000 to £6,450,000.*
9. *Capital increased by Resolution passed 10th June, 1954 from £6,450,000 to £10,450,000.*
10. *Capital increased by Resolution passed 6th February, 1957 from £10,450,000 to £19,450,000.*
11. *Capital increased by Resolution passed 11th June, 1959 from £19,450,000 to £23,450,000.*
12. *Capital increased by Resolution passed 8th June, 1961 from £23,450,000 to £25,450,000.*
13. *Capital increased by Resolution passed 13th June, 1963 from £25,450,000 to £37,450,000.*
14. *Capital increased by Resolution passed 11th June, 1964 from £37,450,000 to £55,450,000.*
15. *Capital increased by Resolution passed 7th June, 1971 from £55,450,000 to £82,600,000.*

# Appendix C

# List of mainly UK companies providing benefits for shareholders

| Company | Brief details of benefits | Minimum shareholding to qualify |
|---|---|---|
| **Alexanders Holdings** | Discount of around 2% on all vehicles at dealerships listed below: Alexanders of Edinburgh Ltd. Alexanders of Kirkintilloch Ltd. Alexanders of Greenock Ltd. Alexanders of Northampton Ltd. | 2,000 Ordinary shares. |
| **All England Tennis** (Stock tightly held and not generally marketable) Cost of two Debentures for 1986/90 series in excess of £8,000. | 1 free Centre Court ticket per day for every 1 £50 Debenture held. Minimum purchase is two Debentures). Entry to Lounge and Buffet Bar at Centre Court, and reserved car parking space adjacent to the Centre Court (for a small fee). Priority for 1986/90 series. | 2 £50 (nominal) non-interest bearing Wimbledon Debentures. |
| **Allied-Lyons** | Periodical offers of cases of wine at reduced price and discount vouchers on Victoria wine purchases. £20 discount voucher towards a Hushaway Break weekend. £3 discount on a meal for two and a free pint at many of Allied Lyons restaurants. | No minimum. |
| **Amber Day Holdings** | 10% discount on normal price of clothing and accessories at group's fashion stores. Card sent with Certificate. | 100 Ordinary shares. |

425

| Company | Brief details of benefits | Minimum shareholding to qualify |
| --- | --- | --- |
| A Arenson (Holdings) | 15% on 'Arvin' domestic furniture and 'Roomsets' bathroom furniture. | Ordinary and Preference shares – no minimum. Unit trusts and investment trusts with holdings may nominate beneficiary. |
| Asprey | Asprey card, sent when holding registered, giving 15% discount on most cash purchases from Aspreys in Bond Street and 153 Fenchurch Street. | 375 Ordinary shares. |
| Associated British Foods | Gift of some of the company's product (approximately 8 grocery items), at AGM. Worth approximately £5–6.00. | No minimum. |
| BSG International | Shareholders may contact company to obtain various discounts on their products, eg child safety seats and seat belts. | No minimum. |
| Barclays Unicorn Group | Special rates on a number of QE2 transatlantic and cruise holidays are available to investors. | All unit holders. |
| Barker & Dobson | 20% discount on retail price of certain lines provided by Charbonnel et Walker Ltd. | Ordinary 6¾% Ln 12% Ln. No minimum |
| Barr and Wallace Arnold | 7½% discount on package holidays on accommodation at Oswalds Hotel, Torquay. 10% discount on a new car, without trade-in, at any of the group's garages. | 250 Ordinary or 'A' shares. |
| Barratt Developments | Discount on purchase of a new house. £500 per £25,000 or part thereof of the purchase of a Barratt property. Thus a shareholder purchasing a property for £30,000 would be entitled to a discount of £1,000. | 1,000 Ordinary shares held at least 12 months. |
| Bass Ltd | Shareholder benefit card entitles holder to 15% discount off full tariff price at all Crest Hotels Monday to Thursday. On Fri, Sat, Sun and public holidays most Crest Hotels offer 'Two for the price of one' charging only the normal single price for a double or twin room. Holders | Ordinary shares – 50 shares OR Preference shares – 50. |

| Company | Brief details of benefits | Minimum shareholding to qualify |
|---|---|---|
| | are entitled to 15% off this rate, which is based on a 1–3 night stay exclusive of meals. Holders also enjoy 15% off all Crest Welcome Breaks. Prices for bed and breakfast only are available in London, Amsterdam and other Crest Hotels on the continent. 10% reduction in the cost of a Pontins UK holiday subject to availability for the shareholder and his family and/or friends. | |
| **Bassett Foods** | Shareholders are invited to an Open Day (at either of the factories, to include lunch plus a gift of confectionery) plus an opportunity to purchase confectionary at discounted prices. | No minimum. |
| **Beecham Group** | Occasional wine offer. | No minimum. |
| **Bellway** | £500–£2,500 discount on price of a new Bellway house. 10% discount on Nixon Kitchen units. | 1,000 Ordinary shares held for one year. |
| **Bentalls** | Discount vouchers entitling shareholder to total discounts of £15 on purchases up to £150. Issued in May and valid until 31st January of the following year. | 100 Ordinary shares. |
| **BL Ltd** | £100 discount on new car (additional to any terms negotiated initially with the dealer). This discount excludes VAT. Only 1 Shardis Authorisation form during period between each annual meeting. | 1,000 Ordinary held at date of most recent General Meeting and held for six months. |
| **Britannia Arrow Holdings** | 2% discount at all times on an investment in any of the group's unit trusts. | 1,000 Ordinary shares on register for 12 months. |
| **British Telecom** (Provisional. Shares not yet issued) | Vouchers of £18 value to be issued for every £250 worth of shares bought on issue. Maximum of 12 vouchers. First voucher sent out 8 months after flotation and then every six months. Vouchers used to offset telephone bills. Shareholders may opt for one-for-ten free bonus in place of voucher scheme if shares kept for 3 years after flotation. | £250 worth. Corporate investors not eligible. |

| Company | Brief details of benefits | Minimum shareholding to qualify |
|---|---|---|
| N Brown Investments | 20% discount on fashion wear of the group's Heather Valley (Woollens) subsidiary. | No minimum. |
| Burton Group | 3 vouchers, usually issued in December, giving 20% discount at Burton/ Top Shop, Evans/D. Perkins, Jackson, Top Man and Peter Robinson. | No minimum. |
| CGA | Free membership to C.G.A. Members entitled to reduced rates on a wide range of goods and services. | 100 Ordinary shares. |
| Cadbury Schweppes | Various discounts on wine. | No minimum. |
| A Caird | 10% discount on clothing and sports goods, on purchases of £50 and over. | 400 Ordinary shares. |
| Ciro | 20% discount at some large stores where they operate jewellery counters. | 500 Ordinary shares. |
| Clifford's Dairies | Buffet lunch at AGM. | No minimum. |
| Comfort Hotels | Application form for membership of Comfort Club International at a special price £2.50 which offers various privileges including 10% discount at the company's hotels and Strikes restaurants. | No minimum. |
| Courts Furnishers | 10% discount on furniture. | 100 Ordinary. 'A' ordinary on register for 3 months. |
| Camphorn | 10% discount on cash purchases excluding sale items at shops and garden centres. Discount card issued. | 100 Ordinary shares held for 1 year. |
| Crossair (Swiss) | Flight vouchers with a value of SFr.7.50, 75 and 150 issued depending on the number of shares held. Vouchers may be used as payment of airfares up to a maximum of 50% of the Crossair fare (charter flights excluded) or as payment for excess baggage. | No minimum. |
| Debenhams | Shareholder Card issued, giving credit limit of £3,000 and 7½% off marked prices at group's stores. | 500 ordinary shares on register for 3 months. |

| Company | Brief details of benefits | Minimum shareholding to qualify |
|---|---|---|
| **De Vere Hotels** | 10% discount on 'Take-a-break' and 'Summer Special' holidays. Booking form in report. | No minimum. |
| **DFDS Danish Seaways** (Shares tightly held and not generally marketable) | 25% rebate on journeys made by shareholders plus one other person on Mondays, Tuesdays, Wednesdays and Thursdays, if booking made not MORE than 8 days before date of departure. Reduction does not apply to cars and registered luggage. Documentary proof of share ownership must be shown before booking is made. | Shares, held since before AGM – no minimum. |
| **Dominion International Group** | Shareholder Benefit Scheme, with right to participate in Annual Draw, held in fourth quarter of each year. 6 shareholders then picked to visit a location of their choice in the UK or overseas wherever Dominion has business interests. Shareholders are also entitled to £250 towards the expense of their funeral or cremation (on register by 30.6.82). This concession will expire on 30.6.87. | 500 Ordinary shares held for at least 12 months prior to date of Draw. |
| **Dunlop Holdings** | Shareholder rebate scheme of 7½% on purchases of the company's products £200 limit, to be spent before 31st May 1985. | 200 Ordinary or Preference shares at the date claim made. |
| **Edenspring Investments** | Offer to shareholders to purchase ORIC personal computer and peripheral products at concessionary prices. (Shares dealt under Rule 535.2) | No minimum. |
| **Eldridge Pope** | Discount on wines, beers, ciders and spirits. Details sent before Christmas. | No minimum. |
| **Emess Lighting** | 25% discount on a range of light fittings. | 100 Ordinary shares. |
| **European Ferries** | Subject to space availability, discount on the normal fare for the carriage of 1 private motor car (or motorised caravan or motorcycle) and 4 passengers (2 fare-paying children count as 1 passanger), including the shareholder, on an unlimited number of return journeys on qualifying routes and sailings, as follows: | 300 Preference shares registered by Feb any year. |

| Company | Brief details of benefits | Minimum shareholding to qualify |
|---|---|---|
|  | Dover to Calais, Dover to Zeebrugge......50% all sailings Felixstowe to Zeebrugge......50% excluding 'A' sailings Southampton to Cherbourg, Southampton to Le Harve......40% excluding 'A' sailings ......and 'B' night sailings Portsmouth to Cherbourg, Portsmouth to Le Harve......40% excluding 'A' sailings Cairnryan to Larne......25% all sailings No single journey or open-date tickets. Applications, specifying sailings and dates must be made by post at least 30 days before first date in July and August, otherwise 7 days, to the company's shareholders' Concessions Department. Holders of 300 or more Preference shares will qualify for the full concessions up to 1.1.88. After then you will have to hold at least 600 Preference to qualify for the maximum discounts. If you have between 300 and 599 Preference shares you will qualify for half the value of the discount after 1.1.88. **Please note that preference is given to full fare paying passengers** |  |
|  | 20% discount off the price of one room for maximum stay of 3 nights for one visit per person at the Magheramorne House Hotel, Co. Antrim. |  |
|  | Reduction on room rates at the Dover Motel from 1st October 1984–25th June 1985 (excluding bank holiday weekends). | 300 Preference shares. |
|  | Selection from an approved range of furniture and furnishings obtainable from a local Spanish supplier, to furnish new accommodation purchased at La Manga, completely free of charge. Refund of up to £500 if you buy an apartment at La Manga after a 1 or 2 week self-catering holiday at La Manga. | 300 Preference shares held for at least 1 year prior to 22 May 1984. |

| Company | Brief details of benefits | Minimum shareholding to qualify |
|---|---|---|
| | Sponsorship at University College, Buckingham. | 1,000 Ordinary shares, registered by 1.1.83 for entry in 1985. |
| **Ferguson Industrial Holdings** | Free entry for up to four people to 12th century Appleby Castle (Co's registered office) on presentation of a copy of the annual report. The grounds are open to the public throughout the summer months. | No minimum. |
| **Fobel International** | Special offers on a variety of goods, covering T.V. games, teletext decoders, radio watches and view data printers, portable telephones and home computers. | No minimum. |
| | Reduced trips to Canada and Hong Kong each year to see factory etc (to be confirmed). | 500 Ordinary shares. |
| **Cecil Gee** | Various discounts at Cecil Gee, Gee, Gee 2, Savoy Taylors Guild and Beale & Inman shops.<br>One 10% discount voucher.<br>Two 10% discount vouchers.<br>A further discount voucher is sent out for each additional 1,000 shares held. (Vouchers may be used during sales.) Discount vouchers are distributed once a shareholder has been on the register for six months. | 500 shares.<br>1,000 shares. |
| **The Gieves Group** | 20% discount on goods purchased from branches of Gieves & Hawkes. Shareholder's Concession Card issued. | 600 Ordinary shares held for three months. |
| **Grand Metropolitan Hotels** | Various discounts on wine, mixed cases of wine & spirits, beer, lager, sherry and spirits.<br>10% discount on Stardust and Camelot mini-holidays; 10% discount on a Warner Continental holiday; or Nova Caravan and camping holidays in the South of France. Grand Metropolitan Account Card issued on request. | No minimum. |

| Company | Brief details of benefits | Minimum shareholding to qualify |
|---|---|---|
| **Greenhall Whitley** | 10% discount on accommodation rates at company's hotels for room charges only. | No minimum. |
| | Periodic. 10% discount on one Summer and one Winter holiday publicised in the current Arrowsmith or Skyfares brochures – Flights from Manchester only. | 400 Ordinary shares or 2,000 'A' Ordinary shares. |
| **Greenfields Leisure** | 12½% discount on purchases of leisure and camping goods made by cash or cheque. Special card sent to new shareholders with interim/final dividend payment. | 100 Ordinary shares. |
| **GRA Group** | Invitation to shareholder and 1 guest to spend an evening at one of the stadiums. 1 free voucher for car park also sent. | No minimum. |
| **GUS** | Reduction of 7½% off the brochure price of a number of Global holidays. This concession only open to shareholders on the register by 28th October 1983. The offer closes on the 31st October 1984. Shareholders should make reservations by telephoning G.U.S. on 01-323 3266 and quoting number of shares held, and registration details. | No minimum. |
| **Hawley Group** | 15% discount on any one purchase of Sharps fitted bedrooms, Dolphin Showers and Alpine Double Glazing installed at the address of the registered shareholder. Valid until 31.3.85. | 500 shares. |
| **Henlys** | Shareholders are offered any make of motor car from the manufacturers the company represents at attractive terms. Also holidays on the Norfolk Broads. | No minimum. |
| **J Hepworth** | 25% discount on one purchase in any Hepworth or Next shop. | 500 Ordinary shares. |
| **Hillards plc** | Discount at Hillards stores. 5 vouchers of £3 each off purchases exceeding £30. (Not on cigarettes or petrol.) Sent out with annual report and account. | 200 Ordinary shares. |

| Company | Brief details of benefits | Minimum shareholding to qualify |
|---|---|---|
| **Hill Woolgar (unquoted)** | Shareholders receive preferential treatment in Co's USM new issues. | No minimum. |
| **Horizon Travel** | 10% discount on Horizon brochure prices, up to a total holiday value of £1,000. Available to one booking per shareholder in any year. Shareholder must travel. Only one concession per booking. | 750 Ordinary, held for 6 months at date of departure. |
| **House of Fraser** | Four £5 discount vouchers on any single purchase exceeding £50. | No minimum (one voucher per one purchase). |
| | Eight 10% discount vouchers on any single purchase exceeding £100. Vouchers may be used in Harrods and any other House of Fraser store. | |
| | Special offer until 29.9.84 for shareholders to purchase cases of wines and spirits from Harrods at attractive prices. Offer form sent with report and accounts. | |
| **Isle of Man Steam Packet** (Shares tightly held and not generally marketable) | On application to head office, return ferry ticket(s) at the time of booking from Douglas to Liverpool, Ardrossan, Dublin, Llandudno, Fleetwood and Belfast. During June, July and August valid Mondays to Fridays only. Those on the register on 15.2.84 will qualify for tickets during the period 3.3.84 to 2.3.85 as shown. | £250–£499 Ord Stk....1 ticket £500–£999 Ord Stk....2 tickets Over £1,000 Ord Stk....3 tickets |
| **Kennedy Brookes Ltd** | 20% discount at any of their restaurants. Including Maxims in London. Credit card issued. | 500 Ordinary shares. |
| **John Kent** | 10% discount on purchases from 'John Kent' and 'Smith' branches. Discount card issued upon registration and renewed with annual report. | 500 Ordinary shares. |
| **Robert Kitchen Taylor (RKT)** | £7 discount on an order of £15–25 worth of group's underwear, including Damart, and outerwear. £15 discount on an order over £25. | 500 Ordinary shares. |
| **Kursaal Company** | Free admission to Dragonara Palace Casino, with a guest. 10% discount on Mediterranean Room or Marquis Room bills (except Saturdays), Lido admission and Reef Club subscriptions. 15% discount on summer rates, 33⅓% discount on winter rates, on | 200 shares of any class. |

| Company | Brief details of benefits | Minimum shareholding to qualify |
|---|---|---|
| | hotel stay at the Dragonara Palace Hotel on booking made direct with MAXOTELS offices in UK or Malta. | 100 Ordinary shares. |
| **Kwik-Fit (Tyres & Exhausts) Hldgs** | 10% discount on any purchase, worth £5 or more, from any of company's depots. Vouchers enclosed with report. Only one purchase per year. | No minimum. |
| **LWT (Holdings)** | 10% discount on holidays with Page & Moy Ltd, Harborough Marine Ltd, Cresta World Travel Ltd and Sunspot Tours Ltd. Discount covers shareholder and family or friends travelling together on the same holiday. | No minimum. |
| **Ladbroke Group** | 10% discount on hotels, motor inns and restaurants, and holiday villages. 7½% discount on marked prices at Lasky stores on all hifi, video and microcomputer products. 10% discount on all restaurants accounts at the Greyhound Stadia. Shareholders privilege card issued. 10% discount on annual membership **only** at the following snooker clubs. Blyth Snooker – Northumberland Cueball Snooker Club – Glasgow, Kirkcaldy & Greenock Cueball Snooker & Leisure Club – Paisley. | |
| **Leyland Paint & Wallpaper** | 10% discount at Leyland DIY shops. | No minimum. |
| **London & Midland Inds** | Discount of 10% on Compton Buildings, Banbury windows, Banbury Homes and Gardens and Falcon Pipe Group. | No minimum. |
| **London and Northern Group** | 17½% discount on list prices of Weatherseal double glazing, patio doors, and replacement windows. Leaflet and form circulated to shareholders, or direct approach to Weatherseal. | 250 Ordinary shares or 250 Preference. Employees of shareholding companies and institutions also eligible. |

| Company | Brief details of benefits | Minimum shareholding to qualify |
|---|---|---|
| **Lonrho** | Periodical discount on Audi & Volkswagen Motor Cars. 20% discount on room rates in UK Metropole Hotels. 10% discount on 'Whileaway Holidays' at all UK hotels. Available March 1984 to 31.1.85 excluding Bank Holidays. 30% discount on full rate bedrooms at the Melville Hotel in Mauritius (valid for bookings through Kuoni Travel). Available March 1984 to 28.2.85 excluding November and December. | At company's discretion. 100 shares on register by 17 Feb. |
| | 15% discount at Brentfords until 31.3.85. | |
| | Privilege subscription rates on certain Scottish Publications. | |
| **Manders Holdings** | Discount of 25% on brushes, 20% on paint and 10% on both wallpaper and sundries. 'Trade cash card' sent to shareholders. | No minimum. |
| **Manor National** | Various discounts on new and used Ford and Austin Rover cars plus Land Rover and Range Rover vans. Discount on all types of insurance cover. | No minimum. |
| **Maynards** | 10% discount on confectionary and toys from Maynards shops plus 25% discount on toys purchased from Zodiac Shops. | No minimum. |
| **Merrydown Wine** | Approximately 20% discount on cases of wine and cider, inclusive of V.A.T. | No minimum. |
| **Milletts Leisure** | 12½% discount on shop goods. Discount card provided. | No minimum. |
| **Moss Bross** | 10% discount on all goods and services, not at sale or Discount card sent to holder. Second card sent to shareholders spouse on request. | 250 Ordinary shares held for 6 months. |
| **Mount Charlotte Investments** | 10% discount on a 'Value Break'. 10% discount at all the Company's Hotels for Room and Breakfast. 15% discount on Weekly Terms for Full Board at the Company's five Family Holiday hotels. For terms other than full board the discount will be 10%. The discount does not apply to Self-Catering holidays. 650ml flagon of Bronte Yorkshire Liqueur at special price of £8.95. Application form for card enclosed with report. | 1,000 Ordinary shares on register 1 March. |

| Company | Brief details of benefits | Minimum shareholding to qualify |
|---|---|---|
| **Norfolk Capital Group** | Vouchers issued with annual report and accounts entitling shareholders to a 10% discount at the Group's Hotels and restaurants. 5% discount on any Greatstay weekend booking and Norbreck Castle holiday package. | No minimum. |
| **The Peninsular and Oriental Steam Navigation Company**<br><br>please ring (0703) 34141. | Holding in joint names will be considered to be held by the first named on register. Subject to space availability, discount on the normal fare for the carriage of 1 motor car (or motorcycle) and passengers as follows:<br>Southampton – Le Harve......50% discount on all sailings except night sailings 30.6.84–15.9.84 inclusive.<br><br>Dover – Boulogne......50% discount.<br><br>Aberdeen – Lerwick (Shetlands)......30% year excluding July and August.<br>Scrabster – Stromness (Orkney)   Restricted to 2 round trips in a 12 month period. Return journeys only. Shareholder must travel. Application form enclosed with interim report in October. Shareholder qualifies as soon as his name is on the register.<br><br>**Please note that preference on bookings is made to full fare paying passengers.**<br><br>Stockholders and/or their spouses are entitled to a 15% discount off tariff fares on selected Sea Princess, Canberra and Swan Hellenic Cruises.<br><br>£1,000 nominal Deferred or £2,500 nominal Preferred stock to he held when the booking is made and on the date of sailing. | 200 Deferred shares<br>or<br>500 units Preferred stock<br>500 units Preferred stock<br>For latest concessions dates<br><br>All sailings except 'D' tarriff in July and August.<br><br>All sailings except July and August. |

| Company | Brief details of benefits | Minimum shareholding to qualify |
| --- | --- | --- |
| **Pentos** | 10% discount on personal cash purchases at any of group's book shops and Athena shops. Application forms in report. Discount card provided. | 500 Ordinary or Deferred shares or a combination. |
| **Peters Stores** | 15% discount on all cash purchases at any branch (general clothing, industrial and protective clothing, camping, sailing and sports equipment). Card with report in November. | No minimum. |
| **Pleasurama** | £10 voucher sent with annual report for use as part payment towards meal for two or overnight stay at selected hotels. | No minimum. |
| **Alfred Preedy & Sons** | 10% discount on purchases in excess of £3, at any of the group's 200 stores and shops, on all goods except cigarettes and tobacco, newspapers and magazines. (Goods include toys and games, books, records, artists' materials, china and glassware, sports equipment, confectionary, greeting cards.) Form with report. | 250 Ordinary shares. |
| **Prince of Wales Hotels** | Concessions under review at time of printing. | No minimum. |
| **Queens Moat Houses** | Two courtesy cheques for £2 towards food and drink when taking a meal in a Queens Moat House hotel. One courtesy cheque worth £15 when taking Town and Country Classics weekend accommodation at a Queens Moat House Hotel. | No minimum. |
| **Rank Organisation** | **Holiday Scheme** 10% discount on brochure price of OSL, Wings, Ellerman Sunflight or Freshfields holidays up to a maximum holiday value of £1,000 for a shareholder and his party. Only one concession per booking. **Shareholder must travel.** **Hotels Scheme** 10% discount on normal published tariff at any Rank Hotel. 10% discount on special weekend rates available at certain times of the year. | 750 Ordinary shares on register for at least 6 months at the date of departure or the holder of any number of Ordinary shares for a continuous period of 5 years up to date of departure. Valid until 31.3.85. |

| Company | Brief details of benefits | Minimum shareholding to qualify |
|---|---|---|
| **Rank Hovis McDougall** | Hamper at AGM | No minimum. |
| **Austin Reed** | 15% discount but not on sale or special promotion prices. | 500 Ordinary or 'A' ordinary shares. |
| **Reliance Industrial Hldgs plc** | 15% discount on installation of Security Alarm Systems. 25% discount on DIY Electronic and radio controlled security alarm equipment and safety products. 15% discount on velvet curtains. | No minimum. |
| **Riley Leisure** | Periodic discounts of 25% on billard tables and accessories. | 500 Ordinary shares on register for 6 months. |
| **Romney, Hythe and Dymchurch Light Railway Co** (Shares tightly held and not generally marketable) | (a) Free personal travel pass.<br>(b) as (a) plus addition free pass for members of shareholder's family.<br>(c) as (b) plus further pass for shareholders' guests and the complete train once per year at no cost. | (a) 100–499 Ord shares<br>(b) 500–4,999 Ord shares<br>(c) 5,000 shares or more. |
| **Savoy Hotel** | Special offer 'Two's Company' at either The Savoy or Claridges, shareholders will receive a special allowance of £5 per person, per night, net price of £115 per person for two nights.<br><br>Any 2 or 3 nights (Fri, Sat, Sun) from 1 April to 2 September 1984.<br><br>Any 2 or 3 nights of the week from 16 July to 2 September 1984. | No minimum. |
| **Sharpe & Fisher** | 10% discount on a purchase at one of Co's DIY supermarkets and Garden centres. Valid following account statement to 30th June. | No minimum. |
| **Scottish & Newcastle Breweries** | £15 voucher for use at Thistle Hotels enclosed with report. Two £3 vouchers for use in Thistle Hotel restaurants. Trumpcard issued to Companies whose business involves overnight stays, offering 10% off total bill, and other benefits. Selection of wines offered at a discount. | No minimum. |

| Company | Brief details of benefits | Minimum shareholding to qualify |
|---|---|---|
| **Sketchley** | 25% discount on normal cost of dry cleaning and ancillary services. Discount card issued on registration and thereafter automatic annual renewal (on 1 August) as long as qualifying shareholding remains on register. | 300 Ordinary or Preference shares. |
| **Southampton, Isle of Wight and South of England Royal Mail Steam Packet Company** (Shares tightly held and not generally marketable) | Free ferry tickets (Southampton to Cowes) and 50% discount on the Standard Single fare on hydrofoil services. Shareholder's pass issued when holding registered. There is no discount on motor cars. | 2,400 Ordinary shares. |
| **Spear and Jackson** | Discount on hand and garden tools, and a range of lawnmowers. Application form enclosed with report. | No minimum. |
| **Stakis** | £10 discount voucher on a Stakis Summer holiday May–October 31 1984.<br>£5 voucher for meals in Stakis Hotels or Inns.<br>£10 voucher for St. Ermins Hotel London.<br>Voucher offering discount on purchase of whisky. | 100 Ordinary shares. |
| **Stylo** | Vouchers giving 20% discount on 2 separate purchases of shoes, sent with report. Company sends copy of latest report to new holders, therefore double vouchers in first year. | No minimum. |
| **Toye & Company** | 15% discount on purchases, from branches of Toye, Kenning & Spencer. (Civil and Military regalia, trophies, awards, medals, badges, jewellery, gold and silverware, cutlery, glassware, watches and clocks.) Does not apply to special offers or on postal orders. 'Special purchase card' issued once name is entered on register. | 250 Ordinary shares. Institutional holders not eligible. |

| Company | Brief details of benefits | Minimum shareholding to qualify |
|---|---|---|
| **Trafalgar House** | 15% discount on accommodation at 4 hotels in UK and 2 hotels in Caribbean. 15% discount on most Cunard voyages aboard QE2, Cunard Countess and Cunard Princess. | 250 Ordinary shares. Institutional and corporate holders may nominate one person to benefit. |
| **Trusthouse Forte** | 10% discount on Leisure Gift Cheques for maximum £2,000 value. Application form enclosed with report. Can be used in settlement of accounts at THF Hotels, restaurants, and other THF establishments. | No minimum. |
| **UMB Group** | 10% discount card for use at UBM Building Supplies branches (valid until June 1985). | No minimum. |
| **E Upton** | 15% discount card for use on goods and services at company's store. | 250 Ordinary or 'A' shares. |
| **Vaux Breweries** | Shareholders may apply for a 'Swallowcard' for use in Swallow Hotels and Restaurants. Anchor Hotels and Taverns. Special discounts will apply from time to time, eg during January and February all holders of 'Swallowcards' allowed 25% discount on Breakaway mini-holidays. 10% discount on accommodation, meals and drinks (with meals) at certain hotels and restaurants. Discount card enclosed with new certificate or reports. | No minimum. |
| **Vectis Stone Group** | 20% discount on tarriff at Albion Hotel, Freshwater Bay during early and late season. Not available during bank holidays. Details on request from the Albion Hotel. | No minimum. |
| **Whitbread** | Special booklet sent with annual report in June offering discounts on articles ranging from whisky to silver cufflinks. | No minimum. |
| **E & OE** | | |

# Appendix D

# Examination Questions

1. When can a newly registered company commence business and what requirements must be met before so doing?

2. Bill and Ben trade in partnership as garage mechanics. They are considering changing their form of business association and trading as a private registered company limited by shares.

Explain to them the legal procedures that they must follow in order to form such a company, and advise them on the advantages of trading as a private company as opposed to a partnership.

3. (a) Examine, with one or more examples, the main consequences of the principle that the company is in law an artificial person distinct from its members.
(b) Give *two* examples of circumstances in which the court will look at the economic reality behind the veil of incorporation.

4. 'Ever since the calamitous decision in *Salomon v Salomon and Co* (1897) a single trader or group of traders are almost tempted by law to conduct their business in the form of a limited company . . .' Kahn Freund (7 MLR). Consider this statement.

5. Examine critically the proposition that the courts will lift the corporate veil wherever the justice of the case requires such action.

6. (a) 'The principle of corporate legal personality is an important and basic fundamental of law in the United Kingdom and Republic of Ireland.' Briefly consider this statement.
(b) 'But there have been several departures from this rule where the court

441

has lifted the corporate veil and looked at the realities of the situation.' Which do you consider to have been some of the more important of such 'departures'?

*(c)* Until 1982 Paul carried on a radio and television repair business as sole trader. In that year he expanded into radio and television sales and incorporated the business, assigning the whole of its assets to the Company known as Brightscreen Ltd. Payment was effected by the allotment to Paul and his wife of 3,000 fully paid £1 shares in Brightscreen Ltd. Paul continued to insure the assets of the business in his own name as he had done prior to the incorporation of Brightscreen Ltd. This year, the premises of Brightscreen Ltd were burgled and some £5,000 worth of audio equipment stolen. Paul has made a claim on the policy but the insurance company refuses to meet his claim. Advise Paul.

7. Advise Graham and Hellen, who wish to form a private company limited by shares, on the following points:
*(a)* The documentation which should be sent to the Registrar of Companies to obtain registration of the company.
*(b)* The provisions which should be included in the company's objects clause to avoid, as far as possible, the company acting ultra vires.
*(c)* The personal liability position of Graham and Hellen as sole shareholders and directors for the debts of the business in the event of winding-up on the grounds of insolvency.

8. What are the differences between the requirements for being a private and a public limited company? In what circumstances would you advise a client to register a company as a public limited company?

9. It has long been common practice to set out in Memoranda of Association a great number and variety of objects together with a subclause that each paragraph shall be read as an independent object.
What is the purpose of such practice and to what extent is it effective?

10. The objects clause of Achilles Ltd states that it was formed to carry on business as a used car dealer and 'to buy and sell any goods whatsoever'. In 1982 the company began to manufacture video recorders and entered into a contract with Brian to purchase 5,000 silicon chips for this purpose. That contract was negotiated by two of the three directors of the company, whilst the third was away on holiday.

In 1983 the company borrowed £50,000 from Charles to purchase a warehouse. Charles was shown a copy of the company's memorandum but refused to read it, stating that he was far too busy.

In 1984 the company agreed to sell, and in fact supplied, 5,000 video recorders to David. Later that year the company went into liquidation.

Advise the liquidator as to the validity of these contracts on the basis that Brian and Charles have not yet been paid by the company and that David has not yet paid the company.

11. Critically examine the proposition that the enactment of s 35 of the Companies Act 1985 provides complete protection to contracting parties who enter contracts with a company which are either ultra vires the company's powers or beyond the capacity of the company's directors.

12. To what extent, if any, has the European Communities Act 1972 affected the operation of the rule in *Royal British Bank v Turquand*?

13. *(a)* By what procedure and for what purposes may a company alter its objects?
*(b)* How may such a proposal be challenged?
*(c)* What is the value of a power to alter the objects since the enactment of the European Communities Act 1972?

14. The directors of Speel plc resolved at a board meeting in 1983 to make a gratuitous payment of a pension to the widow of the company's recently deceased managing director. In 1985 the company is in the process of being wound up.

You are required to explain whether the pension may be recovered by the liquidator of Speel plc as an unauthorised payment.

15. The common law rule was that 'every court is bound to treat a contract, entered into beyond the powers of the company, as wholly null and void'.

How far can such a contract *now* be enforced against the company by the other party? Are any other remedies available to the other party if the contract itself is not enforceable?

16. *(a)* In what ways and subject to what limitations may the shareholders of a company alter its articles of association?
*(b)* The articles of association of Wrongo Ltd attached one vote to each ordinary share in the company and provided that at a general meeting a poll may be demanded by at least two members, or by any member or members

representing not less than one tenth of the total voting rights. The company has issued 20,000 ordinary shares, of which Richard holds 3,000. Richard attended the company's annual general meeting intending to oppose a resolution authorising the directors to borrow a substantial sum of money. On a show of hands Richard's vote was improperly rejected by the Chairman. Richard then demanded a poll but was told by the Chairman that at least two members were necessary for this, and that the resolution had been carried.

Advise Richard whether he may bring an action to have his vote recorded, and whether he can challenge the Chairman's refusal to allow a poll.

17. *(a)* To what extent is it accurate to regard a company's articles of association as constituting a contract between the company and its members?
*(b)* David Bay is a director of Bay Ltd and owns 25% of the Ordinary Shares in the company which carry voting rights. The articles of association of Bay Ltd appointed him as managing director for life.

His fellow directors have recently discovered that David Bay is acting as financial consultant to other companies which are in competition with Bay Ltd. The other directors of Bay Ltd's board wish to propose an alteration of the company's articles to restrict the powers of the managing director by requiring him to seek the approval of the rest of the board for certain major policy decisions.

Advise the directors whether they may so alter the articles and the possible effects of the proposed alteration.

18. The articles of association of Apron Ltd include the following clauses:
*(i)* that Bertram should have the right to nominate the managing director of the company;
*(ii)* that Claude should be the company secretary for life; and
*(iii)* that the company's sales manager should receive an annual bonus equal to five per cent of the company's profits for that year.
David, the majority shareholder has just sold his 75 per cent holding of shares in Apron Ltd to Edward. Edward proposes to alter the articles so that all directors should be appointed by the general meeting, and that the annual bonus payable to the sales manager should be reduced to two per cent of the profits. He also intends to appoint Fred as the company secretary. The sales manager has a contract with the company which makes no provision for the payment of any bonus. Bertram has a contract with the company which states that the company will not alter its articles so as to affect his rights without his consent.

Advise Edward.

19. GBH Ltd has for many years traded as a travel agent. The Memorandum states that the company is in business as 'commission agents in the travel industry . . . and to do all such other things as may be deemed incidental or conducive to the attainment of that object'.

In 1984 the directors proposed to diversify the company's activities as follows:

the purchase of a block of seaside flats at a British resort, for letting to holiday-makers;

the purchase of a fleet of cars for a taxi and car-hire business.

The money for the block of flats was to be found by a loan from Northtown Bank. The bank was given a copy of GBH's Memorandum and Articles at an early stage in the negotiations. The fleet of cars was to be acquired with a loan from Southtown Finance. The finance company asked for a written statement from GBH's secretary that the transaction was within GBH's powers. By an oversight, this statement was not given.

All these transactions were completed by May 1984. The block of flats and the fleet of cars both run at a considerable loss in the first year of operation. The debts outstanding to Northtown and Southtown in each case exceed the value of the relevant assets, although GBH Ltd as a whole is still solvent.

The directors seek your advice. They ask:
*(i)* Can GBH Ltd avoid either loan as ultra vires?
*(ii)* If a loan is void, can GBH Ltd nevertheless keep the assets on which the void loan was expended?

Advise the directors.


20. Alpha Ltd was formed in 1979. Its objects clause stated that it was to manufacture and sell typewriters and other office equipment. In addition it was empowered to do anything which the directors considered could be carried on advantageously with its general business.

In March 1983 Alpha Ltd ceased all productions of typewriters and commenced production of video-recorders for the domestic market. In that month the company obtained printed circuits from Beta Ltd and brochures from Gamma Ltd for use in the venture. Beta Ltd were unaware of the objects clause of Alpha Ltd but the directors of Gamma Ltd had seen but not studied a copy.

In September 1984 Alpha Ltd sold 1,000 video-recorders to Delta Ltd. The relevant documents for all these transactions were signed by Horace, a director of Alpha Ltd.

Beta Ltd and Gamma Ltd have not yet been paid for their goods. Delta Ltd is unwilling to pay for the video-recorders.

Advise Alpha Ltd.

21. The articles of association of Hopeful Ltd include a clause whereby the company has power to purchase its own shares in accordance with the procedure laid down in the Companies Act. The directors, who own 80 per cent of the shares, now wish to alter the articles to include a clause whereby the company may purchase its own shares whether or not the member concerned wishes to sell them, provided that the purchase is at a fair price. Ian, a minority shareholder in the company, suspects that this is aimed at him because he has recently quarrelled with the board of directors and has found employment in a rival company.

Advise Ian whether he may validly prevent either the proposed alteration taking place or any subsequent application of it to his own position. How would your advice differ if the company had been formed with the proposed article?

22. *(a)* Explain how a company may alter its articles and enumerate some of the restrictions applicable to alteration of articles.
*(b)* The shares of the Xlap Co Ltd ('the Company') are held by the members of four families, the Jones, the Smiths, the Browns and the Clarks. The Jones and the Smiths, who together hold 90% of the Company's shares, are concerned about two matters. First, the Company is in need of further capital, but by reason of family differences, neither the Jones not the Smiths are willing to inject additional funds so long as the Browns hold any shares in the Company. Secondly, the Jones and the Smiths have good reason to believe that one of the Clarks is running a business of his own which competes with that of the Company. It is known that he is obtaining information as a member of the Company which he is using to the benefit of this competing business. To resolve both matters of difficulty, the Jones and the Smiths propose to pass two resolutions. The first will enable the majority to acquire compulsorily, at full value, the shares of the minority. The second will require any shareholder who competes with the Company's business, to transfer his shares, at full value, to nominees of the directors. Discuss the validity of each of these resolutions.

23. 'Although they may not be in the strict sense agents or trustees for the company, promoters stand in a fiduciary relation to it.'
(Northey & Leigh, *Introduction to Company Law*)

*(a)* Define the term 'promoter'.
*(b)* What is the extent of the promoter's fiduciary relation to the company he is forming?
*(c)* What remedies are available to the company if its promoter fails to discharge the fiduciary duty which he owes it?

24. James is engaged in the promotion of a company and he seeks your advice on several points relating to promotion activities.

You are required to write a report dealing with the following matters:
*(a)* the restrictions upon the choice of corporate name with which a promoter must comply;
*(b)* the legal duties of a promoter and in particular his responsibilities where he sells property of his own to the company he is promoting;
*(c)* the problem of a promoter obtaining payment for his services from the company once the company has been incorporated.

25. On the basis of a prospectus, North recently applied for, and was allotted, shares offered by South plc. He has now discovered that:
*(1)* the prospectus did not disclose a sale by West, a director, to the company of property of his own on which he made a profit of £100,000;
*(2)* part of a surveyor's report was omitted and what remained gave a misleading impression;
*(3)* the accountants' report contained errors due to incorrect information supplied to them by West.

Advise North of any remedies open to him under the Companies Act.

26. *(a)* The Companies Act requires specified matters to be stated and reports to be set out in every prospectus issued by or on behalf of a company. Explain the purpose of the Act's requirements, illustrating your explanation with a *summary* of the principal matters and reports which must be included in every prospectus.
*(b)* In January 1984 Nib plc. issued a prospectus inviting the public to subscribe for a new issue of shares. The prospectus contained a report by Dr A, an eminent mineralogist, stating that substantial deposits of nickel could be extracted from the Nibelheim mine, which was one of Nib plc's principal assets. Dr A's methods of analysis had been criticised on a number of occasions by other mining experts. By April 1984 Dr A's predictions were proved to be inaccurate, and the Nibelheim mine was found to contain only small traces of nickel.

In January 1984 H applied for 1,000 shares in accordance with the offer in the Nib plc prospectus. He received a letter of allotment for 1,000 shares, containing the usual provision allowing the allottee to assign his allotment by renouncing it in favour of another person. H renounced his allotment in favour of J, who was then placed on the register of members of Nib plc.

In April 1984, as a consequence of the discovery that the Nibelheim mine had failed, Nib's shares fell well below the price at which the January issue had been made. J seeks your advice as to the remedies which he may seek against

*(i)* Nib plc

*(ii)* Nib plc directors

*(iii)* Dr A

in respect of Dr A's inaccurate report in the January prospectus.

Advise J.

27. What legal consequences attach to the issue of a prospectus? What remedies are available to someone who is misled by a misrepresentation or an omission in a prospectus?

28. The directors of Geto plc published, on the company's behalf, a prospectus inviting the public to purchase ordinary shares in the company in June 1984. The prospectus contained false information relating to the value of property which the company had purchased from the managing director in 1983 and failed to include any details of the commission due to be paid to underwriters of the issue.

You are required to discuss the possible liability of the company, and its directors, for the defects in the prospectus.

29–30. Eighteen months ago Zip plc, an unquoted company engaged in the production of motorcycles, issued a prospectus stating that the company had designed and developed a new racing bike which would shortly be patented and distributed to dealers in Britain, West Germany and Japan. The prospectus also contained a detailed technical report from Wye, a professor of engineering, whose conclusions were that the new Zip design was far in advance of developments elsewhere in the world and would succeed in world markets.

On the strength of the prospectus Zip plc issued to X Investment Bank renouncable letters of allotment in respect of £20,000 worth of shares which the bank had undertaken to 'place' with its clients. Most of these securities were taken up by the bank's clients during the initial placing, but the bank itself was obliged to subscribe for 5,000 £1 shares, which it has since managed to sell privately.

The new racing bike is not yet in production; a rival Japanese company, whose research was known to Wye but was not mentioned in the prospectus report, has just marketed a new racing model which is technically superior to the Zip design. It appears that at the time when Zip plc issued the prospectus its new model was at a very early stage of development and is only now undergoing final tests; no arrangements have been made for full-scale production and distribution; and no patent application has been made.

Advise the investors, whose shares have now decreased in value, what remedies may be available to them in respect of the statements contained in the Zip prospectus.

31. Rippoff plc was formed to develop and operate a chain of gambling casinos in some of England's cities.

Its directors became aware of premises for sale, formerly used as a cinema, which they considered suitable for conversion as a casino. Further capital was needed for this project both to acquire the premises and to make the necessary structural alterations. To raise the necessary funds, the directors prepared a circular inviting persons generally to subscribe for shares in the Company. Although 3,000 of such circulars were actually printed, the directors confined their distribution to no more than fifty named persons, known to them as likely to be interested in this business venture. The circular so prepared was accurate in every respect with regard to its express statements. However, it was prepared by the directors without professional advice, and the directors now fear that it may have omitted particulars required by law in the event that the circular is deemed a prospectus. Advise the directors, with your reasons, upon the following questions:
*(i)* Will the circular be deemed to be a prospectus?
*(ii)* If it is so deemed, and there are some omissions, what liability will attach to the directors, and on what grounds may they hope to obtain relief from that liability?
*(iii)* If the circular is deemed to be a prospectus, what remedies does a purchaser of the Company's shares have against the Company, if the circular failed to disclose that the cinema acquired by the Company had been purchased from its promoters, who had made a substantial profit on the sale?

32. *(a)* Explain whether an 'offer for sale' is subject to the requirements of the Companies Act relating to prospectuses.
*(b)* What information must be provided by auditors for inclusion in a prospectus?
*(c)* Explain the statutory provisions whereby a person may escape civil liability for false statements in a prospectus.

33. *(a)* What is the process of 'certification' of a transfer of shares and in what circumstances is it used? Explain the legal effect of certification.

*(b)* In 1983 Tom was the registered holder of shares in the Blaze plc and he deposited his shares in the hands of his broker for safe custody. In 1984 a transfer of the shares was made to Dick by the broker, without the knowledge of Tom, by means of a transfer on which the broker forged Tom's name. The transfer and the certificates were left with the Company Secretary for registration and, in due course, Tom's name was removed from the register being replaced by that of Dick. Dick subsequently transferred the shares to Harry who was duly registered, and certificates were issued to him. The above events have now come to light. Discuss whether the Blaze plc:

*(i)* is obliged to restore Tom's name to the register;

*(ii)* owes any liability to Harry;

*(iii)* has any claim against Dick.

34. *(a)* D is a director of a private company in which he is also the controlling shareholder. For some time the company has been in financial difficulty and has exhausted its available credit with the consequence that D was only able to keep the company in being by making a number of loans to it of £3,000 total value out of his own personal resources. All such loans were unsecured. Realising that a liquidation may ensue at any time, and with the intention of salvaging something for himself from the company, D advanced in July 1984 a further loan of £1,000 to the company causing the company to execute in his favour a deed of debenture by way of floating charge on the company's assets and securing not only the £1,000 currently advanced but also all outstanding debts due to him by the company. This charge was executed on 1 July 1984 and was properly registered with the Registrar of Companies. A compulsory winding up order was made in November 1984. D claims to be a secured creditor to the value of £4,000. Discuss.

*(b)* Tom is a minority equity shareholder in a private company and he wishes to transfer his shareholding to a friend known to be willing to purchase his shares. The company's directors have declined to register the transfer but have given no reasons for such refusal. Advise Tom.

*(c)* What would be the position in *(b)* above, if the company's articles had provided that,

'All shareholders who wish to sell their shares must offer them to the Company's directors who shall purchase them at a price agreed by the Company's auditors'?

35. Consider the proposition that preference shareholders suffer the disadvantage of debenture holders and ordinary shareholders whilst possessing few of the advantages which those investors enjoy.

36. A bank lends money on an equitable mortgage of company shares accompanied by a 'blank transfer' of these shares.

Explain the weaknesses of this type of security and any steps that may be taken to protect the lender.

Jack Smith in his will left all his shares in International Company plc to his son Tom and all his shares in Private Company Ltd to his son Harry. Jack has died recently and his executors are applying for probate of the will.

Explain to them:
(a) How each holding of shares will be transmitted.
(b) Who, if anyone, can exercise the voting rights on each shareholding.
(c) If it makes any difference if Tom and Harry are aged under 18.

37. (a) What are the legal advantages and disadvantages of preference shares?
(b) Thomas wishes to sell 100 of his shares in Vole plc to Ulf. He accordingly sends his share certificate (for 200 shares) to the company, which certifies the transfer document 'certificate lodged.' Thomas exchanges this document for the purchase price from Ulf. Ulf sends the certified transfer document to the company who issue him with a new certificate for the 100 shares purchased from Thomas. By mistake, however, the company returns Thomas' original certificate (for 200) to him. Thomas has used the certificate as security for a loan of £2,000 from Wobble. Thomas has just been declared bankrupt.

Advise Wobble as to any rights he may have against Vole plc.

38. Vernon owned 10 shares in Wobble Ltd. In 1983 he agreed to sell 50 of these shares to Young for £500. The usual transfer procedure was adopted but by accident the company returned the original share certificate for 100 shares to Vernon, in addition to two new certificates of 50 shares each to Vernon and Young. Vernon then used the original certificates as security for a loan of £1,000 from Amble.

Vernon then mislaid the new share certificate which was found by Bumble. By forging Vernon's signature, Bumble 'sold' the 50 shares to Carol, who was registered as shareholder in respect of them. Carol in turn 'sold' the shares to Duncan who has also been registered. Vernon has now discovered the loss.

Discuss.

39. Elf plc engaged Fred as a management consultant for a fee of £10,000. Fred completed his work. He agreed to purchase £10,000 worth of shares from Elf plc. The two contract debts were set-off so that Fred was registered in respect of the shares and no money changed hands.

Discuss the validity of these transactions.

How, if at all, would your answer differ if:
*(i)* the market rate for the work done by Fred was only £500;
*(ii)* Elf plc had been a private company?

40. You are the financial advisor of Apeel plc. The board of directors is concerned at the low profit achieved in the current trading period which will substantially affect the dividend received by shareholders. The board seeks your advice as to whether other funds might be utilised to give shareholders a satisfactory dividend return and how preference shareholders could be bought out, to achieve a uniform capital structure in future years. Write a report for the board, concentrating on the following specific issues:
*(a)* The statutory restrictions upon the company's freedom to distribute funds as dividend.
*(b)* The feasibility of distributing to shareholders any surplus arising from a revaluation of the company's land and buildings.
*(c)* The possibility of using funds held in the company's share premium account for the shareholders' benefit.
*(d)* The methods available to the company to carry out a restructuring of share capital to repay the preference shareholders.


41. Excess plc is a company with substantial assets not fully utilised in the operation of the business and, given its asset worth, with a relatively low stock exchange value placed upon its ordinary shares. These factors have led the board of directors to anticipate that a take-over bid may be made by Combo plc, a competing company. The directors are considering three strategies they might adopt to protect Excess plc from the threatened bid.

You are required to examine the rules of company law relating to the following proposals and to comment on the tactics which Combo plc might adopt to counter the three strategies:
*(a)* An interest-free loan would be made by Excess plc to a trust fund established for the purpose of purchasing ordinary voting shares for the benefit of employees. The company's managing director would be appointed trustee of the fund. His use of the voting power attached to the employees' shares would be used to support the directors in maintaining majority voting power.
*(b)* Surplus funds of Excess plc would be utilised to pay existing shareholders a large interim dividend. This would encourage existing members to retain their shares and could increase the stock exchange valuation of Excess plc's shares.
*(c)* The directors would take no action until Combo plc made a successful bid and took control of Excess plc. If it became apparent that Combo plc intended to run down the business of Excess plc for the benefit of Combo plc, the directors, as shareholders, would petition the court for relief under s 459 Companies Act.

42. Expel plc, a listed company, requires a capital injection of £500,000 to finance a retooling operation in one of its workshops.

You are required to write a report for the board of directors, advising:
(a) on the methods of raising capital that are available;
(b) on the type of capital that might be obtained.

43. Certac plc is a trading company. A and B, the two directors, each hold 40% of the ordinary share capital. The remainder is held by D. A also holds debentures issued by Certac plc redeemable on 1 January 1985. A wishes to dispose of his shares and debentures. B and D are anxious to help A, but do not wish control of Certac plc to pass into other hands. The following schemes are proposed:
(a) Certac plc will raise the necessary funds and purchase the shares and debentures for cash;
OR
(b) B will arrange a private loan so that he may purchase A's shares and debentures. Certac plc will guarantee the loan to B;
OR
(c) Certac plc will raise funds and lend them to D so that he may purchase A's debentures. D will further arrange a private loan, guaranteed by Certac plc, so that he may purchase A's shares.

Advise Certac plc on the legality of these three schemes and on the enforceability of the proposed guarantees.

44. The directors of Speel plc have decided, at a board meeting, that the capital structure of the company, as shown below, is insufficient to meet the future requirements of the company to expand its operations; at the same time they wish to rationalise the capital structure.

|  | £000 |
|---|---|
| Authorised share capital | 1,000 |
| Issued share capital: | |
| 6% (now 4·2% plus tax credit) preference shares of £1 | 110 |
| Ordinary shares of 50p | 500 |
| Ordinary shares of 25p | 390 |
| | 1,000 |

You are required to advise the board of directors on the following matters relating to its capital re-organisation plans:
(a) What provisions of the Companies Acts must be complied with in order to allow the directors to issue new shares?

*(b)* Discuss the methods which Speel plc may adopt to remove the preference shares from the company's capital structure.

*(c) (i)* What procedure must be followed to subdivide the 50p ordinary shares into shares of 25p value to achieve a uniform ordinary share structure?

*(ii)* If the voting rights of the 50p ordinary shareholders (at present one vote per share) are to be effectively doubled to give each new 25p ordinary shareholder one vote per share, could the existing 25p ordinary shareholders complain to the court?

45. In what circumstances may a private company give financial assistance for the acquisition by another of its shares?

46. In connection with the general meeting of a company, compare and contrast:

*(a)* special notice.

*(b)* special resolution, and

*(c)* special business.

47. Counterpoint Limited has adopted articles of association in the form of Table A. The respective shareholdings of the board of directors are: Crotchet: 500 shares; Quaver: 200 shares Minim: 100 shares. The shareholdings of the other members of the company are: Aria: 500: shares; Contralto: 200 shares; Decibelle: 100 shares; Forte: 100 shares.

The board decided to propose a special resolution at the company's next annual general meeting in order to alter the articles by removing the limitation on the directors' borrowing powers. The notice of this AGM accompanied by proxy forms, was posted on 1 April, calling the meeting for 2.00 p.m. on 21 April. The notice just stated that the AGM would be held at the time and place specified, and that a special resolution would be proposed altering the directors' borrowing powers.

The company secretary looked at an out of date copy of the register of members and inadvertently failed to send a notice of the meeting to Aria, but instead sent the notice to Bass, the previous holder of the shares. Contralto returned a form appointing Quaver as her proxy. However, she later telephoned Quaver to revoke her proxy and stated that she would attend the meeting in person. Decibelle returned a form appointing Minim as her proxy and directed him to cast her votes against the resolution.

At the meeting Crotchet was elected as chairman. Forte proposed an amendment to the special resolution which would have required all borrowing by the directors to be subject to the approval of the general meeting. Crotchet refused to accept this amendment. Forte and Contralto then demanded a poll on the special resolution. The voting pattern was as follows:

Crotchet voted in favour of the resolution;

Quaver used both his own shares and Contralto's proxy to vote in favour of the resolution;

Minim used his own shares to vote in favour of the resolution and ignored Decibelle's proxy;

Contralto and Forte voted against the resolution.

The chairman declared the resolution carried by the required majority.

Advise Aria, Decibelle, Contralto and Forte on the validity of the above proceedings.

48. (a) State the rules governing the date for holding the annual general meeting (AGM).
(b) A Limited, registered in 1960 failed to hold an AGM in the year 1984. How can you, as a member of A Limited, remedy the omission?

49. What difference, if any, is there between a special resolution and a resolution requiring special notice?

50. What principles have the courts laid down as to the 'proper purpose' to be applied by company directors when making use of the powers given to them by the company's articles of association?

51. The directors of Merchanting Ltd, a very successful business, have allocated most of the profits to themselves as remuneration and as donations to a charitable institution established by the founder of the company.

Sheila, a shareholder, wishes to challenge the amount of the directors' remuneration, to discontinue the charitable donations and to increase the dividends.

Explain how she could make her proposed challenge.

52. C Ltd has three members and has five issued shares. I and V each owns two shares and are the directors; H. owns one share. The articles of the company provide that on any resolution to appoint or dismiss a director, H's share has five votes. The ordinary rule is that each share has one vote

only. The articles also provide that all directors are appointed for a minimum of four years.

At the Annual General Meeting in 1984 H proposed that he should be elected to the board of directors. As soon as he did this I and V left the meeting. Nevertheless H continued and voted himself in as a director and chairman. H has since discovered that I and V have paid themselves, by way of directors' remuneration, all the profits of the preceding years, although no formal resolution to this effect has ever been put to a general meeting. He has tried since then to convene a meeting of the company on several occasions but I and V have consistently refused to attend.

However, they attended a further meeting in 1985 and purported to pass a resolution that H should be dismissed as a director. They also passed a resolution that H had never validly been a director and must account to the company for the fees he drew as a director during 1984-5.

Advise H what he may do about these matters. The company is financially sound.

53.  The articles of Nunc Ltd authorise the directors to appoint a managing director and to delegate such matters as they think fit to him, except that any purchase of equipment over £10,000 requires the consent of the board as a whole. In fact no managing director has ever been appointed as such but the other directors, Owen and Paul, consistently allowed Quentin to act as such. Quentin has in fact ordered £5,000 worth of equipment from Robin and £12,000 worth of equipment from Steven, in both cases without reference to the board.

The company has refused to pay for the equipment.

Advise Robin and Steven, who have never read the company's articles.

54.  'Information which a director receives in his capacity as such is the property of the company in the same way as the company funds which he controls. If he makes any use of that information for his own personal advantage he must account to the company for it.'

Discuss.

55.  Copperfield Ltd, had a share capital of £100 held as follows:
       Macawber 22 Ordinary £1 shares
       Heap      76 Ordinary £1 shares
       Jim (Heap's accountant) 2 Ordinary £1 shares
For the previous five years Macawber has been a part-time financial consultant to Copperfield Ltd of which Heap was the managing director. Macawber is now in very poor health and is not expected to live for more

than a few years. With the intention of making provision for Macawber's family, Heap invites Macawber to enter a service contract with the Company by which the Company should employ him forthwith at a salary of £10,000 per annum as its only financial director for the rest of his life in consideration of his agreeing to devote the whole of his time and attention to the Company's business. It is also provided that in the event of Macawber's death, his widow shall continue to receive his annual salary by way of a pension payment, for the rest of her life.

You are asked to advise on the following questions:
*(a)* If, contrary to expectations, Macawber's health improves, is there any way in which Heap might remove him from office?
*(b)* Would it make any difference to your advice above if, in addition to the service contract, the Company's articles had been altered so as to provide that Macawber should hold office for life?
*(c)* What would be the legal effect of amending the Company's articles to provide that

'in the event of a resolution being proposed for the removal from office of any director, any shares held by that director shall in respect of such resolution, carry the right to four votes per share'?

*(d)* Should the Company ever go into liquidation, are there any grounds on which the liquidator could contest the validity of the service agreement and refuse to recognise Macawber's widow's claim? (Candidates are not required to discuss the doctrine of privity of contract.)

56. Dennis, Erickson and Frederick have carried on business as partners since 1960. In 1982 they converted their business into a private limited company, P Limited, with an authorised share capital of 1,200 £1 shares. The original partners became the sole shareholders and directors of the company, each holding 200 shares. The Articles of Association of P Limited provided:

'Article 9   The shares of a company shall carry one vote per share except that on any resolution to remove a director from his directorship his shares shall carry three votes per share.'

Over the past three years there has been constant disagreement among the directors and Dennis and Erickson feel that they can no longer work with Frederick. Give Dennis and Erickson advice on the following questions:
*(a)* What is the normal procedure for removing a company director?
*(b)* How could Article 9 affect the possibility of removing Frederick from office?
*(c)* Could the unissued share capital be utilised by Dennis and Erickson to assist them in their plans to remove Frederick?
*(d)* What legal remedies are available to Frederick should Dennis and Erickson be successful in expelling him from office?

57. 'Information which a director receives in his capacity as such is the property of the company in the same way as the company funds which he controls. If he makes any use of that information for his own personal advantage he must account to the company for it.'

Discuss.

58. *(a)* As a condition of granting a loan to a company, the lender may require that one or more of his nominees be appointed as directors of the borrowing company, in order to protect the lender's interests. To what extent (if at all) is this arrangement inconsistent with the rules governing directors' duties?

*(b)* Alfred promoted GBH Ltd in January 1981 to acquire and develop a coastal site as a harbour for pleasure craft. The Articles required each director to hold 1,000 £1 shares as his shareholding qualification. Arthur wished to have Joshua, a well-known yachtsman, on the board of directors but Joshua was reluctant to risk the investment in his qualification shares. Alfred accordingly wrote to Joshua undertaking to purchase, at the price which Joshua had paid for them, any shares which Joshua might acquire in GBH Ltd. Joshua allowed himself to be appointed a director of GBH Ltd, and purchased his 1,000 qualification shares, at par, for cash. The other directors and members of GBH Ltd were not informed of Alfred's undertaking to Joshua.

By late 1983 GBH Ltd was in difficulties and its shares were valued at about 20p each. Joshua resigned from the board of directors and sold his shares to Alfred at £1 each in accordance with Alfred's 1981 undertaking. In June 1984 the other directors of GBH Ltd learned the price at which Joshua had sold his shares to Alfred. They now claim that Joshua must pay over to GBH Ltd the profit of 80p per share which he made from the sale of his shares to Alfred.

Advise Joshua on the merits of the directors' claim.

59 *(a)* Outline the provisions in the Companies Act relating to directors' duties to disclose their interests in contracts with the company. What is the effect of non-disclosure?

*(b)* Artless Ltd was formed to provide publicity for sporting personalities. The directors are A, B and Miss C who between them hold all the shares in the company.

In January 1983 A and B offer Speed, a racing driver, a commission contract under which Artless will have exclusive rights to promote Speed's publicity appearances. Speed rejects this offer. Miss C does not take part in the negotiations, but is told of their outcome.

In October 1983 Miss C meets Speed for the first time, at a social gathering which she is attending for Artless. In December 1983, Speed appoints Miss C as his part-time publicity manager, in return for 25 per cent of all fees he receives for publicity work. Miss C does not disclose her new appointment to the other directors of Artless.

In February 1984 the directors of Artless decide to sell a controlling interest in the company to D. Miss C transfers her shares to D and resigns from the board. She has no service contract with Artless, but A and B agree to pay her £1,000 compensation for loss of office. D has no objection to this course of action.

In May 1984 A, B and D learn of Miss C's business relationship with Speed. A and B are inclined to dismiss the matter but are persuaded by D, who is now a director and holder of the majority of the shares, that there is a case against Miss C. Accordingly, A B and D demand payment to Artless Ltd of all past and future profits arising out of Miss C's contract with Speed; and the repayment of her £1,000 compensation for loss of office.

Advise Miss C on Artless Ltd's claim.

60. The Sludge Mining and Exploration Company plc ('the Company'), an English company, was incorporated in 1972 for the purpose of oil exploration of the North Sea. Harry, a member of the company relates to you the following three events and you are asked to advise on the correctness or otherwise as to each of Harry's contentions:

*(a)* In 1978 the controlling shareholder Slim sold his entire shareholding in the Company to Arthur. This sale was at only 40% of the market value of the business and this was because Arthur could not find enough capital to pay the full value outright. As a solution to his difficulty it was agreed as a condition of Arthur's purchase of Slim's shareholding that Slim should be given a service contract with the Company as its 'Consultant' for ten years at £8,000 per annum. It was mutually accepted that Slim would never in fact be called upon by the Company to advise or perform any other service and the appointment was merely an expedient to enable Slim to be paid a price approximating to the true market value of the shares when sold in 1978. These payments are still being made by the Company but Harry contends that they are illegal.

*(b)* In 1980 the Company's profits had fallen drastically because of increased expenses. Harry was then anxious to sell the bulk of his own shareholding in the Company and made approaches to the directors to ascertain their willingness to purchase the same. Negotiations then ensued in this matter with Harry leading to a sale in 1982 and Harry retained only a token shareholding in the company. However, in 1981 a test hole was drilled by the Company in a new area of the North Sea and this indicated an exceptionally valuable concentration of oil, but the directors kept this fact to themselves and purchased Harry's shares at a low price which reflected

the Company's poor peformance hitherto. Only after the sale was complete did the directors make public the new oil strike. Harry contends that the sale of his shares must be set aside.

*(c)* In 1984 the Scottish Gas Board invited public tenders for the mapping and related geophysical exploration services in the North Sea. The Company tendered for this project. At this time, Smart, a highly qualified civil engineer and a member of the Company's Board resigned his office with the Company and formed his own surveying company which sought, and was awarded the Scottish Gas Board's contract. Harry contends that Smart must account to the Company for the profits his company has made on this contract.

61. Write a report for the board of Malfax plc a listed company, outlining the *statutory* rules which relate to the following activities involving company directors.
*(a)* Janet, the managing director of Malfax plc, has agreed to resign her directorship and managing directorship subject to the company undertaking to pay her a generous compensation sum for loss of office.
*(b)* Kenneth, the finance director, wishes to purchase a greater stake in Malfax plc equity shares, through Stock Exchange transactions, whilst the price is low, Kenneth is aware that another company is about to make a public takeover bid for Malfax plc.
*(c)* Alexander, a director, intends to sell a piece of land to Malfax plc at a price of £60,000.

62. Your client, Happy, has been offered the managing directorship of Grumpy Ltd, with a 40% shareholding in the company. The rest of the shares will be equally divided between Dopey and Sleepy, who at present hold all the shares and who will remain as directors of the company. Dopey and Sleepy are anxious to bring Happy into the company, and are prepared to consider any conditions Happy may seek to impose, save that they are not willing to increase his shareholding.

Advise Happy on any TWO methods by which he might seek to secure himself against dismissal from the managing directorship of Grumpy Ltd, and comment on the effectiveness of these methods.

63. The Land Syndicate Co Ltd was incorporated in 1980 by Abel, Baker, Charles and David, together with their respective spouses, to carry on the business of property development in the South of England. Abel, Baker, Charles and David are the company's directors; each holds 20% of the issued shareholding while their respective spouses each hold a further 5%. You are asked to advise the directors in respect of each of the following matters:

*(i)* No Managing Director of the company has ever been formally appointed, although the articles make provision for such an appointment. In fact Charles, who is the Chairman of the Board, has in the past acted with the acquiescence of the Board in the day-to-day management of the Company's affairs. Very recently, in order to find a purchaser for a 10 acre site in Hampshire, Charles employed a firm of estate agents who successfully introduced a prospective purchaser who has just completed the purchase. The estate agents now claim 2% commission on the sale price in accordance with their express contractual terms. Abel, Baker and David, however, assert that Charles had no authority to bind the Company in this respect.

*(ii)* In 1982 Abel sold a small piece of land owned by himself to the company for £11,000. Only Charles was aware that this land was beneficially owned by Abel.

*(iii)* In 1984 Shyster agreed to sell some land to the Land Syndicate Co Ltd but after the exchange of contracts he changed his mind and refused to complete. To avoid a decree of specific performance against himself Shyster formed a new company with an authorised capital of £100 and conveyed the land to that company. Shyster now protests that as he no longer owns the land any proceedings against him for its possession must fail.

64. The Shaky Box Co Ltd is currently controlled by Tom and Harry who are also the company's directors. Tom has 40% of the company's shareholding, Harry 35%, while the remaining issued share capital is held by the respective spouses and children of Tom and Harry. Harry who has been suffering from ill health for some time has just advised Tom that on medical advice he is to cease all participation in the company and that accordingly he wishes to dispose of his shareholding. Harry has offered Tom his shareholding at a price of £80,000. Tom considers the price asked by Harry to be reasonable but Tom cannot possibly find that amount of money from his own resources, yet he is reluctant to allow Harry's substantial shareholding to pass into the hands of another.

Harry is considering each of the following situations as a possible solution and you are asked to advise on the legality of each of these proposals:
*(i)* whether Tom may refuse to register as shareholder any transferee of Harry's shareholding;
*(ii)* whether Tom may procure that the company shall make an interest-free loan to himself of sufficent funds to enable him to purchase Harry's shareholding;
*(iii)* whether, should Tom's bank agree to make Tom a personal loan of sufficient funds to enable him to purchase Harry's shareholding, Tom may procure that the company shall act as guarantor of that loan;
*(iv)* whether, should Tom consent to Harry's disposing of his shareholding to anyone prepared to purchase it, Tom may effectively retain his

controlling interest by creating a trust fund for the company's employees and allocate to himself and the employees' representatives some of the unissued share capital, paid for by the Company, with special voting rights attached to each share so as to command a majority in general meeting.


65. Lionel, Mark and Neil are the directors of Open Ltd, an investment company. In 1982 the company made several high risk investments which proved to be financially disastrous. It now appears that these contracts were made through another company, Petra Ltd of which Lionel is the managing director. Neither Mark nor Neil were aware of this; Mark because he left all the paper work to Lionel, and Neil because he never bothered to attend board meetings. Petra Ltd received generous commission payments on the deals. All these investments were approved by the general meeting at which Lionel made no reference to his connections with Petra Ltd.

Open Ltd is now in liquidation as insolvent. Advise the liquidator whether there are any possible causes of action against the directors.


66. John is a minority shareholder in Woodly Ltd, a company with three shareholders. The other two shareholders, Adam and Susan, are the company's only directors and John has become increasingly concerned at their conduct as directors over the previous year.

At a board meeting, they had resolved that no dividend should be paid to shareholders in that year.

At a general meeting called to consider the annual accounts, Adam, acting as Chairman, had refused to record John's votes which he had cast against acceptance of the accounts.

John has now discovered that Adam and Susan, at a board meeting, have approved a contract between Susan and the company for the sale of a portion of the company's land to Susan for £10,000.

You are required to explain the legal actions John may bring against Adam and Susan.


67. Beaver, intending to go into the wholesale food business, instructed his solicitor to form a company to be named 'Beaver Foods Limited'. The solicitor prepared the necessary documents which were delivered to the Companies Registration Office on the 10 March this year. The statement delivered under s 10 of the Companies Act 1985 provided that Beaver and his wife should be the first directors, although they are not named as such in the articles of association.

On the 21 March Beaver agreed to purchase a quantity of sugar from Sweet in a letter which he signed, 'For and on behalf of Beaver Foods Ltd, E. Beaver, Director'. The sugar has not yet been delivered and Sweet denies any liability to Beaver or the company.

On 2 April, Beaver, purporting to act on behalf of the company, agreed to supply Texo, a large supermarket chain, with all its requirements for coffee for a period of five years at very competitive prices. The certificate of incorporation of the company, dated 1 April, was received by Beaver on the 3 April. Beaver now considers the agreement with Texo to be disadvantageous and has repudiated it, saying that he had no authority to bind the company to the agreement. There has never been either a board meeting or a general meeting of Beaver Foods Ltd.

Advise Beaver and Beaver Foods Ltd as to their rights and liabilities with regard to:
*(a)* Sweet;
*(b)* Texo.

68. X Ltd has three directors, M, N and O. Its articles of association empower the directors to enter into contracts to buy raw materials for the company up to a total value of £15,000. In addition the managing director may spend up to £20,000 on providing machinery for the company.

In 1983 M entered into a contract with Y Ltd for the purchase of raw materials costing £16,000. In 1984 N made a similar contract with Z Ltd costing £2,000. In 1985 O, who acted as managing director, but had never been officially appointed as such, bought machinery from R Ltd for £10,000.

X Ltd is now in liquidation. Advise the liquidator whether he is bound to pay Y Ltd, Z Ltd and R Ltd, who have submitted claims in respect of these contracts.

69. Heple plc, a construction company, has six directors. Demont, the longest serving director, has not been appointed to the position of managing director but he frequently acts in that capacity, with the other five directors seeking his advice on matters of day to day management. In September 1983, Demont entered into two contracts on the company's behalf. The first contract was with Green Merchant Bank plc, for a loan of £50,000 to assist with a new construction project. The second contract involved the purchase of a warehouse from Jay Limited; Demont considered that the warehouse would be ideal for the extension of the company's activities to the provision of 'do it yourself' building materials for the public. Neither of the contracts had the approval of the company in general meeting or the directors of Heple plc and, in both cases, Demont

signed the contracts as managing director of Heple plc. The Articles of Association of the company provide:

A107 'The directors may appoint any one of their number as managing director on such terms as they think fit.'

A109 'Directors may exercise all borrowing powers of the company but no director may borrow sums in excess of £10,000 without the approval of the company in general meeting.'

The other directors have now discovered the existence of the two contracts.

You are required to explain whether the company is bound to repay the loan to Green Merchant Bank plc and to purchase the warehouse from Jay Limited.

70. You are consulted in respect of the three following events which have occurred in respect of the Fiddle Engineering Co Ltd which received its certificate of incorporation on April 1 1984:

(a) In February 1984 one of the promoters of the Company contracted in the name of the Company for the purchase of machinery, paying 50% of the purchase price on placing the order and undertaking to pay the remaining 50% on delivery. The machinery was supplied in December 1984 and has been in continuous use by the Company since that date. However, the 50% payment due on delivery has not yet been met by the Company which is denying any liability to pay the supplier, on the ground that it did not place the order.

Discuss.

(b) In order to avoid the Company having to pay the full amount of stamp duty due on the Company's purchase of a piece of land, the Company Secretary who carried out the conveyancing work for the Company fraudulently under-stated the purchase-price involved to the Revenue authorities. The evasion has come to light and you are asked to advise whether the Company can be convicted for the false declaration made.

(c) A contract was negotiated by the Company's managing director, without the authority of the board, giving a London based company sole distribution rights of the Company's products in the South of England notwithstanding that the Company's Articles provided that no contract concerning the appointment of factors, agents or concessionaires could be made by the Company without the unanimous resolution of the Board. Is the Fiddle Engineering Co Ltd bound by this agency agreement?

71. John, Keith and Linda are the directors and shareholders of Mouse Ltd, a company formed to create and distribute computer software. John habitually acts as managing director but has never been appointed to that position. Keith has often ordered blank tapes from Nest on behalf of Mouse Ltd with the consent of John. Linda takes no active part in running the

business but is the majority shareholder. John, without consulting the others, has entered into a contract, on behalf of Mouse Ltd, with Owl which gives Owl exclusive rights to sell the Mouse software through his retail shops. Keith, also without consulting the others, has ordered two thousand tapes from Nest.

Linda has discovered these two contracts and wishes to reject both since she disapproves of them. Advise her as to whether and how she may do so, assuming that the articles of the company are in the form of Table A and that both Nest and Owl are aware of this.

72. Antar plc was incorporated under a Memorandum which identified the company's main object to be 'interior decoration wholesalers and retailers'. Benjamin, the managing director of Antar plc, decided in 1984 that the company should diversify its activities into new areas and he entered a contract on the company's behalf to purchase a fleet of lorries for the purpose of operating a transport contracting service. To finance the purchase of the lorries Benjamin arranged a bank loan of £20,000 for Antar plc from C Bank Limited.

Advise Antar plc upon the company's liability to meet the unpaid bill for the lorries and repay the bank loan.

73. *(a)* What is the rule in *Royal British Bank* v *Turquand* (1856), and what defences against its application are available to a company?
*(b)* Beetlecrush Ltd was a company involved in pest control. In 1983 Pellet was appointed as managing director of the company by a board resolution, which gave him exclusive power to manage the company, subject only to a requirement to get the approval of the board for all contracts in excess of £50,000.

On behalf of the company, Pellet began negotiating for the purchase of insecticides from Toxin, who had supplied the company with similar products for a number of years. Before these negotiations were concluded, Toxin accepted an invitation to become a member of the board of Beetlecrush Ltd, and thenceforth duly attended its board meetings. Some months after this, Pellet, without getting the approval of the board, signed a contract with Toxin for the supply of £80,000 worth of insecticides.

Preliminary trials with these insecticides have revealed that they are not as effective as the company had been hoping. The board, with the exception of Pellet and Toxin, is now seeking some way in which the company can claim that it is not bound by its obligation under the contract.

466   Examination questions

74. A, B and C incorporated the Smokease Co Ltd ('the Company') to develop and manufacture a cigarette-substitute with a minimal nicotine content. A, B and C were directors and each held 33% of the Company's shares. Advise C whether he has any cause of action either in his own right, or on behalf of the Company, in respect of each of the following complaints:

(i) A, who was appointed managing director, has managed the business so inefficiently that the Company may now well be insolvent.

(ii) B, who was also the Company's analytical chemist and who carried out research in the Company's laboratories on cigarettte substitutes, incidentally discovered a new product which he claimed was of use as a petrol additive and capable of improving the petrol consumption of cars. He tried, unsuccessfully, to persuade the Company's Board to market this product, but the Board formally rejected it, being unconvinced of its merits. Thereafter, B formed a new company, in which he and his wife were the only shareholders, to market this product. It has proved highly successful, and the value of the shares in this new company has appreciated significantly.

(iii) C has just received a letter signed by A and B, advising him that he has been removed as a director of the Company; yet no meeting has been held for the purpose of considering C's removal from office, nor has C been given any opportunity to make representations on the matter.


75. Richard is a shareholder in Wharfe plc, a listed company, and his wife Amy is employed as a typist by a firm of chartered accountants who are the auditors of the company. Walter, who knows that Richard is a shareholder in Wharfe plc, works in the audit department of the firm and tells Amy that the unpublished accounts of the company show profits at a much lower level than the stock market has been forecasting. The same evening Amy passes on this information to her husband who, on the following day, sells his entire shareholding.

Discuss the legal positions of Richard, Amy and Walter.


76. Explain the need for, and the extent of, statutory regulation of 'insider dealing'.


77. (a) What is the extent of a company secretary's authority to make contracts on behalf of his company?

(b) S Ltd is tenant of 1 Station Road, Ambridge, where it conducts an import agency. Brown, a local accountant in private practice, is the company's secretary. In August 1984 all the directors of S Ltd resigned, and no new directors have yet been appointed. The import agency continues to operate, under the management of S Ltd's senior employees.

On 1 September 1984 Jones, S Ltd's landlord, served on S Ltd a notice to quit 1 Station Road. Under the legislation giving qualified security of tenure to business tenants, S Ltd could seek a new tenancy of 1 Station Road provided it served on Jones, within 2 months of his notice to quit, a counter-notice that S Ltd was unwilling to give up the premises. When S Ltd's senior employees saw Jones's notice to quit, they passed it, without comment, to Brown. On 29 September 1984 Brown returned to Jones a counter-notice that S Ltd was unwilling to give up 1 Station Road because of the goodwill it had built up there. Early in October Jones formally notified S Ltd of his intention to oppose a new tenancy.

In December 1984 Jones discovered that S Ltd had no directors, and had had none on 29 September when Brown stated S Ltd's unwillingness to give up its tenancy. Jones now proposes to challenge the validity of Brown's counter-notice of 29 September on the ground that S Ltd was incompetent to form the necessary intention to continue business at 1 Station Road. If the counter-notice is indeed invalid, S Ltd will not be able to pursue its claim for a new tenancy.

Answer the following questions:
*(ii)* Was Brown competent to give a counter-notice of S Ltd's unwillingness to give up its premises; and
*(ii)* if Brown was not competent, what steps (if any) can S Ltd now take to make effective the counter-notice when Brown purported to give on its behalf?

78. Arthur, an accountant, had for many years provided taxation and general financial advice to Crumble Ltd. Last year, in recognition of his long connection with the company, the board appointed him company secretary and agreed to pay him generous fees for attending the monthly board meetings at which he would present management accounts and give such advice as he considered necessary.

About six months ago the company started trading at a considerable loss.

Arthur continually advised the directors at the monthly board meetings to reduce the company's overheads but he never advised them to stop trading.

During the last six months large quantities of goods have been purchased on credit even though the company, to Arthur's knowledge, has not been able to pay its debts as they fell due. A month ago the company received a large payment from one of its debtors. Since Arthur honestly believed that all creditors of the company would eventually be paid he advised that it was in order for this money to be paid to him in discharge of arrears of his secretary's fees. Unfortunately, Crumble Ltd was at the time hopelessly insolvent and has just gone into liquidation.

Advise the liquidator:
*(a)* whether he may make Arthur or the directors personally liable for the debts of the company;
*(b)* whether he may recover from Arthur the amount paid to him as arrears of secretary's fees.


79. Adam, John and Eric are brothers who have carried on the business of providing transport services since 1970 as a partnership. They have now decided to reorganise their business structure to obtain corporate status but the men are intent on retaining the family nature of the business. The partners consider that an authorised share capital of £100,000 will be sufficient for the proposed company, and they resolve that all three will become shareholders with 25,000 £1 ordinary shares each; the remaining 25,000 £1 shares will be held in five £5,000 blocks by the three partners' wives and by the eldest children of Adam and John. The partners will also be the company's only directors.
*(a)* What types of company may be formed under the Companies Acts? Which type of company would be most suitable for the requirements of this business?
*(b)* Identify the advantages which corporate status will give this business in (i) obtaining business finance, and (ii) protecting shareholders in the event of business failure.
*(c)* How could each director of the company ensure, if at all, that he is not removed from his position as a director against his wishes?
*(d)* How do the provisions of company law assist the partners in ensuring that shareholdings be restricted to members of the family?


80. In 1980 Abel, Baker and Charlie incorporated their partnership business in the name of Nickem Ltd to carry on the business of private detectives and process servers in and around Bournesea. The Company had an authorised ordinary share capital of £100 fully issued and divided equally as between Abel, Baker and Charlie (the remaining £1 share was held by Charlie's solicitor who assisted in the incorporation of the Company). Abel, Baker and Charlie each took a directorship in the company, although no service contracts were entered into with the Company by any of them. Between 1980 and 1984 the Company built up a large amount of work in Bournesea, being used by most of the town's solicitors. Indeed, at the present moment it is the only private process serving agency in the town. Early in 1981 a personality clash developed between Baker and Charlie and in consequence relations became very strained. Abel and Baker accordingly now consult you on each of the following questions:
*(a)* How, if at all, can they exclude Charlie from participation in the management of the Company?
*(b)* If excluded, would Charlie be entitled to any compensation from the Company?

*(c)* In response to the proposal to seek the exclusion of Charlie from participation in the management of the Company, Charlie's solicitor has advised Charlie to petition for a winding up of the Company if those intentions are implemented. What is the basis of this advice?

*(d)* Abel and Baker advise you that, because they have personal guarantees of the Company's liabilities to its Bankers which they cannot at the moment afford to meet, it is unacceptable to them to allow the Company to go into liquidation. As an alternative, therefore, they ask you whether, should it be necessary to abandon their proposal to exclude Charlie from management in the Company, there is any legal objection to their simply forming a new company of their own, without Charlie, to carry on the same type of work in Bournesea?

81. Explain the methods available to the Department of Trade to investigate the affairs and records of a company and the factors which are likely to be taken into account by the Department in selecting which powers are to be employed in an individual case.

82. *(a)* Define and describe the characteristics of a 'derivative action'. Illustrate your answer with decided cases. Is there any disadvantage to the minority shareholder in bringing a derivative action?

*(b)* Small is a minority shareholder in Mighty plc, a public company. He discovered that David, the managing director and majority shareholder had, in breach of his duties as a director, purchased machinery from the company at a gross undervalue. A general meeting of the company, at which David attended and voted, has just ratified the sale.

Advise Small as to the possible causes of action he might take.

83. Lorder was the founder and managing director of Manor Ltd in which he held 60% of the shares. He regarded the company as his own property and resented any interference in its management by the other directors, frequently disregarding any board decisions that he did not like or which purported to curb his powers. Serf, a member of the board who held 15% of the company's shares, protested against this behaviour, and against Lorder's refusal either to present full accounts, or to declare any dividends, despite the company's good profit record.

Lorder was so angered by this criticism that he began diverting work away from Manor Ltd into another company of which he was the sole shareholder. To protect himself he used his voting superiority in Manor Ltd to ratify these actions. Serf objected violently to this, and Lorder promptly used his votes to dismiss Serf from the board.

Advise Serf as to what steps he can take to obtain redress.

84. In what circumstances may a minority shareholder bring an action against the controlling directors of his company:
*(a)* on behalf of the company;
*(b)* on behalf of other shareholders?

85. The issued share capital of Alpha Ltd is 500 ordinary shares with a par value of £2; 100 of these, each carrying four votes per share, are held by the directors of Alpha Ltd and of the remainder, each carrying one vote per share, 100 are held by Exco Assurance Ltd.

A few weeks ago at an extraordinary general meeting of Alpha Ltd a special resolution was passed for voluntary liquidation of the company. Exco Assurance Ltd suspected that Alpha's directors had proposed this resolution, without fully informing shareholders, in order to facilitate a takeover of Alpha Ltd.

The liquidator of Alpha Ltd is now proposing a scheme under s. 459 of the Companies Act 1985 for the sale of Alpha Ltd to Beta Ltd. The terms of the transfer are that Beta Ltd will issue one £2 share, credited as paid up to £1.60, in exchange for each ordinary share in Alpha Ltd and that if any member dissents from the scheme, his shares are to be sold by the liquidator and he will receive the price thus obtained. Exco Assurance Ltd believes, on the advice of its experts, that these terms are based on a substantial undervaluation of Alpha Ltd and has circulated this information to other minority shareholders.

Advise Exco Assurance Ltd and any other dissenting shareholders what courses of action are open to them.

86. When in exceptional circumstances, the rule in *Foss v Harbottle* permits a member of a company to bring an action in respect of some wrong committed by the company's controllers, that action may be framed in one or more of three separate ways; it may be a 'personal' action, a 'representative' action or a 'derivative' action.

In respect of the above statement:
*(a)* explain the nature of the three kinds of action mentioned and the significance of the manner in which the action is framed;
*(b)* consider each of the following situations and explain with reasons whether each is within the category of exceptional circumstances.

*(i)* The controlling members of a company incorporated to carry on the business of retail sale of new and second-hand cars have resolved to diversify the company's business in a time of recession and to commence

trading in agricultural machinery. The minority members object, in view of the large amount of financial outlay this change in trade will involve.

*(ii)* The controlling members of a company appointed Dingle as the company's managing director at an annual remuneration of £15,000, even though he does not hold any qualification shares as required by the company's articles. This appointment was made six months ago and still no shares are held by Dingle. As a result of the objections of minority members, the controlling members intend to hold a general meeting of the company and confirm Dingle's appointment.

*(iii)* The controlling members of a company secured an alteration to the company's articles so as to introduce a power enabling the majority of the shareholders to require any member to transfer his shares at a fair value to a named transferee. A minority member objects.

87. Bert and Fred were for many years the only directors of and shareholders in Job Ltd which carried on the business of builders. Bert held 60 of the 100 issued shares, Fred 40. Both worked full time in the business of the company. No dividends were ever declared and the profits were taken as directors' salaries. Recently, Clarence, an employee of the company, was appointed an additional director and Bert and Fred each transferred five shares to him. Differences then arose because Fred and Clarence found that Bert was diverting building work away from Job Ltd to another company in which he was interested. Bert requisitioned a general meeting at which Fred and Clarence were dismissed as directors. Since then the business of Job Ltd has declined further but Bert has doubled the salary he receives. No dividends have been declared.

Advise Fred and Clarence.

88. Igloo Ltd has three shareholders, Jack, Ken and Lionel. Jack owns 49% of the shares of the company and is the managing director. Ken is the other director and owns 11% of the shares. In 1983 Jack set up another business in premises rented from Igloo Ltd at less than the full market rent. This arrangement was approved by a resolution of the company, despite Lionel's opposition.

In 1984 Ken died. The articles of the company provide that no shares in the company may be transferred without the directors' consent. Jack, who is Ken's executor, has refused to discuss a possible transfer of Ken's shares to Lionel, who wishes to purchase them. Instead he exercises the votes attaching to those shares himself, in his capacity as executor.

Advise Lionel, who does not wish to wind up the company.

89. *(a)* What are the relative advantages and disadvantages of fixed and floating charges as forms of security?
*(b)* What are the statutory provisions for the registration of charges?

*(c)* What is the effect of failure to register a charge within the prescribed time limit?


90. Spokery Ltd, a company engaged in the manufacture of bicycle wheels, approached two bankers, Frank and Mark, who each agreed to lend the company money to purchase new plant for its operations. On 1 January 1984 Frank advanced £40,000 to the company at 12% per annum interest, on the security of a first floating charge over its undertaking and assets. On 18 January 1984 Mark also advanced £40,000 at 10% per annum interest, on the security of a debenture executed that day containing a floating charge over all the company's property.

The debenture stated that it was to rank *pari passu* with the charge to Frank, and also contained a clause prohibiting Spokery Ltd from creating any further charges ranking in priority to or *pari passu* with it. Both debentures were sent for registration at the Companies Registry on 28 January. Frank's debenture however was returned and only registered on 1 March 1984 after an application to the court had been made, and consent granted to late registration, subject to any rights created in the interim.

Spokery was also negotiating for the purchase of another factory to house the new plant. On 1 February 1984 it entered into a contract with Saddler, which provided that Spokery Ltd would purchase a new factory from him for the sum of £150,000, of which £70,000 would be paid on completion and £80,000 left outstanding, secured by a first legal charge over the factory. On 28 February 1984 the conveyance and the legal charge were executed simultaneously.

Unfortunately this venture failed and the company was put into liquidation on 10 January 1985.

Advise the liquidator on the priority and effectiveness of the above charges.


91. *(a)* Describe the characteristics of a floating charge. What are the advantages and disadvantages of the floating charge as a form of security?
*(b)* In April 1984 X Ltd issued to W Bank a debenture secured by a floating charge on all of X Ltd's property and undertaking. It was duly registered at the Companies Registration Office. Six months later a fixed charge on the company's principal factory was created in favour of Z. More than twelve months after the charge in favour of Z was created X Ltd went into liquidation. Prior to taking his charge Z had made a search at the Companies Registration Office and discovered the existence of W Bank's floating charge.

Which charge has priority?

92. *(a)* What are the disadvantages of a floating charge as a security for a creditor?

*(b)* Rusty Ltd borrowed £100,000 for Sandbags Ltd on 1 June 1984, secured by a registered charge. On 10 June 1984, the company borrowed a further £50,000 from Trouble Ltd, secured by an unregistered charge on its factory. On 15 June 1984 the company borrowed £70,000 from Unit Ltd, secured by a floating charge on all the company's assets.

Rusty Ltd is now in financial difficulties. Trouble Ltd has applied to the court for late registration of its charge under the Companies Acts and Unit Ltd has appointed a receiver under the terms of its debenture.

Discuss the rights of the secured creditors.

93. In January 1984, AB Ltd, issued to C bank a debenture for £50,000, secured by a floating charge on all AB Ltd's assets and undertaking; the debenture provided that, in the event of AB Ltd acting in breach of any covenants contained therein, or defaulting on payments of interest or permitting the levying of execution against its assets, the floating charge would immediately attach and become affixed. This charge was duly registered under s 395 of the Companies Act 1985.

In May 1983 AB Ltd granted to E Ltd a legal mortgage of its main office premises as security for a loan of £100,000; this charge too was duly registered. In November 1983 and August 1984 E Ltd advanced further monies to AB Ltd, taking as security the title deeds of development land acquired by AB Ltd; these transactions were not registered.

Eight months ago AB Ltd entered into an agreement with Debt Factors whereby, as security for a loan of £75,000, AB Ltd created a charge on its present and future book debts, undertaking to pay these debts into a separate bank account and not to deal with them without the consent of Debt Factors. The charge was duly registered, but AB Ltd has not opened a separate bank account and has simply continued to pay book debts into its ordinary trading account.

Two months ago, when interest payments due to C Bank and E Ltd were nine months in arrear, E Ltd appointed a receiver to AB Ltd, which has since gone into liquidation.

Advise the liquidator of AB Ltd as to the order of payment of the above debts.

94. Your client, the Mishap Finance Co Ltd relates the two following events:
*(i)* On 1 January 1984 'A' Co Ltd executed a charge over its land in favour of your Client. The charge form was undated. On 1 June 1984 it was noted that by an oversight, the charge had not been registered with the Register of

Companies. On this oversight being discovered, the date on the form was filled in as 1 June 1984. The charge was then registered forthwith by the Registrar of Companies who subsequently issued his certificate in the terms stated on the charge form. 'A' Co Ltd is now in liquidation, but the liquidator maintains that the charge is void on account of non-registration within the requisite period of execution of the charge on the land.

*(ii)* Also on 1 January 1984, 'B' Co Ltd executed a floating charge over its industrial machinery in favour of your Client, and undertook, in the document creating the charge, not to create subsequently, in favour of another, a fixed charge over any of the assets within the floating charge. This charge was duly registered within a few days of its creation, although no mention of the restriction against subsequent fixed charges was made in the particulars supplied to the Registrar. On 1 April 1984 'B' Co Ltd created a fixed charge in respect of three excavators (each having a market value of £20,000) in favour of Bank X Ltd. This charge was registered within a week. 'B' Co Ltd is now in liquidation and Bank X Ltd claims that it has priority as against your Client in respect of the three excavators.

Advise your client, giving reasons, as to the correctness, or otherwise, of the respective assertions of:
*(a)* the liquidator of 'A' Co Ltd, and
*(b)* of Bank X Ltd.


95. Explain the powers, functions and duties of a receiver and manager of a company under a debenture, comparing and contrasting his position with that of a liquidator appointed by the Court.


96. On 2 June 1984 Multiplex Ltd entered into a debenture with Bottle Bank securing the latter's loan of £20,000 by the creation of a floating charge over the company's undertaking and assets. The debenture contained a clause restricting the company's power to create any further charges ranking in priority to or pari passu with it. By an oversight this debenture was left undated in a drawer in the desk of the company secretary for several weeks. It was rediscovered on 30 June 1984 and that date was put on the debenture. It was registered at the Companies Registry ten days later and a certificate of registration was duly issued.

On 20 July 1984 Jars wrote to the company stating that if it did not pay in full within seven days its overdue debt of £10,000 in respect of a delivery of plastic containers, he would forthwith institute legal proceedings. The company did not reply, but Jars received instead a letter from Bottle Bank informing him of their charge over the company's assets. Jars ignored this letter, and subsequently obtained a court judgment for the contract sum, in respect of which he is now seeking to levy execution.

On 1 August 1984 Multiplex entered into a legal mortgage of its office premises to secure a loan of £150,000 from Coffers.

On 2 October 1984 Bottle Bank exercised a power in the debenture to appoint a receiver, because the company had failed to pay any interest due. At that time the company had not for three months paid its production manager, Box, the £400 per month salary that he was entitled to, nor had it paid its local rates demand of £1,500.

Advise the receiver on the priority that the Bank's charge will enjoy in the light of the above circumstances.

97. (a) What are the disadvantages of a floating charge as a security for a creditor?
(b) Rusty Ltd borrowed £100,000 from Sandbags Ltd on 1 June 1984 secured by a registered charge. On 10 June 1984, the company borrowed a further £50,000 from Trouble Ltd, secured by an unregistered charge on its factory. On 15 June 1984 the company borrowed £70,000 from Unit Ltd, secured by a floating charge on all the company's assets.

Rusty Ltd is now in financial difficulties. Trouble Ltd has applied to the court for late registration of its charge under the Companies Acts and Unit Ltd has appointed a receiver under the terms of its debenture.

Discuss the rights of the secured creditors.

98. The articles of Pinkle Ltd provide that if a member wishes to sell his shares they may only be acquired by other shareholders of the company at a fair value to be fixed by the company's auditors. Quentin, a shareholder, wishes to sell his ordinary and preference shares in the company, and has agreed to sell his ordinary shares to Robin and his preference shares to Simon, both of whom are shareholders in the company, in accordance with the articles. The auditors have valued both parcels of shares. Their certificate in relation to the ordinary shares simply provides a valuation figure, but the one relating to the preference shares also sets out the method of valuation adopted. Quentin now wishes to have both valuations set aside on the grounds that they are too low.

Advise him.

99. Justin, an employee of East plc, has been jailed for a computer fraud involving a substantial loss to the company.

Discuss the legal position of the auditors who failed to discover the fraud.

100. (a) Outline the provisions of the Companies Acts relating to the

qualifications, method of appointment and procedures for the removal of a company auditor.

*(b)* Billen is auditor of Leeps plc. He became concerned at the company's recorded stock levels and sought assurances from the directors as to the accuracy of the figures. The directors admitted that there were certain discrepancies, but that these were of a minor nature when considered against the total stock valuation. Billen accepted the directors' view and did not qualify his report attached to the final accounts of Leeps plc. In fact the discrepancies were substantial, leading to grossly inflated stock values and concealed trading losses. Subsequently, the company's poor trading position is revealed and Leeps plc is to be wound-up.

Comment on Billen's possible liability to the company and its shareholders.

101. *(a)* What rules govern the appointment of auditors and what is the consequence if no such appointment is made?
*(b)* To whom does an auditor owe a duty of care in the performance of his professional duties? How extensive is this duty?

102. *(a)* What relationships disqualify an auditor from appointment as auditor to a company?
*(b)* Explain (i) the principal duties of an auditor, and (ii) the powers he has been granted by statute to discharge such duties.

103. *(a)* How far does an auditor owe a duty to exercise care and skill towards prospective investors when he is auditing the accounts of a private company?
*(b)* Marx Bros Ltd is a private company. Its annual balance sheet for the year ending March 1984 showed the company to have made a substantial profit. Laurel and Hardy, a firm of accountants, gave an unqualified auditors' report for that year. On the basis of the balance sheet and auditor's report:
*(i)* a dividend of ten per cent was declared and paid to shareholders; and
*(ii)* Engels, to whom a copy of the report and balance sheet was shown by the chairman of Marx Bros Ltd, was persuaded to purchase 5,000 £1 shares in the company. The shares were transferred to Engels by the chairman and other directors.

It is later discovered that the balance sheet does not reflect the company's true position; it is in fact insolvent. The managing director of Marx Bros Ltd had falsified the accounts by:
*(i)* inflating the stock valuation by including non-existent items;
*(ii)* altering the dates on invoices for goods and services supplied to Marx Bros Ltd so that liabilities did not appear to arise until after March 1984.

Laurel and Hardy had accepted assurances and explanations about the accounts from the managing director, whom they trusted.

On discovering the true position, the company passed a resolution for a creditors' voluntary winding up, and a liquidator was appointed.

To whom, and in respect of what loss, will Laurel and Hardy be liable?

104. A winding-up order has been made against Exe plc following the presentation of a petition by Vee plc, a creditor for £10,000. An investigation of the affairs of the Exe plc reveals the following creditors:

|  | £'000 |
|---|---|
| Wye Insurance plc – loan secured by a fixed charge on freehold property | 300 |
| Zed Finance plc – loan secured by a floating charge on the undertaking of Exe plc | 200 |
| Customs and Excise – VAT | 50 |
| Inland Revenue – PAYE deductions | 30 |
| Dee Bank plc – amount advanced to pay wages | 25 |
| Unsecured creditors (including Vee plc) | 150 |

Compare the position of Wye Insurance plc, Zed Finance plc and Vee plc.

105. (a) Give an account of the difference between a compulsory liquidation and a voluntary liquidation of a company.
(b) In what ways can a company be dissolved, and by what means and with what effects can a dissolved company be revived?

106. In relation to the liquidation of a company, explain *all* of the following matters:
(a) provable debts,
(b) fraudulent preference,
(c) the supervision of the liquidator.

107. (a) In what circumstances may a company be wound up on the just and equitable ground?
(b) Muffin Ltd went into compulsory liquidation in 1984. The following proofs have been received by the liquidator.

Advise him as to how he should deal with them on the basis that the company is hopelessly insolvent:
(i) A claim for two years unpaid value added tax and corporation tax.
(ii) A claim for £7,000 lent by Neil to the company a year prior to the

liquidation. The money was later used to pay the wages of the company's employees.

*(iii)* A claim for repayment of a mortgage granted to Owen by the company four months prior to liquidation. At the time the directors thought that it would still be possible to save the company.

108. *(a)* What is a Declaration of Solvency and what must it contain?

*(b)* When is it made and what is its purpose?

*(c)* What consequences may follow if the declaration is subsequently found to be incorrect?

109. Kant plc has recently made a successful take-over bid for the shares of Lamb plc in that it has received acceptance of its offer from 90 per cent of the Lamb shareholders. Mary, who owns 1 per cent of the Lamb shares has refused the offer.

Advise Kant plc whether and on what terms it may acquire Mary's shares in each of the following circumstances:

*(a)* Mary intends to petition the court on the basis that the take-over offer was too low since Lamb's last profit forecast had been unduly pessimistic;

*(b)* Kant plc already owned 20 per cent of Lamb shares before it made the offer;

*(c)* the percentage of acceptances includes certain convertible debentures which were converted into shares by their holders and then offered to Kant plc, but it does not include those convertible debentures which were not so converted.

110. Multi-mergers plc is an industrial holding company whose directors are proposing to make a rights issue to raise additional finance. Because subsidiary companies have their own classes of share capital with different voting and dividend entitlements the directors are advised that, as a preliminary step, the capital structure of the group should be simplified by exchanging all the subsidiary companies' shares held by minority shareholders for ordinary shares and loan stock in the holding company itself, by means of a scheme of arrangement under s 425 of the Companies Act.

Explain to the directors of Multi-mergers plc the implications of the proposed scheme of arrangement and the steps necessary for its implementation.

111. *(a)* State the methods by which reconstructions and amalgamations can be achieved.

*(b)* How are the rights of shareholders and creditors protected in a reconstruction?

112. The directors of Penny Ltd have agreed to merge their company with Quest plc. The terms of the merger are that the ordinary shareholders of Penny are to receive one Quest share for each Penny share they own, whilst the preference shareholders are to receive one Quest share for each five Penny shares owned. Advise the directors of Penny Ltd as to how they should proceed with the merger in each of the following circumstances:

*(a)* Penny Ltd is solvent with only one significant creditor, the bank, which is in favour of the merger as are all the Penny shareholders.

*(b)* Penny Ltd is solvent but with many creditors not all of whom approve of the merger, although al the shareholders do approve.

*(c)* Penny Ltd is solvent with no significant creditors but some of the preference shareholders, who are not also ordinary shareholders, object to the terms of the merger.

113. In 1983 Quest plc made a take-over bid for all the issued equity share capital of Rubber plc. It offered either one of its own equity shares for each Rubber share, each Quest share at the date of the offer having a value of £2.00, or a cash alternative of £1.00 per share. At the date of the offer Quest already owned 10 per cent of the capital of Rubber plc.

The offer was accepted by holders of 95 per cent of the Rubber shares. Two shareholders, Simon and Tracy refused the offer. Quest now wish to acquire Simon's shares, amounting to three per cent of the total. Simon is opposed to this on the ground that to sell his shares will involve him in severe tax liability and that the offer was in any event too low since it ignored Rubber's potential increased profitability from a proposed joint venture with another company.

Tracy now wants to transfer her shares to Quest but the company have offered her only the cash price of £1.00 per share. Quest shares are currently worth £3.00 on the market.

Advise Simon and Tracy.

114. Provent plc a listed company, is considering making a take-over bid for the equity shares in Retal plc, also a listed company, and in which Provent plc at present holds 29% of the equity shares.

You are required to advise the directors of Provent plc on the following matters which relate specifically to the proposed take-over bid:

*(a)* The proportion of the equity share capital which Provent plc must purchase in Retal plc in order for Retal plc to be classified as a subsidiary company and whether this measure of holding would ensure effective control over all matters which might arise at company general meetings.

*(b)* Whether Provent plc may obtain majority control of Retal plc in secret, without that company becoming aware of the build-up of majority status by Provent plc.

*(c)*  Whether Provent plc may, upon obtaining control of Retal plc, appoint nominee directors who would then authorise the payment of a dividend from the ample reserves of Retal plc, to all shareholders, including Provent plc.

115.  Short one paragraph answers are required to the following five questions:

*(a)*  Explain the difference between a prospectus and an offer for sale as a method of raising funds for public companies.

*(b)*  Identify three distinctions between a public and a private company.

*(c)*  List three types of resolution that may be passed by a company in general meeting with an example of the purpose that each resolution may fulfil.

*(d)*  Distinguish a fixed from a floating charge. What is the effect of failing to register a charge with the Registrar of Joint Stock Companies?

*(e)*  How has s 125 attempted to rectify defects in the existing rules relating to variation of class rights?

116.  Short one paragraph answers are required on the following five matters:

*(a)*  What are the civil law remedies that an investor may pursue against a company and its directors when a mis-statement has appeared in a company prospectus?

*(b)*  Explain the term 'insider-dealing', and identify the legal provisions which attempt to control this activity.

*(c)*  What is the rule in Turquand's Case? Does the rule have any practical significance since the enactment of s 35 of the Companies Act 1985?

*(d)*  Identify three registers which must be kept at a company's registered office with a brief description of their contents.

*(e)*  When would the procedure 'certification of transfer' be utilised by a shareholder? Briefly describe the process.

117.  You are required to give short one-paragraph answers to the following:

*(a)*  What is a 'shadow director'? Give two examples of how such a director may incur liability under the Companies Acts.

*(b)*  Identify three ways in which a directorship may be terminated.

*(c)*  State briefly the decision in *Macaura* v *Northern Assurance Co Ltd* (1925). In what sense does the case illustrate corporate entity theory?

*(d)*  List three situations where a company may purchase its own shares under the Companies Act.

*(e)*  What is the effect of a pre-incorporation contract, entered purportedly on a company's behalf, upon both the company and the promoter who negotiated the contract?

## Appendix E

# Accounts

The following Accounts are those of Marks and Spencer plc and are reproduced with their kind permission.

## Consolidated profit and loss account for the year ended 31st March 1984

| | Notes | 1984 £m | 1983 £m |
|---|---|---|---|
| Turnover | 1 | 2,854·5 | 2,505·5 |
| Cost of sales | | 2,048·9 | 1,807·7 |
| Gross profit | | 805·6 | 697·8 |
| Other expenses | 2 | 526·3 | 458·5 |
| Profit on ordinary activities before taxation | 3 | 279·3 | 239·3 |
| Tax on profit on ordinary activities | 4 | 111·1 | 102·5 |
| Profit on ordinary activities after taxation | | 168·2 | 136·8 |
| Minority interests | | 1·8 | 1·6 |
| Profit for the financial year | 5 | 166·4 | 135·2 |
| **Dividends** | | | |
| Preference shares | | ·1 | ·1 |
| Ordinary shares:— | | | |
| Interim of 2·05p per share | | 27·0 | 24·3 |
| Final of 4·20p per share | | 55·3 | 42·7 |
| | | 82·4 | 67·1 |
| Undistributed surplus | | 84·0 | 68·1 |
| Earnings per share | 6 | 12·6p | 10·3p |

## Report of the auditors

**to the members of Marks and Spencer p.l.c.**

We have audited the financial statements on pages 20 to 35 in accordance with approved Auditing Standards.

In our opinion the financial statements give a true and fair view of the state of affairs of the Company and the Group at 31st March 1984 and of the profit and source and application of funds of the Group for the year then ended and comply with the Companies Acts 1948 to 1981.

LONDON,
1st May 1984

DELOITTE HASKINS & SELLS
*Chartered Accountants.*

# Balance sheets at 31st March 1984

| | Notes | The Group 1984 £m | The Group 1983 £m | The Company 1984 £m | The Company 1983 £m |
|---|---|---|---|---|---|
| **Fixed assets** | | | | | |
| Tangible assets: | | | | | |
| Land and buildings | 9 | 1,115·7 | 1,075·7 | 1,061·4 | 1,023·9 |
| Fixtures, fittings and equipment | 10 | 136·9 | 105·9 | 118·3 | 89·4 |
| Assets in course of construction | 11 | 33·2 | 26·2 | 33·0 | 21·7 |
| Assets leased to third parties | 12 | 100·7 | 44·3 | — | — |
| | | 1,386·5 | 1,252·1 | 1,212·7 | 1,135·0 |
| Investments | 13 | — | — | 69·2 | 66·1 |
| | | 1,386·5 | 1,252·1 | 1,281·9 | 1,201·1 |
| **Current assets** | | | | | |
| Stocks | | 194·1 | 163·3 | 157·5 | 131·1 |
| Debtors | 14 | 48·1 | 57·6 | 92·1 | 73·1 |
| Investments | 15 | 61·9 | 108·9 | 57·9 | 106·6 |
| Cash at bank and in hand | 16 | 73·6 | 63·2 | 10·5 | 14·0 |
| | | 377·7 | 393·0 | 318·0 | 324·8 |
| **Current liabilities** | | | | | |
| Creditors: amounts falling due within one year | 17 | 450·8 | 432·5 | 337·1 | 342·1 |
| **Net current liabilities** | | 73·1 | 39·5 | 19·1 | 17·3 |
| **Total assets less current liabilities** | | 1,313·4 | 1,212·6 | 1,262·8 | 1,183·8 |
| Creditors: amounts falling due after more than one year | 18 | 53·6 | 52·4 | 45·0 | 45·0 |
| **Provisions for liabilities and charges** | | | | | |
| Deferred taxation | 19 | 24·2 | 12·9 | — | — |
| **Net assets** | | 1,235·6 | 1,147·3 | 1,217·8 | 1,138·8 |
| **Capital and reserves** | | | | | |
| Called up share capital | 20 | 330·5 | 329·8 | 330·5 | 329·8 |
| Share premium account | | 15·9 | 11·8 | 15·9 | 11·8 |
| Revaluation reserve | | 391·2 | 393·0 | 395·6 | 395·6 |
| Profit and loss account | | 489·2 | 405·4 | 475·8 | 401·6 |
| **Shareholders' funds** | 21 | 1,226·8 | 1,140·0 | 1,217·8 | 1,138·8 |
| **Minority interests** | | 8·8 | 7·3 | — | — |
| **Total capital employed** | | 1,235·6 | 1,147·3 | 1,217·8 | 1,138·8 |

Approved by the Board
1st May 1984

SIEFF OF BRIMPTON     *Chairman*

THE LORD RAYNER     *Chief Executive*

# Index

**Accountant**
  acting in professional capacity for promoter, 70–71
**Accounts**
  accounting records, 260–261
  accounting reference periods, 261-263
  additional information given in, 278–280
  annual, 261
  auditors' report, 275–276
  balance sheet,
    details required to supplement, 269–270
    documents annexed to, 270
    formula, 264-269
    preparation, 264
  directors,
    remuneration, 195-196
    report, 277–278
  dividends. *See* DIVIDENDS
  exemptions, 263–264
  group, 274–275
  liquidator's duty to keep, 362–363, 371
  Marks and Spencer, 481–483
  modified, 263–264
  oversea company, 29
  profit and loss,
    formats, 270–273
    insurance companies, 301
    items shown separately, 273
    preparation, 270
    supplementary information, 273–274
  responsibility for preparing and maintaining, 260
  unlimited company exempt from filing, 20–21

**Act of Parliament**
  special, incorporation by, 1
**Action**
  debenture holders, 323–324
**Adjournment of meeting.** *See* MEETINGS
**Agent**
  director as, 214–215
**Allotment of shares**
  application,
    conditional,
      condition precedent, 99–100
      condition subsequent, 100
    generally, 99
  consideration for, 103
  discount, at, 106
  irregular, 109–110
  non-cash consideration,
    private company, 105–106
    public company, 103–104
  notice of, 100–101
  power to allot, 101–102
  pre-emption rights, 102
  premium, at, 107–108
  private company, 105–106
  public company,
    irregular allotments, 109–110
    non-cash consideration, 103–104
    restrictions, 108–110
  return as to, 110
**Amalgamation**
  compromise, 379–382
  dissentient members, protection of, 378–379
  meaning, 376
  protection of creditors, 379
  s 582, under, 377–379
  scheme of arrangement, 379–382
**Annual general meeting.** *See* MEETINGS

485

**Borrowing**
floating charge, 8–9
**Breach of contract**
alteration of articles results in, 65
director, 199
**Brokerage**
amount paid by way of, 87
meaning, 87
**Business letter**
publication of director's names on, 201
**Business organisations**
company as member of, 9

**Calls on shares.** *See* SHARES
**Capital**
clause in memorandum of association, 33, 58–59
raising,
prevention of fraud, 96–98
private company. *See* PRIVATE COMPANY
public company. *See* PUBLIC COMPANY
share. *See* SHARES
**Care**
auditor's duty of, 289–290
**Certificate of incorporation.** *See* INCORPORATION OF COMPANY
**Certification**
transfer of shares, 141–142
**Chairman.** *See* MEETINGS
**Characteristics of company**
borrowing, 8–9
constitution, 9
contract, 7
criminal liability, 8
limited liability, 6–7
management, 9
membership of other business organisations, 9
perpetual succession, 7
property, 7
separate legal entity, 5–6
tort, 7–8
transferable shares, 9
**Charge**
avoidance of, 314
fixed. *See* FIXED CHARGE
floating. *See* FLOATING CHARGE
legal, priority of, 315
non-registration, effect of, 320–322
priority of, 314–315

**Charge—**continued
registration,
company's register of charges, in, 318
Registrar of Companies, with, 319–320
**Chartered company**
formation, 18
members' liability for debts, 18–19
powers, 18
**City Code on Take-overs and Mergers.** *See* TAKE-OVER
**Class rights.** *See* SHARES
**Classification of companies**
chartered companies, 18–19
companies limited by guarantee, 22–23
companies limited by shares, 24
holding companies, 29–30
medium-sized companies, 30–31
oversea companies, 28–29
private company, 24–28
public company, 24–28
small companies, 30–31
statutory companies, 19–20
subsidiary companies, 29–30
unlimited companies, 20–22
**Commencement of business**
private company, 4
public company, 4
statutory declaration delivered to Registrar, 4–5
**Committee of inspection**
appointment, 349
cessation of membership, 349
fiduciary position of members, 350
meetings, 349
vacancy, 349
**Company**
characteristics. *See* CHARACTERISTICS OF COMPANY
chartered. *See* CHARTERED COMPANY
classification. *See* CLASSIFICATION OF COMPANIES
corporation, as, 1
damages for misrepresentation and non-disclosure in prospectus, 92–93
holding, 29–30
illegal object, effect of, 4
incorporation. *See* INCORPORATION OF COMPANY
investment, 301

**Company**—*continued*
law and Community law, 15–17
limited. *See* LIMITED COMPANY
limited by guarantee. *See* GUARANTEE
COMPANY
limited by shares. *See* SHARE COMPANY
medium-sized, 30–31
membership of. *See* MEMBERSHIP OF
COMPANY
oversea, 28–29
private. *See* PRIVATE COMPANY
public. *See* PUBLIC COMPANY
small, conditions for qualifying as,
30–31
statutory. *See* STATUTORY COMPANY
subsidiary. *See* SUBSIDIARY COMPANY
unlimited. *See* UNLIMITED COMPANY
**Company secretary**
appointment, 235–236
assistant, 235
chief administrative officer, as, 237
deputy, 235
dismissal, 241
duties, 236–237
joint, 235
liability, 240
limitations,
altering register without approval,
239
binding company by contract, 239
borrowing money on company's
behalf, 238
notice issued without board's
authority, 239
registering transfer of shares, 238
summoning meeting without
board's authority, 239
writ issued in company's name,
239
minimum period of notice, 241
power and authority, 237
qualifications, 236
register, 200, 235
share certificate,
authority to issue, 240
forged, issue of, 240
sole director cannot be, 188, 235
vacancy in office, 235
winding up, 240
**Compensation**
loss of office, director's, 201–203
misrepresentation and non-disclosure
in prospectus, 94–95

**Consideration**
allotment of shares. *See* ALLOTMENT
OF SHARES
**Constitution**
written, 9
**Contract**
breach of. *See* BREACH OF CONTRACT
company secretary binding company
by, 239
freedom of company to enter into, 7
liability on. *See* DIRECTOR
made by director with outsider. *See*
DIRECTOR
pre-incorporation, 73–76
rescission of, as remedy against
promoter, 71–72
service, of director, 199–200
underwriting. *See* UNDERWRITING
*See also* ARTICLES OF ASSOCIATION;
MEMORANDUM OF ASSOCIATION
**Contributory**
first meeting of, 346
liquidator's duty to settle list of,
356–357, 370
meaning, 340
petition for winding up, 340–342
**Convertible debentures.** *See* DEBENTURES
**Court**
disqualification order, 192–193
receiver appointed by, 326–328
rectification of register of members,
159–160
reduction of capital, approval of, 125
winding up. *See* WINDING UP
**Creditor**
execution, 352–353
first meeting of, 346
fraudulent preference, 353–354
petition for winding up, 338–340
protection of, 379
reduction of capital,
involving, 124–125
not involving, 123–124
secured, 358–359
voluntary winding up, 368
**Criminal liability.** *See* LIABILITY
**Crown servant**
insider dealing, 232
meaning, 232
**Damages**
breach of director's contract, 199
breach of fiduciary duty, for, as
remedy against promoter, 72–73